The Arab-Israeli Conflict in American Political Culture

This book surveys discourse and opinion in the United States toward the Arab-Israeli conflict since 1991. Contrary to popular myth, it demonstrates that U.S. support for Israel is not based on the pro-Israel lobby, but rather is deeply rooted in American political culture. That support has increased since 9/11. However, the bulk of this increase has been among Republicans, conservatives, evangelicals, and Orthodox Jews. Meanwhile, among Democrats, liberals, the Mainline Protestant Church, and non-Orthodox Jews, criticism of Israeli policies toward the Palestinians has become more vociferous. This book explores and explains this paradox.

JONATHAN RYNHOLD is the director of the Argov Center for the Study of Israel and the Jewish People in the political studies department at Bar-Ilan University, where he is also a senior researcher at the Begin-Sadat Center for Strategic Studies. Dr. Rynhold's research focuses on Israeli and American approaches toward the Middle East peace process. His work has been published in numerous academic journals, including *Political Science Quarterly*, *Survival*, and the *Review of International Studies*. He has also coedited two volumes on Israeli elections in the Israel at the Polls series and is a member of the editorial board of the journal *Fathom*.

For my mother
Denise Rynhold
1940–1993

The Arab-Israeli Conflict in American Political Culture

JONATHAN RYNHOLD

Bar-Ilan University

CAMBRIDGE
UNIVERSITY PRESS

CAMBRIDGE
UNIVERSITY PRESS

32 Avenue of the Americas, New York, NY 10013-2473, USA

Cambridge University Press is part of the University of Cambridge.

It furthers the University's mission by disseminating knowledge in the pursuit of
education, learning, and research at the highest international levels of excellence.

www.cambridge.org
Information on this title: www.cambridge.org/9781107476400

First published 2015

Printed in the United States of America

A catalog record for this publication is available from the British Library.

Library of Congress Cataloging in Publication Data
Rynhold, Jonathan.
The Arab-Israeli Conflict in American political culture / Jonathan Rynhold (Bar-Ilan University).
    pages cm
Includes bibliographical references.
ISBN 978-1-107-09442-0 (Hardback) – ISBN 978-1-107-47640-0 (Paperback)
1. Arab-Israeli conflict–1993–Foreign public opinion, American. 2. Arab-Israeli conflict–
Foreign public opinion, American. 3. Political culture–United States. 4. Right and left
(Political science)–United States. 5. Jews–United States–Attitudes toward Israel.
6. Protestants–United States–Attitudes. 7. Israel–Relations–United States.
8. United States–Relations–Israel. 9. United States–Politics and
government–1989– I. Title.
DS119.76.R95 2015
956.04–dc23   2014035121

ISBN 978-1-107-09442-0 Hardback
ISBN 978-1-107-47640-0 Paperback

Contents

Acknowledgments

Many people were generous with time, providing invaluable assistance in preparing this book by reading and commenting on parts of the manuscript, or by helping arrange interviews, or simply by being willing to discuss the subject matter of this book with me in depth. In this regard, I would like to thank Carmiel Arbit, Mitchell Bard, Michael Barnett, Ralph Barnett, Peter Beinart, Avi Ben-Zvi, Steve Bickel, Yaeli Bloch Elkon, Daniel Byman, Zoe Clark, Stuart Cohen, Nathan Diament, Alan Dowty, Mike Eisenstadt, Robert O. Freedman, Avi Freeman, Zev Gewurz, Eli Gotlieb, Efraim Inbar, Brian Katulis, Aron Kayak, Michael Kraft, Shimmy Kreditor, Fran and Neil Kritz, Scott Lasensky, Eli Ledledender, Rachel Lerner, David Makovsky, Haim Malka, Henry Nau, Jeremy Newmark, Jeremy Pressman, Natan Sacks, Theodore Sasson, Marcus Sheff, Danny Sherman, David Sloan, Kenneth Stein, Gerald Steinberg, Ken Stern, Elana Sztockman, Kenneth Wald, Michael Weiger, Dov Waxman, Ariella Zeller, and Julie Zuckerman, as well as several interviewees who prefer to remain anonymous. I especially would like to thank the anonymous reviewers, as well as Adrian Daniels and Roy Pinchot, who read and commented on the whole manuscript. Of course, any remaining errors are my sole responsibility.

A significant part of the research for this book was conducted during a sabbatical in Washington, DC, in 2012–2013. In this regard, I would like to thank the Department of Political Science at the George Washington University for hosting me, especially the departmental chair, Paul Wahlbeck, and Professor Emeritus Bernard Reich. I would also like to thank the Kemp Mill synagogue community for being welcoming to myself and my family and for providing a wonderful opportunity for me to immerse myself in American Jewish political culture.

In a wider sense, I would like to thank the members of the Department of Political Science at Bar-Ilan University for providing me with invaluable support and encouragement over the years; special mention to Shmuel Sandler, whose sage advice on this project was invaluable, and to the head of department, my good friend Shlomo Shapiro.

Finally, on a personal note, I especially want to thank my wonderful wife, Elise; our boys, Matan and Tomer; my father, Monty; my sister, Joanna; my uncle and aunt, David and Valerie Rynhold; and my cousin, Professor Daniel Rynhold:

שֶׁהֶחֱיָנוּ וְקִיְּמָנוּ וְהִגִּיעָנוּ לַזְּמַן הַזֶּה.

Introduction

> The United States ... has a special relationship with Israel ... really comparable
> only to which it has with Britain.
>
> —John F. Kennedy[1]

The United States has a special relationship with Israel. A defining feature of the
special relationship is that support for Israel goes beyond an empirical calculation of U.S. interests. This is because the relationship is grounded on deep
cultural foundations that predate the mass immigration of Jews to the United
States. While this special relationship continues to endure; beneath the surface
those foundations are shifting in conflicting directions. For in the first decade of
the twenty-first century, a paradox has emerged in the way America relates to
Israel. On the one hand, Americans identify with Israel and sympathy for Israel
is widespread, surging to new heights. On the other hand, Americans are
increasingly divided about the Arab-Israeli conflict, and this division increasingly aligns with the major political, ideological, and religious divides in
America.

Thus, Republicans and conservatives have become far more supportive of
Israel than liberals and Democrats. At the same time, the most vociferous
evangelical supporters of Israel oppose Israeli concessions to the Palestinians,
while mainline church activists have been pushing divestment from Israel in
order to pressure Israel into making concessions. In the heartland of pro-Israel
sentiment, the organized American Jewish community has become increasingly
divided over the peace process, as exemplified by the formation of the "pro-
Israel, pro-peace" lobby J Street, as an alternative to the established pro-Israel
lobbying organization the American Israel Public Affairs Committee (AIPAC).

What we have here is an "Israel paradox" in American political culture. On
the one hand, sympathy for Israel is deep-seated, widespread, and increasingly

robust. On other hand, there are increasing divisions among Americans over the Arab-Israeli conflict. Surveying and analyzing this paradox is what this book is all about.

APPROACHES TO U.S.-ISRAEL RELATIONS

American support for Israel is a subject of extensive public debate and academic inquiry. Within the public debate a number of clichés have become pervasive. For example, it is often claimed that Americans' sympathy for Israel is primarily due to two factors: apocalyptic evangelicals trying to bring about Armageddon, or the power of the "Jewish" lobby. Certainly, evangelicals are very supportive of Israel, and the pro-Israel lobby in the United States does possess influence. However, such explanations are simplistic and misleading. After all, as we shall see later on, even secular liberal Americans are more pro-Israel than Europeans. Moreover, Americans' support for Zionism was already apparent in the nineteenth century, predating the existence of a Jewish pro-Israel lobby, and at a time when the American Jewish establishment was anti-Zionist.

Others retort that American support for Israel is simply a matter of shared democratic values and that the reason Europeans are more anti-Israel is because of anti-Semitism. Certainly, anti-Semitism is higher in Europe than in the U.S. and is often associated with anti-Israel sentiment, but European countries with democratic values and low levels of anti-Semitism, like the UK, are still more sympathetic to the Palestinians than Israel. So once again, this simplistic explanation does not suffice.

Finally, a common explanation for the growing divide between Republicans and Democrats on Israel is that right-wing Israeli policies are alienating American liberals. Again, there is no doubt that American liberals oppose the policies of the Israeli Right, but the levels of sympathy for Israel among Democrats has actually remained steady, while liberals have been divided among themselves over who is primarily to blame for failure to achieve peace. Clearly then, there is a need to analyze these issues in depth.

In terms of academic studies, broadly speaking, there have been three approaches to U.S.-Israeli relations, one focused on American national interests, another on the influence of the pro-Israel lobby, and yet another on political culture.

THE NATIONAL INTEREST

The Realist approach to international relations views shifts in the balance of power between states and the national interest defined in terms of power and state security as the key to understanding international relations.[2] From this perspective U.S. support for Israel is viewed as stemming primarily from the perception of Israel as a strategic asset for the United States.[3] Indeed, international politics and U.S. interests have clearly played a significant role in influencing U.S. policy to the Arab-Israeli conflict.

However, it is not always clear whether supporting Israel has been in the U.S. interest or not. In fact, there has been a long standing debate among American policy makers as to whether Israel is a strategic asset or a liability. This debate has intensified in the twenty-first century. Crucially, it is not simply a debate over the nature of the empirical reality that can be settled by "facts" alone; rather it is a debate informed by different subjective conceptions of what American grand strategy ought to be.

Grand strategy involves a self-conscious identification and prioritization of foreign policy goals and a selection of a plan and the appropriate instruments such as military power or diplomacy to achieve those goals. It begins with theories about how the world works and what ought to be the role of one's state in that world. Even Realists, such as Walter Lippmann and George Kennan, thought that cultural factors can profoundly affect grand strategy.[4] Thus, in order to explain the influence of strategic factors on U.S. policy, one must first understand the place of Israel in these ideational constructs, which are an integral part of America's political culture.[5]

THE PRO-ISRAEL LOBBY

While Realists generally view domestic politics as at most a secondary factor driving foreign policy, two prominent Realist scholars have argued that U.S. policy toward Israel is an exception to that rule. In the wake of President George W. Bush's strong support for Israel, John Mearsheimer and Stephen Walt argued that U.S.-Israeli relations are primarily a function of a powerful pro-Israel lobby. While the strident polemical tone of their work made a big splash, their argument was not in itself original, but rather echoed earlier works that essentially made the same case.[6] There is no doubt that pro-Israel groups constrain U.S. policy, raising the political costs of pressuring Israel. But Mearsheimer and Walt's claims are exaggerated.[7] Pro-Israel groups do not control U.S. policy, nor are they its main determinant.

Middle East policy is made primarily by the administration, especially the president.[8] Between 1945 and 1984, when the pro-Israel lobby clashed with the executive it won about a quarter of the time, and then primarily on the details of economic issues rather than on the bigger issues of diplomatic or military policy.[9] More recently, Aaron Miller, a former State Department official who dealt with the Middle East peace process in the 1990s, concluded: "I cannot remember a single major decision on Arab-Israeli peace in which AIPAC, either directly or indirectly, prevented us from moving in the direction we [the Administration] wanted."[10] Even allowing for the growth of AIPAC in the twenty-first century, the Center for Responsive Politics ranked the pro-Israel lobby's effectiveness twenty-sixth out of forty industries lobbying Congress.[11]

In any case, whatever the precise level of influence exerted by pro-Israel organizations, that influence cannot be properly understood in isolation from wider public opinion. As Kenneth Wald concluded, foreign policies advocated by ethnic groups succeeded "only to the extent that they had allies outside their own communities; could frame their policy in terms that resonated with American values; and, perhaps most important, offered plans consistent with American national interest as perceived by the president and public opinion."[12] Andrew Kohut, the president of the highly respected Pew Research Center that surveys American public opinion, concurred, stating, "If you didn't have a broad base of public support ... you couldn't create the level of support for Israel that exists on the basis of lobbying."[13] In other words, in order to explain the influence of the pro-Israel lobby, one must first of all understand the resonance of Israel in American political culture.

POLITICAL CULTURE

In terms of International Relations theory, rationalist-materialist paradigms such as Neorealism, Neoliberalism, and Marxist dependency theory view ideas as merely an epiphenomenon, dismissing the role of political culture. However, neoclassical Realism[14] and foreign policy analysis[15] do recognize a significant role for ideational factors, while Constructivism gives culture and ideas pride of place.[16] Indeed, a short Constructivist analysis of U.S.-Israel relations has been published.[17] More generally, there have been a number of works about American political culture and attitudes towards Israel and the Middle East.[18] But these are almost exclusively concerned with the Cold War period or earlier. They also tend to emphasize the "stickiness" of attitudes. This is an important part of the story. However, culture and attitudes are, at least in part, dynamic.[19]

Given changes in American attitudes to Israel and the Middle East since the end of the Cold War, there is an acute need for a new and comprehensive analysis of this subject. This is the purpose of the current work. Below, the concept of political culture is defined and the way in which it is deployed in this book is outlined.

Definitions and Approaches

In the *International Encyclopedia of the Social Sciences*, Lucien Pye defines political culture as "the set of attitudes, beliefs, and sentiments which give order and meaning to a political process and which provide the underlying assumptions and rules that govern behavior in the political system ... encompassing both the political ideals and the operating norms[20] of a polity."[21] As such, political culture incorporates conceptions of collective identity,[22] conceptions as to the nature of politics (ontology), assessments of what is desirable (values), legitimate (norms) and plausible in the political realm, all of which inform the ideological[23] orientations and political objectives of both leaders and citizens, as well as the strategies they deploy to advance these objectives. Moreover, political culture is not only cognitive and evaluative, but also affective. According to Gabriel Almond and Sidney Verba,[24] the cognitive element decodes experience giving it meaning; the evaluative element informs expectations and provide goals towards actions are directed, while the affective element refers to emotions that "move" actors. While some elements of a political culture are consensual, others are contested, often vigorously, by various subcultures.[25]

Some have approached the study of political culture by analyzing the aggregation of individual attitudes through surveys; while others have adopted an interpretative approach that has focused on understanding intersubjective meaning as portrayed in the discourse, in narratives.[26] This involves analysis of how issues are framed, wherein framing is defined as "selecting and highlighting some facets of events or issues and making connections among them so as to promote a particular interpretation, evaluation, and/or solution."[27]

The approach adopted here is eclectic and "bottom-up," driven by the requirements of the empirical case at hand. On the one hand, it looks at long-standing consensual elements of political culture encapsulated in America's national identity, as well as in its shared values and orientations. On the other hand, it analyzes the impact of changes and divisions in American political culture, including the evolution in the ways key subcultures relate to Israel and the Arab-Israel conflict. In each case, the attitudes and orientations of the wider public, as well as the approaches of, and discourse among, intellectuals, opinion formers, commentators, and communal, religious, and ideological elites, are surveyed and analyzed. The attitudes of the former are drawn primarily from many public opinion surveys, whereas the approaches of the latter are drawn primarily from media and public statements that make up the discourse on the subject. While the focus is contemporary, the historical foundations of different approaches are also traced so as to demonstrate the depth of their cultural roots.

CONTENTS AND STRUCTURE

The focus of this book is American political culture, and attitudes and approaches to Israel and the Arab-Israeli conflict, rather than U.S. foreign policy per se. The emphasis is on predispositions, rather than the nitty-gritty of U.S.-Israeli relations itself. While this book does not assess the relative importance of cultural factors in determining U.S. policy compared to other factors – such as the pro-Israel lobby – it does look at the way cultural factors inform both U.S. domestic politics and American strategy toward the Arab-Israeli conflict.

In order to understand the place of Israel and the Arab-Israeli conflict in American political culture, it is necessary to analyze it in two different ways.

First, American attitudes toward Israel must be assessed in a holistic sense and compared to the attitudes of other comparable Western countries, in order to get a sense of what unites Americans and distinguishes them from other nations on these issues. This is done in the first chapter, which focuses on the cultural foundations of American support for Israel and the development of contemporary attitudes; these in turn are compared and contrasted to contemporary European attitudes. Among the questions addressed in this chapter are: Why are Americans more sympathetic to Israel than Europeans, and why has the transatlantic divide over the Arab-Israeli conflict grown?

Second, American political culture must be broken up into a number of key subdivisions that signify core cultural and political divisions in America, and/or groups that are especially concerned and active regarding Israel and the conflict. The most important political and ideological division in America is between Democrats and liberals on the one hand, and conservatives and Republicans on the other hand. Whereas in the past this divide was largely irrelevant to Israel, it has now become increasingly significant. Given that presidents often pay more attention to public opinion among their own supporters than to the public at large,[28] clearly this division warrants serious analysis, and this is undertaken in Chapters 2 and 3.

Chapters 4 and 5 focus on the divide within the largest and most important religious group in America – Protestants. About half of all Americans continue to identify as Protestants. Religion counts in American politics, and as is explained in the first chapter, Protestantism has a particularly important role in American political culture in general, and with regard to Israel in particular. The central dividing line among American Protestants is between the Protestant mainline church and evangelicals. This divide has become increasingly important concerning the Arab-Israeli conflict. Evangelicals provide the largest base of American support for Israel, and they have become mobilized and highly organized for this cause. In contrast, the strongest base of anti-Israel activism in American society is centered in the mainline Protestant churches, which have been at the forefront pushing the campaign to divest from Israel. Consequently, it is important to examine this divide among Protestants in depth.

The final group analyzed in this book is the American Jewish community, the backbone of support for Israel in America. While constituting less than 2 percent of the American population, American Jewry's political influence is magnified by the fact that they are far more engaged in American politics than other ethnic and religious groups, voting in far higher proportions, generous in funding political parties and races, and historically highly organized and active in support of Israel. This is not simply a question of political power, but also more subtle kinds of influence. Because American Jews are understood to be the most invested in Israel, wider American debates about the Arab-Israeli conflict are influenced by debates over the issue among American Jews, much of which takes place in forums that are not specifically Jewish, like the *New*

York Times.[29] Consequently, what goes on inside the community is of great significance to the U.S. relationship with Israel. Chapter 6 examines the growing gap among different Jewish groups in the level of attachment to Israel, while addressing the question of whether American Jews, and especially the younger generation of American Jews, are growing more distant from the Jewish state. Chapter 7 focuses on American Jewish attitudes to the Arab-Israeli conflict and the growing divide within the organized Jewish community over the peace process.

Finally, the conclusion brings together all the different strands referred to above. It addresses the political significance of the "Israel paradox" for U.S.-Israeli relations, with the key question being: will rising support reinforce the pro-Israel tendency in U.S. policy, or do growing divisions signal the weakening of the special relationship?

Overall, each of the chapters is structured in a similar manner. First, they explain the demographic and political makeup of the relevant group. Second, they provide the historical and cultural foundations of approaches to Israel and the conflict within the group. Here the impact of identity, ideology, theology, and/or strategic thinking is examined, as appropriate. These sections focus mainly on elite approaches, though they also help explain the orientations of wider elements of the public. Third, the chapters survey public attitudes within each relevant group toward the conflict from the early 1990s until approximately 2010; in many cases the elite discourse in the relevant media and/or among key organizations is also assessed for the same period. Finally, each chapter demonstrates how cultural factors feed into politics and policy, with the focus on the way culture informs politics, and not on a detailed analysis of U.S. policy per se.

Throughout the book an important distinction is made between a *gap* and a *divide* in opinion. An opinion gap exists when both sides share a basic orientation, the difference being one of degree. An opinion divide exists when the sides adopt opposite positions on an issue, or when one side has a strong opinion pointing in one direction and the other side is equivocal. Finally, a number of recurring questions are addressed. These help provide some overarching benchmarks that aid comparisons across the various groups. They include the following:

Do sympathies lie more with Israel, the Palestinians, or neither/both?

Who is more to blame for the conflict?

On whom does the onus primarily lie, in terms of acting to try to resolve the conflict?

What are people's preferences in terms of key issues at stake in the conflict, such as Palestinian statehood, settlements, and Jerusalem?

How important is the Arab-Israeli conflict to American interests compared to other issues in the Middle East, like terrorism, the proliferation of weapons of mass destruction, and radical Islamism?

How active should the U.S. be in relation to the peace process?
Should the U.S. take sides in the conflict? If so, whom should it support?
Should the U.S. apply heavy pressure on one or both of the parties?

The upcoming chapter looks at how American and European publics answer these questions; but before it does so, it explores the cultural foundations of Americans' support for Israel.

I

Like U.S.: American Identification with Israel

Cultural Foundations and Contemporary Attitudes

There is no nation like us, except Israel.

—Ronald Reagan[1]

INTRODUCTION

American sympathy for Zionism and the State of Israel is widespread, long-standing, and deeply rooted in American political culture. This orientation not only predates the creation of professional pro-Israel lobbying organizations; it actually preceded the mass immigration of Eastern European Jews to the United States at the end of the nineteenth century. In 1948, Jews constituted fewer than 4 percent of all Americans. Even if every American Jew favored Israel, no more than 10 percent of American supporters of Israel could have been of Jewish origin in that year. By 2009, Jews were estimated to be only 1.8 percent of the population, accounting at most for 3 percent of Israel's supporters in the United States.[2] Consequently, the answer to the puzzle of American sympathy for Israel does not lie on the Lower East Side of New York; rather, it is deeply embedded in the very foundations of American national identity and political culture.

The chapter begins by identifying the main strands of American identity and political culture. It then explores the way in which those strands have informed positive orientations toward Zionism and the State of Israel. Subsequently, American public opinion toward the Arab-Israeli conflict is surveyed and contrasted with Western European attitudes, with the focus on the first decade of the twenty-first century. This transatlantic divide is then explained in terms of broader cultural differences between America and Western Europe.

AMERICAN IDENTITY AND POLITICAL CULTURE

There are two main strands of American national identity: the ethnoreligious foundation provided by the white Puritan Protestants who founded the country, and the American creed of classical liberalism.[3]

According to Anthony Smith, national identity is usually constructed on the foundations of a preexisting ethnic identity.[4] In the American case, the preexisting core consisted of white Protestants out of which developed a strong populist sense of American national identity associated with rugged independence, an honor code, and military pride.[5] In the first decade of the twenty-first century, whites still made up more than 70 percent of all Americans, and Protestants (black and white) still constitute the largest religious group by far.[6] In the past, this white Protestant identity often carried racist, anti-Catholic, and anti-Semitic undertones, but since at least the 1970s these prejudices have declined significantly. At the same time, core cultural orientations associated with this identity have spread beyond their original ethnic bounds to incorporate many blacks and Hispanics – the two largest ethnic minorities in America – who serve in the American military in disproportionate numbers.[7]

Alongside this, American identity is also based on a set of beliefs. As G. K. Chesterton remarked, "America is the only nation in the world that is founded on a creed."[8] According to Lipset, "the revolutionary ideology which became the American creed is liberalism in its eighteenth and nineteenth meanings":[9] individualism, meritocracy, democracy, and the free market. Key to this creed is the belief in American exceptionalism, according to which America's allegiance to freedom and democracy make it an exceptionally good country. In 2010, three-quarters of Americans agreed that America's history and constitution made it unique and the greatest country in the world. As Herman Melville, the nineteenth-century novelist, put it, "We Americans are the peculiar chosen people – the Israel of our time; we bear the ark of the liberties of the world."[10]

Influenced by Puritan millennialism, some argue that the creed requires an active foreign policy to build a new liberal world order – Wilsonianism[11] – while others interpret the creed in a passive sense, according to which America should serve as a "shining city on the hill," an example that others should emulate. Aside from this, the fusion of Protestant millennialism – with its sharp dichotomy between good and evil – and the American creed informs a moralistic tendency to divide the world into good nations associated with American values and evil nations associated with antidemocratic values.[12]

THE CULTURAL ROOTS OF AMERICANS' SUPPORT FOR ISRAEL

Protestantism, the Hebrew Bible, and Gentile American Zionism

The historical legacy of Puritan Protestantism is a major foundation of the pro-Israel orientation in American political culture. The Reformation led to a new emphasis on reading the Old Testament – the Hebrew Bible. The Puritans, who left England to set up colonies in America, were among the Protestants most committed to Bible study. They believed that it was important to read the Bible in the original Hebrew in order to understand it properly. Subsequently, the study of Hebrew became a core subject in the early American universities, being compulsory at Harvard from its founding in 1639 until 1787. Ezra Stiles, president of Yale from 1778 to 1795, delivered his commencement greetings in Hebrew. He also made Hebrew a compulsory part of the curriculum at Yale. James Madison spent a year studying Hebrew at Princeton. Samuel Johnson, the first president of Columbia University, concluded that Hebrew was essential to a gentleman's education. By 1917, fifty-five institutes of higher education in the United States taught Hebrew. Hebrew is to be found on the university seals of Columbia, Dartmouth, and Yale.

This contrasts with the great universities of Europe, where the focus was on the classical languages of Latin and ancient Greek. Aside from this, the Bible in English translation was the most widely read book in the colonial era and nineteenth-century America. More than a thousand places in the United States are named after biblical places; during the nineteenth century, thousands of Americans visited the Holy Land and millions more read reports of these travels.[13]

The Bible has also played a significant role in American political culture. The biblical idea of a covenant informed Puritan political thinking and subsequently influenced the framing of the Constitution itself.[14] In addition, Thomas Jefferson, Benjamin Franklin, and John Adams submitted a design for the seal of the United States that depicted the Israelites crossing the Red Sea.[15] To this day, biblical images adorn many national buildings in Washington, DC, including the Supreme Court, the House of Representatives, and the Library of Congress.[16] Biblical metaphors also regularly crop up in presidential inaugural addresses. Thus, Jefferson spoke of "that Being ... who led our fathers, as Israel of old, from their native land and planted them in a country flowing with all the necessities and comforts of life";[17] Lyndon Johnson declared, "They came here, the exile, the stranger ... They made a covenant with this Land";[18] while Bill Clinton referred to an America "guided by the ancient vision of a promised land."[19]

This emphasis on, and familiarity with, the Hebrew Bible and the Hebrew language laid the groundwork for an inclination to support Zionism, even before the founding of the modern Jewish Zionist movement at the end of the nineteenth century. Thus, in 1819 John Adams, the second president of the United States, wrote, "I really wish the Jews again in Judea an independent nation."[20] He was by no means alone. For example, the nineteenth-century scholar Prof. George Bush, an ancestor of both presidents, was also a proto-Zionist.[21] Moving forward to the middle of the twentieth century, when Clark Clifford, the White House chief counsel under President Harry S. Truman, presented the case for U.S. recognition of the State of Israel to the Cabinet in 1947, he quoted God's promise to the Jewish people in the Book of Deuteronomy. According to Clifford, Truman was a student of the Bible who believed that it gave the Jews a historical claim to statehood in at least part of its ancestral homeland.[22] Subsequently, Truman referred to himself as a modern-day Cyrus – a reference to the ancient Persian king who had restored the Jewish people to the Holy Land after the Babylonian exile.[23] Lyndon Johnson was also raised on the Bible, and this informed his support of a Jewish right to a homeland in Palestine.[24] Knowledge of the Bible was not the driving force behind Johnson's or Truman's policies toward Israel, but it informed part of their mind-set, as it did for Bill Clinton. The Clintons visited Israel in 1980 as part of a church group, and in his memoirs Clinton recalls his pastor telling him that God would not forgive him if he abandoned Israel.[25]

This orientation is not confined to former presidents. About half of Americans consistently believe that God gave the land that is now Israel to the Jewish people. This includes not only three-quarters of white Protestant evangelicals but also majorities of black and Latino Protestants, as well as a quarter of mainline Protestants and about a third of non-Latino Catholics. Indeed, there is a strong correlation between belief that the land of Israel was given to the Jewish people by God and support for the State of Israel.[26]

Protestant Millennialism and Biblical Prophecy

As noted earlier in this chapter, Protestant millennialism has played a major role in the forging of American political culture. Consequently, aside from the impact of the Bible per se, the belief that the State of Israel plays an important role in the Second Coming of Jesus is also important. This belief became central to Protestant evangelicals in America toward the end of the nineteenth century, in the form of *premillennial dispensationalism*. Dispensationalism originated in Britain, but it gained much greater currency in America, in part because of the deep-rooted American identification with biblical Israel. One leading American evangelist at the turn of the twentieth century, William Blackstone, developed the idea the United States had a special role in this divine plan: that of a modern Cyrus, to help restore the Jews to Zion.[27]

At the dawn of the new millennium, nearly two-thirds of all white Protestant evangelicals in America believe that modern-day Israel fulfills the biblical prophecy about the Second Coming. Of even greater significance is the influence of this doctrine among other groups in America. Thus, about half of all blacks and Hispanics, a quarter of non-Hispanic Catholics, and about a fifth of mainline Protestants also believe this.[28] This is indicative of the way in which pro-Israel elements of America's core ethnoreligious political culture have spread way beyond their original boundaries to become a part of the wider culture. Sympathy for Israel is lowest among atheist Americans, but even here Israel is consistently more popular than the Palestinians.[29]

The American Creed, Zionism, and Israel

In 1891, Blackstone organized a petition to President Benjamin Harrison that called for the United States to help restore Palestine to the Jews. The petition was signed by 413 prominent Gentile Americans, in an era prior to the mass immigration of Jews into the United States and the formation of major Zionist lobbying organizations. Those who signed the petition included the Speaker of the House of Representatives; the chairs of the House Ways and Means Committee and the House Foreign Affairs Committee; the future president William McKinley; the mayors of Baltimore, Boston, Chicago, New York, Philadelphia, and Washington; the chief justice of the Supreme Court; and the editors of the *Boston Globe, New York Times, Chicago Tribune, Philadelphia Inquirer*, and *Washington Post*. Many university presidents and leading businessmen also signed the petition, including John D. Rockefeller and J. P. Morgan. Other notable supporters of Zionism, even after they had left politics, were presidents Teddy Roosevelt and Herbert Hoover.[30] Neither of them were prophetic Zionists, nor were many who signed Blackstone's petition; they supported Zionism for other reasons.

For alongside biblically inspired Zionism there was a non-Jewish liberal Zionism, which viewed the return of the Jews to their homeland as contributing to improving the world in line with the American creed of liberal democratic values. In 1816, *Niles' Weekly Register*, the leading American news periodical of the time, welcomed the idea of a Jewish independent state with Jerusalem as its capital, with no reference to Holy Writ. It argued that the return to Zion would further American values. Zion would serve as a haven for Jews from persecution, and agricultural labor would improve the Jewish character. Secular Jewish Zionists reached the same conclusion toward the end of the nineteenth century.

In addition, some Americans supported Zionism as a particular example of the universal right of nations to self-determination – a value proclaimed by President Woodrow Wilson in 1917 as part of his famous Fourteen Points. In this vein, the liberal Protestant theologian Reinhold Niebuhr, who rejected the literal reading of the Bible and prophetic Zionism, declared: "The Jews have a right to a homeland. They are a nation ... They have no place where they are not exposed to the perils of minority status."[31]

However, for Americans, Zionism was not just another ordinary case of self-determination; it was much more than that, because they identified Zionism, and later the State of Israel, with the American creed. Americans have generally believed that the creed makes them exceptional; but Israel has often been perceived as an exception to exceptionalism. As Ronald Reagan exclaimed, "There is no nation like us, except Israel."[32] For many years, Americans have admired Israel's rapid economic and social development. Following a visit to Israel in 1959, Eleanor Roosevelt wrote of her deep admiration for Kibbutzim that were "literally reclaiming the desert and making it bloom."[33]

Even before the creation of the State of Israel, Zionist pioneers evoked for Americans their self-image of America as a pioneering enterprise. An example of the political impact this could have came in 1946, when an Anglo-American Commission of Enquiry was established to decide whether or not to let Europe's Jews immigrate to Palestine. One American committee member, Frank Aydelotte, wrote:

I left Washington pretty strongly anti-Zionist ... But when you see at firsthand what these Jews have done in Palestine ... [it is] the greatest creative effort in the modern world. The Arabs are not equal to anything like it and would destroy all the Jews have done ... This we must not let them do.[34]

Frank Buxton, another American member of the committee, wrote:

I came away from those [Jewish] farms [in Palestine] ... not quite so certain that American pioneers left no successors.[35]

Buxton also compared the Haganah (the defense arm of the Labor-led Zionist movement in mandatory Palestine) to the American Revolutionary Army. After the state was already established, President Truman wrote, "I believe it [Israel] has a glorious future before it – [as] not just another sovereign nation, but as an embodiment of the great ideals of our civilization."[36]

More recently, the pioneering theme has found expression in admiration for Israel's technological prowess, particularly in the high-tech field. Because of their pioneering problem-solving mentality, Americans are far more admiring of technological innovation than other nations.[37] As Vice President Joe Biden put it, "Israel's history is a tale of remarkable accomplishment. On a perilous patch of desert with sparse natural resources, you have built perhaps the most innovative economy in the world. You have more startups per capita than any nation on the planet, more firms on the NASDAQ exchange than anyone except the United States, and more U.S. patents per capita than any country, including my own." Biden went on to attribute this "remarkable and yet improbable success" to Israel's "democratic traditions, to its patriotic and pioneering citizens, *and as with my own country*, to its willingness to welcome the persecuted and the downtrodden from far-flung corners of the globe."[38]

Biden is by no means alone in identifying common values that link the State of Israel with America. Once, after crossing from Jordan into Israel, Eleanor Roosevelt reflected that entering Israel was "like breathing the air of the United States again."[39] The United States was founded by immigrants fleeing religious persecution; so was Israel. The United States was built by pioneers on the frontier; so was Israel. The United States had obtained its independence from the British Empire and created a democracy; so had Israel.

Israel's democratic character has been especially important in garnering sympathy among Americans. Its success in maintaining democracy served as a model in American eyes, for other allies. Thus, when in the 1970s, the Taiwanese responded to American prompting to democratize by claiming that it was impossible because they were under threat from mainland China, U.S. officials pointed to the Israeli example of maintaining democracy under the constant shadow of conflict.[40] In 2008, more than 80 percent of Americans agreed that the two countries "share common values, including a commitment to freedom and democracy."[41] In recent times, there has been growing liberal criticism of Israel. This is an important topic fully addressed in a subsequent chapter. But even allowing for this, American liberal opinion remains consistently more sympathetic to Israel than to the Palestinians,[42] in sharp contrast to the Europe Left, as we shall see later.

The Holocaust, the American Creed, and the Commitment to Israel's Security

While the Bible and the American creed created a basis for American identification with Israel, prior to 1945 this orientation was constrained by anti-Semitism. Consciousness of the Holocaust helped delegitimize anti-Semitism, and by the 1960s anti-Semitism had fallen dramatically.[43] Meanwhile, the 1960 Hollywood film *Exodus*, starring Paul Newman, linked the Holocaust directly to the struggle to found the State of Israel, broadening the appeal of Israel in America. In 1978, Holocaust consciousness grew in the wake of the highly publicized threat by American Nazis to march through Skokie, Illinois, home to many Holocaust survivors, and the screening of the NBC miniseries *Holocaust*.[44] The year 1993 was another important one, with the release of Steven Spielberg's film *Schindler's List*, which won seven Academy Awards, and the opening of the United States Holocaust Memorial Museum. The museum is situated in Washington, DC, on the National Mall along with the national museums and monuments. It has more than 2 million visitors per year.

Consciousness of the Holocaust has informed the American commitment to Israel's security. As we saw earlier, there is a strong strain within American political culture that feels the United States has a special duty to support human rights and democracy worldwide. This is perceived to be an important part of what it means to be American, and it became especially pertinent from the 1940s onward, when America left isolationism behind to become a global superpower. In this context, Americans have felt a special duty to protect Israel for two reasons. First, following decolonization after 1945, only two countries have remained consistently democratic: Israel and India. Israel thus stood out as particularly worthy of support, especially as India was closer to the Soviets during the Cold War. The second reason was the Holocaust.

The rise of the Nazis and the Holocaust played a critical role in convincing many Americans, including Eleanor Roosevelt and Reinhold Niebuhr, that the Jewish people needed not only a homeland but also a sovereign state.[45] Presidents Truman, Johnson, and Reagan all felt that the Holocaust placed a special responsibility on the United States to support Israel. As Reagan explained, "I've believed many things in my life, but no conviction I've ever held has been stronger than my belief that the United States must ensure the survival of Israel.

The Holocaust, I believe, left America with a moral responsibility to ensure that what had happened to the Jews under Hitler never happens again."[46] In this sense, the Holocaust is not just something terrible that happened to others; rather, it is *the* symbolic representation of absolute evil, and as such it offends the American creed. As Sen. John McCain wrote, "The Holocaust underlined, in the starkest terms, the moral basis for Israel's founding ... *In standing by Israel, we are merely being true to ourselves.* If we ever turned our backs on Israel, we would be abandoning the principles that built our nation."[47] Thus, while the American public is not generally keen on foreign aid, a majority has consistently supported aid to Israel while opposing aid to the Palestinians and America's Arab allies.[48] When the American public was asked if U.S. troops should be deployed to assist Israel in the event of an Iranian attack on the Jewish state, an absolute majority supported sending troops.[49] Indeed, when the public was asked what U.S. goals in the Middle East should be, "helping to protect Israel" was among the top five answers, with more than three-quarters designating it as an important goal.[50]

Still, the reasons behind support for these commitments to Israeli security have not only been moral and cultural; they are also related to perceptions of U.S. strategic interests.

ISRAEL AS A U.S. ALLY

Over the years, there has been a vigorous debate among the elites as to whether Israel is a strategic asset or liability. This elite debate is dealt with at length in the following chapters. But for now, what is important is that the American public has come to view Israel as a strategic asset. After Israel's spectacular victory in 1967 over the Soviet Union's Arab allies, the idea that Israel could be a strategic asset began to take off. Israel's performance seemed all the more impressive set against the background of Vietnam and the weakness of America's Arab allies.[51] Subsequently in 1979, following the fall of the Shah of Iran, Ronald Reagan referred to Israel as "the only remaining strategic asset in the region on which the United States can truly rely."[52] In the 1980s about a third of Americans viewed Israel as a close ally (a further 40–50 percent viewed it as a friendly country). In the wake of 9/11, the percentage who viewed Israel as a close ally grew to nearly half, while around two-thirds defined Israel as an ally. Only the UK, Australia, and Canada consistently ranked higher than Israel as American allies in the eyes of the public.[53]

Israelis and Americans have also shared a perception of the threat posed by terrorism, radical Middle Eastern states, and Islamism. Since the mid-1970s, terrorism has been the most frequently cited foreign policy problem in surveys conducted by the Chicago Council on Foreign Relations. In the wake of 9/11 the perceived threat from terrorism increased still further.[54] As of 2010, international terrorism remained in the public's view the most significant threat to vital U.S. interests, followed by nuclear proliferation and Iran.[55] Already in the

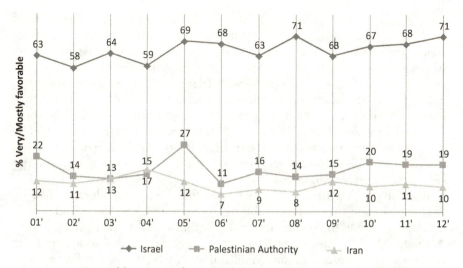

FIGURE I.I. **Favorable Views of Israel, the Palestinian Authority, and Iran** (From Mendes, "Americans Continue to Tilt Pro-Israel." Copyright © 2012 Gallup, Inc. All rights reserved. The content is used with permission; however, Gallup retains all rights of republication. This graph is an interpretation of data compiled by Gallup, Inc. However, Gallup, Inc. had no part in the creation of this graphic interpretation.)[56]

1970s, a spate of hijackings and high-profile terrorist attacks – notably the attack on Israeli athletes at the 1972 Munich Olympics – established a link in the public's mind between Arabs and terrorism.[57] Since 1979 the State Department has maintained a list of states that sponsor terrorism. Most of the countries on this list have come from the Middle East, including Syria, Sudan, Iran, Libya, and Iraq.[58] Moreover, since 1991, most of the countries that the American public has been least favorable toward have also been countries that are very hostile to Israel: Iraq under Saddam Hussein, Iran, Libya, and Syria, and from 2001 to 2004, the Palestinian Authority under Yasir Arafat.[59] (See Figure I.I.) Thus, part of the reason for siding with Israel is the American public's extremely negative perception of such countries.

AMERICAN ATTITUDES TOWARD MUSLIMS AND ARABS

Terrorism is not the only reason why Arab countries tend to be unpopular. For while both strands of American identity forged a sense of identification with Israel, they have also forged a sense of "otherness" regarding Islam and Arabs. In the nineteenth century, what most Americans knew about the region came from the Bible, *A Thousand and One Arabian Nights,* or from popular travelogue books that tended to portray Arabs as alien and Islam as cruel and primitive.[60] Some of these themes continued to inform American attitudes into the 1970s.[61] However, the reach of such negative stereotypes has declined significantly since then. Thus, even in the decade after 9/11 a majority of Americans had a favorable view of Muslim people, double the figure of those who had an unfavorable view.[62] Moreover, a majority reject the idea that 9/11 was part of a clash of civilizations with Islam.[63] Nonetheless, in November 2001, half of Americans felt that their own religion had little in common with Islam, compared to about a third who felt they had much in common. By 2007, this gap had widened to 70 percent and 19 percent respectively. In parallel, in 2002, 25 percent of Americans felt that Islam is more likely than other religions to encourage violence among its believers; by 2007 45 percent agreed with this view, and 39 percent disagreed.[64]

Also in the first decade of the twenty-first century, a plurality had an unfavorable view of Muslim *countries*.[65] These unfavorable attitudes were probably not only to do with terrorism, but also with related perceptions of Arab and Muslim states in the light of the American creed. For in contrast to Israel, most of the rest of the Middle East has lagged behind in terms of economic and social development. By the dawn of the twenty-first century, despite massive oil revenues, the Middle East's GDP was the lowest in world outside sub-Saharan Africa.[66] Furthermore, while Israel has maintained democracy, in the twenty years following the collapse of Communism, Freedom House ranked the Middle East as the most undemocratic area in the world, with only Israel ranked as "free."[67]

AMERICAN POLITICAL CULTURE AND HOSTILITY TO ISRAEL

Many of those who are hostile to the main themes of American political culture tend also to be hostile to Israel per se (as opposed to merely critical of certain Israeli policies). This point is elucidated by comparing the approach of Rev. Martin Luther King and the civil rights movement to Malcolm X and the Nation of Islam. The Nation of Islam is not only anti-Semitic and anti-Israel,[68] but in parallel, rejects both the Protestant foundation of American identity and the American creed. For them America is not an exceptionally good country, but rather an exceptionally bad country. Rather than identifying with America, Malcolm X identified with the Third World, which he viewed as suffering at the hand of white American imperialism, just like the blacks in America. As Malcolm X declared "I don't even consider myself an American ... I don't see any American dream; I see an American nightmare."[69] In contrast, Martin Luther King was a Protestant minister who, in his most famous speech, declared: "I have a dream that one day this nation will rise up and live out the true meaning of its creed."[70] Dr King also supported Zionism, stating, "We must stand with all our might to protect [Israel's] right to exist."[71]

Similarly, the Far Left, which has never believed in the American creed, has also been deeply hostile to Israel.[72] They see America as the prime source of suffering in the Third World, with Israel cast as "a lackey of American imperialism" and as a "colonialist entity." In parallel on the Right, many proponents of the Realist school of international relations, such as John Mearsheimer and Stephen Walt, who believe that foreign policy should be driven purely by material interests and not values like the America creed, have opposed the existence of a special relationship between the United States and Israel. Both these groups are dealt with in depth in forthcoming chapters. But the key point here is that just as the roots of support for Israel stem from identifying Israel with core strands of American political culture, so in parallel, those who reject those strands also tend to be hostile to Israel.

AMERICAN PUBLIC OPINION TOWARD THE ARAB-ISRAELI CONFLICT

In 1948, more than 60 percent of Americans supported the creation of the State of Israel, and only 10 percent opposed it. Since then, the most commonly asked poll question has been whether one sympathizes more with Israel or the Arab states/Palestinians. In the twentieth century, although a plurality of Americans remained neutral, sympathy for Israel remained 2–3 times greater than sympathy for the Arabs. During the Six Day War sympathy for Israel spiked, reaching a ratio of 10:1.[73] But in the 1970s and 1980s the ratio returned to about 3:1 in favor of Israel.[74] Meanwhile, the image of the Palestine Liberation Organization (PLO) was severely damaged by the terrorist attack on Israeli athletes at the 1972 Munich Olympics.[75] Levels of sympathy for Israel and the Palestinians in American public opinion since 1988 are illustrated in Figure 1.2.

Trends in Sympathy, Blame for Violence, and Commitment to Peace

Although there is a clear predisposition to sympathize with Israel over the Palestinians, levels of sympathy fluctuate according to which side is perceived to be more committed to peace. Thus, with the onset of the first Palestinian uprising – *intifada* – sympathy for Israel fell to 37 percent in May 1988, while sympathy for the Palestinians rose to 24 percent as the PLO recognized Israel's right to exist and renounced terrorism. In August 1989, 46 percent of Americans held an unfavorable view of Israel, compared to 45 percent who had a favorable view.[76] Yet during the 1991 Gulf War, when Israel was under rocket attack from Iraq, sympathy for Israel doubled, while sympathy for the Palestinians collapsed to 8 percent after the PLO refused to condemn terrorist attacks on Israel and sided with Saddam Hussein.[77] Sympathy for the Palestinians rose again to more than 20 percent when the PLO signed the 1993 Oslo Accords, with this level of support holding relatively steady until the collapse of the Oslo process in 2000. Still, even during the 1990s when the peace process was in full swing, three times as many Americans sympathized with Israel over the Palestinians.[78]

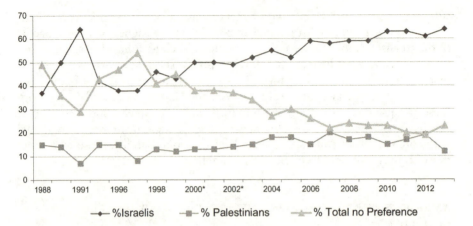

FIGURE 1.2. **Middle East Sympathies, Full Trend** (From Saad, "Americans' Sympathies for Israel Match All-Time High." Copyright © 2013 Gallup, Inc. All rights reserved. The content is used with permission; however, Gallup retains all rights of republication. This graph is an interpretation of data compiled by Gallup, Inc. However, Gallup, Inc. had no part in the creation of this graphic interpretation.)[79]

The collapse of the Oslo process, the onset of the suicide bombings, and 9/11 had a major impact of the levels of sympathy as the number of neutrals declined, and support for Israel *consistently* reached more than 50 percent for the first time. From 2000 until 2010, sympathy for Israel over the Palestinians rose by more than 20 percentage points to 63 percent, a record high.[80] The biggest jump in sympathy came in 2005–2006, following the disengagement from Gaza and the Second Lebanon War. In contrast, from 2001 to 2009 around 75 percent had an unfavorable view of the Palestinian Authority; only 15 percent had a favorable view.[81]

These shifts in the level of sympathy correlate with shifting perceptions of each side's behavior regarding peace. At the beginning of the peace process in the second half of 1991, when the George H. W. Bush administration was in conflict with Israel over settlements and when many Arab states attended the U.S.-sponsored Madrid peace conference, Americans were almost evenly divided over who was a bigger obstacle to peace, Israel or the Arab states. Similarly, in 1997 and 1998, when the Clinton administration was in conflict with the Benjamin Netanyahu government, Americans were again almost evenly divided on attributing blame to Israel and the Palestinians for problems in the peace process.[82] However, when the Oslo peace process collapsed and the violence of the second intifada ensued, the American public perceived the Palestinians as mainly responsible. In polls by Harris, *Newsweek*, and NBC from the start of the violence in October 2000 until its peak in the spring of 2002, less than 15 percent blamed primarily Israel, while around three times that number blamed primarily the Palestinians.[83] In 2006 and 2009, about four times as many thought that the radical Islamist groups Hezbollah and Hamas were primarily responsible for the Second Lebanon War and the Gaza War, respectively.[84] Finally, in 2010, five times more Americans thought that Israel was more committed to reaching a peace agreement than the Palestinians.[85]

A Palestinian State, Settlements, and Jerusalem

While Americans have consistently sympathized with Israel over the Palestinians, their positions on core substantive issues has been more evenhanded. In the 1990s, at the height of the Oslo process, about 40 percent favored the establishment of a Palestinian state, with about 20–25 percent opposed. Despite the collapse of the Oslo process, support for a Palestinians state rose between 2001 and 2003 reaching 58 percent. This rise paralleled the first official U.S. endorsement of Palestinian statehood by President George W. Bush in September 2001 and the promotion of the U.S.-backed Road Map in 2003 which also called for the creation of a Palestinian state. Israel accepted the Road Map with a number of conditions.[86] Overall, support for the ultimate creation of a Palestinian state, *in principle*, has become well established. But support for establishing a state *in practice* has been more conditional. In several polls conducted by *Newsweek* at the height of the suicide bombings in 2001–2002, respondents were asked whether they supported the creation of a Palestinian state *at this time* – and a plurality opposed it.[87] Similarly from 2005 to 2011, a clear majority thought that a Palestinian state should be established only after the Palestinians end terrorism and accept Israel's legitimacy.[88] Yet at the same time an increasing majority of the public has also opposed Israeli settlement construction in the West Bank and Gaza: 52 percent in 2002, 62 percent in 2010.[89] On Jerusalem, things are less clear. Since the 1990s some polls have shown a preference for Israeli sovereignty over all of Jerusalem, others for sharing or dividing the city between Israelis and Palestinians.[90]

U.S. Policy and the Peace Process

According to Gallup and the Chicago Council on Global Affairs polls, between 1998 and 2010 around three-quarters consistently stated than the United States should be evenhanded in the Israeli-Palestinian conflict. Of those who did express a preference, 1–4 percent preferred the Palestinians and roughly 15–25 percent preferred Israel.[91] The National Survey of Religion and Politics came up with a similar figure for the 1990s; however, between 2001 and 2008 it found that the number who thought the U.S. should give Israel preference had risen to 40 percent.[92] Specifically, in the spring of 2002 during Operation Defensive Shield, according to several CBS polls, 40 percent thought the U.S. should support Israel, between a quarter and a third thought the U.S. should say and do nothing, and 11–16 percent thought the U.S. should criticize Israel publicly.[93] Similarly, in the 2006 Lebanon War and the 2009 Gaza War about

40 percent thought the US should take Israel's side, while 1–2 percent less thought the U.S. should say or do nothing. Less than 10 percent thought the U.S. should publicly criticize Israel.[94] In other words, in the abstract the public seemed to prefer an evenhanded approach, especially in the 1990s when the peace process was in full swing. However, once the peace process collapsed and Israel faced suicide terrorism perpetrated by Islamist extremists, a large chunk of the American public evidently felt that the U.S. should side with Israel, as it was fighting a common enemy. In parallel, again in an abstract sense, Americans are willing to pressure Israel, including withholding aid especially if Israel is viewed as unrelenting it its opposition to peace.[95] However, in *practice*, in 2001–2002, there was far more support for pressuring both sides, rather than just Israel.[96] Moreover, since the Second Lebanon War opinion was clearly in Israel's favor. Thus, in 2007–2008, a plurality thought more pressure should be applied on the Palestinians; this rose to nearly 50 percent in 2013.[97]

THE TRANSATLANTIC DIVIDE OVER THE ARAB-ISRAELI CONFLICT

Public Opinion

Americans are far more supportive of Israel than other Western democracies. Between 2002 and 2010 at least double the number of Americans had a favorable opinion of Israel, compared to publics in the UK, France, Germany, and Spain (see Table 1.1).

The transatlantic divide was similarly apparent regarding attitudes to the conflict. The American public sympathized more with Israel by very wide margins. In contrast, in the UK, France, and Spain, a plurality sympathized more with the Palestinians. The Germans were the partial exception in Europe; but even so, the margin by which they preferred Israel was much narrower than among Americans (see Table 1.2).

TABLE 1.1. *Favorable Opinion of Israel (%)*

	U.S.	UK	France	Germany	Spain
2002	58	29	23	29	14
2004	59	24	22	21	13
2005	69	27	26	29	19
2007	63	30	40	27	18
2010	68	19	21	–	23

Data for U.S. is from Gallup and data for Europe is from surveys by Greenberg Rosner Quinlin Research for the Israel Project; a DYM Institute survey undertaken for Casa Sefarad Israel and surveys conducted for the Anti-Defamation League.[98]

TABLE 1.2. *Margin of Sympathy with Israel over the Palestinians (%)*

	U.S.	UK	France	Germany	Spain
2002	+28	−11	−17	−2	−
2006	+35	−5	0	+19	−23
2007	+38	−13	−11	+9	−16
2013	+39	−16	−4	+2	−

Data from Pew Research Center[99]

Between 2001 and 2004, both Americans and Western Europeans were about evenly divided as to whether the Palestinians were serious about reaching a peace agreement with Israel. However, there was a big transatlantic divide regarding Israel. At least 70 percent of Americans thought Israel was serious about reaching a peace agreement. In contrast, in eight out of ten Western European countries, a majority thought Israel was not serious about peace.[100] In the Second Lebanon War in 2006 and the 2009 Gaza War, between a half and two-thirds of Americans thought Israel's military action was "about right" or "had not gone far enough" – just under a quarter thought it had gone too far.[101] In the UK, the opposite was the case.[102] Similarly, in late 2009 to 2010, more than half of Americans thought the Palestinians were mainly to blame for the failure to reach peace, compared to about a fifth who blamed mainly Israel.[103] Again, UK opinion was a mirror image.[104]

Transatlantic differences were narrower when it came to policy, but they were still significant. In both the U.S. and Europe a very large chunk of the public preferred that their own country remain neutral in the conflict. However, among those who thought that their country should take sides, there were clear differences. As we saw above, five to six times more Americans thought their country should side with Israel rather than with the Palestinians. In contrast, in the UK and France, opinion was either evenly divided or pro-Palestinian.[105] The divide was even more pronounced regarding the question of which side should be pressured more. Thus in 2011, in nine Western European countries, more than twice as many, thought that the focus of pressure should be Israel, rather than the Palestinians. The opposite was the case among Americans.[106]

Finally, there was also a major transatlantic divide on Israel's strategic significance. In 2003, the six countries which Americans viewed as the greatest threat to world peace were: North Korea, Iran, Iraq, Afghanistan, Saudi Arabia, and Syria. In a 2003 survey of fifteen EU countries, North Korea, Iran, Iraq, and Afghanistan were also among the top six countries viewed as the greatest threat to world peace. Despite these parallels, there was a major divide over Israel. Europeans viewed Israel as the number one threat to world peace, while Americans put Israel in ninth place, just ahead of America itself.[107]

Political Culture and the Transatlantic Divide over Israel

This transatlantic divide over Israel is largely explained by differences in political culture. First, as demonstrated above, Puritan Protestant theology is an important foundation of support for Israel in the United States, and America remains far more Protestant and far more religious than Western Europe. About half of Americans say religion is very important in their lives, and a similar amount attend a place of worship once a week compared to a fifth or less in Western Europe.[108] In some Protestant European countries, notably England, there was a history of support for Zionism grounded on the Bible.[109] However, due to secularization this outlook has been almost completely marginalized. Meanwhile, predominantly Catholic countries with a relatively high percentage of religious people, like Spain and Poland, are among the European countries least supportive of Israel.[110]

Second, there is significance to the fact that Americans are more patriotic than Western Europeans. In the late 1990s around three-quarters of Americans were proud of their country, compared to about a half of the British, a third of the French, and a fifth of the Germans. Similarly, four-fifths of American youth felt that they wanted to do something to serve their country compared to about a half of the British and the French, who were the most patriotic in Western Europe.[111] There is also a significant stream of European thought that views nationalism as one of the main causes of the two world wars and that therefore seeks to supersede nationalism via European integration. This is important in the Middle East context, because Israel emphasizes its self-definition as the nation-state of the Jewish people, the legitimacy of which the Arabs and Palestinians reject. This leads some federalist Europeans to view Israel's insistence on its national identity in a negative light and as a factor inflaming the Arab-Israeli conflict. Still, national identity remains much stronger than any European identity in Western Europe,[112] and in any case, given that Palestinian and Arab claims are also based on nationalism, the role of this factor should not be exaggerated.

Third, differences of strategic culture inform the divide over Israel. In 2004, more than half of Americans agreed that the best way to ensure peace is through military strength, compared with about a quarter of Europeans. In parallel, 82 percent of Americans believed that under some conditions war is necessary to obtain justice, compared with 41 percent of Europeans.[113] Israel employed force extensively to combat suicide bombings during the second intifada, as well as conducting wide-ranging military operations against Hezbollah in 2006 and Hamas in 2009. Given the transatlantic divide over using military force, it is not surprising that Americans have been more supportive of Israel's use of force. Notable European leaders who were more inclined to support the use of force, such as the former Spanish prime minister José María Aznar and former British prime minister Tony Blair, who supported the 2003 Iraq War, were also more supportive of Israel.

Fourth, as was demonstrated above, Americans' commitment to Israel is informed by the Holocaust, and there is a difference in the way Europeans and Americans relate to the Holocaust.[114] Whereas only about a quarter of Americans agree with the statement that "Jews still talk too much about the Holocaust," more than 40 percent of Europeans surveyed agreed with the same statement.[115] Notable European leaders, who were especially sensitive to the Holocaust, were more likely to be pro-Israel – for example, Per Almark, the former deputy prime minister of Sweden, and Tony Blair, the former British prime minister, who instituted a national day of Holocaust remembrance in the UK.

Fifth, the classical liberal foundations of the American creed continue to differentiate American political culture from its European counterpart. America's lack of an inherited class structure explains the relative weakness of paternalistic conservatism and socialism in the United States, as well as the absence of major political parties representing those ideologies, in contrast to Western Europe.[116] Moreover, support for the radical Right and the radical Left is stronger in Western countries with a history of authoritarianism,[117] which the U.S. lacks entirely. This is important, because the main sources of hostility toward Israel on both sides of the Atlantic come from the Old Right and especially the radical Left, both of which are stronger in Europe than in America.

The Old Right has a paternalistic approach to the lower classes. Historically, it supported social welfare either out a sense of moral responsibility and/or as a means of defending its material interests and privileged position in an attempt to weaken the appeal of social revolution. Similarly, the Old Right tends to adopt a paternalistic attitude towards the Palestinians. In order to protect the material interests of their states, which are connected to oil, they tend to support the Arab side. This tendency is especially strong in Britain and France, where it serves as a means to deflect Arab resentment against their prior imperial role in the Middle East.[118] Aside from this, much of the Old Right is characterized by anti-Semitism. Anti-Semitic attitudes are significantly higher in Europe than in the U.S.,[119] and according to a major survey of the five thousand Europeans in ten countries, the most extreme anti-Israel sentiments strongly correlate with anti-Semitic attitudes.[120]

The American Old Right, often referred to as paleoconservatives, will be discussed at length in the next chapter, but it is important to point out that the Old Right has been in decline in both Europe and the U.S. for some time. In contrast, the New Right/neoconservatives have embraced classical liberalism and democracy with vigor. Against this background, modern conservative leaders such Margaret Thatcher and José María Aznar have admired Israel's democracy and economic innovation, viewing it as an outpost of Western values.[121] More generally, conservative opinion on both sides of the Atlantic is more supportive of Israel than those of the Left.[122]

Indeed, it is on the Left, especially the radical Left, that Israel has been most unpopular. There is a long history of Far Left anti-Zionism. In the early twentieth century, much of radical left-wing politics was anti-Zionist. Most extreme was Marxist-Leninism, which deemed that revolution and assimilation were the answer to anti-Semitism; Jews had to assimilate to be "progressive." In general, Marxist-Leninism viewed national self-determination of oppressed peoples as progressive, with one exception – the Jews. Therefore, because it asserted Jewish collective survival, Zionism was deemed "reactionary."[123]

True, the Holocaust evoked Leftist sympathy for the Jews as the quintessential victims of Fascism. Jean-Paul Sartre came out in favor of the creation of Israel, and even the Soviet Union temporarily reversed its anti-Zionist position, supporting the UN partition plan in 1947. In the early years of Israel, the Left was also sympathetic to Israel because of the Kibbutz movement. However, within a few years the Soviets became hostile, breaking off diplomatic relations in 1967. Similarly, following 1967 the radical Left in the West became vociferously anti-Zionist, viewing the conflict from a postcolonial perspective.

According to postcolonial theory, all the major problems of the Middle East are the result of malevolent outside forces of imperialism, led by the United States with the assistance of its "lackeys" such as Israel.[124] The West and, by extension, Israel are viewed as *essentially* "reactionary," while the status of the Third World, including the Palestinians, as "victims of colonialism" makes them *essentially* "progressive."[125] Their very weakness and their status as victims put them in the right. *Zionism* has become a code word for the forces of "reaction" in general,[126] and since the end of the Cold War, virulent anti-Israel sentiment has become a major unifying theme among radicals within social movements and nongovernmental organizations (NGOs).[127] The radical Left has also been the major force behind the campaign to impose boycotts, divestment, and sanctions (BDS) on Israel. The BDS movement as a whole takes "no position" on Israel's right to exist, but its core activists are anti-Zionists, opposed to Israel's existence in any borders.[128] In the UK, they succeeded in getting the largest trade union – UNISON with several million members – and the Trade Union Congress (TUC) itself to support a partial boycott of Israel.[129]

With the onset of the second intifada a number of important Europeans on the Left questioned Israel's right to exist,[130] while others compared Israeli actions to those of the Nazis[131] (as per Soviet propaganda after 1967) – for example, the Nobel Prize–winning Portuguese author (and self-proclaimed libertarian Communist) Jose Saramago,[132] and the renowned Greek composer and icon of the European Left Mikis Theodorakis.[133]

Meanwhile, according to a poll commissioned by the Italian newspaper *Il Corriere della Sera* in 2004, more than a third of Italians agreed that "the Israeli government is perpetuating a full-fledged genocide and is acting with the Palestinians the way the Nazis did with the Jews."[134] According to the European Monitoring Centre on Racism and Xenophobia,[135] denying the Jewish people the right to self-determination and drawing comparisons of Israeli policy to that of the Nazis constitute a new form of anti-Semitism. A core motif of traditional anti-Semitism is that Jews represent absolute evil. Nowadays Nazis are considered the embodiment of absolute evil. In this sense comparing Israel per se to the Nazis, constitutes anti-Semitism.In addition, the 2006 report of All-Party Parliamentary Inquiry into Anti-Semitism in the UK[136] concluded that left-wing activists and Muslim extremists were using criticism of Israel as a pretext for anti-Semitism and that as such anti-Semitism was entering the mainstream.

Leaving aside the new anti-Semitism, it is clear that the discourse within the highbrow press in Europe was far more anti-Israel than in the U.S. This is evident when comparing the discourse in the five broadsheet British papers: the *Daily Telegraph*, the *Times*, the *Guardian*, the *Independent*, and the *Financial Times*; with their closest U.S. equivalents: the *Washington Post*, the *New York Times*, the *Los Angeles Times*, the *Wall Street Journal*, and the *Chicago Tribune*.[137] Between September 1991 and April 2010, 1,703 articles in all these publications combined contained articles in which Israel or Israelis were tied to the words: *Apartheid*, *racist/racism*, and *colonial(ism)*. These phrases are usually associated with the Palestinian narrative or with especially harsh criticism of Israeli actions and policies. Two-thirds of these articles appeared in the British papers, and two-thirds of the British articles appeared in the left-wing newspapers the *Guardian* and the *Independent*.[138] Anti-Zionism and comparisons between Israel and the Nazis were also made by the American radical Left, as is discussed in depth in Chapter 3. However, because both the Marxian Left and traditional anti-Semitism are much stronger in Europe than in the US, those ideas have been far more marginal to the American discourse compared to Europe.

In addition, Europe's history of imperialism and colonialism means that postcolonial guilt has had greater resonance there than in the United States. Consequently, the Far Left's anti-Zionism and support for the Palestinians based on their status as victims has had greater resonance in Europe, especially since the late 1960s. During this period, the rise of postcolonial guilt coincided with the decline of Israel's own victim status, as the Holocaust became more distant and Israel became stronger, occupying the West Bank and becoming increasingly allied with the "imperial" United States.[139]

Regarding the identification with the Palestinians as victims, there is an important qualitative distinction here between liberal criticisms of Israeli policies, which are increasingly common in the United States, and left-wing identification with the Palestinians as victims – which has far greater purchase in Europe. A defining characteristic of liberalism is its belief that the choices people make are meaningful and significant, and that consequently they are responsible for those choices. Accordingly, liberals reject in principle the postcolonial premise that because the Palestinians are weak, suffering, and hail from the Third World they are ipso facto in the right and a progressive force. Also, in contrast to much of the postcolonial left, liberals are unwilling to explain away Palestinian terrorism and political extremism with the excuse that it is the inevitable and desperate response of the victim for which the powerful Israelis are ultimately responsible.[140]

Thus, virtually all of Israel's mainstream friends in Europe actually oppose settlements and support the creation of a Palestinian state, including those on the liberal Left, like the journalist Nick Cohen (not Jewish) in the UK and Pascal Bruckner in France. Cohen and Bruckner reject the postcolonial guilt complex and are highly critical of the radical Left *across the board*, because they perceive it as representing a threat to liberal values per se, not simply to Israel.[141]

Finally, it is important to note that the Muslim factor plays little or no role in explaining the transatlantic opinion divide on Israel. In the first decade of the twenty-first century, far fewer Americans held negative views about Muslims than did the citizens of France, Spain, and Germany, and yet the public in those countries were far less sympathetic to Israel than were Americans.[142] As for Muslims themselves, there are many more in Europe than in the U.S.,[143] but they still constitute less than 5 percent of the population of the European Union. So even though they are much more sympathetic to the Palestinians than non-Muslim Europeans, they do not constitute a large enough group to explain the breadth and depth of the transatlantic divide on Israel.

CONCLUSION

Public sympathy for Israel in America is akin to a large oak tree. It has very deep roots in American political culture and many different branches. The seed was planted prior to the establishment of a large Jewish community in the United States, and it continues to flourish for reasons largely independent of that community. The deepest roots are the very foundations of American identity itself: Puritan Protestantism, the American creed, and a pioneering spirit. Aside from this, Americans also support Israel because they view it as a strategically important and reliable ally against the common threats posed by terrorism, Islamism, and weapons of mass destruction. Indeed, the rising strength of this conviction provides the main explanation for the increase in sympathy for Israel to record levels in decade following 9/11, though it was also reinforced by the belief that the Palestinian side was mainly responsible for the failure to achieve peace. On this issue, Americans' pro-Israel disposition means that the burden of proof is generally on the Arab-Palestinian side, but the behavior of the parties causes significant variation. Moreover, when it comes to the question of whether U.S. foreign policy should favor Israel or adopt a more evenhanded policy, American have been more divided. A closer look at public attitudes reveals that important subgroups hold significantly different opinions on this issue and others related to the conflict. The most important division is between Republicans and conservatives on the one hand, and liberals and Democrats on the other hand; this divide is examined in the following two chapters.

PART I

PARTY AND IDEOLOGY

2

Republicans, Conservatives and the Right: The Surge in Support for Israel

The acrid and unexpungable odor of terrorism, which has hung over Israel for many years, is now a fact of American life ... Americans are targets because of their virtues – principally democracy, and loyalty to those nations that, like Israel, are embattled salients of our virtues in a still-dangerous world.

—George Will, September 12, 2001[1]

INTRODUCTION

For many years support for Israel was associated more with liberals and Democrats than with Republicans and conservatives. However, in the first decade of twenty-first century, this was no longer the case. George W. Bush is widely regarded as the most pro-Israel president ever, while in the 2012 Republican primaries, candidates were falling over themselves to demonstrate support for Israel. The candidates were not just expressing their own convictions, they were responding to the fact that Israel has become an important issue for the Republican base. Indeed, between 2000 and 2010, sympathy for Israel over the Palestinians among Republicans rose from 60 to 85 percent, far outnumbering the percentage for Democrats,[2] and conservative Republicans were the most pro-Israel of all.[3]

This chapter surveys and analyzes conservative and Republican approaches to Israel and the Arab-Israeli conflict. The chapter begins with a look at levels of identification with conservatism among the general public and within the Republican Party. A brief survey of conservative attitudes to Israel during the Cold War is then presented. Subsequently, the three main approaches to the Arab-Israeli conflict and the Middle East among Republicans and conservatives in the post–Cold War era are sketched out, with the focus being on the intellectual and political elites. First, there is the "old conservative

establishment," whose approach towards Israel is one of "unfavorable neutrality." Second, there is Kissingerian realism, which adheres to an approach of
"favorable neutrality" toward Israel. Third, there is the "new conservative
mainstream" that strongly identifies with, and sides with, Israel. This has
become the dominant approach among Republicans and conservatives in the
twenty-first century. Following this, narratives of the rise and fall of the peace
process from the early 1990s until the end of the first decade of the new
millennium are surveyed through the coverage of the relevant issues in the main
conservative magazines and columns of a number of leading conservative
columnists. Finally, attention turns to the attitudes of rank-and-file Republicans
and conservatives.

CONSERVATIVES AND THE REPUBLICAN PARTY

In the United States, conservatives tend to favor limited government; many are
also nationalistic, socially conservative and hawkish on foreign policy. Between
1992 and 2010 the percentage of self-identifying conservatives among the
general public rose from 36 to 40 percent. As a consequence, conservatives
became the largest ideological group in America, overtaking moderates.[4] Moreover, since the 1980s, the amount of conservatives who identify as Republicans

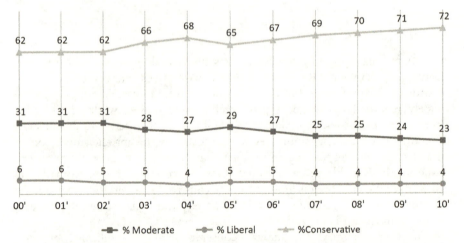

FIGURE 2.1. **Recent Political Ideology Trend among Republicans** (From Saad,
"Conservatives Continue to Outnumber Moderates in 2010." Copyright © 2010
Gallup, Inc. All rights reserved. The content is used with permission; however, Gallup
retains all rights of republication. This graph is an interpretation of data compiled
by Gallup, Inc. However, Gallup, Inc. had no part in the creation of this graphic
interpretation.)[5]

has almost doubled,[6] so that in 2010, almost three quarters of Republicans defined themselves as conservative (see Figure 2.1);[7] while about half were evangelicals.[8]

AMERICAN CONSERVATIVES AND ISRAEL, 1948–1991

Before 1967, conservatives were generally cool toward Israel, and sometimes hostile. The leading conservative publishing house, Regnery, published a stream of books championing Arab culture and sympathizing with the Palestinians. Ironically, at a time when the leading conservative magazine, *National Review*, was still defending Jim Crow segregation, the magazine referred to Israel as "the first racist state in modern history."[9]

There were numerous reasons for this bias. In the 1940s and 1950s the largest domestic anti-Zionist lobby was located in the mainline Protestant church, which in that period was closely associated with the Republican Party, and had a lot of influence in the Bureau for Near East Affairs inside the State Department.[10] Then, there was the anti-Semitism of the Old Right, which viewed Jews as outside their definition of a white Christian American national identity. The fact that Israel was run by social democrats and that it generally received strong support from American liberals served to further tarnish Israel in conservative eyes. Moreover, while the Holocaust was an important factor in generating sympathy for Israel in liberal eyes, *National Review* tended to belittle the evils of Nazism, including the Holocaust. Finally, mainstream conservatism in the 1950s was stanchly anti-Soviet, and to the eye of a senior editor of *National Review*, James Burnham, Israel looked like a strategic liability. Supporting Israel, it was held, would alienate the strategically more significant Arabs.

The turning point was Israel's victory in the Six Day War, which highlighted Israel's military prowess as a strong, independent American ally, at a time when America was suffering greatly from the absence of just such an ally in Vietnam. Subsequently, conservatives began to relate to Israel as a strategic asset. This shift was facilitated by *National Review* founder William F. Buckley Jr.'s campaign to remove anti-Semitism from the conservative movement.

The first significant practical expression of this shift came during the first administration of Richard M. Nixon, which dramatically increased military aid to Israel. However, the influence of solidly pro-Israel groups within the GOP, namely evangelicals and neoconservatives, did not begin to be felt seriously until the Reagan presidency. In the 1980s and 1990s Republicans and conservatives were divided between these pro-Israel groups and more neutral and hostile groups led by, among others, George H. W. Bush and Pat Buchanan. However, in the wake of 9/11, the pro-Israel outlook came to dominate Republican politics and the conservative discourse. The section below examines the three main conservative approaches to Israel in detail, with a focus on the post–Cold War era.

THE OLD CONSERVATIVE ESTABLISHMENT: UNFAVORABLE NEUTRALITY

Foundations

Old-establishment conservatism in America contains within it three interrelated orientations: paleoconservatism, libertarianism, and Arabist Realism. The roots of these groups are in the Old Right that supported isolationism in the 1930s.

For paleoconservatism, the particularistic Anglo-Christian culture that prevailed in the eighteenth century defines the American nation, not the universal values of the American creed.[11] In the 1960s it opposed civil rights legislation. Today, they are conservative on social issues, favor limited government, states' rights, and protectionism, while remaining hostile to immigration.[12] Russell Kirk was the intellectual mentor to contemporary paleoconservatives like Paul Gottfried. There was also the syndicated columnist Robert Novak. The main organs for disseminating paleoconservatism have been the Rockford Institute's *Chronicles* magazine, and the *American Conservative* magazine founded in 2002 by Pat Buchanan, who previously campaigned for the Republican Presidential nomination. Buchanan summed it up thus: "We are old church and old right, anti-imperialist and anti-interventionist, disbelievers in Pax Americana."[13]

Libertarians champion limited government, civil liberties, individualism, and market economics. They oppose an interventionist foreign policy, because they fear it will strengthen central government, lead to increased taxes, and threaten civil liberties. Their leading politician was long-serving congressman Ron Paul, the presidential candidate of the Libertarian Party in 1988 who ran for the Republican nomination in 2008 and 2012. The libertarian perspective is promoted by the Cato Institute. Then there is Andrew Sullivan, one of the first prominent political journalists to start his own blog.

Arabist Realism is a version of the Realist approach to international relations that favors the Arab side in the Arab-Israeli conflict. Realism defines itself in opposition to Wilsonian liberal idealism. For Realists, foreign policy is about state interests understood in terms of material power and physical security, not spreading democracy or constructing international institutions.[14] While more internationalist than libertarians and paleocons, the dread of getting bogged down and being overstretched is central to Realist thinking, as is evident in the (Caspar) Weinberger and (Colin) Powell doctrines, which severely circumscribed the terms under which the U.S. would commit military forces abroad to combat.[15]

For them, the Vietnam War is a powerful symbol. The lessons of Vietnam, especially the Tet offensive of 1968, are understood as demonstrating the strategic futility of military interventionism, for while the U.S. won many battles militarily, including Tet, it was the willingness of its indigenous opponent to suffer greater losses that ultimately determined the course of the war.

Realism is influential among the old Republican business elites and diplomats, as well as figures such as George H. W. Bush, James Baker, Brent Scowcroft, Colin Powell and Robert Gates. Within academia, Stephen Walt and John Mearsheimer are leading proponents.

Grand Strategy: Defensive Realism in the Middle East

The "old conservative establishment" views international relations in terms of state interests and nationalism, while discounting other ideologies. Thus, in the 1930s, the Old Right's support for isolationism and appeasement was grounded in the perception that Nazi Germany's agenda was driven by nationalism in a way that was not qualitatively different from that of traditional German nationalists. Some even ended up as apologists for Fascism.[16] Even with the benefit of hindsight, Buchanan referred to General Francisco Franco as a "patriot" while rejecting the existence of Fascism as a coherent ideology.[17]

Indeed, nationalism is central to their strategic thinking. As they see it, direct intervention in the affairs of other countries always breeds resentment from the locals, a resentment that easily translates into violent resistance. As the isolationist Republican senator Robert Taft (1939–1953) argued, "However benevolent we might be, other people simply do not like to be dominated."[18] From their perspective, this dynamic was compounded following the end of the Cold War by the gulf in power between America and other states, which was viewed as leading other countries to be especially fearful of America. When the U.S. is militarily assertive, this is said to generate a strong counteraction. Hence, defensive Realists advocate that direct U.S. intervention abroad should be extremely limited.[19] Consequently, they opposed humanitarian intervention in the Balkans in the 1990s.[20]

Also in the 1990s they rejected the idea that Islamism represented a major threat to the U.S.,[21] and 9/11 did not fundamentally alter their outlook. Instead, they posited that while America had discreet conflicts of interests with a variety of different actors in the Middle East, the vast majority could be handled by political accommodation.[22] What united these actors and turned them into enemies of the U.S. was not religion or ideology, but blowback from American intervention in the Middle East,[23] including the stationing of U.S. troops in Saudi Arabia, the Iraq War,[24] and support for Israel.[25] As Ron Paul put it, "They don't come here to attack us because we're rich and we're free, they come and attack us because we're over there."[26]

The antidote was therefore to reverse all these policies. Thus, the Baker-Hamilton Report advocated a speedy withdrawal from Iraq; Mearsheimer and Walt recommended removing American ground troops from the region and relying on a strategy of "offshore balancing," while libertarians advocated a wholesale American military withdrawal from the region.[27] In the case of Iran, they reasoned that Teheran's pursuit of the nuclear option was driven by power considerations, national prestige, and the threat they felt from the U.S., not ideology. Consequently, they felt that a nuclear Iran would be rational and hence manageable. They advocated engagement to reassure Iran; Buchanan was prepared to reach a deal that left the Islamist regime in possession of nuclear weapons.[28]

Strange as it seems, there has been something of an unholy alliance between the paleocons and the progressive-postcolonial Left based on their shared opposition to an activist interventionist American foreign policy. This convergence has roots going back to the late 1930s, when the conservative-led America First Committee merged with the left-wing Keep America out of War Committee. Indeed, in 1940 Russell Kirk supported the socialist Norman Thomas for president because of his antiwar stand. Another contemporary strand of convergence has been shared hostility to Israel. Indeed, articles in the *American Conservative* drew heavily on virulent left-wing critics of Israel.[29]

Israel

The defensive Realist approach of the old conservative establishment rejects the idea that the United States should have a special relationship with Israel. As Brent Scowcroft put it, "I think we have a relationship that is natural with a small, courageous democracy in a hostile land. *But I don't think we have any special commitment there. And I think we have an equal commitment to Palestinians.*"[30] Yet in practice, there has not been an "equal commitment" but rather a strong tendency to lean towards the Arab side. This is because they view Israel as a strategic liability.[31] This view rests on the linkage[32] theory, according to which the Arab-Israeli conflict is regarded as the lynchpin of regional instability and anti-Americanism in the Middle East. Many of them advocate ending American aid to Israel.[33]

Back in the 1930s and '40s, adherents of unfavorable neutrality opposed the creation of Israel, fearing it would drive the Arabs into the pro-Soviet camp.[34] Later, they blamed Western support for Israel for the penetration of Soviet influence into the Middle East. To counter this, they sought to distance the U.S. from Israel while advocating the imposition of a settlement to the conflict on pro-Arab terms.[35] The Palestinian issue was deemed the key because of its resonance in Arab nationalist mythology. This was viewed as constraining America's Arab allies from adopting pro-American policies, while simultaneously allowing America's opponents to rally support to their cause. Consequently, after Anwar Sadat's dramatic visit to Jerusalem in 1977, they *opposed* a separate Israeli peace treaty with Egypt, fearing it would simply draw the rest of the Arab world closer to the USSR. For the same reason they opposed the development of strategic cooperation between Israel and the U.S. in the 1980s. This approach continued to drive their thinking in the post–Cold War era. Thus they rejected the idea that Israel and the U.S. were both in conflict with radical Islamist enemies.[36] Instead, American intervention in the Middle East and its support for Israel were identified as the major cause of opposition to the U.S. in the region.[37] As Scowcroft put it, "[It] creates a sense of grievance and hatred for us ... [and] at some point those chickens will come home to roost."[38]

To assuage this sense of grievance they advocated heavy pressure on Israel. Mearsheimer and Walt went so far as to recommend that the U.S. "[line] up international support to isolate Israel, much the way South Africa was singled out and shunned."[39] In any case, in nearly all their schemes the practical onus for concessions fell squarely on Israel and involved the creation of a Palestinian state, irrespective of its internal nature and its approach to reconciliation with Israel.[40] Libertarians took a different tack, advocating American strategic disengagement from Israel and the peace process altogether.[41]

In terms of ascribing blame for the conflict, the old conservative establishment placed the burden overwhelmingly on Israel. Palestinian terrorism was viewed as an understandable response to nationalist grievances. It was defined as merely a tactical problem that would disappear once Palestinian grievances were resolved.[42] On occasion, a moral equivalence was drawn between the Likud and Hamas.[43] Robert Novak even called Hamas "freedom fighters."[44] There was also a tendency in the *American Conservative* magazine to whitewash Israel's enemies. For example, the paramilitary Shiite organization Hezbollah was presented as "a nonsectarian organization that is able to cooperate with people of all faiths,"[45] while the brutal dictator of Syria, Bashar Assad, was presented as an unassuming head of state, a "wonkish professor" eager for peace and interreligious accord.[46]

Arab Nationalism, Oil, Anti-Semitism

Many State Department area specialists who first developed this approach were committed to Arab nationalism as a result of being the children and grandchildren of Americans who set up universities in Beirut, Cairo, and elsewhere in the Middle East – for example, John Foster Dulles and his brother Allen.[47] While their influence is no longer felt directly, it lingers to a small degree in the culture of the State Department.[48] In addition, some Realists, like James Baker and President George H. W. Bush, have extensive business ties in the Arab world.[49] In addition, there has been very strong criticism of the pro-Israel lobby and the neoconservatives.[50] On occasion, the language used has echoed anti-Semitic tropes[51] with references to "the fifth column"[52] and "the transparent cabal"[53] "controlling" the media and Capitol Hill[54] to fight wars for Israeli interests.[55]

To sum up, there are differences between the various strands that make up the old conservative establishment. Yet what unites them regarding Israel and the Middle East is more important than what divides them. They all advocate a defensive Realist grand strategy and neutrality in the Arab-Israeli conflict. They all oppose a special relationship with Israel, and they all believe that the special relationship is a major cause of anti-Americanism in Middle East. Paleoconservatives and Realists explicitly place the onus for concessions on Israel and call for heavy U.S. pressure on Israel in this regard. While libertarians call for American disengagement from the peace process, the practical implications of this stance would be similar, because in the absence of American diplomatic support for Israel, there would be enormous international pressure to impose a settlement on Israel, on Arab terms.

KISSINGERIAN REALISM: "FAVORABLE NEUTRALITY" TOWARD ISRAEL

Unburdened by the isolationist strand within the old conservative establishment, Kissingerian realism has been comfortable with the U.S. playing a leading role in international politics, while simultaneously opposing the more offensive orientated strategy of the new conservative mainstream. Unlike Arabist Realism, it has not adopted an unwaveringly negative approach to Israel, though without completely embracing Israel, as has the new conservative mainstream.

Favorable neutrality began to emerge at the end of the 1950s, when elements within the Dwight Eisenhower administration, including Vice President Richard Nixon, began to change their strategic assessment of Israel. The Egyptian president, Gamal Abdel Nasser, was accepting Soviet weapons, continuing to ferment revolution against U.S. allies in the region, while ignoring American support for Egypt during the Suez Crisis. All of this after he had rejected a pro-Arab American plan to settle the Arab-Israeli conflict. Against, this background, some Realists began to understand that the key regional dynamic was not the Arab-Israeli conflict after all, but the "Arab Cold War"[56] for leadership of the region in which pro-Soviet Nasserite forces were ranged against pro-American conservative regimes. Shared Arab hostility to Israel was a secondary issue in this strategic environment. At the same time, the weakness and unreliability of America's Arab allies contrasted with Israel's military strength and clear pro-Western orientation such that the Eisenhower Administration, which had previously thought that American support for the creation of Israel was an error, reached the conclusion in 1958 that it made sense for the U.S. "to support Israel as the only strong pro-West power left in the [Middle] East."[57]

In the wake of Vietnam, Henry Kissinger and Richard Nixon shared the Realist conviction within the old conservative establishment that America was strategically overstretched and that it needed to retrench and move to a policy of détente with the Soviet Union. However, they differed from the Arabist Realists regarding the implications of this for Middle East policy. Arabist Realists took a regional approach; for them détente meant working with the Soviet Union to pressure Israel into a comprehensive settlement of the Arab-Israeli conflict on Arab terms. In contrast, Nixon and Kissinger took a global approach in which containment of the Soviet Union, especially in areas of vital interest like the Middle East, was the primary concern. Given the need for retrenchment, the Nixon doctrine placed greater emphasis on burden-sharing with allies in place of direct U.S. intervention. Israel and Iran were considered the American allies best placed to play this role in the Middle East. Israel's victory in the Six Day War had demonstrated its strength, and its designation as a strategic asset was sealed in September 1970, after Israel saved the pro-American regime in Jordan from collapse at the hands of the PLO and Syria, then Soviet allies. In the aftermath, Kissinger increased American aid to Israel tenfold.

Still, viewing Israel as a strategic asset did not mean giving it unconditional support. During and after the Yom Kippur War, the U.S. put enormous pressure on Israel, first to accept a cease-fire and then to withdraw from Egyptian territory in the Sinai desert. Initially this was done to contain the threat of escalation to a global nuclear confrontation and later in order to entice Egypt to switch sides in the Cold War. Nonetheless, Kissinger continued to view a strong Israel as a strategic asset; hence he increased military aid to the Jewish state. In any case, Kissinger absolutely opposed the idea that a comprehensive peace settlement on Arab terms with the active involvement of the Soviets and their radical allies was in the American interest; the whole purpose of his strategy was to exclude the Soviets.[58]

In the post–Cold War era, Kissingerian realists continued to support active U.S. engagement in international politics. In the 1990s they soberly supported the Middle East peace process as something that strengthened a pro-American balance of power in the region. This strategy also sought to bring Syria and the Palestinians under the U.S. wing through the promotion of a peace process that was designed to lead to Israeli withdrawal, in return not only for peace but for an enhanced security relationship with the United States.[59] As under Kissinger, the aim was not simply to benefit Israel, but to reinforce America's strongest and most reliable ally and thereby reinforce a pro-American balance of power by preventing America's and Israel's radical enemies exploiting Israel's weakened geostrategic position following withdrawals.

One of the main proponents of Kissingerian realism in the conservative discourse was William F. Buckley Jr. in *National Review*, the leading highbrow conservative magazine in America. Although Buckley sympathized with Israel, he argued that strategic considerations rather than pro-Israel sentiment should guide US foreign policy.[60]

THE NEW CONSERVATIVE MAINSTREAM: "ISRAEL IS US"

Foundations

This pro-Israel approach is articulated by an intellectual elite of neoconservatives and by populist nationalists who form the base of the Republican Party. Both these groups became politically mobilized in the late 1960s and early 1970s, and both shifted their political allegiance from the Democrats to the Republicans thereafter. In the first decade of the twenty-first century, this staunchly hawkish pro-Israel approach was absolutely dominant among conservatives and Republicans. They share an offensive grand strategy and a perception of Israel as a "strategic asset," which is complemented by a strong commitment to Israel independent of strategic considerations.

Populist nationalism[61] consists of the instincts, emotions, beliefs, and values of a large section of the American public who put a premium on an "old-fashioned" sense of honor, and who favor a foreign policy based on a strong military and unilateralism. Populist nationalism is historically rooted in the feeling of belonging to a folk community prevalent among the white family farmers in the American heartland. It remains strong among white evangelicals in the South, but it has expanded beyond its geographic and ethnic core to include many black and Hispanic Americans, who have become disproportionally represented in the American military. Populist nationalists have come to form the base of the Republican Party in the South. Populist nationalism has a strong resonance with Tea Party supporters,[62] as well as among many white working-class swing voters in the North, known as Reagan Democrats. Within the media, it is expressed by people like Rush Limbaugh and Glenn Beck. Among the political elites, former secretary of defense Donald Rumsfeld and former vice president Richard Cheney qualify as the more secular representatives of this tradition, while religion has played more of a role for people like the former Republican vice presidential candidate Sarah Palin and the former Republican congressman and House majority leader Dick Armey.

Neoconservatism emerged in the late 1960s and early 1970s in reaction to the counterculture, the antiwar movement, and affirmative action – all of which it opposed. At that time, neoconservatives were Democrats who viewed themselves as classical liberals. They had strongly supported the civil rights movement and been skeptical about the Vietnam War. But after the Democratic Party moved leftward under George McGovern and Jimmy Carter, they shifted their allegiances to the Republican Party. Many of the first generation of neoconservatives had been Trotskyites in their youth. Among these founders were Irving Kristol and the editor of *Commentary*, Norman Podhoretz. Many of the second generation of neoconservatives also had early ties to the left. However, their dominant influence was the hawkish New Deal Democratic senator Henry "Scoop" Jackson, for whom many of them worked, including Elliot Abrams, Richard Pearle, Paul Wolfowitz, and Doug Feith; these figures went on to serve in senior posts under George W. Bush. More broadly, neoconservatism draws on the American tradition of conservative internationalism, which Henry Nau argues is embodied in the foreign policies of previous presidents such as Thomas Jefferson, James Polk, and Ronald Reagan.[63] Neoconservatism is particularly strong in intellectual circles; as such, their ideas gained significant influence through conservative think tanks such as the American Enterprise Institute, the Heritage Foundation, the Hudson Institute, and the Center for Security Policy.[64]

An Offensive Grand Strategy

For both neoconservatives and populist nationalists, the world is sharply divided between America ("the children of light") and its friends and allies on the one hand, and the enemies of America ("the children of darkness") on the other hand. The preferred strategy for dealing with these enemies is a hawkish, offensive one, in which the use of force, deterrence, and resolve are key; compromises by the West are viewed as appeasement, which will only be exploited by the enemy. After 9/11 they advocated an offensive interventionist grand strategy to combat the threat from radical Islamic terrorism. Below, a more detailed account of each group's approach is presented.

Neoconservatism

For the neoconservatives, the divide between liberal democratic ideology and totalitarian ideologies is the most important strategic divide in world politics. It was this antitotalitarianism that caused them to break with the Trotskyite Left in the 1940s. They came to utterly reject the view, which had been influential in their Trotskyite circles, that that there was little difference between imperialist Britain and Nazi Germany. They were deeply disturbed by the failure of a decadent, uncertain, demoralized West to prevent the collapse of the Weimar Republic; deeply disturbed by the failure of appeasement to contain Hitler, and deeply disturbed by the consequences of those failures: the Holocaust. This was true not only for first generation Jewish neocons, but also for Scoop Jackson, who visited Buchenwald just after its liberation, as well as for second-generation neocons like Paul Wolfowitz who lost family in the Holocaust. For the neocons, the cardinal sin is appeasement symbolized by the Munich agreement of 1938; the key lesson is that democracies must stand strong against totalitarianism; which during the Cold War meant Soviet Communism.[65] As they saw it, the Cold War was, in essence, a struggle between two ideologies, one good and the other evil. When the Realists promoted détente as a prudent adjustment to shifts in the balance of power; the neoconservatives vehemently retorted that such "appeasement" would fail because Soviet hostility was driven by an inherently aggressive ideology that could not be reasoned with. Instead, they argued for a more offensive strategy of military buildup.[66]

Following the end of the Cold War, neoconservatives eventually converged around a forceful, interventionist, unilateralist grand strategy designed to preserve American primacy while promoting free markets and democratization. While they remained wedded to these classical liberal goals, they rejected contemporary liberal methods of achieving these aims through multilateralism and international institutions. Instead, they argued for a vigorous unilateralism or a coalition of democracies willing to follow America's lead. Despite the collapse of the USSR, they thought that the international arena remained a dangerous place, with the key threat being posed by the proliferation of weapons of mass destruction to revisionist "rogue" states that supported

terrorism in areas of vital interest to the U.S., like the Middle East.[67] By the end
of the 1990s, one particular rogue state moved to the top of their agenda: Iraq.
Saddam's regime was founded on Ba'athist ideology with elements borrowed
from both European fascism and Communism. Once again, neoconservatism
was on a mission to combat totalitarianism.[68] The historical "lesson" of
Munich 1938 rang true for Iraq 2003.

Saddam's Iraq was not the only neo-Fascist enemy identified by the neocons.
Already in 1989, *Commentary* urged the U.S. to confront radical Islamism,[69]
and this call was echoed by leading Republican politicians, like Dan Quayle
and Newt Gingrich, who compared Islamic radicalism to Nazi and Communist
totalitarianism.[70] After 9/11 the neocons argued that the lack of democracy in
the Middle East was a major underlying cause of Islamist terrorism.[71] Once
again, American foreign policy was about an absolute struggle against evil –
this time against the totalitarian ideology of Islamic fascism– what Podhoretz
termed World War IV.[72] These ideas lay behind the Bush doctrine, which spoke
of creating a "balance of power for freedom" against the "axis of evil."

Populist nationalism[73]

Populist nationalism is based on a sharp distinction between the folk community –
the American nation – and those outside it. This distinction is reinforced for many
populist nationalists by fundamentalist religious beliefs that emphasize the
unbridgeable gap between the "saved" and the "unsaved" – good and evil. In
light of these sharp distinctions, populist nationalists view the international arena
as essentially anarchic and violent. In such a setting, the U.S. can trust no other
nation and must rely only on itself. Consequently, they advocate an assertive
unilateralist approach that seeks to maximize American military power and keep
it unbound by multilateral alliances and international organizations. For many
populist nationalists, fundamentalist Protestantism informs a profound skepticism
of human schemes to improve the world through international cooperation and
the like, associated with liberal internationalism. The world cannot be redeemed
by humanity, only by the return of Jesus. In war, populist nationalists support
using force at the highest possible level of intensity to crush the enemy as quickly
and decisively as possible. This is necessary, because the aim is not simply to
disarm the enemy but to deter the enemy society from even thinking about going
to war against the U.S. again. Honor plays a role in restraining the treatment of
adversaries, but adversaries who are deemed to break their honor code – for
example, terrorists – forfeit that consideration, irrespective of the demands of
international law.

In the interwar period populist nationalists tended to be isolationist. With
the Depression, which hit family farms in the South especially hard, they
wanted government to focus on sorting out the domestic economy. What
pushed populist nationalists to support American entry into World War II
was not the immorality of Nazism, but rather the Japanese attack on Pearl
Harbor. Subsequently, their support for internationalism was sustained by a

powerful sense of the threat posed to the United States by the Soviet Union. In the late 1940s some called for a preemptive strike on Moscow, while later on Barry Goldwater and others criticized containment as too defensive in nature, arguing instead for an offensive strategy of rollback. With the demise of the Soviet threat at the end of the Cold War, they retreated from internationalism, opposing intervention in Bosnia, but 9/11 led them to once again support activism abroad to combat the threat of Islamic radicalism and terrorism.

Grand Strategy in the Middle East and the Commitment to Israel

Because we share the same values, we also share many of the same adversaries ... We know that Israel is America's most ardent ally in the Middle East.

—Mitt Romney[74]

For the new conservative mainstream Israel is a Western-oriented democracy that shares with the U.S. common enemies and thus common interests.[75] The Six Day War turned Israel into a "strategic asset" in their eyes. Subsequently, Israel came to be viewed as the front-line strategic ally in the struggle against Soviet totalitarianism.[76]

In this scheme, the peace process was viewed as, at best, a distraction from confronting America's radical enemies. In fact, they were deeply skeptical toward the Oslo process. In 1996, they put forward a strategy which, as the title of a policy paper made clear, called for making a "clean break"[77] from the peace process. It proposed that the U.S. work closely with the most moderate democratic and pro-U.S. countries in the region (Israel, Turkey, and Jordan) to "contain, destabilize and *roll back*" radical anti-U.S. forces (Iraq, Iran, Syria, and Hezbollah), the aim being to forge a pro-American, pro-freedom balance of power. They also advocated removing Yasir Arafat and the democratic reform of the Palestinian Authority.[78]

After 9/11, Israel came to be seen as a key ally in the war on terror. The surge in populist nationalist support for Israel was reflected in the large rise in the number of Republicans sympathizing with Israel over the Palestinians: from in 60 percent in 2000 to 85 percent in 2010.[79] They approved of Israel's tough response to terrorism, which fitted their own preferences for U.S. policy. Critically, they viewed the U.S. and Israel as facing a common threat from radical Islamic terrorism and from Iran. Thus, when asked why America should have a military option for dealing with Iran when the threat is mainly directed against Israel, John McCain, the 2008 Republican candidate for the presidency, replied:

I think these terrorist organizations that they sponsor, Hamas and the others, are also bent, at least long-term, on the destruction of the United States of America ... We've heard the rhetoric – the Great Satan, etc.[80]

Mitt Romney, the 2012 Republican candidate for president, went further, declaring:

The Iranian regime is unalloyed *evil* ... [that] threatens not only Israel, but also every other nation in the region ... [It] is the greatest immediate threat to the world since the fall of the Soviet Union, and before that, Nazi Germany ... Stop thinking that a charm offensive will talk the Iranians out of their pursuit of nuclear weapons ... Once an outstretched hand is met with a clenched fist, it becomes a symbol of weakness and impotence.[81]

Against this background, support for Israel, and its tough response to terrorism, has become something of a litmus test by which the new conservative mainstream judges political leaders. The more clearly you support Israel, the more you are viewed as a reliable American patriot.[82]

Although supportive of Israel, they could also be very critical when Israeli actions contradicted the strategic and ideological logic of their commitment. Thus, they took a very strong line against Israeli military sales to China.[83] They were also opposed to foreign aid in general; indeed, the policy paper "A Clean Break" advocated ending civilian aid to Israel.

Ideology, Theology, and Underlying Sympathy for Israel

Aside from the strategic foundations of their support for Israel, neoconservatives and populist nationalists also share a special commitment to Israel. Neoconservative support for Israel has an emotionally Jewish side to it.[84] Until the mid-1960s, *Commentary* was the home of liberal Jewish intellectuals who were ambivalent about their own Jewish identity and about Israel. However, in the period immediately preceding the Six Day War – when many felt Israel stood on the precipice of a second Holocaust – a strong sense of Jewish collective identity and a new assertiveness regarding the promotion of Jewish interests emerged.[85] For at the very time the neocons were speaking out about the dangers of Soviet totalitarianism and the New Left, Israel came under vicious attack in anti-Semitic Soviet propaganda, echoed in New Left anti-Zionism. The victims of the totalitarian Nazi Holocaust were now being targeted by the totalitarian Soviet Union and their fellow travelers. Still, Jewishness is not primarily responsible for neoconservative support for Israel. Many of the original leading neoconservatives were non-Jews, and they too were very pro-Israel – for example, James Q. Wilson, Daniel P. Moynihan, Michael Novak, Richard Neuhaus, William Bennett, George Weigel, and Jeanne Kirkpatrick. Actually, in the 1970s the core issue for neoconservatives was their opposition to both Kissinger and McGovern's approaches to the Soviet Union, not Israel.[86]

For many populist nationalists there is a religious dimension to supporting Israel. They are evangelicals who believe that the Bible is the word of God, that God promised the land of Israel to the Jews, and that this promise is still valid. As explained in the previous chapter, from the second half of the nineteenth century onward, the theology of Restorationism – according to which Biblical prophecies predicting the return of the Jews to Palestine are viewed as the first step toward the Second Coming of Jesus – gained widespread support among conservative evangelicals. The Six Day War greatly boosted their support for Israel, because it seemed to fulfill biblical prophecy. Not only did Israel achieve a "miraculous" victory, it also gained control over a united Jerusalem, including the site of the ancient Jewish Temple that, according to their interpretation of biblical prophecy, needs to be rebuilt. The timing of this upsurge was especially significant politically, because it coincided with the demographic growth of evangelicals and their return to the political arena for the first time since the 1920s.

Against this background, in 2011, nearly two-thirds of white evangelicals thought that helping protect Israel should be a very important goal for U.S. foreign policy – virtually double the national average.[87] The same outlook was expressed by many leading Republicans, including Sarah Palin,[88] Rick Perry, and Rick Santorum, candidates in the 2012 primaries.[89] Most powerfully, President George W. Bush, in a speech to the Knesset in 2008, declared that the State of Israel represents "the redemption of an ancient promise given to Abraham and Moses and David – a homeland for the chosen people."[90]

Religiously inspired support for Israel is a major force in its own right; it is dealt with at length in a separate chapter. But aside from theology, it was also a matter of identity. Until the 1960s, populist nationalists' white Christian conception of American identity was often tied to anti-Semitism, a fact that constrained identification with Israel. However since then, one symptom of the more inclusive shift in populist nationalism is the way its leaders now talk about America being a country built on a *Judeo-Christian* culture, rather than simply being a Christian country. The inclusion of *Judeo* as part of the quintessential national "us" makes more room for identification with the State of Israel. At the same time, Islam would appear to lie outside that definition: of all partisan-ideological groups, conservative Republicans have the least favorable view of Muslims.[91]

Final Status Issues: Supporting the Israeli Right?

Many evangelical populist nationalists are sympathetic to the territorially maximalist "whole land of Israel" ideology of Israel's Far Right, which seeks to incorporate the West Bank into the State of Israel. Consequently, they tend to be supportive of Israeli settlements and oppose American pressure on Israel to compromise.[92] Thus, Tom DeLay, the Republican whip from 1995 to 2003 and House majority leader from 2003 to 2005, spoke against trading land for peace, as did Rick Santorum.[93] Mike Huckabee opposed the creation of a Palestinian state and supported the expansion of Jewish settlements in the West Bank and Gaza – as did Sarah Palin.[94] Sen. James Inhofe (R-OK) declared, "Hebron is in the West Bank. It is at this place where God appeared to Abram and said, 'I am giving you *this* land' – the *West Bank*. This is not a political battle at all. It is a contest over whether or not the word of God is true."[95] Most extreme, the former House majority leader Dick Armey supported the "transfer" of Palestinians from the West Bank as advocated by the fringe of the Israeli Far Right.[96]

Nonetheless, it is the tendency to favor Israel, rather than opposition to Israeli compromises per se, that stands at the core of the approach of populist nationalists who are not theologically committed to the settlements. For them the most important thing is not the details of any potential peace deal, but rather that the U.S. firmly takes Israel's side in the diplomatic and political struggle over such a deal. As Mitt Romney put it in 2011:

Inexplicably, the United States [under President Obama] now places the burden on Israel to make still more unilateral concessions ... We can encourage both parties in the conflict, but we must never forget which one is our ally... Keeping our word to our allies is a matter of honor, but it is also a matter of self-interest.[97]

As for the neoconservatives, Doug Feith has roots in the Revisionist Zionist movement, out of which grew the Likud. There were also strong ties between neoconservatives like Elliot Abrams and leading Likud figures that had spent extended periods in the U.S., especially Benjamin Netanyahu and Moshe Arens.[98] However, these figures came from that part of the Likud that, while hawkish, was also firmly committed to the values of classical liberalism – just like the neoconservatives. Arens is well-known for his advocacy of the need for Israel to invest more in the integration of Israel's Arab citizens, a position also advocated by the neoconservatives.[99] Arens was also one of the first of the leading Likudniks to abandon the party's "whole land of Israel" ideology[100] – an ideology that the neoconservatives do *not* support. Thus Charles Krauthammer praised Netanyahu when he broke with Likud ideology by accepting the principle of partition in the late 1990s.[101] While in 2006, the *Weekly Standard* expressed support for the centrist party Kadima's election platform, which advocated a unilateral disengagement from most of the West Bank.[102] Even before then, a senior editor at *National Review*, David Pryce-Jones, referred to the capture of the West Bank and Gaza as "a poisoned cup."[103] The outlier was Paul Wolfowitz, who was sympathetic to the Geneva draft peace agreement authored by figures from the Israeli Left and moderate Palestinians. It advocated Israeli withdrawal from all of the West Bank (with territorial swaps), and the division of Jerusalem.[104] The rest of the neoconservatives rejected the Geneva plan. For many years, they opposed to the creation of a Palestinian state. But the primary rationale behind this was strategic rather than ideological,[105] and later on leading neoconservatives came to accept the eventual creation of a Palestinian state,[106] excluding the Jordan Valley, which they considered vital for Israel security.[107] They also opposed the division of Jerusalem, apparently as a result of their general identification with the Jewish state.[108]

Clearly, there are differences between populist nationalists and neoconservatives. Populist nationalists are staunchly nationalistic and conservative, while neoconservatives retain elements of liberal idealism. Populist nationalists are interested only in security, while neoconservatives are also concerned with democratization. Many populist nationalists sympathize with the Israeli settlement movement, while neoconservatives are willing to endorse Israeli withdrawals and the dismantling of many settlements. Nonetheless, both have been strong supporters of a vigorous offensive American grand strategy in the Middle East. Both identify with Israel and view it as an ally, both are committed to favoring Israel over other actors in the Middle East, and both were deeply skeptical of the peace process. They also put the overwhelming blame for the conflict and onus in peacemaking on the Arab side, while opposing Israeli concessions such as a return to the 1967 border and the division of Jerusalem. Overall, then, what unites them on Israel and the Middle East was more significant that what divides them.

Table 2.1 summarizes and compares the different approaches toward Israel and the Arab-Israeli conflict among conservative elites.

THE CONSERVATIVE DISCOURSE: NARRATING THE RISE AND FALL OF THE PEACE PROCESS

This section surveys the elite conservative discourse regarding Israel and the peace process since the early 1990s. The survey is based on relevant articles in the major highbrow conservative magazines: *National Review*, *Commentary*, the *Weekly Standard*, the *American Spectator*, and the *American Conservative*. The most established and most widely read conservative magazine in America is *National Review*. Taken together, the circulation of the pro-Israel *National Review*, *Commentary*, *Weekly Standard*, and *American Spectator* from 1991 to 2010 was approximately 250,000–380,000; in contrast, the circulation of the anti-Israel *American Conservative* was about 8,000.[109] Also surveyed are the columns of the leading conservative columnist George Will in the *Washington Post*, William Safire in the *New York Times*, and the syndicated columns of Pat Buchanan; all of whom wrote consistently on the issue over the years.[110]

The Heyday of the Peace Process

In the 1990s the conservative discourse was generally sympathetic to Israel, but there was a divide over the peace process. In this period *National Review* generally followed the approach of Kissingerian "favorable neutrality" and in 1993 came out in support of the Oslo process, while expressing concern about the PLO's reliability and the fear that giving the PLO a foothold might eventually allow them to threaten US allies Israel and Jordan.[111] The magazine supported the cautious approach of Israeli Realists like Yitzhak Rabin, who viewed the peace process as a test of Palestinian intentions. Right-wing Israeli settlers were presented as a threat to the peace process and by extension to US interests.[112] When Netanyahu came to power, he was praised for continuing

TABLE 2.1. *Elite Conservative Approaches to the Arab-Israeli Conflict*

	Old conservative establishment	Kissingerian realists	New conservative mainstream
Subcomponents of each approach	*Arabist Realists, Paleoconservatives, Libertarians*	*Pro-Israel Realists*	*Neoconservatives, Populist Nationalists (inc. evangelicals)*
Grand Strategy	Defensive	Balanced Internationalism	Offensive
Resonant Historical Symbols	Vietnam, Tet Offensive 1968	–	Nazism, 1938 Munich Agreement
Roots of instability and anti-Americanism	Arab-Israeli Conflict – "Linkage" "Blowback" vs. U.S. "imperialism"	Pro-U.S. moderates vs. Anti-U.S. radicals Arab-Israeli conflict significant but secondary	Islamist Extremism
Israel in U.S. strategy	Liability	Asset (though not always)	Asset
Ideology, theology, prejudices	Secondary: residual anti-Semitism	Secondary: "Anti" anti-Semitism	Primary: Special Commitment to Israel, some Islamophobia
Taking sides	Unfavorable Neutrality	Favorable Neutrality	Favor Israel
Outline of peace settlement	Pro-Palestinian State Vs. Settlements 1967 Borders Divided Jerusalem Equivocal re recognizing "right" of return	Pro-Palestinian State (if = pro-U.S.) Vs. Settlements – – Vs. "right" of return	Equivocal re Palestinian State Equivocal re Settlements Vs. 1967 border United Jerusalem under Israel Vs. "right" of return
Blame for the conflict	Israel	Mainly Arab/Muslim radicals Radical Israeli Settlers too	Palestinians, Arab states, Islamists
Morality	Moral Equivalence	Palestinian Terror worse Israel also criticized	Palestinian Terror worse
Onus for concessions	Israel	Both sides; shifts around	Palestinians

Oslo, and for being the first right-wing Israeli leader to accept partition.[113] Although there was some concern over the way Netanyahu handled the peace process, the main threat was viewed as coming from Hamas and other radical forces tied to Iran. Gradually skepticism increased about whether Arafat and Assad were really committed to peace.[114] Nonetheless, the magazine remained cautiously supportive of the peace process, right up to its collapse in 2000.[115]

By this time the old conservative establishment approach had very little traction in mainstream conservative magazines. In 1992 *National Review* endorsed Pat Buchanan for the presidency. But this was the last time it expressed support for the conservatism of the old establishment. Following a long essay in the magazine in which he declared Buchanan to be anti-Semitic, Buckley fired the columnist Joseph Sobran for "contextual anti-Semitism." Subsequently, the old establishment approach to the Middle East was almost entirely missing from *National Review*. Nor did it receive much of an airing in the other major conservative magazines in the 1990s. In any case, the old establishment was quite subdued on the peace process in the 1990s, because they were generally supportive of the direction of American policy. Only in 1998, when the right-wing Israeli government was in conflict with the Clinton administration, did Buchanan call for the U.S. to pressure Israel by cutting aid and by formally coming out in support of the creation of an independent Palestinian state.[116]

Meanwhile, in line with the neoconservative approach, the *Weekly Standard*, *Commentary*, the *American Spectator*, George Will, and William Safire saw the PLO and Syria's engagement in negotiations as a tactical ruse, believing that they remained ideologically opposed to the existence of the Jewish state and practically committed to its destruction in phases.[117] Evidence for this thesis was brought from Arafat's statements in Arabic and from the Palestinian Authority's role in facilitating Hamas terrorism.[118] In any case, the neoconservatives did not think real peace was possible with the dictatorial Arafat and the Ba'athist regime in Syria.[119] They argued that Arab dictators would misconstrue Israel's willingness to compromise as weakness and they would then exploit it. Indeed, America's embrace of the peace process reminded them of the appeasement of dictators in the 1930s.[120] In a phrase Netanyahu used a lot, they demanded "reciprocity" – making further Israeli concessions conditional on the Palestinians doing far more to combat terrorism and incitement, while simultaneously demanding changes to the PLO charter (which negated Israel's right to exist), as the Likud demanded.[121] The key was deemed to be rebuilding Israeli deterrence and avoiding further concessions until the Palestinians changed.[122]

The Collapse of the Peace Process and the Rise of Radical Islamism

The Dominant Narrative: Overwhelmingly Pro-Israel

When the peace process collapsed in 2000, the bulk of the conservative discourse placed the blame unequivocally at the Arab door for rejecting generous (they thought too generous) Israeli offers. This was viewed as demonstrating that they had been right all along regarding Arab intensions and the effect of "appeasement." The mainstream conservative discourse called for Israel to deliver a knockout blow to terrorism. Further negotiations or Israeli forbearance were deemed not only futile but very bad, because they effectively rewarded, and thus encouraged, terrorism.[123] Thus, following the Passover Massacre at the Park Hotel in 2002 in which thirty Israeli civilians were murdered and a further 140 injured, strong support was given to Israel's major offensive against terrorist infrastructure – Operation Defensive Shield – and there was strong opposition to U.S. pressure on Israel to resume negotiations until terrorism was vanquished and Arafat replaced.[124] The onus was thus completely on the Palestinians. George W. Bush's June 2002 speech conditioning a Palestinian state on the removal of Arafat was viewed as a vindication of their approach.[125]

Following 9/11, the influence of the neoconservatives expanded as theirs became the dominant orientation within *National Review*. As such, the mainstream conservative discourse totally rejected the idea that American support for Israel was the cause of the attacks. Instead, anti-Americanism, Islamist extremism, and terrorism were understood as emanating from a hatred of American values, with the core of the problem being the dominant political culture in the region.[126] The key objective for the United States was to create "a balance of power for freedom," and in this conflict democratic Israel was viewed as a frontline ally. As such, Israel's fight against terrorism was the same as America's fight against terrorism. Israeli victories against terrorism were American victories against terrorism, while a defeat for Israel would be a defeat for the U.S.[127]

However, the mainstream conservative discourse was not all about defeating terrorism with military might. Paradoxically, another theme was the advocacy of unilateral concessions by Israel. In 1998 Charles Krauthammer first suggested that Israel should unilaterally set its own border by withdrawing from the majority of the West Bank and Gaza.[128] With the onset of the second intifada, the priority became the defeat of terrorism, and any idea of withdrawal was shelved as it would demonstrate weakness. However, the idea of a "short war" followed by the construction of a "big wall" behind which Israel would unilaterally withdraw continued to have support among columnists like Krauthammer, David Brooks, and George Will.[129] Furthermore, once Israel had effectively defeated terrorism, Safire and Podhoretz came out in favor of the disengagement from Gaza.[130] Writing in *Commentary*, Hillel Halkin went further, advocating a withdrawal from the vast majority of the West Bank that would make the security barrier the de facto border.[131] A necessary part of this plan involved the removal of all Israeli settlers east of the security barrier. While Halkin noted that settlements were not the main obstacle to peace, and that under a real peace these Jews would be able to live under Palestinian sovereignty, he argued that such a peace was not in the offing, and that therefore the only way to secure them was by deploying the Israel Defense Forces throughout the West Bank. If made permanent, such a situation would amount to a policy of Bantustans; therefore Israel had to withdraw.[132] This was in line with the position of the centrist party Kadima, not the Likud.

However the Second Lebanon War in July 2006 once again buried talk of unilateral withdrawals, and the emphasis swung back to enhancing deterrence against the Iranian-led axis that included Syria, Hamas, and Hezbollah.[133] Conservatives felt solidarity with Israel in that war, but when Israel failed to crush Hezbollah, they were disappointed.[134] The rise of Hamas in Gaza was obviously viewed as a setback for the democratization agenda. Yet at the same time the democratization agenda was not entirely abandoned, as it was advocated that the U.S. should strongly support Palestinian prime minister Salam Fayyad's economic and institutional reforms.[135] Though, when the U.S.-sponsored peace process restarted at Annapolis, it was dismissed as a farce and criticized as a renunciation of the Bush doctrine that political reform had to precede peace diplomacy.[136] Finally, when Israel launched the Gaza War in December 2008, it received strong support in the mainstream conservative discourse, where it was viewed it as part of a wider civilizational struggle.[137]

Minority and Marginal Narratives
Following the collapse of the Oslo process, Kissingerian Realism was relegated to a minority viewpoint in *National Review*. According to this approach, the failure to achieve a deal at Camp David was not a function of Palestinian wickedness but simply reflected the fact that the positions of the parties were too far apart, and that such ethnic conflicts take a very long time to resolve.[138] Once the violence started, Buckley came out in favor of a decisive Israeli campaign to defeat Palestinian terrorism by targeting Arafat and his henchmen directly.[139] But he denounced Israel's major attack on the terrorist infrastructure launched after the 2002 Passover massacre – Operation Defensive Shield, which he thought would only intensify Palestinian hatred of Israel.[140] Buckley was also very skeptical of Bush's June 2002 speech, in which he conditioned Palestinian statehood on the replacement of Arafat and democratic reforms in the Palestinian Authority.[141]

Simultaneously Buckley was very critical of the settlements, which he viewed as an "endless source of tension"; he called on the U.S. to pressure Israel to dismantle them, once Israel had began to defeat Palestinian terrorism.[142] Indeed, against this background an editorial in the first week of September 2001 advocated that Israel unilaterally withdraw from most of the West Bank and erect a security barrier.[143] This was the position being given by figures within the Israel Labor Party at the time, a position staunchly opposed by the Israeli Right. Later on, when Israel was in the midst of erecting the barrier, another editorial called for U.S. pressure on Israel to ensure the route of the barrier did not preclude the future creation of a Palestinian state, while calling on Israel to "retrench" from settlements outside the barrier.[144] While cautious at the time, after the disengagement had occurred, the magazine unequivocally praised the withdrawal from Gaza.[145] Indeed, *National Review* never became a cheerleader for the ideology of the Israeli Right. Consequently, Israeli moderates on the peace process who also took a tough stand on Iran and Islamic extremism received very positive coverage.[146]

While the approach of the Kissingerian realists was very much a minority position, the approach of the old conservative establishment was marginal within the conservative discourse, being reduced to the columns of Pat Buchanan and some articles in *Chronicles* and in the *American Conservative*. Here the blame for the collapse of the peace process was placed primarily on Israel.[147] Hamas on the one hand and Ariel Sharon and Likud on the other hand were viewed as constituting equal and equivalent obstacles to peace; though the onus for concessions was placed primarily on Israel.[148] 9/11 intensified their hostility to the special relationship with Israel. Al Qaida's attacks were presented as a reaction to America's "neocolonial" presence in Saudi Arabia,[149] with Israel being identified as "among the greatest crosses" that the U.S. "had to bear in the war on terror."[150] When Israel assassinated the spiritual head of Hamas, Sheik Ahmed Yassin, in 2004 using an American-made helicopter gunship, the act was presented as playing "straight into [Osama] Bin Laden's hands" by implicating the U.S. in Israel's actions and thereby serving to unite Muslims and Arabs against the United States.[151] To improve America's standing in the Arab world, it was argued that the U.S. distance itself from Israel by applying pressure on the Israeli government to freeze settlements and impose a permanent status settlement.[152] After Hamas seized control of Gaza, they advocated bringing it into the negotiations.[153]

Finally, one of the main themes in the *American Conservative* was virulent criticism of the mainstream pro-Israel lobby and the neoconservatives. It was argued that these groups promoted policies that were not in the American interest.[154] One article bombastically declared that the pro-Israel lobby received orders from the Israeli government in a similar manner to which American Communists received orders from Joseph Stalin.[155] In venomous attacks, the neoconservatives were referred to as that "cabal behind the Iraq War."[156] Indeed, blaming the pro-Israel lobby for the Iraq War was a major theme,[157] popularized by the academics John Mearsheimer and Stephen Walt.[158]

Having surveyed the various approaches in the elite discourse among conservatives, one question remains: how much support did these elite approaches have among the mass of Republicans and Conservatives?

PUBLIC OPINION AMONG REPUBLICANS AND CONSERVATIVES

Grand Strategy and the Middle East

In the first decade of the new millennium, most Republicans identified with the grand strategy of the new conservative mainstream. From 2001 to 2009 a majority supported an internationalist strategy, and conservative Republicans were the most internationalist of all.[159] Two-thirds of Republicans justified the application of preemptive force against countries that threaten the U.S.,[160] and a similar percentage was also skeptical of multilateralism and international institutions.[161] Meanwhile, between 1997 and 2009 the percentage of Republicans who agreed that the best way to ensure peace was through military strength increased from two-thirds to three-quarters.[162]

After 9/11 this hawkish approach was directed mainly at forces emanating from the Middle East. Between 2002 and 2011 the percentage of Republicans who thought that Islam encouraged violence more than other religions doubled, reaching 59 percent.[163] In addition, around three-quarters of Republicans viewed Islamic extremist groups and Iran's nuclear program as the greatest threats to the United States. About the same percentage approved using force if it were certain Iran had produced a nuclear weapon.[164] Clearly then, a majority of Republicans believed that Israel and the United States faced common threats deriving from common enemies. Consequently, it is no surprise that three-quarters of Republicans also perceived Israel as a strategic ally.[165] Indeed, when asked in 2010 to identify the two best reasons for supporting Israel, the most popular answer among Republicans was "Israel is our most important ally in the Middle East" (40 percent) and the third most popular answer was "Israel is a partner with the U.S. in our fight against terrorism" (26 percent). The belief that "God gave the land to the Jews who had lived there for thousands of years" came in fourth with 21 percent (common democratic values came in second with 34 percent).[166]

Israel and the Arab-Israeli Conflict

Just as support for Israel in the elite conservative discourse skyrocketed after 9/11, so did support for Israel among the Republican and conservative public. From 1967 until 9/11 a little more than half of Republicans sympathized more with Israel;[167] whereas in the decade after 9/11 this figure shot up to more than three-quarters of Republicans.[168] Similarly, in terms of ascribing blame for the conflict, Republicans became increasingly pro-Israel. In 2002, at the height of the second intifada, a majority thought that neither Ariel Sharon nor Yasir Arafat really wanted peace; however, they were far more negative about the Palestinian leader by a margin of 27 percentage points.[169] In 2006, Republicans blamed Hezbollah rather than Israel for the outbreak of the Second Lebanon War by a margin of 46 percentage points. And in 2011, Republicans thought that Israel was making more effort that the Palestinians to achieve peace by a margin of 50 percentage points.[170] All of this had consequences in terms of the onus for peacemaking. Thus, in 2007, when asked whom the U.S. should pressure more, more than half of conservatives said the Palestinians, and only a fifth answered the Israelis.[171]

On the substantive issues, more than half of Republicans favored Jerusalem remaining united under Israeli control even if there were a two-state solution, compared to a quarter who preferred to divide the city between Israelis and Palestinians.[172] Yet, on the creation of a Palestinian state, Republicans were about evenly divided,[173] as they were regarding settlements.[174] This indicates that some Republicans who are generally supportive of Israel oppose settlements and support Palestinian statehood.

Concerning U.S. policy, in 2002 at the height of the second intifada, nearly half of Republicans thought the Bush administration's supportive policy toward Israel was appropriate, a further 12 percent thought it was too little support, while slightly more than a third thought it represented too much support.[175] During the Second Lebanon War and the Gaza War, more than half of Republicans preferred that the U.S. take Israel's side, while about a third thought that the U.S. should say or do nothing.[176] Finally, despite a general hostility to foreign aid, more than 60 percent of Republicans thought that Israel should receive aid; in contrast, three-quarters thought that aid to Arab countries should end.[177]

Overall, opinion among the rank and file of Republicans and conservatives roughly reflected the balance within the elite discourse. Positions associated with the pro-Israel approach of the new conservative mainstream generally received the highest levels of support. On the issue of a Palestinian state, Republicans were more or less evenly divided. This reinforces the conclusion that Republican and conservative support for Israel is not primarily driven by the "whole land of Israel" ideology of the Israel Right, since support for Israel was much higher than opposition to Palestinian statehood.

U.S. POLICY UNDER THE REPUBLICANS

At the level of policy, the struggle has been primarily between Realist approaches and the approach of the new conservative mainstream. There was no automatic correlation between orientations and policy, as many other factors also influenced American policy.[178] Nonetheless, ideas did matter. While it is beyond the scope of this chapter to analyze the impact of conservative discourse and attitudes on policy in detail, a brief survey of this relationship is sketched out below.

As the peace process took off in the early 1990s, the George H. W. Bush administration adopted a moderate version of the Realist approach, which combined aspects of pro-Israel and anti-Israel neutrality. It was willing to intervene militarily in the Persian Gulf to expel Saddam from Kuwait, though not to drive him from power in Iraq itself. Following this it vigorously promoted the peace process, convening the Madrid conference, while pressuring the right-wing Israeli government to freeze settlements. Despite such pressure, the administration focused on facilitating the peace process, rather than attempting to impose a settlement.

From the mid-1990s, the new conservative mainstream began to rise. Jesse Helms, who chaired the Senate Foreign Relations Committee from 1995 to 2001, was a former Southern Democrat and a very conservative Republican. After visiting Israel in the 1980s he became an active supporter of Israel for a mixture of religious and strategic reasons. It was Helms who initiated the Middle East Peace Facilitation Act, which monitored Palestinian compliance. The initiative was born of a deep-seated skepticism about the Palestinians' willingness to make peace and an equal measure of skepticism concerning the Clinton administration's willingness to call the Palestinians out on this.[179]

Matters ratcheted up a notch when the leading Republican in Congress, Newt Gingrich, led a campaign to prevent the Clinton administration from applying pressure on the right-wing government of Benjamin Netanyahu. Nonetheless, it was not until the 107th Congress (2001–2003) that conservative and Republican support for Israel in the House outweighed that of liberals and Democrats. The motions of that Congress relating to Israel were mainly sponsored by Republicans, and they took Israel's side in the conflict against the Palestinians. For example, a House resolution sponsored by Rep. Eric Cantor (R-VA) and Rep. Roy Blunt (R-MO), contained a lengthy condemnation of Arafat and a call for a prohibition on providing aid to the Palestinian Authority.[180] Subsequently, left-wing organizations, like Americans for Peace Now, felt a noticeable drop in support from Realist-oriented Republicans, as their numbers dwindled in Congress.[181]

The surge in Republican support for Israel in the wake of 9/11 was also evident in the White House itself, although it took until March 2002 for this to become fully evident. Until 9/11 the administration was relatively disengaged from the peace process, focusing on conflict management. In the immediate aftermath of 9/11, the administration seemed to shift toward a more Realist position, when it became the first administration to *officially* endorse the creation of an independent Palestinian state. However, once the president became convinced that Arafat was behind the acts of terrorism directed against Israelis, and that he was receiving weapons from a member of the "axis of evil" – Iran – he switched to the approach of the new conservative mainstream championed by Vice President Dick Cheney, Secretary of Defense Donald Rumsfeld, and other people in the administration like Elliot Abrams and Doug Feith. The fact that Arafat lied to President Bush himself about his receiving arms from Iran and supporting terrorist groups had a major impact on the President, who took such matters of honor seriously.[182]

Subsequently, President Bush swung behind the approach of the new conservative mainstream by more or less acquiescing in Israel's military campaign to defeat Palestinian terrorism, known as Operation Defensive Shield. As he explained:

I refused to accept the moral equivalence between Palestinian suicide attacks on innocent civilians and Israeli military actions intended to protect their people. My views came into sharper focus after 9/11. If the United States had the right to defend itself and prevent future attacks, other democracies had those rights, too.[183]

Later, in June 2002, he conditioned the creation of a Palestinian state not only on an end to terrorism but also on the replacement of Yasir Arafat and the institution of political reforms in the Palestinian Authority. In a wider sense, the president also adopted an offensive grand strategy, as witnessed by the initiation of the Iraq War in 2003.

Neoconservative influence was also evident when the administration came out in favor of the Sharon government's plan to unilaterally disengage from Gaza. This plan was similar to ideas put forward in the conservative discourse in the preceding years. In return for this unilateral Israeli concession, the president sent an official letter to Israel in April 2004, which laid out his administration's positions regarding final status issues. The letter was also influenced by neoconservative thinking. First, it reiterated that American support for Palestinian statehood was conditional on their fighting terrorism and internal reforms. Second, the letter referred to American support for changes to the 1967 cease-fire lines as well as support for Israel's continued ability to defend itself by itself along "defensible borders," which is usually understood as referring to an Israeli security presence in the Jordan Valley. Still, Bush also declared that any settlement was dependent on an agreement resulting from negotiations between Israel and the Palestinians; in other words, the administration would not impose the letter on the Palestinians.

In late 2006, the administration's policy shifted toward Realism. As the situation in Iraq became more chaotic, representatives of the new conservative mainstream associated with the Iraq policy, such as Donald Rumsfeld and Doug Feith, resigned. Replacing Rumsfeld in 2006 was the Realist Robert Gates, who had served under George H. W. Bush as deputy national security advisor. Gates also served on the Baker-Hamilton Commission studying the Iraq War, which recommended placing a new emphasis on the peace process, in line with the preferred Realist strategy.

Two other events served to cripple the credibility of the neoconservative approach. First, the election victory of Hamas in January 2006 demonstrated that democratic elections could increase the power of forces opposed to both peaceful relations with Israel and the US. Second, as a result of the Second Lebanon War, in which Israel failed to impose a major defeat on Hezbollah, that radical Islamist organization went on to achieve greater political power at the expense of the American-backed pro-democracy government of Lebanese prime minister Fouad Siniora. Subsequently, the Bush administration put a new emphasis on peace negotiations with the convening of the Annapolis summit. Still, rather than seeking to impose a settlement or focus on pressuring Israel, the administration confined its role primarily to facilitation.

CONCLUSION

In the wake of the Six Day War, Republicans and conservatives began to be more supportive of Israel. After 9/11, support for Israel surged and the approach of the new conservative mainstream became dominant. For them, Islamic radicalism is the main cause of instability and anti-Americanism in the Middle East. In this struggle, Israel is viewed as a key frontline ally and as a strategic asset. Aside from this, their commitment to Israel has deep ideological and theological roots, and they advocate taking Israel's side in the Arab-Israeli conflict.

Could this overwhelming support for Israel recede, or even be reversed? Since the surge in support for Israel in the wake of 9/11 correlates with the surge in support for an offensive interventionist grand strategy, it is conceivable that the shift of the Republican base away from support for an interventionist grand strategy in the wake of the Iraq War and the economic crisis[184] may lead to a parallel decline in support for Israel. One indication of a potential change came in the 2012 Republican primaries, when leading candidates endorsed the idea of starting the aid budget from zero, with every country, including Israel, having to make the case.[185]

Although "distancing" is conceivable, it is also highly unlikely. Even if Republicans were to cut aid to Israel, such aid is no longer of critical economic importance to Israel. What is critical is American willingness to supply Israel with advanced weaponry and diplomatic support. There is no indication that Republicans and conservatives would reverse these policies even if they adopt a strategy of retrenchment, because they would continue to view Israel as an ally engaged in a struggle against common enemies. In this vein, it is worth remembering that in 1970 a Republican administration which sought to retrench actually increased aid to Israel tenfold, precisely because it took the view that having strong reliable allies like Israel had become of greater strategic significance.

So Republicans and conservatives are likely to remain staunchly pro-Israel. On the surface, this would appear to reinforce America's pro-Israel orientation. However, the strident nature of Republican and conservative support for Israel raises the prospect that supporting Israel may shift from being uncontroversial to become a partisan issue. In 2010, Republican supporters of Israel set up a partisan Israel lobby named the Emergency Committee for Israel,[186] and in the 2012 presidential primaries, all the Republican candidates tried hard to make support for Israel a partisan issue by strongly attacking Obama's policy toward the Jewish state. At the very least, such developments demonstrated that bipartisan sympathy for Israel masks significant partisan and ideological disagreements on U.S. policy toward Israel, the peace process, and the wider Middle East. The nature and extent of these differences are revealed in the next chapter.

3

Democrats, Liberals, and the Left:
Rising Criticism of Israel

This explosion of violence would be totally understandable if the Palestinians had no alternative. But ... it came in the context of a serious Israeli peace overture, which Mr. Arafat has chosen to spurn. That's why this is Arafat's war. That's its real name.

—Thomas Friedman, October 2001[1]

Israel's continued control and colonization of Palestinian land have been the primary obstacles to a comprehensive peace agreement in the Holy Land.

—Jimmy Carter, 2006[2]

INTRODUCTION

Since Vietnam, and especially since the 2003 Iraq War, American opinion over foreign policy has grown more polarized along partisan and ideological lines, with Democrats and liberals on one side, and Republicans and conservatives on the other.[3] At the same time, Democrats have become increasingly divided among themselves over foreign policy.[4] For a long time both of these divisions bypassed the Arab-Israeli conflict, however this is no longer the case.

This chapter surveys and analyzes liberal, Democratic, and left-wing approaches to the Arab-Israeli conflict. It begins with a look at levels of identification with liberalism among the general public and within the Democratic Party, followed by a brief survey of the development of liberal attitudes to Israel prior to 1990. It then focuses on three elite approaches to the conflict: robust liberal internationalism, which is the most supportive of Israel while also promoting a two-state solution; the approach of dovish Democrats who favor an evenhanded approach to the conflict; and the progressive-postcolonial approach that sympathizes primarily with the Palestinians. The chapter then goes on to survey liberal narratives of the rise and fall of the peace process from the early 1990s until the end of the first decade of the new millennium through the coverage of the main liberal magazines and columns of a number of leading liberal columnists. Attention then turns to the attitudes of rank-and-file Democrats and liberals. Following this, the chapter briefly demonstrates the impact of liberal approaches on U.S. policy towards the conflict in the Clinton and Obama administrations, as well as among Democrats in Congress. Finally, it is argued that there is a decline in support for Israel over the Palestinians, particularly among the younger generation of liberals.

LIBERALISM AND THE DEMOCRATIC PARTY

Classical liberalism is central to the American creed. However, in contemporary political discourse, liberals are inclined to believe in government intervention to deal with socioeconomic problems, they support the right to abortion, separation of church and state, and minority rights. They also tend to be more dovish on foreign policy. Between 1992 and 2010 roughly half the number of Americans identified as liberals, compared to those who identified as conservatives.[5] However, conservatives' advantage is eroding as successive generations of Americans are increasingly liberal. Thus by 2014 within the "millennial" generation – those born between 1980 and 2000 – more voters identified themselves as liberals (31 percent) than as conservatives (26 percent). In every other age group, more voters identified as conservative.[6] This is demonstrated

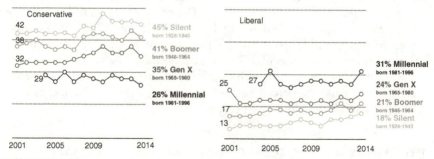

FIGURE 3.1. **Self-Reported Ideology by Generation: 1997–2009** (From "Millennials in Adulthood: Millennials Less Conservative Than Older Generations." Reprinted with permission from the Pew Research Center.)

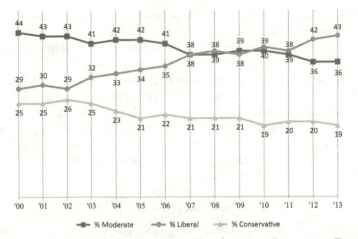

FIGURE 3.2. **U.S. Political Ideology – Recent Trends among Democrats** (From Jones, "Liberal Self-Identification Edges Up to New High." Copyright © 2014 Gallup, Inc. All rights reserved. The content is used with permission; however, Gallup retains all rights of republication. This graph is an interpretation of data compiled by Gallup, Inc. However, Gallup, Inc. had no part in the creation of this graphic interpretation.)

in Figure 3.1. Overall, the percentage of self-identifying liberals rose from 17 to 23 percent in the period 1992–2013.[7]

The trend toward increased liberalism is especially strong within the Democratic Party. Since the mid-1960s Democrats have become increasingly liberal, and this trend intensified between 2000 and 2013 as the share of liberals rose among Democrats from 29 to 43 percent; making liberals the largest ideological grouping in the Party (see Figure 3.2).[8] The other part of the Party's base is composed of disparate elements including ethnic minorities, two-thirds of whom are blacks and Hispanics. Aside from becoming more liberal, Democrats are also becoming more secular. In the early years of the twenty-first century, the percentage of Democrats with "no religion" rose from a quarter to more than a third, while the percentage of white evangelicals identifying as Democrats fell to an all-time low of 9 percent.[9]

THE AMERICAN LEFT, DEMOCRATS, LIBERALS, AND ISRAEL 1917–1991

In 1917 President Woodrow Wilson backed the Balfour Declaration in which the British government committed itself to the "establishment in Palestine of a national home for the Jewish people." By the 1940s – in the wake of the rise of Nazism, the closing of America to mass Jewish immigration, violent Arab opposition to Jewish immigration to Palestine, and finally the Holocaust – Democrats, liberals, and organized labor were overwhelmingly in favor of the creation of a Jewish state. Subsequently, they became very strong supporters of Israel. As was discussed in the first chapter, there were a variety of reasons for this: the universal principle of national self-determination, the provision of a refuge for victims of the Holocaust, and solidarity with a fellow democracy run by social democrats under threat from its undemocratic neighbors. Democrats also had a domestic political incentive for supporting Israel, given the importance of the Jewish vote.

Until 1967, the liberal consensus on Israel ran parallel with the liberal internationalist consensus on containment of the Soviet Union. In the wake of Vietnam and the Six Day War, things changed. At first, the change was confined to the fringes. The New Left emerged as a force in the antiwar movement. From their postcolonial perspective, the PLO leader, Yasir Arafat, was a hero. At the same time, there was a retreat from liberal internationalism and containment among Democrats represented by the rise of progressive, antiwar elements associated with George McGovern. McGovern was considered likely to weaken support for Israel; indeed, the Israeli ambassador, Yitzhak Rabin, effectively endorsed Richard Nixon in the 1972 election campaign. Subsequently, hawkish pro-Israel elements like the neoconservatives and white Southerners left the Democratic Party, while organized labor shrank in size, becoming less important within the Party.

While liberals and Democrats continued to sympathize with Israel by large margins, the liberal media became increasingly critical of right-wing Israeli government policy toward the Palestinians in the wake of the 1982 Lebanon War and even more so in the wake of the first intifada, which began in December 1987. As the Palestinians and the Arab states began to take diplomatic steps toward peace with Israel, and as Israelis became deeply divided as to how to handle the peace process, so liberals began increasingly to support the Israeli center Left, while increasingly coming to view the Israeli Right as a major obstacle to peace.[10] The section below examines the three main liberal approaches to Israel in more detail, with a focus on the post–Cold War era.

ROBUST LIBERAL INTERNATIONALISM AND "CRITICAL FRIENDSHIP" WITH ISRAEL

Roots and Grand Strategy

Among liberals and Democrats, adherents of robust liberal internationalism stand out as being both the most willing to use force – though they are less hawkish than the Republican mainstream – and the most supportive of Israel, while being critical of illiberal Israeli policies. There are two subgroups within this approach: liberal interventionists, and centrist Democrats.[11]

For liberal interventionists, radical antidemocratic regimes are viewed as implacable enemies that must be confronted because of their ideological nature. This outlook was forged in the fight against Fascism and Nazism in the 1930s and 1940s. It was dominant in the Democratic Party and anti-Communist elements of the labor movement from the early days of the Cold War until Vietnam. Leading adherents included Harry Truman, Hubert Humphrey, and Scoop Jackson. They supported labor rights, the New Deal, and civil rights at home, while simultaneously supporting liberal international institutions and foreign aid, combined with a tough policy of containment toward the Soviet Union abroad. The purpose of foreign aid, such as the Marshall Plan, was to limit the popularity of Communism by demonstrating that democracy would improve the material condition of ordinary people.[12] The Vietnam War led to the decline of these liberal hawks within the Democratic Party, and some left the party altogether in the late 1970s.

Another strand of liberal interventionism stems from liberal intellectuals associated with the magazine *Dissent*, founded by Irving Howe in 1954. Howe abandoned his former Trotskyite compatriots over their opposition to entering World War II, and he was extremely critical of the New Left. He emphasized the moral distinction between totalitarian regimes on the one hand and democracies – however imperfect – on the other. Howe died in 1993; nonetheless, many people associated with the magazine continue to adhere to his approach, such as Michael Walzer and Paul Berman.

Alongside liberal interventionists are the centrist Democrats. They share a commitment to a domestic liberal agenda and anti-totalitarianism; however, their approach to foreign policy is tempered by political realism. Thus, centrist Democrat Dennis Ross – who became the most important U.S. official dealing with the Middle East peace process in the 1990s – was more cautious about the ability of U.S. intervention to impose democracy than neoconservatives.[13] Bill Clinton summed up the centrist foreign policy creed thus: "When our national security interests are threatened, we will act with others when we can, but alone if we must. We will use diplomacy when we can, but force if we must."[14] In the 1980s the centrist approach regained some traction inside the Democratic Party with the rise of the New Democrats, such as Al Gore and Joe Lieberman, who were more willing to support Reagan's interventionist policies in Central America than most Democrats.[15] The Democratic Leadership Council (DLC) and the *New Republic* magazine, which was influential in Washington circles during the 1980s, also promoted this outlook. Bill Clinton served as president of the DLC, and its centrist approach played an important role during the Clinton presidency.

Post–Cold War
Supporters of robust liberal internationalism constituted the minority of Democratic congressmen who supported the 1991 Gulf War; which *Dissent* editor Michael Walzer defined as a "just war." They also led the campaign for

humanitarian intervention to save Bosnian Muslims. Their support for the use of force stood out even more starkly regarding the 2003 Iraq War. For Paul Berman at *Dissent*, the key reason to support the war was the fascist nature of Saddam Hussein's regime and its massive crimes against its own people. Senators Joe Lieberman and Hillary Clinton, as well as Richard Holbrooke, also supported the war, though they argued for a more multilateral approach than that adopted by the Bush administration, with greater emphasis on postwar institution building.[16] Much as after Vietnam, the Iraq War led to a decline in support for the robust approach among Democrats, as it became tainted by both the situation in Iraq and its association with the major policy of the conservative Bush administration.

America, Israel, and the Middle East

Adherents of robust liberal internationalism recognize that the Arab-Israeli conflict is one of many sources of instability in the Middle East, but they believe that even if Israel did not exist, the region would remain very unstable and anti-American.[17] Instead, they put forward a number of different reasons for regional instability, all of which are primarily related to the *internal* dynamics of the region.

First, they argue that instability and anti-Americanism is driven by extreme Islamist theologies and radical Arabist ideologies that fuel terrorism and dictatorship.[18] This is especially important for liberal interventionists, who view such ideologies as essentially pathological, which, they argue, makes political accommodation impossible.[19] From this perspective, Israel warrants support as a democracy in the frontline of an ideological battle. Centrists' greater political realism means that they are more willing to engage diplomatically with radical states. They believe that a mixture of carrots and sticks can affect such states' calculations, especially those related to regime survival. Yet ultimately, they agree that such extremism, as embodied in Hamas and Hezbollah, cannot be accommodated in a strategic sense. Hence they preferred to build up Palestinian moderates like Mahmoud Abbas and Salam Fayyad, rather than an unreconstructed Hamas. More generally, in line with the logic of Marshall aid, this approach argues that the U.S. should support liberals in Arab and Muslim countries through the provision of aid and development assistance to compete with the Islamists, who often gain support through charitable good works. The importance of ideology is also reflected in their belief that it is unlikely that the U.S. will be able to deter a nuclear Iran under the ayatollahs' regime.[20]

Indeed, robust liberal internationalists – especially the centrists – have viewed the threat posed by Iran's potential possession of WMD as of vital strategic importance, because of the dependence of the global economy on Middle Eastern oil. Moreover, they fear that allowing Iran to obtain nuclear weapons would be a tipping point that would lead to a dangerous proliferation of nuclear weapons in the region. This would signal the death knoll of the nonproliferation regime while simultaneously boosting the prestige of radical Islam. Against this background,

Israel has been perceived as a strategic asset, as it is the strongest and most reliable U.S. ally in the region.[21] Finally, they argue that excessive state interference in the economy, the lack of a self-critical educational culture, and the lack of good governance are significant causes of instability in the Middle East[22] – hence their support of economic, social, and political reform.

The Peace Process

Robust liberal internationalists value a two-state solution in and of itself, as an expression of the universal value of national self-determination. They also think that the peace process assists in managing the conflict by preventing the development of a dangerous vacuum. Yet while they strongly favor heavy U.S. engagement in the peace process, they oppose the idea that the United States should seek to impose a settlement, since the successful implementation of any peace agreement is primarily dependent on the parties themselves. Without their willingness, an imposed deal would be likely to unravel quickly with dire consequences. As a result, they tend to focus on providing incentives for peace rather than pressure. In this connection, aid to Israel is designed not only to strengthen an ally against common enemies, but also to reassure Israel and thereby encourage it to take the risks required to make peace.[23]

Consequently, when an Israeli government was seriously committed to making compromises, Centrists tended to promote the idea that the US should coordinate its strategy toward the peace process with Israel more closely than with America's Arab partners. For the key to successful U.S. mediation was deemed to be not neutrality per se but having leverage over the parties and recognizing that the key to reaching an agreement was to meet the needs of both sides.[24] According to David Makovsky, in the Israeli-Palestinian case, the core needs were deemed to be security for the Israelis and dignity for the Palestinians.[25]

Given their belief that peace ultimately depends on the parties themselves, they were willing to actively support attempts to reach a comprehensive peace settlement when they perceived that both sides were genuinely committed to that objective. But they were not always convinced that there was a genuine Arab-Palestinian partner able and willing to deliver a permanent status peace agreement.[26] As a consequence, and especially after the failure of the Clinton administration to achieve permanent status agreement, they preferred to focus on partial agreements.[27] For example, during the Obama administration David Makovsky and Dennis Ross of the Washington Institute for Near East Policy think tank[28] put forward the idea that the U.S. should promote a deal on borders and security first rather than focus on a comprehensive settlement.[29] Equally, the bad experience of Arafat's Palestinian Authority in terms of corruption and terrorism led robust liberal internationalists to promote internal Palestinian bottom-up institutional reform and economic development alongside traditional top-down diplomacy in the 2000s. Part of the purpose of this aid was to help moderate Palestinians at the expense of Hamas.

Critical Friendship with Israel

Robust liberal internationalists are united by sharing a critical commitment to a democratic Israel.[30] While underlyingly supportive of Israel, they criticized Israeli policies regarding settlements, the treatment of the Palestinians, Israel's Arab citizens, and issues related to religion and state.[31] Though completely rejecting the idea that Israel *is* an apartheid state,[32] they feared that the expansion of settlements would prevent a future Israeli withdrawal, thereby forestalling the chance for peace and threatening to turn Israel *into* an apartheid state in which a Jewish minority with full political rights rules over a Palestinian majority without those rights indefinitely.[33] This was a central theme in their thinking. But they were also strongly critical of Leftists who reject a Jewish state per se and advocate boycotting Israel.[34]

DOVISH DEMOCRATS: 'EVENHANDEDNESS' AND LINKAGE

Identity and Roots

From 1968 onward Democrats and liberals became divided about the level of military assertiveness appropriate for American foreign policy, with the majority increasingly adopting a defensive, dovish line. These dovish liberals remained supportive of foreign engagement in terms of trade, diplomacy, and the promotion of human rights, but they became very cautious about extending military commitments and the extensive use of force. Thus, during the 1980s most Democrats opposed American intervention in Central America, and in 1991 most Democrats in Congress opposed the Gulf War. This tendency retreated somewhat in the 1990s, but following the 2003 Iraq War, dovishness rose sharply among Democrats, becoming dominant inside the party.[35]

Supporters of this approach include Howard Dean, who ran unsuccessfully for the Democratic nomination for president in 2004. It has also been represented inside left-of-center think tanks like the Center for American Progress, as well as within the Obama administration. Aside from dovish liberals, this cautious defensive approach to the use of force was supported by Realists within the Democratic Party, such as Zbigniew Brzezinski, national security advisor during the Carter administration, and later on by Realist Republicans who served in the Obama administrations, such as Robert Gates (who worked for Brzezinski during the Carter administration) and Chuck Hagel.[36]

Grand Strategy

Dovish Democrats tend to believe that the best way to handle conflict is to deal with its root causes by addressing legitimate grievances. This faith in rationality leads them to evaluate hostile ideologies as less strategically significant than robust liberal internationalists. Democratic doves believe that the use of force should be a last resort. They emphasize the importance of "soft power" – cultural appeal. And they tend to advocate treating countries equally, regardless of their internal ideological character, through open inclusive multilateral diplomacy, trade and economic interdependence, and membership in international institutions. This they believe will encourage those countries in the long term to become more democratic, cooperative and peaceful.[37]

For dovish Democrats, the Vietnam War holds important lessons for U.S. foreign policy. As they see it, U.S. policy in Vietnam was driven by misplaced idealism, a failure to recognize the limited strategic utility of military force, and a failure to understand that North Vietnam was driven primarily by local nationalism rather than by a commitment to world revolution and Communism. It was these misconceptions that led to America getting bogged down in a war it could never win. For dovish Democrats, the George W. Bush administration repeated these mistakes in Iraq.[38]

Post-Cold War, 9/11, and the War on Terror

According to dovish Democrats, the U.S. faces a diffuse array of threats and challenges including WMD proliferation, jihadist terrorism, and the rise of China, as well as global warming, health pandemics, and energy scarcity.[39] They are at least as worried about economic and humanitarian threats as about military ones.[40] The way to deal with these threats is said to be by strengthening the liberal-internationalist order founded by the U.S. after 1945. They believe that by binding itself to international norms and institutions, U.S. leadership will be more readily accepted. As they see it, expanding the reach of international institutions to deal with issues of development and unconventional security threats (such as public health, refugees, and emergency aid) is akin to investing in social services and education in the domestic arena – it all helps make for a more stable, safe, and better functioning community.[41]

From their perspective, 9/11 required a tough U.S. response against al Qaida and the Taliban. But they did not view the U.S. as facing a major geostrategic threat from radical Islam in the way that it had from Nazi Germany and its Fascist allies or from the Soviet Union. This is not only because radical Islam lacks the equivalent military power, but also because they do not view Islamism as having a unified revolutionary agenda.[42] According to this view, unlike al Qaida, most Islamists are focused on gaining control of existing nation-states, not bringing about a return to the caliphate. Rather, they see the Middle East as containing a series of discreet conflicts driven primarily by specific local issues. Hence, they favor engaging "moderate" Islamists, placating them with local political compromises and co-opting them against al Qaida.[43] They also reject a predominantly military approach as futile, since they believe it only fuels public support for al Qaida.[44] Against this background, they believed that the 2003 Iraq War increased the threat from jihadis because it divided the U.S. from key allies in Europe damaging the multilateral liberal international order,[45] while greatly increasing America's unpopularity with the Arab public.[46] America's

Iraq intervention was seen as having produced a backlash, similar to that produced by U.S. intervention in Vietnam. To combat this required not only withdrawing from Iraq, but also making resolution of the Arab-Israeli conflict a priority.[47]

Israel and the Palestinians

There are four distinctive features of the dovish Democrats' approach. First is its embrace of the concept of "linkage," according to which resolving the Arab-Israeli conflict is viewed as the key to resolving or at least greatly ameliorating all other major sources of instability and anti-Americanism in the Middle East. From this perspective, Israel is often perceived as a strategic liability. It might help the United States here and there with intelligence cooperation and anti-terror tactics, but in the absence of a peace deal that would satisfy the legitimate demands of the Palestinians, American support for Israel is viewed as a major cause of hostility to the U.S., exploited by radical Islamists to gain wider support. Only by addressing the Palestinians' grievances would support for terrorism diminish and America's position improve.[48] As Daniel Kurtzer and Scott Lasensky put it, "A just and comprehensive peace is one of the strongest arguments against Islamic militancy in the Arab world."[49] Or as Bill Clinton's national security advisor, Sandy Berger, wrote in 2012, "There is perhaps no more intractable, yet vital, issue in U.S. foreign policy ... None of these challenges [the threat of a nuclear Iran, the Syrian civil war, the rise of China] means that Israeli-Palestinian peace is less important now. Indeed, it is more important."[50]

While many dovish Democrats identify more with Israel than with the Palestinians, others are more ideologically and emotionally neutral. Either way, the second distinctive feature of the dovish approach is that when it comes to U.S. policy, they advocate an evenhanded approach to the conflict. They argue that the U.S. should encourage Israel to make compromises through the offer of aid and security cooperation.[51] But support for such carrots is tied to the prospect of Israeli withdrawal, not wider U.S. strategic interests; after all, as one Middle East expert from a liberal think tank put it, "why should the U.S. continue to subsidize the occupation?"[52] Moreover, they are more willing to put heavier pressure on Israel to promote a permanent status agreement than robust liberal internationalists.[53] Indeed, the third distinctive element of the dovish approach is the belief that the U.S. should vigorously promote its own outline for a comprehensive settlement,[54] preferably in coordination with European allies.[55]

Fourth, while dovish Democrats support reforms in the Palestinian Authority, they do not imbue those reforms with the same degree of significance as do robust liberal internationalists. As a Center for American Progress report put it: "For all of the institutional problems and corruption of the Palestinian Authority, the core of the problem remains the Israeli occupation."[56] Against this background, after Hamas took control of the Gaza Strip in 2007, some supported engaging the organization or at least including it in a Palestinian national unity government that would empower the moderate PA leader Abbas to negotiate with Israel. They feared that without Palestinian unity, no deal would be possible. Some argued that Hamas would go along with this, because they viewed Hamas as being primarily driven by local nationalist considerations, rather than implacable, transnational religious extremism.[57]

THE ANTI-ISRAEL LEFT: PROGRESSIVE POSTCOLONIALISM

Identity, Roots and Grand Strategy

There are two overlapping elements within the anti-Israel Left. First, there is the progressive tradition. In the twenty-first century it has been present among supporters of Ralph Nader's presidential bid and on the left of the Democratic Party, where it is more prominent among the liberal base than among party elites – where it is marginal. Their most vocal spokesman in the media was Michael Moore. The second element is postcolonialism, which is strong in academia, notably in the humanities and Middle Eastern studies, inspired by the work of Edward Said and Noam Chomsky. These approaches are popular within social movements and many human rights NGOs.[58] They are also prevalent in the leading progressive magazine the *Nation* and the radical newsletter *CounterPunch*, as well as getting a hearing at mainstream liberal websites such as the *Huffington Post*, which carries anti-Zionist bloggers like Mondoweiss.

For progressives and postcolonialists, America needs to minimize its "imperialist" intervention abroad and concentrate instead on reducing poverty at home. In the 1930s they were strongly represented in the Keep America out of the War Coalition. Back then, many of them argued that there was little moral difference between the British Empire and Nazi Germany. Indeed, hostility was more focused on the British Empire, as they were strong supporters of nationalist movements under colonial rule; irrespective of these movements' lack of democratic credentials.[59] In 1948 the former Democratic vice president Henry Wallace formed the Progressive Party. It argued that American imperialism provoked a defensively orientated Soviet Union. The party opposed Truman's policy of containment, which it declared benefited only Wall Street. Soviet oppression and aggression were never condemned. After Truman won the 1948 election, progressivism declined. But the protest movement against the Vietnam War led to a resurgence – notably inside the Students for a Democratic Society (SDS) movement. The Democratic presidential candidate in 1972, George McGovern, represented the progressive outlook. He referred to the U.S. bombing of Vietnam as the most barbaric action taken by any country since the Holocaust.[60]

Later, the Carter administration drew on postcolonialist ideas, emphasizing "North-South relations." Postcolonialism grew out of the Non-Aligned Movement and the intellectual milieu of the New Left in the late 1960s. Its axiom is that "many of the wrongs, if not crimes, against humanity are a product of the economic dominance of the north over the south."[61] In the 1960s and 1970s they supported violent resistance of anti-imperialist forces in the Third World, even if such forces were antidemocratic. Since the 1990s, its strategy has focused on nonviolent resistance such as boycotts, divestment, and sanctions (BDS), though it does not always condemn Palestinian terrorism. It uses a quasi-Marxist analysis that transfers the old class division of European society into a new race-based class division between colonizers and the colonized.[62] In the post–Cold War era, progressives and postcolonialists opposed intervention in Bosnia and saw 9/11 as "blowback" – a consequence of anger generated by U.S. imperialism, including support for Israel. Some were willing in theory to use of force in Afghanistan. But their demand that any operation not lead to any civilian casualties rendered this meaningless. They also vehemently opposed the 2003 Iraq War.[63]

Israel and the Palestinians

In the aftermath of the Second World War, progressives were generally supportive of the fledgling State of Israel. The Holocaust cast the Jewish people as the quintessential victims of Fascism, while Israel itself was led by social democrats and was the home of the kibbutz. Thus, the leading progressive magazine, the *Nation*, supported the creation of Israel. The turning point was the Six Day War. Suddenly, Israel was no longer the underdog and it was now allied with the "imperialist" U.S. At the same time, the Palestinians came to be viewed as the victims of Western "imperialism" and Israeli "colonialism." As of 2010, progressive elites were the only subgroup of Americans where sympathy for the Palestinians reached double figures (27 percent); although the Arab-Israeli conflict has not been a major political priority for American progressives.[64]

While some progressives retain sympathy for Israel, postcolonialists are unequivocally anti-Israel. The West, and by extension Israel, are viewed as *essentially* reactionary, while the status of the Third World, including the Palestinians, as victims of colonialism makes them *essentially* progressive.[65] In this vein the Black Power leader Stokely Carmichael referred to "white Israel's" oppression of the "colored Palestinians."[66] Hard-core Postcolonialists, view Israel as illegitimate and favor dismantling or destruction of the Jewish state.[67] In contrast, progressives like Jimmy Carter and George McGovern accept Israel's right to exist and support a two-state solution. This has been the dominant progressive position. The distinction between the minority of one-staters and the majority of two-staters is significant. However, both groups sympathize more with the Palestinians, because they are perceived as the victims[68] and both frame the conflict in the same way, as comparable to the displacement of Native American peoples and apartheid. Progressives clearly place the fundamental blame for the conflict on Israel. Correspondingly, they place the overwhelming onus for concessions on the Israelis.[69] They argue that the US should pressure Israel into making concessions;[70] consequently, they have been very hostile to the pro-Israel lobby.[71]

In line with their general tendency to single out the West for opprobrium while whitewashing Third World dictatorships,[72] the progressive-postcolonial discourse was characterized by the demonization and singling out of Israel combined with the whitewashing of Israel's enemies. Thus, in the first decade of the twenty-first century the leading human rights NGO, Human Rights Watch, heaped disproportionate criticism on Israel;[73] a fact recognized by the founder of HRW himself.[74] On the one hand, Jimmy Carter alleged that Israeli actions towards the Palestinians were worse that the Rwandan genocide![75] On the other hand, Carter whitewashed Hezbollah as interested only in ending the occupation and conducting good works in the community.[76] At the extreme, anti-Israel prejudice flirted with anti-Semitism by comparing Israel to the Nazis[77] including on the popular *Daily Kos* website.[78]

In addition, Islamist extremism was downplayed or viewed as a form of resistance to imperialism and as a function of internalized "Orientalist" traits for which the West is ultimately to blame.[79] In 1979, Princeton law professor Richard Falk argued that Khomeini's "entourage of close advisers is uniformly composed of moderate, progressive individuals … who share a notable record of concern for human rights."[80] In March 2009, Falk then serving as United Nations Special Rapporteur on Human Rights in the Palestinian Territories published a report on the Gaza War that concluded that Israel's operation constituted "an unprovoked assault," "a war crime of the greatest magnitude," and a "crime against humanity." Meanwhile in 2010, Professor Judith Butler determined that "understanding Hamas, Hezbollah as social movements that are progressive, … that are part of a global Left, is extremely important."[81] Table 3.1 summarizes and compares the different approaches toward Israel and the Arab-Israeli conflict among liberal elites.

THE LIBERAL DISCOURSE: NARRATING THE RISE AND FALL
OF THE PEACE PROCESS

This section surveys the elite liberal discourse regarding the peace process since the early 1990s. The survey is based on relevant articles in the major highbrow liberal magazines: the *New Republic* (TNR), the *Nation*, the *Atlantic*, the *New York Review of Books* (NYRB), *American Prospect*, *Mother Jones*, *Dissent*, and *Salon*.[82] Also surveyed are the articles of liberal columnists Thomas Friedman of the *New York Times* and Richard Cohen of the *Washington Post*, both of whom wrote the largest amount of opinion pieces on the subject in their respective newspapers throughout the period.

TABLE 3.1. *Elite Liberal Approaches to the Arab-Israeli Conflict*

	Robust liberal internationalism	Dovish democrats	Progressive postcolonialism
Grand strategy	Centrist; Interventionist	Anti-military intervention	Isolationist
Roots of instability and anti-Americanism	Indigenous to the Middle East Arab-Israeli conflict secondary	U.S. policies in the Middle East Arab-Israeli conflict primary	Extraneous to the Middle East Blowback vs. U.S. "imperialism"
Israel in U.S. strategy	Asset (esp. if supports the peace process)	Liability (neutral if supports peace process)	Liability
Ideology, theology, prejudices	Critical friendship with Israel Support liberals on both sides	Many identify more with Israel	Flirts with anti-Semitism at extreme Sympathize with the "victims"
Taking sides	Pro-Israeli Center-Left	Evenhanded	Pro-Palestinian
Strategy toward the conflict	Equivocal re Interim/Permanent deal	Heavy U.S. pressure for permanent deal	BDS: Impose pro-Palestinian settlement
Outline of peace settlement	Palestinian State 1967 Borders +/- Divided Jerusalem vs. settlements vs. "Right of Return" to Israel	Palestinian State 1967 Borders +/- Divided Jerusalem vs. settlements vs. full implementation "Right of Return"	Palestinian State/One State vs. settlements Pro "Right of Return"
Blame for the conflict	Mainly Palestinian/Arab extremists Also Israeli ideological Right	Both sides	Israel
Morality	Palestinian Terror worse	Palestinian Terror worse But increasingly equivocal	Moral equivalence/Israel worse
Onus for concessions	Both sides	Both sides, Israel more	Israel

The Liberal Discourse in the 1990s: The Heyday of the Peace Process

In the 1990s the liberal discourse was heavily concentrated in the *Nation*, which gave voice to the progressive-postcolonial approach, and *TNR*, which gave voice to the approach of robust liberal internationalists, also expressed by Thomas Friedman and Richard Cohen. The other magazines' coverage of the issue was extremely sparse. *TNR*, *Dissent*, Thomas Friedman, and Richard Cohen were very supportive of the peace process, albeit with the regular expression of concerns and criticisms of both sides. They praised the Rabin government and urged it to constrain settlements and confront settlers whom they viewed as a threat to the peace process and Israeli democracy.[83] Criticism of the Palestinian side, especially in the *New Republic*, peaked following the spate of suicide bombings in 1995 and 1996. But ultimately they remained committed to the peace process.[84] One important figure, Marty Peretz, the owner of *TNR*, was more hawkish. He never believed that Arafat was genuinely committed to peace.[85] He was hostile to the settlements, but unprepared to divide Jerusalem or commit to a full withdrawal from the Golan Heights.[86]

In any case, Friedman, Cohen, and *Dissent* remained very critical of the Israeli Right, strongly supporting Shimon Peres over Benjamin Netanyahu in the 1996 election.[87] Netanyahu's victory was referred to as a "disaster"[88] and a "tragedy."[89] They advocated U.S. pressure on Netanyahu.[90] They also argued that mainstream American Jewish organizations should take a stronger stand in favor of the peace process and were critical of right-wing supporters of Israel in the U.S.[91] Nonetheless, they gave Bibi some credit for agreeing to further withdrawals and promoting a partition plan.[92] Nor did they place the onus for concessions only on Israel. They strongly criticized Arafat and the Arab states for demonizing Israel in their state-controlled media and for their refusal to speak out loudly and clearly against terrorism in Arabic. They argued that Arab leaders were not doing enough to demonstrate to Israelis that their concessions would lead to genuine coexistence.[93]

The *Nation* supported the 1993 Oslo Accords,[94] but it also gave significant space and legitimacy to Palestinian opposition – which argued that the peace process constituted a nauseating sell-out[95] – including two cover stories by Edward Said.[96] When Hamas carried out a spate of bus bombings, the dominant response in the *Nation* was that it was ultimately fault of the occupation and that only further Israeli concessions would end the violence.[97] Still, the magazine continued to support the peace process.[98]

The Collapse of the Peace Process and the Rise of Hamas and Hezbollah, 2001–2009

The collapse of the peace process and 9/11 led to a massive surge in the quantity and intensity of liberal comment on the peace process. Whereas in the 1990s the liberal discourse was basically united in support of the peace process; following the collapse of the peace process and 9/11 it became characterized by deep divisions. Robust liberal internationalism provided the basis for the dominant narrative in *TNR*, *Dissent*, the *Atlantic*, the columns of Richard Cohen and Thomas Friedman, and the blog of Jeffrey Goldberg. The progressive-postcolonial approach dominated in the *Nation*. While in *American Prospect*, *Salon*, and the *NYRB*, the dovish liberal approach dominated, and after 2006, these magazines moved closer to the progressive approach.

The Narrative of Robust Liberal Internationalism and Critical Friends of Israel

Israel has tried, over and over again, to make peace with a recalcitrant and unforgiving enemy.

—Richard Cohen, the *Washington Post*[99]

When the Oslo process collapsed and violence erupted, robust liberal internationalists identified the Palestinians, and especially Yasir Arafat, as the primary culprit. Thus, Thomas Friedman labeled the conflict "Arafat's War."[100] Criticisms were made of U.S. and Israeli policy, but ultimately they argued that had the Palestinians truly wanted a state based on 1967 borders, with Arab East Jerusalem as its capital, they could have had it. Their rejection of the Clinton Parameters and the suicide bombing campaign targeting Israeli civilians signified that the Palestinians had not really given up on the goal of destroying Israel.[101]

Arafat and the Arab states were once again criticized for their failure to prepare their peoples for peace and for their active discouragement of necessary Palestinian compromises. The demonization of Israel was viewed as a significant obstacle to generating legitimacy for the concessions required for peace. They drew attention to the hatred nurtured in school textbooks and wider Arab media and public statements by leaders, such as when Bashar Assad, standing next to the Pope, called for Christians and Muslims to unite against "Jews who betrayed Jesus and tried to kill Mohammed." This was contrasted with the Israeli public's willingness to pay the necessary price for peace.[102]

Another major factor underlying strong support for Israel was Palestinian terrorism. Terrorism was viewed primarily not as a function of desperation but as a strategic choice.[103] The fact that more Palestinians were dying was deemed less significant than the fact that the Palestinians, unlike Israel, were *deliberately* targeting civilians.[104] They were disgusted by the Palestinian public's celebration of suicide terrorism involving their own children.[105] As Richard Cohen put it, "One engages in the inhumane murder of civilians while the other strives, sometimes vainly, to retain its humanity."[106] Over the next decade, there was criticism of Israel's military actions, but Israeli behavior was virtually always reckoned to be more ethical than that of its enemies.[107]

Overall this added up to a reframing of the conflict. From at least the first intifada until 2000, Arafat and Fatah had been given the benefit of the doubt, and the main stumbling block was deemed to be the Israeli Right. But after 2000, the main stumbling block was deemed to be on the Arab and Palestinian side.[108] This shift was reinforced by 9/11, which was viewed not as a result of U.S. support for Israel but rather as an expression of radical Islam's hatred of America's liberal democratic values.[109]

Still, while they viewed Israel and the U.S. as sharing a common fight against radical Islamic terrorism,[110] they argued that, unlike al Qaida, the Palestinians had legitimate grievances that needed to be addressed.[111] So although they supported the construction of the security barrier in the West Bank, they criticized the route arguing that it should be closer to the pre 1967 border.[112] Moreover, while they understood Israel's military response to prevent terrorism in Operation Defensive Shield, they urged the administration to be more proactive in promoting negotiations and tougher on Israeli settlements.[113]

While remaining supportive of genuine Palestinian moderates and extensive U.S. involvement in the peace process, they were divided about the merits of plans for a permanent settlement like the 2003 Geneva draft agreement and the 2002 Arab League plan.[114] The disengagement from Gaza was viewed as a strategic defeat for the settlement movement, as well as a step toward a Palestinian state, with Sharon cast in the role of De Gaulle,[115] though some argued that Sharon should have reached an agreement with the moderate Palestinian leader Abbas, instead of acting unilaterally.[116] But others advocated an additional unilateral civilian withdrawal from many settlements in the West Bank, a proposal similar to that put forward by Ehud Olmert, the leader of the centrist Kadima party in the 2006 election.[117]

The rise to power of Hamas in Gaza and the Second Lebanon War against Hezbollah deepened their support for Israel. Hamas and Hezbollah were viewed as anti-Semitic extremists committed to Israel's destruction.[118] They completely rejected any moral equivalence between democratic Israel and its Islamist enemies and they supported a tough Israeli response,[119] though not all Israeli actions.[120] Leftists who focused their condemnation on Israel rather than Hamas and Hezbollah were dismissed as "useful idiots"[121] who thought they were being humanitarian while actually serving the interests of antidemocratic forces opposed to a two-state solution.[122] In contrast, they understood the rockets fired by Hamas and Hezbollah as detrimental to peace, since it undermined the Israeli public's support for compromise by creating the impression that what Israel got in exchange for withdrawals from Gaza and Lebanon was not peace but war.[123]

The Second Lebanon War also led them to identify an increase in the security threat posed to Israel by the risk that a Palestinian state would be taken over by religious zealots, who would rain down rockets on Israeli cities.[124] This did not change their minds about the urgency of an Israeli civilian withdrawal from the West Bank, but it did lead them to argue that a military withdrawal would have to come later, after it was clear that there was a partner able and willing to counteract such threats effectively.[125] In this regard, great hopes were raised by the state-building efforts of the Palestinian prime minister Fayyad, which they hoped would lay foundations for a decent Palestinian state that would coexist peacefully alongside Israel.[126]

The return to power of a Likud-led government in Israel in 2009 led to an upsurge in criticisms of Israeli policies. Netanyahu was taken to task for not extending the settlement freeze and for not taking the diplomatic initiative. Israel's foreign minister, Avigdor Lieberman, was castigated for using racist language and for contradicting the values that made Israel "worth supporting."[127] Yet at the same time, they thought that Abbas did not seem much interested in negotiating an agreement, either.[128] Nor did they believe that removing Lieberman and the settlements was a panacea that would, by itself, unlock the door to peace between Israel and the Palestinians or regional stability,[129] given the strength of extremist forces among the Palestinians and in the region in general.[130]

The Progressive-Postcolonial Narrative

The *Nation* placed the bulk of the blame for the collapse of the peace process in 2000 on Israel. Israeli concessions under Barak were portrayed as grossly insufficient. Some argued for abandoning the negotiations and creating a boycott movement, while others called for a return to negotiations.[131] The *Nation* condemned suicide bombings while continuing to place the primary responsibly on Israeli policies.[132] One article referred to suicide bombing against Israeli civilians as "counter-attacks,"[133] and another implicitly accused Israel of attempting genocide, claiming, "The Israelis are trying ... to do to Palestinians ... what Ahmadinejad seems to suggest should be done to Israel."[134] Even the unilateral withdrawal from Gaza was dismissed as merely a means of strengthening Israel's grip on the West Bank.[135] Unsurprisingly, Israel was also deemed primarily responsible for the Second Lebanon War,[136] and there was deemed to be no moral difference between Israeli and Hezbollah actions.[137] A similar approach was taken to the Gaza War in 2008–2009, with the emphasis being on Palestinian suffering.[138]

The Dovish-Liberal Narrative: Tilting Towards Progressive Postcolonialism

In *American Prospect, Salon,* and the *NYRB,* both sides were blamed for the collapse of the peace process and the cycle of violence.[139] The Israelis had to stop settlements; the Palestinians had to stop terrorism.[140] By far the most influential of the articles in this genre was authored by Robert Malley and Hussein Agha in the *NYRB,* which argued that part of the reason for failure was that the U.S. was too supportive of Israel.[141] Although it triggered an exchange of views, the net effect of this article was to erode the idea that the Palestinians were primarily responsible for the collapse of the peace process. The former U.S. negotiator Aaron Miller concurred, arguing that the U.S. had erred at Camp David by acting as "Israel's lawyer."[142]

While the thrust of the discourse was to blame both sides, prior to 9/11 there was a tilt toward the Progressive pro-Palestinian narrative, especially in *Salon*, where some articles cast Israel as engaged in colonization, racism, and apartheid.[143] One article gave a sympathetic portrayal of a Palestinian mother who felt not only anguish but also pride that her son had been killed in a suicide attack on Israeli civilians. The Israeli view that such pride constituted a culture of brutality that rendered peace impossible, was characterized as racist.[144]

In contrast, in the wake of Palestinians cheering the 9/11 attack,[145] the discourse tilted the other way, laying the blame primarily on Arafat[146] while strongly rejecting attempts to delegitimize and boycott Israel.[147] However, it was also emphasized that Sharon sought to create "Palestinian Bantustans" instead of a genuine Palestinian state.[148] When the Sharon government launched Operation Defensive Shield, it was argued that such attempts to resolve matters by force would fail and that only addressing legitimate Palestinian grievances through negotiations would succeed. In this vein, they endorsed the 2002 Arab League peace plan and the 2003 draft Geneva peace agreement.[149]

While on balance, the view of the Gaza disengagement was positive,[150] the tilt toward Israel began to erode before then, with the onset of the Iraq War in 2003. The most significant article in this regard was Tony Judt's "Israel: The Alternative" in the *NYRB*,[151] in which he declared that the very idea of a Jewish state was anachronistic. He referred to Israel as a colonial state and to the then deputy prime minister of Israel, Ehud Olmert, as a Fascist. This article caused a storm. However, it was not until the Second Lebanon War that the expression of anti-Israel positions grew substantially, when Israel was accused of "methodically smashing Lebanon into the dust," of "pounding civilians," and seeking to "ethnically cleanse" South Lebanon. The Israeli claim (later proven to be true) that Hezbollah was hiding among civilians was declared a myth.[152] A few articles that were relatively neutral or sympathetic to Israel did appear, but they were in the clear minority. Much of the strong criticism of Israel was heavily linked to strong criticism of the Bush administration's support for Israel in the war.[153]

The same perspective was prevalent in relation to the conflict between Israel and Hamas. In the wake of Hamas's seizure of power in Gaza in 2007, there was a groundswell of opinion in favor of the U.S. opening a dialogue with Hamas and the construction of a Hamas-Fatah coalition, without Hamas having to accept the three Middle East Quartet (U.S., EU, Russia, UN) conditions adopted by much of the international community: recognition of Israel, acceptance of past agreements, and the complete cessation of terrorism. They argued that its anti-Semitic ideology was not that important as, in their view, Hamas was a complex, pragmatic grassroots organization.[154] As Gary Kamiya, the executive editor and cofounder of *Salon*, argued, "Hamas is not the problem; it is a symptom. The problem is ... the dispossession of Palestinians and the ongoing Israeli occupation of their land."[155]

Given their assertion that U.S. pressure on Israel was a sine qua non for peace, it is not surprising that much ink was spilt arguing that the mainstream pro-Israel lobby, the Christian Right, and the neoconservatives[156] were preventing the exertion of the necessary pressure. The most influential article on the subject was penned by a former editor at the the *New Republic*, Peter Beinart, who took the American Jewish leadership to task its refusal to adopt an openly dovish stand when that involved opposing the Israeli government.[157] Liberal hostility toward the foreign policy of George W. Bush also spilled over into hostility toward Israeli policy under Sharon, which like the Bush doctrine emphasized unilateralism and the use of force. Opposed to the Iraq War for a variety of reasons, they also viewed it as a diversion from dealing with the key issue – the Israeli-Palestinian conflict.[158]

Having surveyed the elite approaches and discourse, the question remains as to how much support these approaches had among the mass of Democrats and liberals.

PUBLIC OPINION AMONG DEMOCRATS AND LIBERALS

Grand Strategy

Democrats are divided over U.S. grand strategy. Though the trend is increasingly dovish, a large minority favor robust liberal internationalism. On the one hand, Democrats share a strong belief in the efficacy of diplomacy. Between 1997 and 2009, the percentage of Democrats who agreed that "good diplomacy is the best way to ensure peace" increased from about two-thirds to three-quarters,[159] reaching 90 percent among liberal Democrats.[160] On the other hand, a large minority of Democrats continue to believe that "the best way to ensure peace is through military strength."[161] In parallel, Democrats have been divided about multilateralism. A majority favors multilateralism,[162] yet a large minority of 45 percent believe the U.S. should "go its own way in international matters regardless of what other countries think."[163] Finally, Democrats are divided about the degree to which the U.S. should engage internationally, though the trend is toward a defensive or even an isolationist position. Thus, between 2002 and 2009 the number of Democrats agreeing that the U.S. should "mind its own business internationally and let other countries get along the best they can on their own" increased from 40 to 53 percent.[164]

The Middle East and the Arab-Israeli Conflict

Democrats' attitudes toward the Middle East are also mixed. Between 2002 and 2011, an absolute majority of Democrats consistently *disagreed* with the idea that Islam encourages violence more than other religions. Liberal Democrats were the most opposed to this claim.[165] Despite this, a majority of Democrats viewed Islamic extremist groups and Iran's nuclear program as the greatest threat to the United States. Yet in March 2012, they were evenly

TABLE 3.2. *Sympathy for Israel and the Palestinians, 2002 to March 2006 (%)*

	Israel	Palestinians	Pro-Israel Margin
All Americans	51	15	+36
Democrats	47	20	+27
Liberals	43	25	+18
Republicans	72	07	+55

Data from Gallup[166]

TABLE 3.3. *Sympathy for Israel over the Palestinians August 2006 to January 2009 (%)*

	Aug. 2006 (2nd Lebanon War)	Jan. 2009 (Gaza War)
All Americans	52	49
Democrats	45	42
Liberals	42	33
Republicans	68	69

Data from Pew Research Center[167]

divided between those who were concerned about the U.S. "acting too quickly" against the Iranian nuclear program and those who were concerned that the U.S. might wait too long.[168] Among liberal Democrats, doves outnumbered hawks on Iran, by a margin of 2–1.[169] However, a majority of Democrats would approve of using force if it were certain Iran had produced a nuclear weapon.[170] As regards the peace process, despite major divisions within the liberal discourse, Democrats level of sympathy for Israel in opinion polls has remained stable since 1967, hovering at 45–50 percent, at least double the number for those who sympathized more with the Palestinians.[171] In the 2000s the level of Democrats sympathy for Israel was slightly below the national average (see Tables 3.2 and 3.3).

During times of heightened violence, the liberal preference for Israel over the Palestinians eroded considerably. Thus in 2002, at the peak of the second intifada, as well as during the Gaza War in 2008–2009, about a third of liberals sided with Israel, while about a quarter preferred the Palestinians, thereby constituting a slim pro-Israel margin of 8 percentage points among those taking sides.[172] In these cases, the gap between Democrats and liberals was especially pronounced. In 2002 Democrats sympathized with Israel over the Palestinians by a margin of 27 points, more than three times the figure for liberals.[173]

While most Democrats are more sympathetic to Israel than the Palestinians, they are also supportive of Israel ultimately making concessions for peace. In 2002 Democrats supported the creation of a Palestinian state by a margin of 44–28; by 2009 the margin had grown to 59–22.[174] On Jerusalem, in the event of a two-state solution, nearly half of Democrats supported dividing the city, while only a third supported complete Israeli control.[175] Also in 2009, when President Obama called on Israel to freeze settlements, more than two-thirds of Democrats agreed that the United States should get tough with Israel.[176]

When it comes to attributing blame, the pro-Israel margin among Democrats is much narrower than it is on the sympathy index. Thus in June 2002, a majority of Democrats thought that neither Ariel Sharon nor Yasir Arafat wanted peace. The margin by which they were more skeptical of Arafat's intensions was only 9 percentage points.[177] In 2011, they believed that both sides were making a serious effort to reach peace. The margin by which they were more positive regarding Israel was 13 percentage points. By a similar margin Democrats favored Israel concerning the appropriate level of force used in the 2006 Lebanon War and the 2009 Gaza War.[178] However, on some aspects of these wars, Democratic opinion ran against Israel. In 2006 a narrow plurality thought Israel was mainly responsible for civilian causalities.[179] While in 2009, a larger plurality of Democrats *disapproved* of Israel's military action.[180] Such attitudes contrasted sharply with the unequivocally pro-Israel stance of Republicans (see Tables 3.4 and 3.5).

On the issue of the U.S. taking sides in the conflict, the majority of Democrats favored the even-handed approach espoused by the dovish Democrats. In 2002, about a half of Democrats thought George W. Bush's policy was too supportive of Israel; approximately a third thought it was about right.[181] During the Second Lebanon War and the Gaza War, around 40 percent of Democrats thought that the U.S. should say or do nothing: around a third thought the U.S. should support Israel, while about a tenth thought the U.S. should publicly

TABLE 3.4. *The Second Lebanon War, 2006: Pro-Israel Margin (%)*

	Republicans	Democrats	Partisan Gap
Responsibility for the war	+46	+18	+28
Responsibility for civilian casualties	+26	− 05	+31
Too much Force (−) vs. (+) Too little/Just right	+64	+16	+48

Data from Pew Research Center[182]

TABLE 3.5. *The Gaza War, 2009: Pro-Israel Margin (%)*

	Republicans	Democrats	Partisan Gap
Dis/approve of Israel's military action	+35	−16	+51
Too much Force vs. Too little/Just right	+66	+15	+51

Data from Pew Research Center[183]

criticize Israel.[184] In 2007, a plurality of liberals thought the U.S. should apply more pressure on Israel rather than on the Palestinians.[185]

Focus groups

Focus groups in 2010–2011 with well-informed mainstream and liberal-leaning Democrat opinion formers in the Washington, DC, area revealed a similar picture to that portrayed by opinion polls.[186] These Democrats were friendly towards Israel, they felt that the U.S. has a special commitment to Israel, and they were sensitive to its difficult security environment. At the same time they were critical of Israeli settlements and strongly supportive of Palestinian state-hood in the context of a negotiated peace. While critical of many aspects of Palestinian behavior, they also sympathized with them as "oppressed" and "abandoned" victims. Their support for the peace process was very strong and central to their view of American interests in the Middle East. They felt both sides were responsible for the conflict and that the onus for peacemaking fell equally on both parties. They also argued that the U.S. should serve as an honest broker in the peace process and about half thought that Obama's policy was too favorable to Israel. About half also agreed with the linkage theory, while the other half argued that even if the U.S. distanced itself from Israel, it would make little difference to America's standing in the region.

U.S. POLICY UNDER THE DEMOCRATS

The Clinton Administrations, 1993–2000

U.S. policy to the peace process under Democratic administrations has been influenced, but not dictated, by the different approaches outlined above. During the Clinton presidency, the dominant approach was the centrist version of robust liberal internationalism. The administration tried to create a Pax Americana through two policies that were supposed to be mutually reinforcing.[187] On the one hand, it pursued a tough policy of "dual containment" directed at the radical regimes of Iran and Iraq. On the other hand, it devoted great energy to the peace process.

There was a high degree of coordination with Israel regarding the peace process. Thus, the administration accepted Rabin's initial preference to focus on the Syrian track.[188] Meanwhile, on the Palestinian track the U.S. initially played the role of a facilitator. Although Washington had not brokered the 1993 Oslo Accords, it was happy to adopt the agreement. Indeed, Dennis Ross argued that since dealing with the PLO was extremely controversial in Israel, it was a decision only the Israelis could make for themselves.[189] Following the agreement, the administration once again coordinated its strategy toward the peace process with Israel. It blamed Hamas terrorists for Israel's policy of closure, and it refused Arafat's demands that the U.S. intervene directly in the talks when Israel opposed that intervention, in order not to give the Palestinians the impression that the U.S. would "deliver" Israel. Furthermore, to reassure Israel and to encourage it to continue with the peace process, every time an agreement was signed the administration upgraded the strategic relationship between the two countries.[190] In the run-up to the 1996 Israeli election, the administration sought to help the Labor leader, Shimon Peres, against his right-wing rival, Benjamin Netanyahu, for example, by organizing an antiterrorism conference and granting Israel extra aid.

The defeat of Peres led to a period of tension with the Netanyahu government. Indeed, between 1996 and 1999, Arafat visited the White House many more times than Netanyahu. Nonetheless, when Netanyahu eventually succumbed to U.S. pressure and agreed to withdraw from a further 13 percent of the West Bank in the 1998 Wye Agreement, he did get in return a package of strategic benefits, which included cooperation in the field of missile defense and a memorandum of strategic understanding which stated that the U.S. would "consult promptly with the Government of Israel with respect to what support, diplomatic or otherwise, or assistance, it can lend to Israel" in the event that Israel was threatened by intermediate- or long-range ballistic missiles.[191] The victory of Ehud Barak in the 1999 election re-inaugurated close coordination, which was in evidence at the Camp David summit. The summit was Barak's initiative; he convinced Clinton to endorse it. The U.S. also acceded to Barak's request that no formal written notes of the summit should be taken in order to protect Israel's negotiating position. Indeed, when the administration finally presented its own parameters for a permanent status agreement in December 2000, they did so only in oral form.[192]

The Clinton Parameters were an attempt to bridge the positions between the two sides undertaken with the support of both parties. They would have given the Palestinians 100 percent of the Gaza Strip and 97 percent of the West Bank including territorial swaps, plus the addition of safe passage across Israeli territory from the West Bank to Gaza. The parameters called for the creation of a nonmilitarized Palestinian state with a permanent international force in the Jordan Valley to replace the Israeli military presence there. While allowing for three Israeli early warning stations in the West Bank, it gave the Palestinians sovereignty over their airspace. On Jerusalem, it divided the city along ethnic lines, with Jewish areas coming under Israeli control and Arab areas under Palestinian control; it also gave the Palestinians sovereignty over the holiest site in Judaism: the Temple Mount. On refugees, the parameters spoke about Israel being the homeland of the Jewish people while rejecting a specific right of return for Palestinian refugees and their descendants to Israel that would stand in contradiction to Israel's sovereign rights and threaten its Jewish character. The guiding principle was that a Palestinian state would be the focal point for refugees, without ruling out that Israel would accept some of them.[193] Overall, then, the parameters gave the Palestinians the viable territorially contiguous state that they had claimed had been their objective since the beginning of the peace process. Consequently, when Yasir Arafat rejected those parameters, which Israel accepted, Dennis Ross and many others laid the blame for the failure of the peace process at Arafat's door. On the other hand, both Ross and Martin Indyk[194] felt that tactical errors by Ehud Barak played a significant role in the failure to achieve an Israeli-Syrian peace deal.[195]

The First Obama Administration

The Obama administration came into office with a dovish grand strategy, which, it was hoped, would allow the president to devote more time and resources to domestic issues. Obama sought to improve America's standing through direct engagement of the Arab-Muslim public and radical states that Bush had shunned, like Iran. As a result, he made a series of public speeches in the Middle East. The most important of these was in Cairo in June 2009 where he adopted the evenhanded approach favored by dovish Democrats. On the one hand, Obama asserted that denial of the Holocaust and other anti-Semitic slurs prevalent in the region were unacceptable. He also reaffirmed that America's bond with Israel was "unbreakable" and stated that America's historical support for "the aspiration for a Jewish homeland [was] rooted in a tragic history that cannot be denied."[196] On the other hand, this was balanced by a reference to Palestinian suffering.[197] In addition, Obama failed to mention the Jewish people's deep historical ties to the land of Israel, which lies at the heart of Zionism. The speech did not stand alone. The administration's initial strategy was to create distance between the U.S. and Israel. Consequently, Obama pointedly did not visit Israel, and when the head of a major pro-Israel organization told the president that he should not allow there to be any daylight between Israeli and U.S. positions on the peace process, Obama disagreed, arguing that under Bush there had been "no daylight, and no progress."[198]

Again, in line with the dovish approach Obama put the onus for peacemaking on Israel. One of his first acts after taking office was to appoint the former senator George Mitchell as special envoy for the peace process.[199] This demonstrated that the administration intended to make the peace process a priority. Mitchell was also known to support an evenhanded approach.[200] To begin with, the administration demanded that the new Likud-led government endorse the establishment of a Palestinian state and freeze settlements. Subsequently, Netanyahu publicly endorsed the establishment of a Palestinian state, while also implementing a ten-month settlement freeze and agreeing to immediate unconditional negotiations.

Within the administration this approach was promoted by four key staffers: Dan Shapiro, director of Middle East and North Africa at the National Security Council; Mara Rudman, Mitchell's chief of staff; Ben Rhodes, the chief foreign policy speech writer; and Denis McDonough, the chief of staff at the National Security Council. All four had previously worked for the former Democratic senator Lee Hamilton. Hamilton advocated opening a U.S. dialogue with

Hamas, and he cochaired the Iraq Study Group, whose report urged an aggressive U.S. push for Arab-Israeli peace. He also claimed that Israel's war against Hezbollah in 2006 increased hostility to U.S. troops in Iraq.[201]

However, the administration's approach began to change as it began to realize that the Israeli government was not the sole significant block to peace, and that a peace agreement was much harder to obtain that it initially thought.[202] Abbas refused to enter into negotiations with Netanyahu until the last month of the settlement freeze and then demanded an extension, including in Jerusalem, before he would continue to negotiate; Syria did not break with Iran, as Obama had hoped, nor did it stop assisting Hamas and Hezbollah. In addition, Saudi Arabia refused to enact the confidence-building measures that Obama had requested, such as providing overflight rights for Israeli airlines.

Against this background, the approach of robust liberal internationalists began to gain traction. The first sign of this came when the administration switched its approach toward Israel from sticks to carrots, as Dennis Ross began to play a larger role in policy making.[203] The administration offered Israel a large military aid package if it would agree to extend the freeze by a further three months; the Israeli government did not formally respond, and eventually the administration removed the offer from the table. When indirect talks resumed, the U.S. made a gesture to Israel by granting it an additional $205 million in military aid to help it expand its antimissile defense system.[204]

The second sign of the switch came when the president decided that he would not present an American peace plan, as per the dovish approach. While Obama restated his commitment to engaging with the peace process, he declared, "No matter how much pressure the United States brings to bear … the United States can't impose solutions unless the participants in these conflicts are willing to break out of old patterns of antagonism … We can't want it more than they do."[205] The third sign came when the administration moved toward David Makovsky's plan for dealing with the conflict by dealing with borders and security issues first, while leaving the more difficult issues of Jerusalem and refugees to later. Subsequently, Obama endorsed a permanent status peace agreement based on the 1967 borders, which annoyed the Israeli government, while also stating that "a lasting peace will involve two states for two peoples: and the state of Palestine as the homeland for the Palestinian people, each state enjoying self-determination, mutual recognition, and peace" – which annoyed the Palestinians, who oppose recognizing Israel as a Jewish state.[206] Obama also came out against involving Hamas in the peace process until they recognized Israel's right to exist, while firmly opposing the Palestinian attempt to get UN recognition of a Palestinian state on the 1967 border outside of the negotiating framework.[207] These positions were closer to the approach of robust liberal internationalism, than that of the dovish Democrats.

Congress

Congressional Democrats have traditionally been very pro-Israel. From the 1970s until the end of the century, Democrats and liberals in Congress were marginally more supportive of Israel than Republicans and conservatives. However, by the 107th Congress (2001–2003), conservative and Republican support for Israel in the House outweighed that of liberals and Democrats.[208] This reflected trends in public opinion and elite discourse among Democrats and liberals, as presented above.

During the Obama administration, Democrats in Congress were willing to back the administration in its demand for a settlement freeze from the Likud-led Israeli government in 2009. Rep. Gary Ackerman (D-NY), the pro-Israel chairman of the House Foreign Affairs Committee panel on the Middle East, equated "terrorism and the march of settlements" as part of a pattern of "shallow calculation and venal self-interest" through which "the two-state solution to the Israeli-Palestinian conflict is finally rendered impossible." Another strong advocate of Israel, Rep. Robert Wexler (D-FL), declared: "The notion that Israel can continue to expand settlements, whether it be through natural growth or otherwise, without diminishing the capacity of a two-state solution is both unrealistic, and, I would respectfully suggest, hypocritical."[209]

In addition, the small minority of congressmen who were not supportive of Israel came mainly from Democratic Party ranks. Thus, during Operation Cast Lead, the House of Representatives passed a Resolution siding with Israel against Hamas. The resolution received 390 yea votes, 5 nay votes, and 37 abstentions. Democrats cast 4 of the nay votes and 29 of the abstentions. In November 2009, Congress passed House Resolution 867 condemning the Goldstone Report; 344 congressmen voted for the resolution, 36 voted against it, and 52 abstained. Among those voting against, 33 were Democrats; 44 Democrats abstained.[210]

Nonetheless, after the Israeli government accepted the establishment of a Palestinian state and agreed to a settlement freeze, and the Palestinians proved extremely reluctant to enter direct negotiations with Israel, while the Arabs states refused to offer any confidence-building measures, Democrats in Congress began to take Israel's side. Another factor here was concerns regarding the impending midterm elections. In this vein, the majority of Democrats, led by US House majority leader Steny Hoyer, put the onus on the Palestinians and the Arab side to make concessions, and they put the blame for the failure of the peace talks squarely on the Arab side rather than Israel.[211] When differences arose between Israel and the administration over settlements in Jerusalem, leading Democrats backed Israel.[212] Subsequently, bipartisan letters from both houses of Congress urged the administration to only express their disagreements with Israel in private, because progress toward peace required that there be *no space* between the U.S. and Israeli positions.[213] Indeed, bipartisan support for Israel in Congress was so strong that dovish pro-Israel groups like J Street criticized such congressional declarations for being too one-sided.[214]

Congressional Democrats' support for Israel was more conditional on the policies pursued by the parties to the conflict than their Republican counterparts' approach. At the same time, congressional Democrats' support for Israel was stronger and less conditional than both public opinion and elite liberal approaches. Part of the reason might be that those Democrats with the lowest levels of support for Israel, the religiously unaffiliated, are not represented in Congress; in 2011 not a single member of Congress declared themselves to be religiously unaffiliated.[215] Another important reason for this gap is likely to be the influence of AIPAC. This is the reason why the dovish J Street lobby was established. Yet while J Street had some influence, it was dwarfed by that of AIPAC.

Nonetheless, there are signs that attitudes among liberals and Democrats may be shifting. One of these sign came during the 2012 election campaign, when the initial version of the Democratic Party platform did not refer to Jerusalem as Israel's capital or to Israel as "America's strongest ally in the region." The party convention eventually amended the platform, but the change was not popular with the floor of the convention, with some doubt as to whether it really received the required majority.[216]

DEMOCRATS, LIBERALS, AND ISRAEL: OPINION TRENDS AND THEIR IMPLICATIONS

Hispanic Catholics and the Religiously Unaffiliated

In 2003, Hispanics surpassed African-Americans as the largest minority group in the United States. In 2010 they comprised about 15 percent of the total US population and this figure is projected to double by 2050.[217] Hispanic Catholics, who make up more than two-thirds of all Hispanics in the US, were an especially strong source of support for the Democrats from 2000 to 2010.[218] The secular and the religiously unaffiliated also constitute a growing segment of the American population that heavily identifies with the Democrats.[219] Between 2000 and 2010 the percentage of Democrats who professed no religion rose from a quarter to more than a third, double the national average.[220] Among all the major ethnoreligious groups in the U.S., sympathy for Israel was lowest among Catholic Hispanics and the religiously unaffiliated (see Table 3.6). On the other hand, sympathy for the Palestinians was also lowest among Catholic Hispanics. Moreover, sympathy for Israel has actually increased among the religiously unaffiliated while at least holding steady for Hispanic Catholics.[221] Consequently, while the growth of the religiously unaffiliated and Hispanics might lower the level of pro-Israel support among Democrats, it is unlikely to reverse the pro-Israel orientation. A more significant challenge is posed by attitudes among young liberals.

TABLE 3.6. *Catholic Hispanics and the Religiously Unaffiliated Sympathy for Israel over the Palestinians, 2006 (%)*

	Israel	Palestinians	Pro-Israel Margin
All Americans	44	9	+36
Democrats	40	13	+27
Catholic Hispanics	24	4	+20
Religiously Unaffiliated	26	10	+16

Data from Pew Research Center[222]

The Generation Gap

Young Liberal Bloggers and Israel

In the first decade of the twenty-first century, young Americans were more likely than older people to identify with the Democrats and to have liberal attitudes.[223] This generational gap was also apparent over the Arab-Israeli conflict.[224] The gap was particularly pronounced on the question of whether helping to protect Israel should be a very important goal of American foreign policy. In 2001, about a third of Americans aged 18–50 agreed with this statement, compared to about 50 percent of those aged 50 and over.[225]

Among liberal commentators, a generational divide was also present. The leading robust liberal internationalists like Richard Cohen, Thomas Friedman, and Michael Walzer were born between 1935 and 1953; only Jeffrey Goldberg, born in 1965, was significantly younger. In contrast, leading liberal bloggers born between 1969 and 1984 – Josh Marshall, Peter Beinart,[226] Matthew Yglesias, Spencer Ackerman, and Ezra Klein – were closer to the evenhanded approach of dovish liberalism. Most of these bloggers identified personally with Israel and liberal Zionism.[227] But unlike robust liberal internationalists, their criticism of Israel lacked the counterbalancing effect of the former's extensive criticism of Arab, Muslim, and Palestinian extremism. In fact, they tend to downplay the seriousness of threats to Israel's physical security.[228] They remained convinced that the Arab side was willing and able to deliver peace.[229] Tellingly, for Marshall, the key negative turning point in the peace process was the assassination of Rabin in 1995 and his replacement by Netanyahu, and not Arafat's rejection of the Clinton Parameters and the second intifada.[230] In other words, for these bloggers the blame for the conflict and the onus in peacemaking lay on Israel's shoulders.[231] Spencer Ackerman went so far as to refer to the Gaza War as "disgusting,"[232] while Ezra Klien referred to Israel's actions as "disproportionate"[233] and "vengeance."[234] The bloggers also argued that America's association with Israel was damaging American interests during the Gaza War by fomenting an increasing hatred of America.[235] In addition, Yglesias argued that the U.S. should bring Hamas into the diplomatic process, without requiring the organization to first recognize Israel.[236] Klein argued that the U.S. should pressure Israel to freeze settlements by withdrawing aid.[237]

University Students

American university students are more likely to be liberal and Democrats than the statistical average among Americans.[238] Until the mid-1980s more educated Americans sympathized with Israel by more than average.[239] However, in the twenty-first century, college students are less likely to sympathize with Israel than the statistical average.[240] In a focus group study of top graduate schools for business, law, government and journalism conducted in 2005,[241] most of the students had started from a pro-Israel position that has eroded toward neutrality or hostility, with this tendency strongest among more liberal students. In addition, a 2011 survey by The Israel Project (TIP) revealed that a quarter of American students thought Israel an apartheid state; a further 50 percent were unsure.[242] But it is important to bear in mind that the 2005 focus group consisted of only 150 students, while wider surveys indicate that most students are *not* anti-Israel. Indeed, a plurality favors Israel over the Palestinians.[243] Moreover, that same 2011 TIP survey indicated that among the minority of student who took sides, Israel supporters outnumbered supporters of the Palestinians by extremely large margins. For example, while 32 percent thought that Israelis share American values, only 1 percent thought the Palestinian Authority did so; 17 percent thought the Israelis are "morally right" compared to 4 percent for the Palestinians.[244]

The Significance of Generational Differences: From Kibbutz to Kibush [occupation]

It could be suggested that the opinions of these students and young liberal bloggers will soften as they mature – the life-cycle effect. Many young people have more extreme liberal-Left opinions that change altogether as they get older. However, there was no shortage of student radicalism on American campuses in the late 1960s and early 1970s, yet then more educated Americans sympathized with Israel more than average, unlike today. Aside from the life-cycle effect, there is also a well-documented generational effect, whereby basic orientations formed in response to key events and generational experiences in earlier life continue to inform opinions thereafter.[245] Opinion polls seem to indicate that the generational effect has become more pronounced since 2001.

In this case, for the older generation of liberals supporting Israel was about supporting the weak against the strong and about righting an historical wrong. It was also about implementing a shared political vision, as Israel was run by secular, social democratic kibbutzniks. However, for younger generations growing up after 1967, it is the Palestinians who are cast as the underdog. Moreover, since the late 1970s, Israel has been run primarily by center-Right governments. Finally, the Holocaust has far less resonance; victims of genocide in Rwanda and Sudan demand attention. This is particularly important for liberal interventionists, traditionally the liberals most supportive of Israel. Indeed, the person most identified with liberal interventionism in the Obama administration, Samantha Power, while not hostile to Israel, has at times advocated positions closer to the dovish Democrat approach to the peace process.[246]

Moreover, especially for liberals who came of age in the shadow of 9/11, the 2003 Iraq War seems to be a constitutive event affecting their attitudes toward Israel and the Middle East. When liberals rejected U.S. foreign policy in Iraq, they also came to reject policies associated with that stance, notably robust U.S. support for Israel.[247] In the case of Yglesias, a look at 2002 entries in his blog demonstrates that he was far more supportive of Israel[248] than he was later on. By his own admission, his stance changed in the wake of the Iraq War and the Second Lebanon War, which appeared to him as a rerun of Iraq.[249] A senior congressional Democrat also noted how the Iraq War had a negative impact on Democratic opinion toward Israel in Congress, with many being influenced by the charge that Israel and its American supporters were responsible for the war.[250]

CONCLUSION

Democrat and liberal opinion as a whole sympathizes more with Israel than with the Palestinians, albeit by less than the national average. Although Democrats and liberals are significantly more divided over the peace process than Republicans, they share a consensus centered on three basic positions: they support the peace process and a two-state solution, they oppose settlements and are critical of the Israeli Right; and they think that the U.S. should be actively engaged in trying to resolve the conflict. The section below brings together the findings of this chapter and the previous one to directly compare liberal and Democratic attitudes toward the Arab-Israeli conflict with those of Republicans and conservatives.

Partisan and Ideological Differences

There are certain common themes shared by liberal and conservative approaches that are favorable to Israel. First, they tend to favor an internationalist approach to grand strategy, one which is relatively more willing to use military force. Second, they think that the Arab-Israeli conflict is *not* the central cause of anti-Americanism and instability in the Middle East. Third, they tend to believe that cultural and ideational factors are very significant in political life. In contrast, liberal and conservative approaches that are relatively unfavorable to Israel tend to favor a defensive grand strategy. They also tend to the view that U.S. policies, notably excessive support for Israel, play a critical role in empowering anti-Americanism and engendering instability in the Middle East. Finally, they tend to emphasize the role played by material power in political life.

The key point is that the first set of attitudes is much more common among Republicans than among Democrats, while the opposite is true of the second set of attitudes. Consequently, differences over the Arab-Israeli conflict increasingly run parallel to the growing partisan-ideological divide. This is symptomatic of the fact that Republicans and Democrats have also become increasingly divided over how to view the Middle East as a whole. For example, double the number of Republicans, as compared to Democrats, believed that "Islam encourages violence more than other religions." As is illustrated in Table 3.7, whereas in 2002, the partisan *gap* was 11 percentage points on this question by 2011, it had become a *divide* of 30 points. Furthermore, as of 2012, while Republicans were overwhelmingly concerned that the U.S. might take too long to act against the Iranian nuclear program, Democrats were divided over the issue, with 44 percent fearing the U.S. might act too quickly (see Table 3.8).

These divides have clear implications for attitudes toward Israel. Hence, while a majority of Republicans thought that the U.S. should support Israel if it attacked Iran to stop its nuclear program, a majority of Democrats thought the U.S. should remain neutral (see Table 3.9). More generally, for Republicans in 2010, the most positive thing about Israel was that it "stands by the United States as an ally and fights against Islamic extremists," whereas for Democrats, the most positive things about Israel was that it "supports a two-state solution where both Israelis and Palestinians can live in peace."[251]

Since the collapse of the Oslo process and 9/11, this difference explains why Republicans and conservatives sympathize with Israel by much larger margins than do Democrats and liberals (see Tables 3.10 and 3.11). Indeed, this **sympathy gap** has doubled since the 9/11 from around 20 percentage points to around 40 percentage points. Meanwhile, among young liberals the preference for Israel over the Palestinians is at its narrowest and support for U.S. pressure on Israel at its highest. This indicates that the partisan divide over the Arab-Israeli conflict could well widen in the future.

TABLE 3.7. *Agree That "Islam Encourages Violence More Than Other Religions"* (%)

	2002	2005	2008	2011
Republicans	33	57	61	59
Democrats	22	43	39	29

Data from Pew Research Center[252]

TABLE 3.8. *Main Concern Regarding U.S. Policy to Iran's Nuclear Program* (%)

2012	Act too quickly	Take too long to act
Republicans	17	75
Democrats	44	42

Data from Pew Research Center[253]

TABLE 3.9. *"If Israel Attacks Iran to Stop Its Nuclear Weapons Program, What Should the U.S. Do?" (%)*

2012	Support Israel	Stay neutral	Oppose Israel
Republicans	62	33	3
Democrats	34	57	7

Data from Pew Research Center[254]

TABLE 3.10. *Partisanship and Sympathy for Israel over the Palestinians: Pro-Israel Margin (%)*

	Republicans	Democrats	Partisan Gap
1993–8/2001	+43	+25	+18
2002–2006	+61	+27	+34
Gaza War 2009	+64	+24	+40
2011	+73	+33	+40

TABLE 3.11. *Ideology and Sympathy for Israel over the Palestinians: Pro-Israel Margin (%)*

	Conservatives	Liberals	Ideological Gap
1993–8/2001	+41	+20	+21
2002–2006	+56	+19	+39
Gaza War 2009	+52	+12	+40
2011	+65	+19	+46

Data for both tables from Gallup and Pew Research Center[255]

In addition, on the substance of the conflict, there is an **opinion divide**. A clear majority of Democrats and liberals favor the establishment of a Palestinian state and oppose settlements, while Republicans are equivocal on those issues (see Table 3.12). Similarly, among Republicans and conservatives, a majority support taking Israel's side in the conflict, while a large minority prefers neutrality; among liberals and Democrats these positions are reversed. Given these differences, it is hardly surprising that liberals and conservatives have different narratives concerning the peace process. In the 1990s the conservative discourse was divided over its merits, while the thrust of liberal discourse was very supportive. In the 2000s the conservative discourse overwhelmingly blamed the Palestinians and Arab side for the failure of the peace process and put the onus on them, while the liberal discourse was divided over whom to blame and where to put the onus.

TABLE 3.12. *Partisanship and Attitudes toward the Establishment of a Palestinian State (%)*

	Republicans			Democrats			Partisan Gap/Divide	
	Favor	Oppose		Favor	Oppose			
2002	42	38	(+4)	44	28	(+16)	12	Gap
2009	39	43	(−4)	59	22	(+37)	41	Divide

Data from Gallup[256]

   Thus, while sympathy for Israel remains bipartisan, there is a clear **partisan-ideological gap** regarding the magnitude and intensity of that sympathy. Even more significantly, attitudes toward the Arab-Israeli conflict have become increasingly **divided** along partisan and ideological lines, and there are clear political consequences that result from this. Thus, a Republican administration, especially a more conservative one, will have a predisposition to lean toward Israel's side in the conflict. In contrast, a Democratic administration, especially a more liberal one, will have a predisposition towards evenhandedness in the conflict, including a greater likelihood of pressure focused on Israel – that would make U.S. support for Israel, in effect, more conditional.

PART II

PROTESTANTS

4

Evangelicals and Christian Zionism: Standing with Israel

To stand against Israel is to stand against God.

—Rev. Jerry Falwell[1]

INTRODUCTION

One of the most talked-about elements of America's relationship with Israel is the rise of evangelical support for Israel. Critics view this group as a "bunch of crazy extremists" working to block peace and induce Armageddon.[2] Their defenders claim they are driven less by end-times theology and more by a sense of being commanded by the Bible to support the "Children of Israel," and that they express this through financial and political support for Israel in general, as opposed to the Israeli Far Right.[3] This chapter will address these issues by analyzing the nature and extent of evangelical support for Israel. The chapter begins by examining what evangelicals believe and the relationship between evangelicals and American politics in general. Following this, the historical development of Christian Zionism is outlined and the reasons for contemporary evangelical support for Israel are analyzed. Subsequently, the approaches of the evangelical public and elites towards the Arab-Israeli conflict are presented and their influence over U.S. policy assessed, along with their relationship to the wider pro-Israel lobby and the American Jewish community.

EVANGELICALS AND FUNDAMENTALISTS

Definitions

The term *evangelical* refers to a religious movement within Protestantism formed in the eighteenth century. The deliberate use of the term in twentieth-century

America dates from the formation of the National Association of Evangelicals in 1942, led by Billy Graham. Today, this movement has three irreducible characteristics: being "born again," which involves submitting to the authority of Jesus and accepting that one is saved solely by faith in him; belief in the authority of the Bible as the actual word of God; and sharing faith – either through missionary work or charitable activities known as "lifestyle evangelism." Evangelicals have been willing to engage with modern culture and society, far more than Fundamentalists.[4]

The term *fundamentalism* comes from a series of essays published in the 1910s called "The Fundamentals," which became the statement of a movement to return to the fundamentals of traditional doctrine regarding the inerrancy of the Bible, the creation of the world ex nihilo, the virgin birth, and the bodily resurrection. The movement developed in reaction to the great wave of theological modernism which overtook much of American Protestantism as it came to accept the findings of critical biblical scholarship. After the Scopes "Monkey Trial" in 1925, Fundamentalists split from mainline Protestant denominations that had fallen under control of the modernists, and they withdrew from politics until the 1970s. In contemporary terms, Fundamentalism can be understood as a movement within evangelicalism that maintains the same core beliefs but more militantly holds to a literal interpretation of scripture and separatism.[5] Belief in biblical prophecies concerning Armageddon and the Second Coming is especially pronounced among fundamentalists.[6] Fundamentalists are often referred to as conservative evangelicals or as the Christian Right.

Demography and Politics

From World War I until the 1990s mainline Protestants dominated the worldview of the U.S. political class and outnumbered evangelicals among the general population. Since the 1990s there has been a reversal of fortunes. Whereas in 1988, 59 percent of American Protestants were mainline and 41 percent evangelical, by 2008 these figures had reversed. In the first decade of the new millennium, a little more than a quarter of all Americans defined themselves as evangelical Christians.[7] In parallel, there has been a big increase in the percentage of self-identified evangelicals in Congress, from around 10 percent in 1970 to more than 25 percent in 2004.[8]

Evangelicals can be divided into three main groups. About half of all evangelicals are traditionalists in theological terms and conservative in ideological terms. They are characterized by a high level of church attendance, and support for the Republicans and the Christian Right. They tend to be hostile to the theory of evolution, and they believe the world will end with the battle of Armageddon and the coming of the Antichrist. Leading figures have included Jerry Falwell, Pat Robertson, and John Hagee. Second, there are centrist moderates who make up 30–40 percent of evangelicals. About half of this group identifies as Republicans, and slightly more than half are hostile to the theory of evolution and believe in Armageddon. Finally, theological modernists and ideological liberals compromise a little more than 10 percent of evangelicals. They identify more with the Democrats (44 percent) than the Republicans (33 percent), and only a minority believe in Armageddon.[9] Leading figures include Jim Wallis, Tony Campolo, and Jimmy Carter. Although the smallest group, they do have some political influence; for example, Campolo was close with former president Bill Clinton, while Barack Obama chose to give his first major speech on religion in the public sphere at Jim Wallis's Sojourners' Call to Renewal conference in 2006.[10]

The Rise of the New Christian Right

The social change of the 1960s, alongside of Supreme Court decisions on prayer in schools, abortion, and sex education, led conservative evangelicals to return to politics. Subsequently, there was a resurgence of evangelicalism that helped to make the new Christian Right a mass political movement. The key political organization of the Christian Right in the 1980s was the Moral Majority, headed by Jerry Falwell, which had a membership of more than six million at that time.[11] In the 1990s the Christian Coalition, headed by Pat Robertson, was the most important organization. In parallel, there has been a rise in evangelical identification with the Republicans. Up to the late 1960s a majority of evangelicals, especially in the South, identified with the Democratic Party. But as the Democrats moved leftward, so evangelicals began to move toward the Republican Party. By the late 1980s, evangelicals favored the Republicans over the Democrats by a narrow margin, and by the 2000s evangelicals had became the most important element of the Republican base, with more than two-thirds identifying as Republican or leaning Republican.[12]

THE DEVELOPMENT OF CHRISTIAN ZIONISM

For most pro-Israel evangelicals, religion is the cornerstone of their support for the Jewish state. Such people are known as Christian Zionists, namely a "Christian whose faith, often in concert with other convictions, emotions, and experiences, leads them to support the modern state of Israel as the Jewish homeland."[13]

Restorationism and Premillennial Dispensationalism

From the fifth century until the sixteenth century, St Augustine's replacement theology was dominant within Christianity. According to replacement theology, following the crucifixion, God's covenant with the Jews was broken and all future related promises in the Bible have been rendered void or applicable to the new "Israel" – the Church. At the same time, the main theological position concerning biblical prophecy was *a*millennial, expecting the return of Jesus in a remote future; biblical passages with messianic overtones tended to be interpreted allegorically. The Reformation changed this. Protestantism insisted that the Bible itself was a source of authority and that any believer could correctly interpret scripture when inspired by the Holy Spirit. This led some to adopt a literalist reading of the biblical prophecies of Isaiah, Daniel, and the book of Revelation in the New Testament, which seemed to anticipate an imminent Second Coming. In contrast to replacement theology, such "restorationists" saw the Jews as *continuers* of the biblical children of Israel, heirs to the covenant between God and Abraham, and the object of biblical prophecies about a restored Davidic kingdom in the land of Israel. In their messianic scenarios, the return of the Jews to Palestine was the first step in the advancement of the messianic timetable, which would end with the Second Coming of Jesus. Subsequently, the Jews would remain a distinct nation, but be converted to Christianity. This restorationism flourished especially among the Puritans because they put greater emphasis on the Hebrew Bible than other dissenters.[14]

One particular version of restorationism became popular in America in the second half of the nineteenth century – premillennial dispensationalism. It was developed by John Darby in Britain, who brought it to the United States after the civil war. According to Darby, rough times would befall humanity before the return of Jesus. Those who have accepted Jesus as their personal Savior will be spared this turmoil through the Rapture, whereby the true believers will be snatched from earth by Jesus. During the following seven years, there will be natural disasters and terrible wars in which two-thirds of humanity will perish. Meanwhile, the Jews will return to their ancient home-land without accepting Jesus. They will establish a state there ruled by the Antichrist posing as the Messiah. The Antichrist will inflict a reign of terror. The arrival of Jesus at the end of the Great Tribulation will end Antichrist's rule and establish the millennial kingdom. Those Jews who survive will accept Jesus. Jesus will then rule, with the Jews inhabiting David's ancient kingdom. The Temple will be rebuilt, and Jerusalem will serve as the capital of the entire world.[15]

Dispensationalism started as a minor part of the evangelical movement, but it gained support though populist preachers, like D. L. Moody, who were part of the revival movement. Dispensationalists were also prominent in the Bible Conference and Bible school movements, and they gained influence through the popular Scofield Bible, which has a dispensationalist commentary. Dispensationalists' emphasis on the Bible gave them a prominent role as part of the conservative coalition against modernist liberal forces within the Protestant church.[16]

In the late nineteenth century, many Dispensationalists were excited by the rise of the Zionist movement and later by the foundation of the State of Israel itself in 1948. From the 1890s onward, Christian Zionists, most notably William Blackstone, became involved in pro-Zionist lobbying. However, these efforts were quite limited. This was both because, in the wake of the Scopes

Monkey Trial, conservative evangelicals were politically quietist, and because the Zionist movement focused on winning the support of the liberal mainline, which it viewed as more influential.[17] Apart from supporting Zionism, the premillennialist evangelical movement also gave rise to a large wave of missionary activity targeting Jews. The aims were to teach the Jews about their special role in history and to save them from the Great Tribulation. Blackstone himself was involved in such missionary activity.[18]

In 1967, the Six Day War gave a huge boost to evangelical support for Israel. Not only had Israel achieved what appeared to be a miraculous victory, but it also gained control over a united Jerusalem, including the site of the ancient Jewish Temple that, according to prophecy, needs to be rebuilt before the Second Coming. As the then editor of *Christianity Today*, the main evangelical magazine, reflected:

That for the first time in more than 2,000 years Jerusalem is now completely in the hands of the Jews gives the student of the Bible a thrill and a renewed faith in the accuracy and validity of the Bible.[19]

Contemporary Christian Zionism: Organizations and Elites

The rise in pro-Israel sentiment generated by the Six Day War was translated into political support because it coincided with the rise of the Christian Right. The relationship took off when Menachem Begin became Israeli prime minister in 1977. The Begin government encouraged evangelical tourism to Israel, and by 1980 the Israeli government estimated that nearly half of all American visitors to Israel were Christian tourists.[20] Begin also forged links with Jerry Falwell. Support for Israel was one of the four elements that made up the founding manifesto of the Moral Majority. During the 1980s Falwell sponsored many Christian Zionist tours of Israel, in which pilgrims heard right-wing Israeli speakers. Falwell was awarded the Jabotinsky Medal by Begin in 1980.[21] In the 1990s, Pat Robertson formed the Christian Coalition, which claimed to have more than a million members. His Christian Broadcasting Network donated hundreds of thousands of dollars to support Jewish immigration to Israel.[22] According to Rabbi Yechiel Eckstein, the director of the *International Fellowship of Christians and Jews* (IFCJ), 'Evangelical support for Israel would not be so broad without Pat Robertson. He and Jerry Falwell were the first to really stand up ... Because of them Christian support for Israel went from a tendency to a movement.'[23]

The first specifically American Christian Zionist organization was Bridges for Peace, founded in 1976. It was active in assisting Soviet-Jewish immigration to Israel. It also carries out large-scale programs of assistance to the needy Israelis, with a special emphasis on the absorption of new immigrants. The organization founded the first and largest food bank in Israel. Most of its contacts in Israel are at the municipal level.[24] The second major Christian

Zionist organization was founded in 1980 was the International Christian Embassy in Jerusalem; though this is not a specifically American organization, it has eighty-two branches worldwide. It is most famous for its annual parade through the streets of Jerusalem on the Jewish festival of Succoth.

In 1983, Yechiel Eckstein, an Orthodox American Jewish Rabbi, founded the International Fellowship of Christians and Jews, which mobilizes evangelicals for more than 250 welfare projects in Israel.[25] During the Israel-Hezbollah war in 2006, the organization paid for the renovation of bomb shelters in the north of Israel and in the area near Gaza. In 2002 Eckstein founded Stand for Israel, which is focused on political campaigning for Israel. That year it organized a nationwide day of prayer for Israel in which 15 000 churches and 5 million parishioners took part.[26] Between 1993 and 2005 Eckstein is estimated to have raised between $100 million and 250 million from a base of more than 300,000 Christian donors, primarily by advertising on Christian TV channels in the U.S.[27] In 2007 Eckstein was given a seat on the Jewish Agency for Israel's highest governing committee, in return for pledging $45 million to the agency over three years.[28] In 2008 the IFCJ claimed contributions of $84 million, reaching approximately $100 million in 2009.[29] The IFCJ is ranked in the top 400 US charities, and the Israeli newspaper *Haaretz* listed it as Israel's second largest charitable foundation.[30]

In the first decade of the twenty-first century the leading Christian Zionist has been John Hagee, the pastor of an eighteen-thousand-member megachurch in Texas. He is also the president and CEO of Global Evangelism Television, which is said to reach nearly 100 million homes across the world. He has been a pro-Israel activist since 1981. Hagee has given millions of dollars to Jewish organizations to help fund Jewish immigration and absorption in Israel.[31] In 2006, Hagee re-formed the Christians United for Israel (CUFI) organization as a national grassroots movement focused on the support of Israel – a kind of Christian AIPAC. It has directors in every state, and city directors in more than ninety of America's leading cities, with a purported 1 million members in 2012, and an annual conference attended by five thousand people. In July 2006, at the time of their conference, CUFI arranged 280 meetings for their members with congressmen.[32] Hagee's importance was recognized by AIPAC when he addressed its annual policy conference in 2007.

At the national level, in the first decade of the twenty-first century, several leading congressman belonged to the Christian Right and were avid Christian Zionists, included Sen. Jesse Helms (1980–2002) who was chair of the Foreign Affairs Committee, the former House Republican majority whip: Tom DeLay, a former House Republican leader: Dick Armey and Sen. Sam Brownback, who chaired the Senate subcommittee on Near East and South Asian Affairs. Other leading politicians in this mold were Gary Bauer and Mike Huckabee. President George W. Bush was also sympathetic to Israel, in part for religious reasons, but his approach to Israel diverged significantly from that of the Christian Right, as will be discussed later on.

WHY DO AMERICAN EVANGELICALS SUPPORT ISRAEL?

Biblical Prophecy

According to Blackstone, America has a unique role to play in bringing about the final redemption by supporting Zionism. In this vein, Jerry Falwell declared, "God has raised up America for the cause of world evangelization and for the protection of his people, the Jews. I don't think America has any other right or reason for existence other than for those two purposes."[33] Falwell also called the existence of Israel, "the single greatest sign indicating the imminent return of Jesus Christ."[34] Other Christian Zionist leaders such as Hagee and Robertson often referred to the prophetic element in their support for Israel.[35] In his 1998 book *Final Dawn over Jerusalem*, Hagee wrote: "We are racing toward the end of time, and Israel lies in the eye of the storm."[36] Nearly two-thirds of evangelicals believe in biblical prophecy relating to Israel[37] and, according to a 2002 Tarrance survey, for about a third of evangelicals this is the number one reason they support Israel.[38] This explains the popular success of Hal Lindsey's book, *The Late Great Planet Earth*, which linked the birth of Israel and the Six Day War with the divine plan for the Second Coming. The book has sold more than 15 million copies and was the nonfiction bestseller of the 1970s. The *Left Behind* series of novels by Tim LaHaye, which provide fictional accounts of the Second Coming, sold more than 60 million copies from 1995 to 2004. Six titles in the series reached number one on the *New York Times* bestseller list in that period.[39]

The Biblical Promise to Bless Israel and the Jewish people

In Genesis 12:3 God told Abraham: "I will bless them that bless thee, and curse them that curse thee." This is the verse cited most by Christian Zionists to explain their support for Israel, including Pat Robertson, former Republican presidential candidate Gary Bauer, Pastor John Hagee, Ted Haggard, who was head of the National Association of Evangelicals, and Dr. Richard Land of the Southern Baptist Convention, the largest Protestant denomination in the U.S., who was highly influential on the Bush administration public policy. The verse also appears in the statement of faith of Hagee's seventeen-thousand-member megachurch.[40] As Falwell put it:

God has blessed America because America has blessed the Jew ... If this nation wants her fields to remain ripe with grain, her scientific achievements to remain notable, and her freedom to remain intact, America must continue to stand with Israel.[41]

I personally believe that God deals with all nations in relation to how these nations deal with Israel ... I premise that on what God said to Abraham: "I will bless them that bless thee, and curse them that curse thee." I therefore think America should without hesitation give financial and military support for the State of Israel. My political support for Israel in unconditional.[42]

About three-quarters of evangelicals believe in the biblical promise that God gave the land that is now Israel to the Jewish people. Twice as many evangelicals who held this belief expressed sympathy for Israel than those who did not.[43]

"Judeo-Christian Civilization" and "Islamic Fascism"
Another reason cited by evangelical leaders regarding their support for Israel is the sense of common religious-cultural foundations.[44] Related to this is a sense that Israel and America are part of a shared democratic, Judeo-Christian civilization. Indeed, according to a 2002 Tarrance survey, 24 percent of evangelicals said they supported Israel primarily because it is a democracy that values freedom.[45] This sense of commonality is reinforced by the fact that evangelicals have a strong tendency to view Islam as being involved in a clash of civilizations with the Judeo-Christian West, especially since 9/11. Evangelicals tend to view God and Allah as wholly distinct and the contemporary conflict with radical Islam as part of an ancient struggle, of which the Arab-Israeli conflict is apart. As one evangelical leader put it, "God's covenant is with Isaac, not Ishmael."[46] Falwell referred to Mohammed as a terrorist;, Robertson called him a robber and a brigand, arguing on one occasion that Islam at its core teaches violence. A 2002 poll indicated that more than three-quarters of evangelical leaders held a negative view of Islam, and they were far more disapproving than other religious groups; the same goes for the evangelical public vis-à-vis the general public.[47] Thus, during the 2000s a plurality of Americans had a favorable view of Islam. In contrast, most white evangelicals had an unfavorable view of Islam. In parallel, white evangelicals were far more likely to believe that Islam is more likely to encourage violence than other religions. This gap widened in the decade after 9/11 so that by 2011, while the general public was divided over the question 42–40, evangelicals' negativity was reflected in their numbers: 60–24.[48] In this confrontation with Islam, many evangelicals see Israel as a strong country on America's side. Thus, in 2002, 19 percent of evangelicals said their main reason for supporting Israel was that it is a longtime ally that works with the U.S. in the war on terror.[49]

Remorse for Anti-Semitism
The final reason cited by evangelicals regarding their support for Israel is remorse for Christian anti-Semitism. In this vein, the Christian Zionist organization *Eagles Wing* created a "Watchmen on the Wall" program that denounces anti-Semitism.[50]

How Important are the Various Reasons for Supporting Israel?

The question of what is the primary motive for evangelical support for Israel is one with important political consequences. Critics of Christian Zionism emphasize prophecy. This could mean that Christian Zionists are supporting Israel only as a means to bring Armageddon, which would involve the deaths of millions of Jews and the conversion of those who remain. It also implies that Christian Zionism may actually threaten the State of Israel, since it might support moves that would bring Armageddon closer. This is a charge that Christian Zionists and their Jewish supporters deny. They accept that the prophetic element is the wellspring of Christian Zionism without which the movement would not exist, but they deny that this is dangerous. Instead, they emphasize Genesis 12:3 as the key reason.[51]

A 2003 Pew survey found that nearly two-thirds of white evangelical Protestants who believe that Israel fulfills biblical prophecy say they sympathize with Israel compared with just under half of white evangelicals who do not hold this belief.[52] Evangelical pro-Israel activists are particularly inspired by prophetic Zionism;[53] and pastors who speak most frequently in church about Israel come from denominations where belief in biblical prophecy is especially strong. Support for Israel among congregants rises significantly after they have spoken.[54] Moreover, evangelical philanthropic donations to Israel are focused on immigration and absorption, issues that relate directly to Biblical prophecy. For example, *Bridges for Peace's* promotional piece is: "Don't just read about prophecy, when you can be a part of it."[55]

As for the issue of "hastening the end times," there are many Christian Zionists who look forward to the rebuilding of the Temple. The Temple Institute, a museum in Jerusalem that reconstructs Temple utensils, has become a pilgrimage site for many Christians who believe in biblical prophecy. During the 1980s a Christian Zionist organization called the Jerusalem Temple Foundation was active. Its goal was the rebuilding of the Temple on the Temple Mount in Jerusalem. They received backing from Christian Zionists in America. Gershon Salomon, the leader of the Temple Mount Faithful – a very small group of Israeli Jews who want to rebuild the Temple – is very popular with evangelical tour groups. The Temple Mount Faithful and the Jerusalem Temple Foundation reportedly receive significant funds from evangelicals. A few evangelicals are also involved in efforts to breed a red heifer, a religious prerequisite for the conducting sacrifices in the Temple.[56]

The construction of a Third Temple would presumably involve the destruction of the mosques on the mount. This could lead to a massive war between Israel and Muslim Arab states. Hence, the Israeli security services are concerned about such activity. This concern reached its height toward the end of 1999, as the new millennium was identified by some believers as a possible date for the Second Coming. At that time, Israel's security services rounded up members of a messianic group called "Concerned Christians" who planned to commit mass suicide or perhaps damage the mosques on the Temple Mount. Israel also arrested, deported or refused to entry to dozens of Christians who came to Jerusalem to witness the Second Coming of Jesus.[57]

Another concern is that Christian Zionists are trying to hasten end times by encouraging a confrontation between Israel and Iran. In his 2006 book *Jerusalem Countdown*, Hagee charts the way in which a future confrontation with

Iran will lead to Armageddon. At the same time, Hagee has supported a preemptive Israeli strike on Iran's nuclear facilities. This has led to speculation that Hagee and his followers support for Israel represents a cynical and highly dangerous attempt to trigger the end times. Hagee has strongly denied this. He claims that his support for an Israeli strike is motivated by his concern for Israeli and U.S. security. In any case, he explained, "we don't believe that we can speed up the end of days one second. Why? Because we believe that God is sovereign. That He has set the time. We are powerless to change God's time-table. That's what makes Him God."[58]

Indeed, despite the fact that biblical prophecy drives some evangelical extremists to undertake dangerous activities, for the overwhelming majority of Christian Zionists this is not the case. Christian Zionists are not, generally speaking, driven by a desire to hasten the end times, nor is biblical prophecy the most important reason for their support of Israel. Thus, of the hundreds of evangelicals interviewed by Prof. Chris Smith, not one stated that they were trying to hasten end times.[59] Moreover, according to the 2002 Tarrance poll, when evangelicals were asked to cite their *main* theological reason for support-ing Israel, 59 percent said it was the Hebrew Bible's promise to bless Israel and the Jewish people, while only 28 percent cited Biblical prophecies.[60] The 2008 National Survey of Religion and Politics confirmed this order of priorities.[61]

EVANGELICALS, CHRISTIAN ZIONISTS AND APPROACHES TO THE ARAB-ISRAELI CONFLICT

Public Opinion among Evangelicals

About 20 percent of all Americans cite religious beliefs as the *primary* reason for their position on the Arab-Israeli conflict, and most of those are evangelic-als.[62] White evangelicals are significantly more sympathetic to Israel than the national average, as well as far more sympathetic than any other Christian group in America. In parallel, the percentage of those who sympathized more with the Palestinians among evangelicals is about half the national average.[63] (See Tables 4.1 and 4.2.)

When it comes to U.S. policy, the difference between the general public and evangelicals grew more significant over the course of the 2000s, from an opinion gap to an opinion divide. By the end of the decade a majority of

TABLE 4.1. *Percentage Sympathizing with Israel over the Palestinians, 2001–2009*

	Pre-9/11 (9/2001)	8/2006	1/2009
General public	40	52	49
White evangelicals	54	64	70

Data from Pew Research Center[64]

evangelicals thought that the U.S. should take Israel's side, while a majority of the general public thought the U.S. should remain neutral (see Tables 4.3–4.5). Evangelicals were also more likely than any other group (apart from American Jews) to oppose U.S. pressure on Israel.[65]

On the question of whether Israel should build settlements in the West Bank, 67 percent of fundamentalists endorsed settlements, compared to about a third of other religious groups in America.[66] Yet according to a poll conducted in 2003 by *Christianity Today*, a plurality of 49 percent of evangelicals would support a Palestinian state that recognized Israel and did not threaten its security, compared to 39 percent who rejected the idea. Similarly, 52 percent of evangelical leaders were in favor of the creation of a Palestinian state so long as it did not threaten Israel.[67] Even Pat Robertson reckoned that President Bush

TABLE 4.2. *Percentage Sympathizing More with the Palestinians, 2001–2009*

General public	12
White evangelicals	6

Data from Pew Research Center[68]

TABLE 4.3. *Percentage Agreeing that "the U.S. Should Support Israel over the Palestinians"*

	1992	2008
General public	28	40
Evangelicals	40	55

Data from National Survey of Religion and Politics[69]

TABLE 4.4. *"What the U.S. Should Do If Israel Attacks Iran's Nuclear Program,"* 2012 (%)

	Support Israel	Neutral	Oppose Israel
General public	39	51	5
White evangelicals	64	32	1

Data from Pew Research Center[70]

TABLE 4.5. *Percentage Agreeing That "Protecting Israel Should Be a Very Important Goal of U.S. Foreign Policy,"* 2011

General public	39
White evangelicals	64

Data from Pew Research Center[71]

TABLE 4.6. *Evangelical by Theology and Political Ideology: Percentage Agreeing "The U.S. Should Support Israel over the Palestinians"*

	1996	2008
Evangelical traditionalists	50	73
Evangelical centrists	32	46
Evangelical modernists	24	36

Data from National Survey of Religion and Politics[72]

would not have lost many evangelical votes by encouraging Israel to give up parts of the West Bank.[73]

This difference between fundamentalist attitudes towards settlements and evangelical attitudes to Palestinian statehood is part of a wider divide among evangelicals regarding the Arab-Israeli conflict that mirrors the broader theological and ideological divisions between traditionalist-conservatives, centrist-moderates, and modernist-liberals referred to earlier. Polling indicates that traditionalist-conservative evangelicals have been the most supportive of Israel (see Table 4.6). The different approach among evangelical elites is outlined in greater detail below.

Evangelical Elites and Christian Zionist Organizations

Traditional-Conservative Evangelicals and Christian Zionist Organizations

Christian Zionist organizations draw their support overwhelmingly from those evangelicals who believe that the U.S. should support Israel over the Palestinians; and the overwhelming majority of these evangelicals are traditionalist-conservatives. The basic position of Christian Zionist organizations toward the Arab-Israeli conflict is close to that of the religious right in Israel and was summed up in the proclamation of the Third International Christian Zionist Congress held in 1996. It stated that:

the Land of Israel has been given to the Jewish People by God as an everlasting possession by an eternal covenant. The Jewish People have the absolute right to possess and dwell in the Land, including Judea, Samaria [the West Bank], Gaza and the Golan.[74]

At the same time, most Christian Zionists believe that the Arabs and Muslims are determined to sabotage this "eternal covenant."[75] Consequently, at the Christian Coalition's 2002 rally, speakers exhorted Israel's leadership to never give up any territory to the Palestinians,[76] while Hal Lindsey compared the 2007 Annapolis peace conference to the 1938 Munich conference.[77] These positions seemed to have a wide resonance among traditionalist evangelicals if the sales of Mike Evans's book *Beyond Iraq: The Next Move* are anything to go by. The book which adopts the Far Right perspective outlined above, reached the *New York Times* best-seller list and briefly ranked at number 2 on Amazon.com.[78]

Christian Zionists are particularly strongly opposed to the division of Jerusalem. Thus, while Hagee was willing to concede that Israel may give up land if all the Arab terrorist groups lay down their weapons, he insisted that Jerusalem never be divided "for any reason with anyone."[79] Meanwhile Robertson referred to the idea of giving the Palestinians East Jerusalem as "Satan's plan." Robertson remained supportive of George W. Bush even after the latter promoted Palestinian statehood. However, he declared that if Bush pressured Israel to divide Jerusalem, he would leave the Republicans and form an alternative party.[80] Christian Zionist leaders also view God as punishing those who give away territory in the Holy Land. Thus, Robertson declared that Rabin's assassination was a punishment from God for withdrawing from territory as part of the Oslo process.[81] Later on, he declared that Ariel Sharon's stroke was a punishment from God for Israel's disengagement from Gaza in 2005. Robertson later apologized for these remarks. Similarly, following the disengagement, Hagee wrote, "I do not consider it an accident that the very same week Jews were driven out of Gaza and placed in tent cities in Israel, the hand of God, through Hurricane Katrina, drove Americans out of their homes to live in tent cities in America."[82]

Christian Zionists have forged links with the Israeli Far Right, especially the former Member of Knesset Benny Elon, who often travels to the U.S. to raise funds and cultivate support from Christian Zionists. Elon even wrote a book specially designed for the Christian market entitled *God's Covenant with Israel: Establishing Biblical Boundaries in Today's World*.[83] There are also links with the *Zionist Organization of America* (ZOA), a right-wing American Jewish organization. Some of the money raised by evangelicals has gone to settlements.[84] In 1995, the *Christian Friends of Israeli Communities* was founded to aid Israeli settlements in the West Bank. It has gotten about fifty churches to "adopt a settlement." It claims to have raised a few million dollars.[85] Its leader estimates that more than half of the settlements in the West Bank receive direct or indirect funding from Christian communities.[86] It is estimated that the settlements received more than $200 million in tax-deductable gifts from Christian Zionist organizations from 2000 to 2010.[87]

Against such claims, Hagee has stated that the vast majority of his donations are made within the 1967 boundaries. Indeed, while Christian Zionism is ideologically close to the Far Right in Israel, its support for Israel is not narrowly defined by a right-wing political agenda. Thus, the overwhelming bulk of the money raised by Christian Zionists does not go to settlements, nor does it go toward causes that are directly related to the Arab-Israeli conflict or Israeli politics. Rather, the focus has been on social welfare, especially immigration and absorption.[88]

Pro-Israel Moderate Evangelicals

Like traditionalist-conservatives, moderate evangelicals also tend to be Christian Zionists. As such, they generally affirm that Israel plays a special role in the Second Coming and feel a biblical duty to support the State of Israel, but not in an unconditional or uncritical way. In the 1990s they thought that biblical promises gave Israel a right to *at least* its pre-1967 borders and guaranteed security. At the same time they were willing to support the peace process and a two-state solution on condition that they perceived there to be a genuine partner willing to recognize Israel and committed to peaceful coexistence.[89] In this vein, Richard Land, president of the Southern Baptist Ethics and Religious Liberty Commission, stated, "I would argue that nothing could be more secure for Israel than creating a viable, self-sustaining Palestinian state that agrees to live in peace and agrees to suppress terrorism."[90] While for Richard Mouw, president of Fuller Theological Seminary, there was no theological reason to either require or forbid the creation of a Palestinian state: "The question for me is one of prudence, and not of theological principle."[91]

In the wake of the collapse of the Oslo process and 9/11, centrists primarily blamed Arafat and the Palestinians for the failure to achieve peace.[92] Yet like Richard Land, they tended to support the 2005 Disengagement from Gaza. The fact that the Disengagement was an Israeli initiative was an important factor in this. As Land explained, "If our American government were perceived as putting pressure on the Israeli government to make decisions that it was felt by the Israeli people ... to endanger their security, it would cause a serious and cataclysmic failure in the level of support for George W. Bush or any American [president]."[93] Another leading prominent evangelical supporter of Israel, Jack Hayford, described the Disengagement as 'Christ-like' because its purpose was to try to make peace. Going one stage further, Ted Haggard, leader of the National Association of Evangelicals from 2003 to 2006, told Israeli prime minister Ariel Sharon in 2004 that Israel's security barrier should not cut into Palestinian land.[94]

Still, even moderate evangelicals, who are not deeply committed to eschatological theology, appear to put Jerusalem in a different category from the rest of the West Bank.[95] Thus, in the estimation of Richard Land, if Israel were to give the Palestinians the Temple Mount and part of the Old City of Jerusalem, evangelicals would rise up and protest – though even here Land estimated that they would ultimately acquiesce so long as it was a decision freely taken by Israel.[96]

Evenhanded and Pro-Palestinian Evangelicals

As explained above, modernist-liberal evangelicals are the smallest ideo-theological evangelicals group. They tend to advocate an evenhanded approach or a clearly pro-Palestinian approach to the peace process. The leading theologist promoting this approach is Rev. Dr. Gary Burge. In his book, *Whose Land? Whose Promise?* Burge affirms Israel's right to exist while also invoking passages in the New Testament to portray Israel's existence as a violation of Christian theology. Additionally, he makes Jewish sovereignty in modern Israel contingent on faithful adherence to Judaism. In taking this position, Burge singles out Israel. No other people in the world have their right to statehood made contingent on such a requirement. Like Jimmy Carter, Burge also equates Israel with apartheid South Africa.[97] David Neff, the editor of *Christianity Today*, effusively praised the volume and the magazine gave it an "award of merit." Indeed, since the early 1990s most articles about the conflict in *Christianity Today* adopted either a balanced or a pro-Palestinian approach to the conflict, which has involved significant criticism of Israeli policies.[98] Almost no articles adopted the position of the conservative Christian Zionists, though several articles adopted a moderately pro-Israel position.[99] Meanwhile, in the political arena, pro-Palestinian evangelicals have adopted a moderate tone. For example, two letters sent to President George W. Bush by more than thirty evangelical leaders in 2002 and 2007 supported a negotiated two-state solution and condemned Palestinian terrorism and Israeli settlements, while calling for the U.S. to adopt an evenhanded approach to the conflict.[100] In any case, such lobbying has been massively overshadowed by the efforts of conservative Christian Zionists. It is to this that we now turn.

CHRISTIAN LOBBYING FOR ISRAEL: "*RIGHT* OR WRONG?"

There are two key questions concerning Christian Zionist lobbying for Israel. First, do Christian Zionists lobby for the elected government of Israel even if it clashes with their own policy preferences? Second, how much influence has Christian Zionism had over U.S. policy toward the Arab-Israeli conflict, especially during the administration of George W. Bush, who is himself an evangelical Christian? These issues are addressed below.

The Likud Party came to power in 1977. It recognized that Christian Zionists shared its positions, and so it encouraged them to lobby, though Christian Zionists were only a very minor player in the 1980s.[101] In 1989, Dispensationalists founded the Christian Israel Public Action Campaign (CIPAC), which was the first registered Christian pro-Israel lobby. It fostered ties with AIPAC and other pro-Israel organizations. In the 1990s CIPAC lobbied on a variety of issues; some of these were directed *against* the policy of the Israeli government.[102] For example, when Labor was in power (1992–1996), CIPAC sought to prevent the stationing of U.S. peacekeepers on the Golan Heights in the event of an Israeli withdrawal and fought against giving U.S. aid to the Palestinian Authority; both policies were supported by the Rabin government.

The issue of Jerusalem was the focus of Christian Zionists' limited lobbying efforts in the 1980s and 1990s. In 1995 they worked with other pro-Israel organizations like AIPAC, and their efforts led Congress to pass the Jerusalem Embassy Act in 1995, which called for the embassy to be moved to Jerusalem by 1999. (However, the bill contained a waiver that allowed the president to suspend implementation at six-month intervals, which is what every president has done since then.) The Israeli government did not want to proceed with the campaign, fearing that raising the issue at this stage would cause serious damage to the peace process.[103] A year later, when Netanyahu came to power, he worked closely with the Republican-led Congress and Christian Zionists to ease pressure from the Clinton administration on Israel regarding the peace process. Thus, in early 1998 Netanyahu met with Falwell and also spoke at a large public meeting attended by evangelicals who, following his speech, chanted, "Not one inch." This occurred just prior to Netanyahu's planned meeting with President Clinton, to maximize the political effect.[104]

Nonetheless, in the 1980s and 1990s, Israel remained a secondary issue for most evangelicals, even for the Christian Right. In 1981, although the Moral Majority strongly opposed the sale of AWACS to Saudi Arabia, no senators with ties to it voted against the sale.[105] In 1992, Falwell endorsed George H. W. Bush for president despite Bush's major clash with Israel over settlements. In 1996 Falwell endorsed Pat Buchanan despite Buchanan's anti-Israel positions. Moreover, studies from the mid-1990s demonstrate that there was no positive correlation between the pro-Israel activities of congressmen and the number of evangelicals in a congressmen's constituency, which reinforces the impression that Israel was not a major political concern at that time for most evangelicals.[106]

However, after 9/11 and the collapse of the Middle East peace process, Israel did take on a more central role. Thus, at the 2002 Christian Coalition conference, foreign policy, including support for in Israel, was the main topic for the first time; there was even a "Solidarity with Israel" rally at the conference.[107] This shift was also evident in Congress. In the latter half of the 1990s, evangelical members of the House of Representatives were not especially supportive of Israel; however, from January 2001 to December 2003, evangelical conservatives in the House became strong supporters of Israel, promoting resolutions that clearly took Israel's side against the Palestinians.[108]

George W. Bush, Christian Zionism, and the Second Intifada

It has been argued that George W. Bush is a Dispensationalist and that this heavily influenced his policy toward the Middle East.[109] On the one hand, the president's underlying attitude toward Israel was at least partly influenced by his faith. Bush described a visit to Israel before becoming president as one of the most moving experiences of his life. In a speech to the Knesset in May 2008, Bush stated that the modern State of Israel represents "the redemption of an ancient promise given to Abraham, Moses and David – a homeland for the chosen people."[110] However, there is a big difference between an underlying sympathy for the State of Israel based on the Bible and adopting a foreign policy based on end-times theology. Indeed, according to numerous people who worked in the Bush White House as well as personal friends of the president, end-times theology was alien to Bush and his administration's approach to the Middle East.[111]

Most significant, Bush adopted policies diametrically opposed to the position of the Christian Right and Dispensationalists. For example, after 9/11 he became the first American president to officially endorse the creation of a Palestinian state – in the face of opposition from the Christian Coalition.[112] He also supported Israel's disengagement from Gaza and sponsored the Annapolis process. Finally, in September 2008, Bush himself tried to convince the Palestinian president Mahmoud Abbas to accept the Israeli prime minister Ehud Olmert's peace plan. The plan involved Palestinian statehood, a shared Jerusalem, and an Israeli withdrawal from about 94 percent of the West Bank, including a territorial swap of about 6 percent to make up the difference.[113] Abbas rejected the offer, but the fact that Bush favored the plan in the face of a lot of opposition from the Christian Right makes the point.[114]

Furthermore, whereas the Christian Right believes that America should always support Israel, Bush's practical support for Israeli policy ebbed and flowed, influenced by a variety of political and strategic factors. In this context it is worth recalling that following his endorsement of a Palestinian state, Bush applied pressure on Prime Minister Sharon, forcing him into a cease-fire and into allowing Arafat to meet Foreign Minister Peres, while refusing to put Hamas and Islamic Jihad on the official U.S. list of terrorist organizations. Against this background, Sharon compared Bush's policy toward Israel to Chamberlain's policy at Munich.[115]

Leaving Bush himself aside, there is still the question of the lobbying of the Christian Zionists during his presidency. This became particularly intense at the height of the second intifada. Gary Bauer and others have claimed that Christian Zionist pressure was responsible for the shift in American policy toward the conflict between late 2001 and the summer of 2002.[116] In October 2001, Bush became the first U.S. president to officially endorse a Palestinian state and the administration worked for a ceasefire with the ultimate goal of restarting peace negotiations. However, when Israel launched Operation Defensive Shield in the spring of 2002, the administration allowed Israel time to pursue, what was the largest military operation in the West Bank since 1967. Furthermore, in June 2002 Bush made a speech in which he conditioned restarting the peace process on transformation of the Palestinian leadership. Certainly, in the spring of 2002, there was plenty of Christian Zionist lobbying of the President in favor of giving Israel a free hand to strike a military blow against the terrorist campaign. They organized a demonstration in Washington DC with Jewish organizations attended by an estimated 100 000 people. They also organized a massive email and letter writing campaign. During April and May, the Middle East dominated the weekly telephone conference call between the White House and evangelicals leaders who were very concerned that the Administration not abandon Israel.[117] In May, after protracted negotiations with the administration, both Houses of Congress passed pro-Israel resolutions. The House resolution, sponsored by the conservative Christian Republican Tom DeLay, was especially critical of the Palestinians; it was passed by a massive majority.

All of this probably had some effect, but the fact of the matter was that the balance within the administration was strongly in favor of shifting policy in that direction, anyway. Bush, Rumsfeld, Cheney, and Wolfowitz were never really enamored with the peace process. When it became clear that Arafat had accepted arms from Iran and was directly involved in funding terrorist operations, this greatly strengthened the hand of the hawks against the relatively dovish Powell, and policy shifted accordingly.[118] Furthermore, even allowing for the fact that Christian Zionist activities may have helped to encourage that shift by touching the president's conscience, there is no way they can be said to have pressured the president. For as David Frum, a speechwriter for the Bush administration, has pointed out, Bush would have easily won a trial of strength with Bauer and Robertson over the Republican base.[119] Indeed, this is exactly what happened when Bush launched the Road Map in 2003, which was a staged plan designed to lead to the establishment of a Palestinian state. The Far Right Israeli politician Benny Elon used his contacts to mobilize Christian Zionists against the Road Map.[120] Despite receiving more than fifty thousand postcards from Christian conservatives in the fortnight following the announcement of the Road Map, the Bush administration still pressured the Israeli government to accept the Road Map – which it did, albeit with several reservations.[121] Actually, rather than Christian Zionists influencing Bush, Bush actually moderated the stance of Jerry Falwell, who reversed his opposition to the creation of a Palestinian state.[122]

Again in 2004 and 2005 the Israeli Far Right tried to mobilize Christian Zionists against the disengagement from Gaza that involved removing eight thousand settlers from their homes. Although most Christian Zionist activists opposed the move, they did not lobby against it.[123] The key factor, according to the then Israeli ambassador to Washington, Danny Ayalon, was that the initiative came from the Israeli government itself and was not the result of U.S. pressure.[124] As Falwell explained, "I personally have a problem with trading land for peace but that's not our business. If Sharon wanted to say no to a withdrawal, okay, we would have supported him. And if he [Sharon] said yes, well, that's okay with me, too."[125] Other Christian Zionist leaders such as Robertson, Inhofe, and Hagee also made the exactly the same point,[126] and this position has become central to the operational code of leading Christian Zionists in America.[127] As Hagee explained in relation to his own lobbying organization:

From our founding . . . we decided that CUFI would never presume to tell Jerusalem how to conduct its foreign or domestic affairs. We have never, and will never, oppose Israeli efforts to advance peace. Our involvement in the peace process will continue to be restricted to defending Israel's right to make decisions free of international interference or pressure – including U.S. pressure.[128]

Thus while various Christian Zionist organizations have favored the Israeli right, what stands out about their lobbying during the Bush era is that it was mainly reactive and defensive. It was less concerned with promoting settlements or preventing Israeli withdrawals, and more focused on blocking U.S. pressure on Israel, especially on allowing Israel to prosecute its war against terrorism as its saw fit. Evangelicals were more energized in April 2002 in support of Israel's counterterrorism operation than they were by the withdrawal from Gaza. In any case, neither end-times theology nor Christian Zionist lobbying were central factors in the Bush administration's policy. They had political influence, but it was not decisive.

A COMPLEX RELATIONSHIP WITH AMERICAN JEWRY

One factor that facilitated the growing activism of Christian Zionist lobbying was the shift in attitudes toward cooperation within the American Jewish community. Prior to 2000, Christian Zionists' relationship with most of the organized American Jewish community had been strained. On core domestic issues like church and state and abortion, the Christian Right and the majority of American Jews are on opposite sides. Against this background, in 1994, the Anti-Defamation League (ADL), a mainstream Jewish organization, produced a two-hundred-page report that warned that the religious Right was a source of intolerance. In addition, there is widespread Jewish opposition to missionary activity. In the early 1990s, *Voices United for Israel* was established to promote Jewish-Evangelical cooperation regarding support for Israel. At the outset, its executive committee included senior representatives of the Anti-Defamation League and Rabbi Eckstein's International Fellowship of Christians and Jews. Within a couple of years these organizations had pulled out, citing proselytization of Jews and overt support for the Republicans as major reasons. At the same time, the Jewish community's relations with evangelicals were further strained by the passing of a resolution to focus missionary activities on the Jews by the Southern Baptists.[129]

Despite the general antipathy toward the Christian Right, some American Jews have long advocated a political alliance in support of Israel, notably the neoconservatives. Indeed, neoconservatives and evangelicals worked together to form the *New American Century* foundation in 1997.[130] Jewish advocates of cooperation pointed to the fact that three-quarters of evangelicals have a positive view of Jews, and less than 10 percent have a negative view. In addition, about 90 percent of evangelicals believe that God hears prayers of all people, not only Christians, and that Jews are basically similar to other Americans. All these figures are almost identical to the national average. Even on the vexed question of whether Jews need to be converted, evangelicals were about evenly split.[131]

But it was only following the collapse of the peace process in 2000 and the subsequent onslaught on Israel's legitimacy at the UN sponsored anti-racism conference held at Durban in 2001 that mainstream Jewish organizations began to shift.[132] Symbolically, in 2002 the ADL's leader, Abe Foxman, endorsed working with Christian Zionists on Israel.[133] In 2003, Ralph Reed, former head of the Christian Coalition, was a keynote speaker at the ADL's National Leadership Conference in Washington. Also in 2003, former presidential candidate and evangelical leader Gary Bauer was the keynote speaker at the annual AIPAC conference. Meanwhile, at its annual plenum for 2003, the Jewish Council on Public Affairs (JCPA), the umbrella organization of Jewish community relations bodies across the country, adopted a resolution in favor of working with evangelicals on issues of common concern – namely Israel – that would have been unfathomable several years earlier.[134] Subsequently, in 2006 Hagee was the recipient of the Humanitarian of the Year Award by the mainstream Jewish organization, B'nai B'rith, and in 2007 he addressed the AIPAC annual conference. Yet evangelical-Jewish cooperation over Israel remains controversial. In 2008, Rabbi Eric Yoffie, then head of the Reform movement (the largest Jewish religious denomination in America) came out strongly against cooperation with the evangelicals.[135]

CONCLUSION

White evangelicals are more supportive of Israel than any other group in America, except for American Jews. A sense of being biblically commanded to support the Jewish people coupled with a sense that support for Israel is linked to biblical prophecies about the end times undergird that support, along with other more common and prosaic reasons, like a perception that Israel and the U.S. are on the same side in the war against terror. The wider one casts the net, the less knowledgeable evangelicals are about modern-day Israel and the hazier are the political implications of their general sympathy in terms of concrete political issues. In contrast, the most activist core of evangelical supporters, Christian Zionists, hail from the most conservative wing of the evangelical movement and they share a political orientation with, and have ties to, Israel's religious Right. Nonetheless, the bulk of their donations and lobbying are focused around what most Israelis and American Jews would consider consensual positions, namely giving money to underprivileged Israelis and lobbying against U.S. pressure on Israel.

On the one hand, this would seem to indicate that evangelical support for Israel, *in practice*, is guided more by the generic biblical command to support Israel than by a messianic ideology tied to territorial maximalism. On the other hand, much of the donations go to causes related to biblical prophecy: immigration and absorption. The key here is to recognize that while Israel's religious Right and Christian Zionists share a messianic orientation, its details differ, and not only in the obvious theological sense. For most of the Israeli religious Right, settlements and territorial maximalism are the touchstones of their mission; they tend to believe that their actions will eventually lead to the onset of the messianic age. In contrast, for most Christian Zionists, settlements and territorial maximalism are not as central to their worldview; only Jerusalem has such an elevated status. For most, "end times" is something preordained rather than a practical program; it is primarily about being on the right side when Armageddon strikes.

In terms of the political influence of Christian Zionism, there is no doubt that it has grown significantly and that they became an important part of the pro-Israel coalition in the first decade of the new millennium. They have demonstrated the ability to mobilize hundreds of thousands of people to donate money to Israel and tens of thousands of people to write e-mails and letters, and attend demonstrations for Israel. Meanwhile, at the pinnacle of the political pyramid, they had some influence over policy under the Bush Administration (2000–2008), but they did not determine any critical decision. As per the received wisdom on lobbying, their influence was greatest when they adopted positions that had a wide resonance in public opinion – such as taking Israel's side in the war against terror. Conversely, when they came out against an Israeli government and an American president pursuing the peace process, they became peripheral, allied with small right-wing American Jewish organizations but alienated from the Israeli and the American Jewish mainstream.

In terms of demography, the religious Right and the religious Left are approximately the same size in America.[136] However, on the Left, foreign policy toward Israel is not a major priority, and in any case opinion is divided. In contrast, the religious Right is solidly behind Israel and it is able to mobilize tens of thousands of people on the issue, people who tend to vote in disproportionately large numbers.

Still, Christian Zionist influence is limited to the Republican Party. If the Democrats are in power, they have little sway. Moreover, there is the possibility that Christian Zionists' loud support for Israel could erode bipartisan consensual support for Israel. It may cause liberals with little direct interest in the Middle East to instinctively take the other side, given that liberals are strongly opposed to traditionalist evangelical positions on many other key political issues. There are already some indications of this within the liberal discourse, which has been highly critical of evangelical support for Israel. This is likely to be particularly the case for liberal mainline Protestants, who to a certain degree can be said to define themselves in opposition to conservative evangelicals. It is to the mainline that we now turn.

5

The Mainline Protestant Church and Anti-Zionism: Divesting from Israel?

> The occupation is ... **the root of evil acts** committed against innocent people on both sides.
>
> —Presbyterian General Assembly Divestment resolution, 2004[1]

INTRODUCTION

In 2004, the General Assembly of the Presbyterian Church in America PC(USA) voted to initiate a process of "phased selective divestment" from companies operating in Israel. Israelis and American Jews were shocked. Most Israelis had no idea that significant organized hostility to Israel existed in America. American Jews were taken aback, as many were used to looking on the mainline Protestant churches (here on in – the mainline) as allies in the struggle for civil rights and the preservation of the separation of church and state. Yet the Presbyterian divestment resolution was not an aberration but part of a broader trend in mainline policy.

But what exactly is the nature and extent of mainline hostility to Israel? Does it reflect widespread feelings within the mainline, or is it driven by a small but politically active group of Far Left extremists? Is that hostility primarily a function of changes in the Middle East since 1967, especially changes in Israeli policy? Does it reflect, in fact, an evenhanded approach, in which the moral faults of the policies pursued by both sides in the conflict are criticized? Alternately, is this hostility of a more longstanding and fundamental nature? Does it, in fact, extend beyond criticism of specific Israeli policies into outright hostility to the Jewish state by singling out Israel among all the nations of the world for particular opprobrium?

The chapter begins by surveying the institutional, theological, and ideological makeup of the mainline in general terms. It then looks at the historical roots of approaches to Israel within the mainline. Following this, the discourse and political activity of the mainline regarding Israel and the conflict are outlined. Finally, the sources of the rise of contemporary hostility toward Israel are assessed.

THE MAINLINE

The dominant theology in the mainline has been liberal and modernist. The mainline generally accepts modern critical Bible scholarship, rejecting the literalist position on the Bible characteristic of evangelicals. They also tend to regard Jesus primarily as a moral teacher, whereas evangelicals tend to treat Jesus primarily as the source of personal salvation. In terms of social theology, the mainline emphasizes social justice, and it is active on issues such as economic, racial, and gender equality, in line with a liberal approach that seeks to establish the "kingdom of God" on earth. In contrast, evangelicals are generally associated with a conservative approach that emphasizes personal morality.[2]

Demography and Politics

From the 1920s until the 1990s mainline Protestants dominated the worldview of the U.S. political class, while also outnumbering evangelicals among the general population. However, since their peak in the mid-1960s, mainline denominations have lost up to a quarter of their membership, during a period in which the overall size of the American population has grown substantially.[3]

Despite their numerical decline, the mainline churches remain important politically. First, mainline Protestants still account for more than 40 million American adults and around a quarter of all voters. They constitute sizable portions of each party's vote and have become a potential swing constituency in many states.[4] Second, the mainline churches retain a significant amount of moral prestige, which grants them influence beyond their membership. This prestige derives from the mainline's historical legacy. Members of the mainline denominations played a major role in authoring the Declaration of Independence and the Constitution, as well as in successful reform and protest movements such as the abolition of slavery, women's suffrage, the civil rights movement. and the antiwar movement. Indeed, according to Lester Kurtz, "Mainline Protestantism provides an institutional infrastructure for dissent that has no rival on the contemporary American political scene."[5] Third, members of mainline churches are generally better educated and wealthier than both the general public and evangelicals.[6] Greater wealth and education correlate with greater political involvement and influence. For example, President Obama was a longtime member of the largest United Church of Christ (UCC) congregation.

The Rise of the "New Christian Left"

In the 1950s the mainline Church was generally viewed as part of the establishment and its members were generally associated with the Republican Party. However, from the 1960s onward there was a decline in mainline identification with the GOP.[7] More dramatically, in the 1960s mainline clergy and organizations began to play a major role in progressive causes including opposition to the Vietnam War, fair housing, and civil rights. These actions were rooted in the social gospel tradition, which had been very influential in the early part of the twentieth century.[8] They also reflected the growing influence of liberation theology.[9] Liberation theology began to develop among Catholic intellectuals in Latin America in the early 1970s. It demands that the church concentrate on liberating the people of the Third World from poverty and oppression. It contends that the Third World has been victimized by colonialism, imperialism, and multinational corporations, which have placed it in a situation of dependency to the U.S. and its First World allies. These ideas run parallel to those of the postcolonial ideology of the New Left, which emerged at about the same time. Indeed, liberation theology consciously drew on Marxism. A leading American exponent of liberation theology was Robert McAfee Brown who declared: "What my nation did in Vietnam was not an exception to US foreign policy, but an example of it."[10] Liberation theology also inspired mainline opposition to U.S. intervention in Nicaragua in the early 1980s. Left-liberalism remains dominant within the mainline clergy and among mainline political activists, but since the mid-1980s the mainline has devoted fewer resources to political action at the national level. Instead, mainline clergy have prioritized local social welfare projects, for example, running soup kitchens and clothing centers for the poor. Still, the mainline does not ignore political issues. The political issues most regularly addressed by the clergy were race and civil rights and the environment.[11]

The Ideological and Political Divide within the Mainline

While the clergy and national bureaucracies that lead political campaigns have shifted leftward since the 1960s, a majority of the mainline laity has remained moderate or conservative.[12] Between 1989 and 2008 around half of the clergy identified as Democrats and liberals, while around a third identified as Republicans and conservatives.[13] In contrast, between 1992 and 2011 about a third of the white mainline public identified as conservative, about a fifth as liberal, and the rest as moderates. In the same period about half of the mainline public identified with or leaned toward the Republicans, while the percentage identifying with or leaning toward the Democrats ranged from about a third to about 45 percent.[14] These divisions also found expression on some big foreign policy issues. Thus, while two-thirds of the mainline clergy opposed the 2003 Iraq War, a majority of the white mainline public was moderately supportive.[15] A similar divide within the mainline is apparent regarding the Arab-Israeli conflict.

THE MAINLINE PUBLIC AND THE ARAB-ISRAELI CONFLICT: PRO-ISRAEL

On the one hand, the mainline public is less pro-Israel than the evangelical public; on the other hand, they are more pro-Israel than mainline political activists. The mainline public has been broadly supportive of Israel, though at a slightly lower level than the average for the American public as a whole. Indeed, while both evangelicals and mainliners sympathize with Israel over the Palestinians; the pro-Israel margin has been about 20 percentage points higher for evangelicals. Regarding attitudes toward U.S. policy, there is a divide, with a majority of evangelicals preferring to side with Israel and viewing support for Israel as a very important foreign policy goal, while a majority of the mainline public prefer a neutral policy to the conflict; nor do they view support for Israel as a very important goal (see Tables 5.1–5.4).

Nonetheless, throughout the 2000s, whereas mainline institutions became increasingly hostile to Israel, the mainline public became increasingly pro-Israel, with the ratio by which they sympathized with Israel over the Palestinians rising from 2:1 to 4:1.[16] The level of mainline public support for America taking Israel's side in the conflict was highest among theological traditionalists, where it formed a majority, and lowest among modernists, a clear majority of

TABLE 5.1. *Sympathize with Israel over the Palestinians (%)*

	(Pre 9/11) 2001	2003	2006	2009	2012
General public	40	41	52	49	50
Mainline	35	34	44	48	47
Evangelicals	54	55	64	70	67

Data from Pew Research Center[17]

TABLE 5.2. *Percentage Agreeing "The U.S. Should Support Israel over the Palestinians"*

	1996	2000	2004	2008
General public	30	29	36	40
Mainline	28	28	33	40
Evangelicals	36	39	54	55

Data from National Survey of Religion and Politics[18]

TABLE 5.3. *Percentage Agreeing "Protecting Israel Should Be a Very Important Goal of U.S. Foreign Policy," 2011*

Mainline	34
Evangelicals	64

Data from Pew Research Center[19]

TABLE 5.4. *"What Should the U.S. Do If Israel Attacks Iran's Nuclear Program?" (%)*

2012	Support Israel	Neutral	Oppose Israel
Mainline	42	51	2
Evangelicals	64	32	1

Data from Pew Research Center[20]

TABLE 5.5. *Presbyterian Attitudes toward the 2004 Divestment Resolution (%)*

	Pro-Divestment	Anti-Divestment	Margin
Lay Presbyterians	28	42	−14
Pastors	48	43	+5
General Assembly	87	13	+74

Data from Presbyterian Church (USA) Research Services[21]

whom rejected the proposition. Nonetheless, between 1992 and 2008, the preference for Israel increased across the board among traditionalists, centrists, *and* modernists by very similar margins.[22] Yet at the very time support for Israel was on the rise among the mainline, mainline institutions were moving in the opposite direction, toward a policy of divestment from Israel. An indication of the gap between the mainline laity, the clergy, and the political activists in this regard was apparent over the 2004 Presbyterian divestment resolution. For mainline political activists divestment was a central cause, and they succeeded in getting the divestment resolution passed by a massive majority of 431–62 in the General Assembly. Yet only a slim majority of pastors favored the resolution. It was not a priority for them; indeed, Israel ranked only tenth on a list of sixteen major issues addressed regularly by mainline clergy.[23] In contrast, a clear plurality of lay members opposed divestment (see Table 5.5).

Clearly, the policy of the Presbyterians on Israel was being driven by something other than the general will of its members. In fact, it stemmed primarily from the political activism of a relatively small group, who were more active and more committed on the issue than anyone else in the mainline. The historical foundation of this approach and its contemporary character are examined below.

THE HISTORICAL ROOTS OF MAINLINE APPROACHES TO THE ARAB-ISRAELI CONFLICT

Mainline Anti-Zionism

Traditional Anti-Jewish Theology
Early Christians believed that because Christianity grew out of Judaism, Jews would recognize it as their own. When this did not happen, it led to the development of an anti-Jewish literature, *Adversos Judeos*, or "teachings of

contempt." In the Middle Ages, contempt became demonization – as the Jews were presented as an active force for evil.[24] Mainline anti-Zionism was also informed by St Augustine's replacement theology, according to which the covenant between God and Israel was replaced by the covenant between God and the "new Israel" – the Church – as divine punishment for rejecting Jesus. According to Augustine, the Jewish people were destined to survive but not to thrive, as evidence of its "perfidy."[25] For this reason, according to the mainline theologian Roy Eckhardt:

The entire movement to re-establish the Jewish people in their ancient homeland ... has been a traumatic experience from which the collective Christian psyche has never entirely recovered. How presumptuous for Israel to be "reborn" in clear violation of Christian eschatology![26]

Prior to 1948 this anti-Jewish theology was a major source of mainline anti-Zionism.[27] The Jewish people represented a special case to be judged by a different measure from other peoples. This double standard was consciously applied to Zionism. For example, a 1933 editorial in the leading mainline magazine, the *Christian Century*, opined:

The Christian mind has never allowed itself to feel the same concern for Jewish suffering that it has felt for the cruelties visited upon the Armenians, the Boers, the people of India, American slaves or the Congo Blacks. Christian indifference to Jewish suffering has for centuries been rationalized by the tenable belief that such sufferings were the judgment of God upon the Jewish people for their rejection of Jesus.[28]

The editorial went on to urge it readers to reject the idea that all Jews should be held responsible for the crucifixion. But at the same time it asserted that *nationalist* Jews *were* responsible, as it explained:

He was crucified because he had a program for Israel which ran counter to the cherished nationalism of Israel's leaders.

Mainline Protestantism was not concerned with an all-out assault on nationalism per se, but rather focused its opposition on the Jewish national movement – Zionism. Only the Jewish national movement was singled out for demonization. Anti-Zionists in the *Christian Century* railed against Jewish communal distinctiveness, which was juxtaposed against Christian universalism. Against this background, in the 1930s the *Christian Century* constantly compared Zionism to Nazism, arguing that the two ideologies shared a "privileged race mentality."[29]

Mainline Missionaries and Arab Nationalism

In the nineteenth century, especially after the American Civil War, American missionaries were sent to the Middle East, mainly by the Presbyterians and the Congregationalists. By 1900, twenty-five thousand students were enrolled in American missionary educational institutions in the Middle East.[30] Among the institutions founded was the Syrian Protestant College in 1866, which was renamed the American University of Beirut (AUB). Having failed to convert many Muslims, the missionaries focused instead on trying to instill American ideals in the form of a secular Arab patriotism that would transcend the religious divide between Muslims and Christians. Indeed, the Syrian Protestant College played an important role in the development of Arab nationalism, as recognized by its leading ideologue, George Antonius.[31]

Many American missionaries in the Middle East and their descendants became active supporters of Arab nationalism and opponents of Zionism. For example, Howard Bliss, the president of the Syrian Protestant College, lobbied for Arab nationalism and against Zionism at the Versailles peace conference. In a similar vein, the 1919 King-Crane Commission appointed by President Woodrow Wilson came out against a Jewish state in Palestine, favoring instead the creation of a large Arab/Syrian Republic. Charles R. Crane was a Presbyterian trustee of Robert College, another missionary institution in the Middle East. Antonius dedicated his book *The Arab Awakening* to Crane. Crane was also a rabid anti-Semite with an intense admiration for Hitler, who once proposed to the Mufti of Jerusalem[32] that he prepare an anti-Jewish campaign with the Vatican.[33]

Some of the children and grandchildren of American missionaries entered the State Department's Bureau of Near East Affairs – for example, Allen Dulles, the grandson of a Presbyterian missionary, who as a young diplomat promoted an anti-Zionist stance.[34] Dulles went on to become the first director of the CIA, which funded the anti-Israel American Friends of the Middle East, founded in 1951 and headed by Dorothy Thompson, the daughter of a Methodist minister. Its board included figures such as Daniel Bliss, the head of the AUB. They all regarded American support for the creation of Israel as a tragic mistake.[35]

The existence of such anti-Zionism among American Protestants was not confined to missionaries in the Middle East. Although American Protestant public opinion as a whole was supportive of the creation of the State of Israel, significant elements of the mainline clergy were actively anti-Zionist. From the Balfour Declaration until the mid-1940s, the *Christian Century* reflected this view. The rise of Nazism changed things somewhat so that by the early 1940s mainline Christian clergy were divided over Israel. Still, major figures such the former and then current presidents of Union Theological Seminary, Henry Sloan Coffin and Henry Van Dusen, remained anti-Zionist.

Mainline Pro-Zionism: Niebuhr, Christian Realism and the Holocaust

Yet there were also pro-Zionist mainline theologians. The most important of these was Reinhold Niebuhr, the most influential theologian in America in the 1940s and 1950s. Niebuhr helped found the pro-Zionist Christian Council for Palestine in 1942 that later merged into the American Christian Palestine Committee, which by 1946 had the support of 3000 American clergymen.

In the 1950s and 1960s this organization was more effective within the mainline than the anti-Israel organization, American Friends of the Middle East.

In his early years, Niebuhr was part of the social gospel movement, and was active in the pacifist Fellowship of Reconciliation. However by the mid-1930s Niebuhr had become a harsh critic of the social gospel and pacifism. He argued that the messianic dream of universal perpetual peace and brotherhood can never be fully realized on earth because of the limits of human nature. At the same time, Niebuhr rejected the conservative position that preached only other-worldly salvation. While it was impossible to achieve absolute justice on earth, that did not absolve Christians from seeking a more limited proximate form of justice.[36] In this vein, Niebuhr actively campaigned against racial discrimination, in favor of American involvement in World War II (against the position of the Federal Council of Churches), and in favor of Zionism and Israel.

Unlike evangelicals, Niebuhr's support for Zionism was grounded in moral and political considerations, not a literal reading of the Bible. The rise of Nazism, the West's impotence, and its refusal to accept mass Jewish immigration pushed Niebuhr to look for a solution. This led him away from binationalism toward support for Jewish sovereignty. Theologically he continued to stress a universalist message and he continued to promote equal rights for individual Jews in liberal societies. However, his moral and political realism led to him to be skeptical that anti-Semitism would every fully disappear, and he viewed the Holocaust as evidence regarding the limitations of the democratic creed's ability to prevent evil.[37] But Niebuhr went further – he supported Zionism not only to save individual Jews but also to promote the right of the Jews to survive and flourish *as a collective*. Niebuhr rebuked his liberal anti-Zionist colleagues who advocated Jewish assimilation for "implicitly making collective extinction the price of provisional tolerance."[38] Writing in the early 1940s Niebuhr declared:

The Jews have a right to a homeland. They are a nation ... They have no place where they are not exposed to the perils of minority status ... The fact that the Arabs have a vast hinterland and the Jews have nowhere to go establishes the *relative* justice of their cause ... Arab sovereignty over a *portion* of the debated territory must undoubtedly be sacrificed.[39]

It is important to note two things here. First, that as per his moral realism, Niebuhr aspired only to relative justice; and second, that this involved support for a Jewish state in only part of Palestine, because the Arabs also had legitimate interests that needed to be taken into account. Indeed, while Niebuhr supported Israel's preemptive strike in 1967 and was exhilarated by its victory, he hoped that the U.S. would subsequently take an active role in pursing peace. After Niebuhr's death in 1971, his protégé, the theologian Roy Eckhardt, defended Israel and the right of the Jewish people to exist as a sovereign nation, along with a few other mainline theologians such as Franklin Littell, who felt an especially strong commitment to Israel in the wake of the Holocaust.

THE MAINLINE AND ISRAEL, 1949–1999

Following the Holocaust, the mainline churches came to accept the creation of Israel, primarily for humanitarian reasons. Nonetheless, the new State of Israel received overwhelmingly negative coverage within the *Christian Century* even before Israel's victory in the Six Day War, which Henry Van Dusen castigated as "the most violent, ruthless aggression since Hitler's blitzkrieg."[40] Following the Six Day War, the mainline increasingly adopted far more pro-Arab positions than mainstream Americans. In 1980 the main umbrella organization of mainline American churches, the National Council of Churches (NCC), endorsed the establishment of a PLO state alongside Israel, at a time when most Israelis and American Jews opposed the idea. At the same time the NCC called on the PLO to recognize "Israel as a sovereign state and its right to continue as a Jewish state," though that section passed the 250-person body by a majority of only nine votes.[41] A few years later, in the wake of the first intifada, there was an upsurge in official mainline criticism of Israel combined with calls to make U.S. aid to Israel contingent upon freezing settlement construction.[42] The rise of the Oslo process dampened down these voices. It was only when the peace process collapsed in 2000 that mainline hostility exploded.

THE MAINLINE DISCOURSE ON ISRAEL AND THE CONFLICT SINCE 2000

The Christian Century

Between 2000 and 2008, approximately a hundred articles appeared in the *Christian Century* focused on Israel or the Arab-Israeli conflict. The thrust of the discourse was anti-Israel with a heavy dose of anti-Zionism, especially in the articles by the main contributor on the issue, James Wall,[43] a senior contributing editor to the magazine. Some articles presented a more balanced picture, including perspectives from the Zionist left, but these were in a clear minority.[44] The magazine reviewed nine books on Israel and the conflict. Of these, six were by anti-Zionist authors that received positive reviews, as did a book that claimed that U.S. policy is "controlled" by "the Israel lobby."[45]

The magazine overwhelmingly placed the blame for the conflict on Israel.[46] One article on the 2005 Disengagement even laid the ultimate blame on Israel for the destruction of synagogues in Gaza by the Palestinian Authority.[47] Israeli military actions were generally presented as a form of cruel punishment rather than a function of security, and moral equivalence was expressed regarding the actions of Israel and those of Hamas and Hezbollah.[48] Wall even denied the latter were terrorist groups.[49] He argued that the massive campaign of Palestinian suicide attacks that targeted Israeli civilians mainly within pre-1967 Israel was "resistance to occupation, not terrorism."[50] No articles focused on the extremist ideologies of Israel's enemies and the threat they pose to Israel.

The Mainline, Israel, and Human Rights

The mainline discourse tends to single out Israel for disproportionate criticism and opprobrium. According to a study of mainline human rights advocacy from 2000 to 2003, 37 percent of mainline statements issuing criticism of human rights were focused on Israel; 32 percent were focused on the United States, and the remaining 31 percent were spread across twenty nations. Eighty percent of NCC resolutions targeting foreign nations for human rights abuses were aimed at Israel. Meanwhile, of the fifteen worst human rights offenders in the world, only five were criticized.[51] Not a single human rights criticism was made by any mainline body of the Palestinian Authority or of any of the countries bordering Israel. This despite the fact that Freedom House rated Israel as "free" while its neighbors were rated as "not free" or, in the case of Jordan, "partly free." Other Middle Eastern states with particularly bad human rights records like Saudi Arabia, which was both a U.S. ally and one of the fifteen worst human rights offenders in the world, according to Freedom House, also received no criticism.

Official Mainline Statements and Resolutions

Between 2000 and 2006 official statements and resolutions by mainline bodies were characterized by strongly anti-Israel positions. First, Israel was indicted as primarily responsible for the violence. For example, an NCC statement asserted at the start of the violence in October 2000 declared, "The *fundamental* source of the present violent confrontation lies in the continued failure to make real the national rights of the Palestinian people."[52] Other official statements went further by blaming Israeli "apartheid" for the outbreak of violence.[53]

Second, much greater detail and much more emotive language were used to describe Palestinian suffering and losses than Israeli suffering and losses. The practical demands made of Israel tended to be specific and detailed, while only a vague demand was made of the Palestinians to halt violence. For example, the 2004 Presbyterian resolution on Israel's security barrier conjured up images of the Holocaust and the dispossession of Native Americans by declaring that "the current wall ghettoizes the Palestinians and forces them onto what can only be called reservations."[54] Nothing in that resolution or any other mainline resolution on the issue mentioned the fact that the barrier was a response to terrorism and that it dramatically reduced Israeli civilian casualties.

Third, mainline statements usually referred to a "cycle of violence" while emphasizing "disproportionate" use of force by Israel.[55] For example, during the Second Lebanon War in 2006,[56] the General Secretary of International Affairs and Peace at the NCC declared: "While we ... certainly condemn the attacks of Hezbollah into Israel, we see that the response of Israel is so damaging to the people and to the infrastructure in Lebanon that we see it as more destabilizing."[57] Two years earlier, Ronald Stone, a Church elder who had served on the Advisory Committee on Social Witness Policy and as a professor at Pittsburgh Theological Seminary, along with other American Presbyterians, met with Hezbollah leaders in Lebanon. In that meeting Stone stated: "We treasure the precious words of Hezbollah and your expression of goodwill towards the American people ... As an elder of our church, I'd like to say that ... relations and conversations with Islamic leaders are a lot easier than dealings and dialogue with Jewish leaders."[58] This was not the only meeting between American Presbyterians and Hezbollah.[59] Meanwhile, in contrast to their criticism of Israel, mainline churches were virtually silent over the occupation of Lebanon by Syria, which had been going on in one form or another since the late 1970s. Finally, a Presbyterian resolution in 2003 implied Israel was a foreign entity *within* its pre-1967 borders by referring to "over *fifty* years of Israeli rule in Palestine."[60]

THE POLITICS OF DELEGITIMIZATION AND DIVESTMENT

These resolutions and statements were not spontaneous or confined to rhetoric; rather, they were part of an orchestrated international campaign of boycotts, divestment, and sanctions (BDS) led by the Palestinian Solidarity Movement. Within the mainline, the centerpiece of this campaign has been the push for divestment from Israel. The campaign was led by a relatively small group that typically operates in "Peace and Justice" departments and church committees responsible for dealing with world conflicts.[61] Also central to the divestment campaign have been Palestinian clergy, especially those associated with the Sabeel Ecumenical Liberation Theology Center. Their strategic aim is to broaden support for their anti-Zionist position among the soft liberal center-left of the mainline. As we noted earlier, most of the mainline clergy are liberal and dovish, but their main focus is on tackling local poverty. They have no particular animosity to Israel. While they know little about the conflict, they generally favor the peace process and mutual reconciliation. The goal of the BDS activists is to shift the mainline discourse away from a general discussion about the rights and wrongs on both sides, and in the region more generally, toward a conversation focused on the degree of Israeli iniquity. They seek to achieve this objective by presenting issues of general concern, such as settlements, as an expression of Israel's innate moral corruption. They are assisted in these efforts by the mainline clergy's hostility towards conservative evangelical theology, which is associated with strong support for Israel.[62]

The BDS campaign made a significant breakthrough in 2004 when the Presbyterian General Assembly voted to initiate a process that could lead to divestment. The resolution termed the occupation the root of evil acts committed by both sides. At the same time two other resolutions were passed, one calling for the removal of Israel's security barrier and the other denouncing Christian Zionism. The Presbyterian decision catalyzed the divestment campaign in other denominations. Two local regions of the United Methodist Church passed divestment resolutions. Subsequently, the Episcopal Church, the United Church of Christs' General Synod, and the Evangelical Lutheran Church in America's churchwide assembly all seriously considered divestment.

THE FOUNDATIONS OF CONTEMPORARY MAINLINE HOSTILITY TO ISRAEL

Israeli Policy?

It could be posited that it was Israel that changed rather than the mainline. From this perspective, mainline hostility is related to the fact that before 1967 Israel was the underdog, surrounded by Arab states implacably opposed to its existence. Whereas after 1967, Israel became a regional power, occupying the West Bank, Gaza, the Golan Heights, and Sinai, and building settlements there. At the same time, Israel refused to recognize the legitimacy of Palestinian nationalism and was staunchly opposed to the idea of establishing a Palestinian state until the 1990s. The first intifada further cemented the image of Israel as the powerful side and the Palestinians as the underdog. Meanwhile, the Arab states grudgingly began to move toward coming to terms with Israel by accepting UN Resolutions 242 and 338, which implied at least a formal recognition of Israel's right to exist. Egypt then made peace with Israel in 1979. In 1988 the PLO formally recognized Israel's right to exist and promised to stop terrorism. Indeed, once Israel recognized the PLO and opened negotiations in 1993, the intensity of mainline opposition subsided. Even Israel's most prominent mainline supporter, Reinhold Niebuhr, had supported the creation of Israel in terms of relative justice, and this had led him to support partition as a means of reconciling Jewish and Arab claims. He was categorically opposed to the type of messianic theology that inspired unequivocal support for Zionism among evangelicals. So when, after 1967, Israeli policy under the Likud was directed at preventing partition in alliance with the messianic religious Right in Israel, it is not surprising that the mainline became more critical of Israeli policies.

The limitations of this thesis become apparent when one tries to apply it to the period after 2000, in the wake of the collapse of the peace process. In that year a left-wing Israeli government made an unprecedented offer to fully withdraw from the Golan Heights, subject to some minor and mutual border rectifications. Syria rejected the offer. Israel then unilaterally withdrew from Lebanon in any case. Meanwhile, that same government accepted the Clinton Parameters, which would have given the Palestinians a state in 100 percent of Gaza and 97 percent of the West Bank, with free passage between the areas, and with its capital in East Jerusalem including Palestinian sovereignty over the surface of the Temple Mount. Arafat rejected the offer, while the Palestinians initiated a campaign of suicide bombing directed against Israeli civilians. If the mainline discourse was primarily exercised by a benevolent neutral concern for both sides, one would expect both their opposition to Israel and their support for the Palestinians to at least be reduced in the aftermath. But the opposite is the case; their hostility towards Israel increased dramatically to an all-time high. Moreover, much of the mainline discourse was not simply characterized by criticism of Israeli policies, but by a rejection of Jewish sovereignty per se. Clearly then, the direction of Israeli policy is of limited utility in explaining the thrust of the mainline discourse and the divestment campaign.

Historic Mainline Ties with the Middle East

Historic ties between American mainline denominations and the Middle East forged in the nineteenth century continue to influence mainline approaches to the Arab-Israeli conflict. Those denominations with historic and contemporary ties to the Middle East have been most active politically on the conflict, including the UCC, the Episcopalians, the Quakers, the Mennonites, and most of all the Presbyterians.[63] The Quakers established educational institutions in the Middle East in the nineteenth century, notably in Ramallah. They were also active in assisting Palestinian refugees after 1948.[64] Although few, they exercise a moral influence beyond numbers. This is particularly true with the American Friends Service Committee (AFSC), which has won wide international recognition, including the Nobel Peace Prize. A fact sheet about the conflict available on a Quaker website[65] denies that the historic connection of Jews to the Land of Israel is any more meaningful than the connection between ancient extinct biblical peoples like the Canaanites and the Holy Land. It designates Israel as an "apartheid" state and refers to Hamas's position as being characterized by good faith and a "willingness to negotiate with Israel on equal terms." The pamphlet calls for economic sanctions against Israel.[66] The Presbyterians were most active in setting up educational institutions in the Arab world in the nineteenth century. They have also been the most supportive of the Palestinians. According to a 1988 survey of mainline and evangelical denominations, the Presbyterian clergy were the most likely to support Palestinian statehood.[67] In the twenty-first century, Presbyterian missionaries with strong ties to the Palestinians were at the forefront of the divestment campaign.[68]

Most influential of all has been the development of a close relationship between the mainline churches and the Sabeel Ecumenical Liberation Theology Center in Jerusalem. Sabeel is run by Rev. Naim Ateek, a Palestinian Anglican priest. While Ateek publicly accepts the two-state solution for pragmatic reasons, he emphasizes rejection of Israel's *right* to exist. Statements by Ateek and many other speakers at Sabeel conferences indicate that their support for a two-state solution is provisional.[69] Sabeel's ideal is the replacement of Israel by single state for all Palestinians and Jews,[70] in which the Jews will become a minority. Delegations from mainline churches regularly visit the Sabeel Center and they routinely send missionaries to work in Sabeel's office in Jerusalem.

Sabeel is an official partner of the Presbyterian Church (USA) and the ecumenical Churches for Mideast Peace, which lists among its members major mainline denominations like the Episcopal Church, the Evangelical Lutheran Church of America, and the United Methodist Church. Various mainline congregations have sponsored Sabeel conferences,[71] and in 2006, Ateek was awarded the Episcopal Peace Fellowship Award. Sabeel has been one of the moving forces behind the divestment campaign in the U.S.[72]

Liberation Theology

Sabeel's influence is not simply a function of the historic ties between the mainline and Arab nationalism. Sabeel promotes a narrative of the conflict grounded on liberation theology; as already noted, liberation theology has had significant influence within the mainline since the 1970s and a significant influence on the mainline discourse on Israel, especially since the first intifada.[73] In this vein, liberation theologist Rosemary Ruether referred to "the Zionist concept of a Jewish state" as "a remnant of a racist concept of nationalism."[74] She defined the State of Israel as, in its very *essence*, a colonialist power dependent on American imperialism, even *within* the pre-1967 boundaries.[75] Ruether also asserts (incorrectly) that the aim of Zionism per se was to expel the Palestinians, and that as such it is at one with the displacement of indigenous peoples carried out by European colonists against Native American peoples.[76]

This approach is echoed by various mainline pro-Palestinian activists such as David Wildman, who has served as executive secretary for Human Rights and Racial Justice in Mission Contexts and Relationships at the United Methodist General Board of Global Ministries, a $150 million church agency that used to support Marxist liberation movements in Latin America. At a Sabeel conference in 2005, Wildman exclaimed: "The U.S. represents a country where the settlers won and all but exterminated the indigenous population after seizing most of the land by force. Israel is one of the last places where a colonial settler project is actively seizing land from the indigenous population."[77] Wildman has been a strong advocate for anti-Israel divestment. The American Friends Service Committee has also been strongly influenced by liberation theology,[78] as has Rev. Jeremiah Wright, Obama's longtime pastor.[79] Wright and the AFSC have consistently adopted a virulently anti-Israel line.[80]

While liberation theology provides the broad theological framework for mainline hostility to Israel, it does not explain the peculiar focus on Israel. After all, perhaps the leading Protestant American liberation theologist, Robert McAfee Brown, took a far more balanced position on the conflict. Liberation theology dictates that its followers should side with the poor and oppressed. While Brown recognized the Palestinians as being in this category, he argued that the Israelis were *also* in this category because they are threatened militarily by the Arabs; he therefore argued that *both* sides required liberation. He supported Palestinian national aspirations, but argued that this could not happen until Israelis were liberated from the threat to their security, because there is always the danger that when an oppressed people gains liberation they will deny it to others. He argued that it was legitimate to criticize Israel from a theological perspective; but that Israel should be held to the *same* standards as all others. Only Israelis had the right to hold themselves to a higher standard, and Brown argued that Israel's vigorous internal debate over the first intifada was a model of how to go about this.[81]

Consequently, taken alone, liberation theology is an insufficient basis for explaining the intense antipathy to Israel in the mainline discourse. Rather to understand the particular intensity of hostility to Israel, it is necessary to examine the ways in which it interacts with the residue of traditional anti-Jewish Christian theology.

Liberation Theology and the Legacy of Traditional Anti-Jewish Theology

In post–World War II America, the legitimacy of both anti-Semitism and replacement theology declined very significantly, and this was reflected in the attitudes and official positions of the mainline church. Nonetheless, Prof. Dennis Hale, a lay minister in the Episcopalian Church, and Holocaust theologian Richard Rubenstein have argued that the extraordinary amount of attention and depth of hostility focused on Israel within the mainline reflects a double standard born of the residual effects of old anti-Jewish theological themes.[82] They argue that the Jewish people remain a special case in the contemporary Christian imagination, albeit sometimes unconsciously. The idea of the Jews as an archetype rather than a normal people continues to exist because of the "witness-people" mentality according to which the Jews, and by extension the State of Israel, retain symbolic meaning for Christians.[83]

The residual effects of traditional anti-Jewish theology are clearly present in liberation theology as applied to the Arab-Israeli conflict, notably in the work of Ateek and Sabeel.[84] Such works tends to view "the oppressor" in the light of the Gospels, not as Rome but as Jewish Pharisaism. They recast standard Christian anti-Jewish motifs and combine them with anti-Jewish themes absorbed from Western New Testament scholarship in the 1970s. While liberation theologists do not specifically endorse replacement theology, in the spirit of this theology they diminish the particular role of the historic people of Israel, sometimes even denying this role completely, for example with regard to the Exodus. This provides a foundation from which to delegitimize Jewish historical claims to self-determination in Israel. In addition, they tend to glorify Jewish exile. They either overlook the intense suffering of the Jewish people in the exile or advocate exile for the Jews, because without sovereignty, the Jews demonstrate the virtues of nonviolence and powerlessness. However, the so-called virtues of Diaspora powerlessness are applied only to the Jewish people. No liberation theologists ever suggest that non-Jews should disavow their legitimate aspirations for sovereignty and self-determination. *Only the Jews are asked to live in vulnerability and impotence.* Thus, all liberation theologians strongly support Palestinian self-determination, while self-determination is never presented as being equally applicable to the Jewish people. Thus continues the Christian practice of singling out the Jews as categorically different from other peoples.[85]

Liberation theology also demonizes Israel using classical anti-Jewish images, notably the idea of the Jews as Christ killers. A statement from the World Alliance of YMCA on the Israeli-Palestinian conflict from the perspective of liberation theology repeatedly used this image; as have many Sabeel publications.[86] Indeed, Ateek has even presented the Israeli-Palestinian conflict as a metaphysical struggle in which Israel symbolizes "the spiritual forces of evil."[87]

The Decline of Pro-Israel Elements

Two intertwined factors, related in part to generational change, led to the decline of pro-Israel sentiment in the mainline. First, there was the decline of Niebuhr's Christian Realism and its replacement by liberation theology and the social gospel as the dominant theologies in the mainline. The worldview of Christian Realism is far more understanding of the use of force by states to defend their legitimate interests than the social gospel or liberation theology. It is also far more skeptical of the ability of well-meaning people to bring about conflict resolution. This type of outlook is bound to be more sympathetic to Israel's strategic dilemmas.

Second, the resonance of the Holocaust as a factor mandating sympathy and support for the State of Israel declined considerably. The generation for whom World War II and the Holocaust were the defining experiences was gradually replaced by the generation for whom Vietnam was the defining experience. In the 1970s and 1980s the centrality of the Holocaust restrained virulent anti-Israel sentiment. For example, prior to World War II, Brown had been a pacifist, but he chose to renounce this position and become a navy chaplain because of Hitler's war against the Jews. He was later appointed to the U.S. Holocaust Memorial Council, as well as writing a book about Elie Wiesel. For Brown, Christian complicity in the Holocaust and centuries of Christian persecution of Jews made a big moral claim on Christians.

Finally, these factors were reinforced by the decline in Israeli and American Jewish engagement with the mainline. With the success of the civil rights agenda in the 1960s, the mainline alliance with the American Jewish community waned. In the 1990s Israeli foreign policy focused on peacemaking, reducing the resources dedicated to public diplomacy. Equally, however, the increase in American Jewish engagement with the mainline was a factor in restraining the anti-Israeli campaign in the mainline, in the wake of the Presbyterian divestment resolution of 2004.

STEMMING THE DIVESTMENT TIDE?

Although the 2004 Presbyterian divestment resolution led to a spate of efforts to get other denominations to follow suit, in the end they all rejected divestment. Moreover, at their 2006 General Assembly, the Presbyterians took a step away from divestment. The 2006 resolution did not formally reverse the 2004 resolution, but instead of talking about divestment, it spoke about identifying positive investment opportunities to help build peace in Israel, the West Bank, and Gaza. Instead of calling for the complete dismantling of the security barrier, as it did in 2004, the 2006 resolution called only for those parts of the barrier that were in the West Bank to be moved to areas on or within the Green Line. Significantly, the resolution added: "The General Assembly does not believe that the Presbyterian Church (USA) should tell a sovereign nation whether it can protect its border or handle matters of national defense." The resolution passed 483 to 28, with 1 abstention. Another resolution was also passed, which declared suicide bombings a "crime against humanity." The net result was to make the probability of divestment extremely remote. In 2007, the UCC's General Synod approved a resolution acknowledging its previously one-sided resolutions by declaring that it had "yet to fully address other forces contributing to the ongoing violence, oppression and suffering in the region" and calling for the establishment of "a Task Force to engage in ongoing and balanced study of the causes, history and context of the conflict."[88]

What then, led to the stemming of the divestment tide? First, there were changes in the situation on the ground that lessened the wider resonance of some of the core messages of the BDS campaign. Thus, the assumption that the Israeli-Palestinian conflict was primarily a function of the occupation became less tenable when, following Israel's unilateral withdrawal from the Gaza Strip in 2005, Hamas won the Palestinian elections in January 2006 and later took control of Gaza by force. The Islamist Hamas charter quotes from the anti-Semitic forgery, "The Protocols of the Elders of Zion." It is ideologically opposed to Israel's existence and committed to terrorism. Meanwhile in the summer of 2006 Hezbollah, which shares the ideology of Hamas and which is closely allied with Iran, attacked Israel, triggering a war from Lebanon, six years after Israel had unilaterally withdrawn from southern Lebanon. These changes in context were not enough to block divestment on their own; rather, they served to blunt the wider credibility and legitimacy of the divestment campaign.

Second, the American Jewish community mobilized and engaged. While the reaction of some Jewish groups alienated the mainline; intensive engagement with centrist Jewish groups like the American Jewish Committee, which had a long history of working with the mainline on issues such as civil rights, had more of an impact. Especially significant was the very strong disproval of dovish liberal Jewish groups whose voices could not easily be dismissed. One of the ways that mainline anti-Israel activists have traditionally sought to broaden their legitimacy has been to highlight their cooperation with Jewish anti-Zionists.[89] Anti-Zionism has been an extremely marginal position within the American Jewish community since at least 1948. But by bringing a few such Jews onboard, mainline anti-Israel activists sought to blur the distinction between this handful of Jews and the much wider constituency of dovish liberal Jews, who, while critical of certain Israeli policies, are fiercely pro-Israel. However, this blurring strategy was exposed over divestment, which alienated the overwhelming bulk of dovish liberal Jewish groups. For example, *Rabbis for Human Rights* wrote a strong condemnatory letter in response to the divestment resolution, which stated:

Like you we hate the Occupation, condemn it and work for its speedy end in a peace accord ... Yet you direct not one word of criticism to the Palestinian Authority ... It is not just that your resolution ignores the homicidal ideologies that have so sadly taken hold among some of our Palestinian neighbors. Nor is the problem just that it averts its eyes from the attempts to destroy our country that transcend the Occupation and precede it by decades. *Its deepest flaw ... is the allegation that the Occupation is somehow "at the root of evil acts committed." This is a restatement of the paradigmatic allegation that Jewish sins are somehow especially significant ... The result is a descent into discriminatory behavior against Jews and their State.*[90]

Third, for all the Jewish activity, the thrust of the reversal came from within the Church. Until the 1980s there had been active mainline pro-Israel organizations, but these had been allowed to wither in the 1990s as the peace process seemed to suggest they were redundant. But following the divestment resolution, they reemerged in organizations such as End Divestment Now and Presbyterians Concerned for Jewish-Christian Relations, and ecumenical organizations like the National Christian Leadership Conference for Israel and Christians for Fair Witness on the Middle East. Many of those who were actively opposed to divestment were heavily involved in interfaith dialogue with the Jewish community. Their approach to the conflict was quite dovish, similar to the center-left of the American Jewish community. They were able to mobilize opposition to divestment by virtue of the fact that the 2004 resolution was out of sync with the position of the majority of Presbyterians, a fact which severely damaged the legitimacy of the resolution.[91] The mobilization of this generalized opposition was viewed by Jewish organizations involved in the campaign to reverse the 2004 decision as decisive.[92] At the same time, with the pro-Israel camp now mobilized, the Presbyterian leadership feared that the argument over the Middle East within the denomination would widen the growing split between conservatives and liberals within the denomination to crisis point; they therefore sought to defuse the situation.[93] Despite this, the BDS campaign in the mainline church continues, and in 2014 the Presbyterians voted narrowly to reinstitute a limited policy of divestment. More generally, the thrust of the struggle is over the Kairos Palestine document, written by Palestinian Christians, which calls on Christians throughout the world to target Israel with BDS. The document itself promotes the usual one-sided anti-Israel narrative that is hostile to the idea of Jewish self-determination.[94]

CONCLUSION

In the first decade of the new millennium the mainline discourse towards Israel was hostile, culminating in the campaign to divest from Israel. The thrust of the mainline approach has been one-sided, blaming predominantly Israel both for the lack of a peace settlement and for the ongoing violence. Threats to Israel are largely ignored, discounted, or dismissed. Similarly downplayed is the larger picture of indigenous political and religious extremism, unrelated to Israel, which drags down the Middle East. The mainline has, in effect, singled out Israel for particular opprobrium. Israel has not been treated as a normal country, rather it has been judged according to a separate standard. This discourse is informed by a variety of influences, including liberation theology intermingled with new versions of old anti-Jewish themes – replacement theology and the witness mentality. Historical and contemporary mainline ties to the Palestinians and Arab nationalism also played a significant role. These are the ideas behind the divestment campaign, which has been spearheaded by a relatively small but well-organized group of activists.

No doubt the anti-Israel activists' call for peace, along with some of their more reasonable criticisms of Israeli policy, resonates among the wider circle of liberal mainline clergy. Without this it would be extremely difficult for the activists to impose their agenda on the mainline at large. On the other hand, the clergy do not identify en masse with the vehemently one-sided approach of divestment advocates. For most mainline clergy, Israel and the conflict are not a major concern. Moreover, mainline anti-Israeli activists are completely out of sync with the mainline public, which has remained more sympathetic to Israel than to the Palestinians, albeit to a lesser extent than evangelicals. Nonetheless, for much of the time it has been the interested minority rather than the largely passive majority that has shaped the discourse and the politics of the mainline toward Israel.

Some may question whether any of this matters politically. Who cares about a minority of anti-Israel Church activists? American public opinion is consistently and overwhelmingly pro-Israel, and the amount of evangelicals that can be mobilized for Israel at the grassroots level dwarfs the number of committed mainline opponents of Israel. No divestment has actually taken place and even if it did, the direct and immediate economic impact on Israel would be marginal. Yet the mainline divestment campaign does matter. The importance of divestment is not primarily economic but rather political, in that it increases the resonance of the idea of Israel as a pariah state. Divestment advocates are promoting an analogy with apartheid South Africa; mainline denominations did divest from South Africa. In this way, they hope to broaden support for their position by associating Israel with something that is very widely recognized as not only illegitimate but a defining symbol of politically constructed evil.

The fact that the activists themselves are a relatively small group does not mean that their political influence is commensurate with their numbers. On the question of the Middle East, this minority has the upper hand in very large and prestigious mainline institutions with millions of members. The fact that they can speak in the names of these institutions dramatically multiplies their political standing, influence, and leverage. Nor is divestment simply a domestic American issue. The mainline has strong connections with churches worldwide, and the divestment campaign is part of a broader global campaign of boycotts, divestment, and sanctions. So in Britain, for example, there was a strong campaign within the Anglican Church to promote divestment. Also in Britain, a relatively small group of anti-Israel activists have managed to push through boycott resolutions in trade unions with hundreds of thousands of members, the overwhelming majority of whom are entirely indifferent to Israel and the Palestinians. Taken together in a global sense, such a campaign could eventually have economic as well as political significance if it were to take off, because Israel's economy is highly globalized and thus very dependent on international economic interactions that could be stymied by boycotts, divestment, and sanctions.

Yet despite all this, there is no reason to assume that divestment will achieve its objectives within the mainline. Israel has friends in the mainline, and there are many who oppose the divestment agenda for reasons largely unconnected to the Middle East. Once Israel's supporters mobilized, once the issue was brought out into the wider political discourse that is sympathetic to Israel, once Israel itself took steps like the Disengagement, which enhanced its credentials with liberals while Hamas gained power in Gaza, it was possible to stem the divestment tide.

Finally, in a sense, the mainline discourse is a kind of mirror image to the evangelical discourse. Both single out Israel as a country to be treated differently. Evangelicals do so consciously, and it manifests itself in support; while mainline anti-Israel activists would no doubt vehemently deny that they are consciously or unconsciously engaged in negative discrimination, that is what it often amounts to. Both flirt with the idea of a one-state "solution," one out of commitment to Jewish ascendancy without apparent regard for democracy and Palestinian rights, the other out of apparent naiveté regarding the consequences for the safety and well-being of Israeli Jews under Palestinian ascendancy combined with a disregard for a Jewish right to self-determination. Similarly, both sides engage in political acts that damage the prospects of a stable and peaceful two-state solution by providing political backing for groups and positions that threaten such a solution. Christian Zionists do so through their ties with Israel's Far Right and by supporting settlements; the mainline do so by endorsing the so-called right of return for Palestinian refugees and their descendants to Israel within its pre-1967 boundaries, and by backing the BDS campaign aimed at demonizing and delegitimizing Israel per se. Both sides make a positive contribution to the parties through their humanitarian work and charity, but a fair proportion of their activity hinders rather than helps the cause of peace and stability in the Middle East.

PART III

JEWS

6

American Jewish Attachment to Israel: Mind the Gap

We Are One.

—campaign slogan of the United Jewish Appeal, 1967

There exists a distance and detachment between young American Jews and their Israeli cousins that ... has not existed until now.

—Frank Luntz, *Israel in the Age of Eminem* (2003)[1]

INTRODUCTION

For many years a deep attachment to Israel united American Jewry. After 1967, Israel achieved a heroic status and many Jews thought that not supporting Israel was "a great, if not the greatest 'crime' that could be committed by a Jew."[2] To this day American Jews' *attachment* to Israel remains deeper than the widespread *sympathy* for Israel expressed by the general public. However, since the late 1980s, an increasing number of voices have argued that American Jews have become more distant from Israel.

This chapter argues that while American Jews no longer view Israel through rose-tinted glasses, a large majority continue to feel attached to the Jewish state. Yet, there is a clear *attachment gap* that mirrors the wider polarization within the community between those with a more intense sense of belonging to the Jewish people and greater Jewish communal involvement, and those with a weaker sense of belonging and a lesser degree of involvement. The Orthodox are most strongly represented at the pole of strong attachment, while the intermarried and the unaffiliated are dominant at the other pole. In the middle are Jews from the Reform and Conservative movements.

Below, the chapter begins by surveying the development of American Jewish attitudes to Zionism and Israel from the late nineteenth century until the present day. It then examines the contemporary process of polarization within the community, including the decline in the sense of peoplehood, before surveying the gap in attachment to Israel among different segments of the community. Finally, the distancing debate is assessed and its political implications analyzed.

AMERICAN JEWRY, ZIONISM, AND ISRAEL

By the middle of the nineteenth century, there were about 250,000 Jews in the United States, most of them immigrants from Germany. The strongest religious movement was the liberal Reform movement, whose roots also lay in Germany. From the 1880s until the early 1920s, more than two million Jews immigrated to America, transforming the nature of the community. These immigrants were more religiously traditional than their German predecessors, and though most shed their religious Orthodoxy, they formed the backbone of the centrist Conservative movement, which became the largest religious movement in twentieth-century American Jewish life.

Zionism: From the Periphery to the Consensus, 1885–1948

Towards the end of the nineteenth century, as the Zionist movement emerged in Europe, major elements of American Jewry adopted an anti-Zionist stance. Thus, the Reform movement's 1885 Pittsburgh Platform declared, "We consider ourselves no longer a nation but a religious community and therefore do not expect a return to Palestine."[3] The Reform movement's rejection of Jewish peoplehood informed its anti-Zionism.Two additional factors served to shape their anti-Zionism. First, a fear that the foundation of a Jewish state would lead to charges that American Jews had dual loyalties, which in turn could lead to a rise in anti-Semitism that could threat Jews' civil and political rights in America. Second, the Reform movement's liberal universalism inclined it against the idea of Jewish statehood, which seemed to them at the time a particularistic project. In a similar vein, a little later, the National Conference of Jewish Labor, influenced by the Bundist Jewish socialist party in Russia, also adopted an anti-Zionist position.

During the First World War, the situation began to change and by 1918 membership in the Zionist Organization of America (ZOA) had reached 120,000. By the end of World War II, the combined membership of American Zionist organizations was more than 700,000. Three factors lay behind this pro-Zionist shift. First, a large proportion of the new immigrants from Russia had a strong attachment to Jewish peoplehood. This informed the newcomers' support for fellow Jews who sought to return and build up the ancient Jewish homeland. Second, the first major American Zionist leader and first Jewish Supreme Court justice, Louis Brandeis, developed a specifically American

Zionist ideology, which cast Zionism as an expression of progressive American values, and which succeeded in muting concerns about particularism and dual loyalty. Unlike classical Zionism, Brandeis's American version did not advocate the immigration of American Jews to the Jewish homeland; rather, it supported the creation of such a homeland as a refuge for Jews suffering from persecution in *other* countries. A major theme of American political culture has always been the country's democracy as an exemplar, a model to emulate. Brandeis applied this theme to Zionism by promoting the idea that American Zionists should work to make the Jewish homeland a model of progressive democracy. Against this background, Brandeis presented Zionism as a patriotic *American* act involving the promotion of American values, such as that of national self-determination proposed by President Woodrow Wilson.[4]

Against the background of these twin factors, American Jewry became increasingly supportive of Zionism. The largest religious movement, Conservative Judaism, was strongly pro-Zionist. Among the much smaller Orthodox movement, opinion was split. Modern Orthodoxy's support for Zionism was strong, but the Ultra-Orthodox minority was predominantly non-Zionist or anti-Zionist. Meanwhile, there was a dramatic reversal of positions in the Reform movement. In 1930 a survey of students at Reform's Hebrew Union College found that more than 90 percent either favored or were neutral regarding Zionism. By 1937 the movement's Columbus Platform affirmed "the *obligation* of all Jewry to aid in its [i.e., Palestine's] upbuilding as a Jewish homeland."[5]

The shift in Reform attitudes to Zionism in the 1930s was also related to a third factor that was extremely important: the growing threat to Jewish survival, specifically European Jewry. In the 1930s support for unlimited Jewish immigration into Palestine as a refuge grew exponentially in the wake of the rise of Hitler and the closing of America to mass immigration. But the idea of Jewish statehood was still controversial. It was not until the end of the Second World War, in the shadow of the Holocaust, that American Jewry became mobilized en masse to lobby for the creation of a Jewish state, including the largest non-Zionist organizations such as the Jewish Labor Committee and B'nai B'rith. Support for the creation of a Jewish state had become the consensual position of American Jewry. The anti-Zionist American Council for Judaism had only 2 percent of the membership of the American Zionist movement.[6]

The Six Day War: Israel as a Symbol of American Jewish Identity

Following the creation of the State of Israel, the focus of American Jewry shifted away from Zionism toward a domestic agenda of synagogue construction and support for civil rights. Membership in the ZOA declined substantially, but at the same time American Jews donated money to Israel, instituted regular synagogue prayers for the welfare of Israel, and developed programs to study Hebrew.[7] On the eve of the Six Day War, with Israel surrounded by states threatening its destruction, American Jews feared that another Holocaust was imminent. The sense of impending disaster awakened very deep feelings of Jewish solidarity with Israel. As one young volunteer wrote, "Two weeks ago Israel was *they*; now Israel is *we*." At the height of the war, polling showed that 99 percent of American Jews expressed strong sympathy for Israel.[8] Whereas in 1966 the United Jewish Appeal (UJA) raised $64 million, in 1967 it raised $240 million, $100 million of which was raised in the first three weeks of the crisis.[9] The effect of the Six Day War on American Jewish identification with Israel was profound. As Thomas Friedman put it, "After the 1967 War, the perception of Israel in the minds of many American Jews shifted radically, from Israel as a safe haven for other Jews to Israel as the symbol and carrier of Jewish communal identity."[10] Daniel Elazar, an American Zionist who immigrated to Israel, even went so far as to call this sensibility: *Israelolotry*.[11]

Indeed, the Six Day War represents the high watermark of American Jewish attachment to Israel. All the key elements underlying support for Israel were present. There was a strong sense of Jewish peoplehood, a strong sense that Israel was under serious threat, and a strong sense that Israel was a good liberal American cause, being surrounded by authoritarian enemies backed by the totalitarian Soviet Union. Moreover, the rapid decline of anti-Semitism meant that American Jews felt more confident about publicly demonstrating their support for Israel, without fear of being charged with dual loyalty.

Controversies in the 1980s

In the latter half of the 1980s Israel's heroic, pristine image among American Jews began to erode in the wake of a series of controversies. In 1986 Jonathan Pollard, a Jewish intelligence officer in the U.S., was convicted of spying for Israel. U.S. Jews were extremely angry as they felt that Israel had raised the spectre of an anti-Semitic backlash on the basis of dual loyalty. Moreover, by the 1980s, Israel's existence was no longer perceived by American Jews to be as threatened as it has once been. Indeed, Israel was clearly the stronger party in the 1982 Lebanon War and the first Palestinian uprising (intifada), which began in December 1987. Moreover, in the eyes of many American Jews, Israel's liberal credentials were challenged due to the massacre of Palestinian refugees by Israel's Lebanese allies in the Sabra and Shatilla refugee camps during the 1982 Lebanon War.[12] The outbreak of the intifada had a more sustained and a more traumatic effect than the Lebanon War. One symptom of this was the growing public criticism of Israel by well-known Diaspora Jews such as Woody Allen. The most emotionally charged of these controversies was the "Who is a Jew" crisis of 1988, which tarnished the image of Israel as the symbol of Jewish peoplehood among many American Jews. At that time, Israeli prime minister Yitzhak Shamir agreed to change Israel's Law of Return, which allowed automatic immigration to Israel for Jews, so that it applied only to persons defined as Jewish by Orthodox Jewish law. While the overwhelming majority of American Jews are affiliated to non-Orthodox streams of Judaism, in practice this change would have affected only a handful of Diaspora Jews each year. However the non-Orthodox saw the proposed amendment as the delegitimization of their Jewish identity by Israel. Israel was, in a symbolic sense, rejecting their Judaism and their family members.[13]

These controversies led some to suggest that the American Jewish love affair with Israel was waning. American Jewry, they claimed, was distancing itself from Israel. Indeed, this issue has not gone away; rather, it attracts ever-increasing attention.[14] It is addressed directly after the following section on the trends within the contemporary American Jewish community and their effect on American Jews' attachment to Israel.

AMERICAN JEWS IN THE TWENTY-FIRST CENTURY: INCREASED POLARIZATION, DECREASED PEOPLEHOOD

In the first decade of the twenty-first century, an estimated 5.2 to 6.4 million Jews live in the U.S., with the best estimate likely to be closer to the higher end of the spectrum.[15] Synagogue membership is the most widespread form of communal affiliation. Among the different religious movements, the Reform movement is the largest, followed by the Conservative and then the Orthodox. But among the children of synagogue members, the Orthodox constitute a plurality (see Tables 6.1 and 6.2). At the other end of the religious spectrum, the number of self-defined nonreligious Jews almost doubled from 1990 to 2008.[16]

All of this adds up to a process of religious polarization. In the center, the previously dominant Conservative movement is in decline. On the Right, the Orthodox movement, which has become more right-wing in religious and political terms,[17] is the fastest-growing religious movement. Meanwhile, about a third of American Jews are married to non-Jews, with the rate of intermarriage rising from 13 percent before 1970, to around a third by the early 1980s, to 58 percent in 2013.[18]

TABLE 6.1. *American Jews by Religious Denomination, 2000 (%)*

	Adults	Children
Orthodox	10	23
Conservative	27	24
Reform	35	30
Reconstructionist	2	3
Just Jewish	26	21

Data from United Jewish Communities, National Jewish Population Survey 2000–2001. (From Jonathon Ament, *American Jewish Religious Movements* [New York: United Jewish Communities, 2005], table 2. Reprinted with permission from Jonathon Ament and the Jewish Federations of North America.)

TABLE 6.2. *American Jews, Synagogue Members, 2000 (%)*

	Adults	Children
Orthodox	23	38
Conservative	32	25
Reform	37	32
Reconstructionist	2	3

Data from United Jewish Communities, National Jewish Population Survey 2000–2001. (From Ament, *American Jewish Religious Movements*, table 9. Reprinted with permission from Jonathon Ament and the Jewish Federations of North America.)

This religious polarization overlaps to a significant extent with a wider pattern of polarization regarding Jewish communal and educational engagement. The more engaged group is quite religiously observant, and its members tend to have many Jewish friends. They are evenly divided among Orthodox, Conservative, Reform, and nondenominational Jews; but their most dynamic and committed segment is the Orthodox. The non-Orthodox are more likely to be a part of the unengaged segment than the Orthodox, but the core of the unengaged segment are the intermarried.[19] Overall, increased intermarriage has served to decrease the number of Jews committed to an ethnically based sense of Jewish peoplehood.[20]

However, it is not only among the intermarried and the Jewishly unengaged that an ethnically based sense of Jewish peoplehood is in decline. This is also the case among the younger generation of non-Orthodox Jews who *are* engaged in Jewish matters. Here there has been a generational shift in the *meaning* of Jewish identity. Surveys indicate that around 75 percent of Jews more than sixty-five years old agree with this statement: "I have a strong sense of belonging to the Jewish people," but the proportion strongly agreeing drops steadily with age to only 47 percent for adults under thirty-five.[21] Previous generations were characterized by a strong sense of ethnic Jewish identity – peoplehood. This informed a strong commitment to protect the welfare of all Jews, including those abroad. It also found expression in strong opposition to intermarriage, charitable donations focused on Jewish causes, the dominance of the Conservative movement, and centralized communal "defense" organizations like the Anti-Defamation League (ADL) and the American Jewish Committee (AJC). Support for these orientations is significantly lower among the younger generation of non-Orthodox American Jews. They are less committed to aiding Jews abroad, less committed to specifically Jewish charitable giving, less concerned by the need to combat anti-Semitism, and more open to intermarriage.[22]

Younger non-Orthodox Jews have shifted from communally orientated normative constructions of being Jewish to more individualistic, aesthetic understandings. Fewer Jews regard being Jewish as a matter of norms and obligations; fewer relate personally to the very notion of the Jewish people, and most have a weaker sense of Jewish peoplehood. This "expressive" orientation is accompanied by a "progressive" orientation identified with promoting universal moral causes, mainly focused among non-Jews (or not specifically targeted at Jews), including environmentalism and social justice, which are viewed as more important than communal needs. The old sense of ethnicity has not disappeared, but it is no longer dominant among the younger generation. Again this trend is not confined to the less Jewishly engaged. It is also true of many young non-Orthodox Jewish leaders who have received more Jewish education and have better knowledge of Hebrew than the older generation of leaders and communal professionals.[23]

This general process of polarization among American Jews is also reflected in differences regarding the degree of attachment to Israel among various segments of American Jewry.

MIND THE GAP: AMERICAN JEWISH ATTACHMENT TO ISRAEL

According to regular AJC surveys, a majority of between two-thirds and three-quarters of American Jews feel close to Israel and between 70 and 80 percent cares about the Jewish state.[24] Furthermore, an absolute majority across all age cohorts "strongly agree" that "Israel is the spiritual center of the Jewish people."[25] Nonetheless, there are substantial gaps regarding the extent of attachment to Israel among different Jewish groups.

Religious Movements

Historically, the Conservative movement had the strongest connection to Zionism and Israel. However, since at least the late 1980s, Orthodox Jews have much stronger Israel connections than other Jews. Conservative Jews come next, followed by the Reform and "Just Jewish" groups who have a similar level of attachment.[26] Theologically, the Orthodox differ from the other movements in that they view themselves as being in exile in America. The Orthodox have a stronger sense of Jewish peoplehood, they are generally more knowledgeable about Israel, and they travel to Israel far more than the other groups. Indeed, it is almost the norm for Modern-Orthodox teenagers to study in a religious seminary in Israel for a year between high school and college. At the same time, as is made clear in Table 6.3 and Figure 6.1, a majority of all the religiously defined groups feel attached to Israel.

Affiliation

According to the National Jewish Population Survey in 2000, 28 percent of American Jews are highly affiliated, 28 percent are moderately affiliated, and

TABLE 6.3. *Attachment to Israel, 2000 (%)*

	Very/Somewhat Attached	Very Attached
Orthodox	92	68
Conservative	80	39
Reform	64	21
Just Jewish	55	24

Data from United Jewish Communities, National Jewish Population Survey 2000–2001. (From Jonathon Ament, *Israel Connections and American Jews* [New York: United Jewish Communities, 2005], report 12, table 5. Reprinted with permission from Jonathon Ament and the Jewish Federations of North America.)

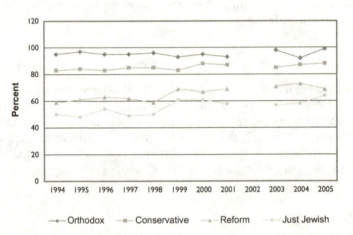

FIGURE 6.1. **Close to Israel, by Religious Denomination** (From, Sasson, Kadushin, and Saxe, *Trends in American Jewish Attachment to Israel*, p. 10. Reprinted with permission from Theodore Sasson and the Cohen Center for Modern Jewish Studies.)

44 percent are unaffiliated. As is illustrated in Table 6.4, highly affiliated Jews have the strongest connections to Israel and unaffiliated Jews have the weakest.

Intermarriage

Intermarriage has a strong effect on attachment to Israel, especially among the under-35s, where it is far more prevalent.[27] This is illustrated in Table 6.5 and Figure 6.2. Among the intermarried, those with low attachment to Israel are more than double the number with high attachment. Among the in-married and unmarried, under 5 percent qualify as "alienated" from Israel compared to 15 percent for the intermarried.[28] Similarly, the children of the in-married were twice as likely to feel connected to Israel, compared to those of the intermarried.[29]

TABLE 6.4. *Communal Affiliation and Attachment to Israel, 2000 (%)*

Level of Affiliation	Very/Somewhat Attached	Very Attached
High	85	47
Moderate	75	34
Unaffiliated	55	20

Data from United Jewish Communities, National Jewish Population Survey 2000–2001. (From Ament, *Israel Connections and American Jews*, table 5. Reprinted with permission from Jonathon Ament and the Jewish Federations of North America.)

TABLE 6.5. *Marital Status and Attachment to Israel 2000 (%)*

Marital Status	Very/Somewhat Attached	Very Attached
In-married	78	52
Intermarried	41	15

Data from United Jewish Communities, National Jewish Population Survey 2000–2001. (From Ament, *Israel Connections and American Jews*, table 7. Reprinted with permission from Jonathon Ament and the Jewish Federations of North America.)

Age

Among the biggest gaps in attachment are those between the oldest and youngest.[30] According to a 2007 survey, among the over-65s those highly attached to Israel vastly exceed those with low attachment. Among the 35–49 cohort, the low-attached vastly exceed those with high attachment. Among the under-35s, the gap in Israel attachment widens further.[31] This is illustrated in Figure 6.3. Similarly, other studies indicate that only about a third of the young view caring about Israel as very important to their Jewish identity.[32]

Partisanship

More than two-thirds of American Jews either identify as Democrats or lean toward the Democratic Party, while about a fifth identify as Republicans or lean toward the Republican Party. This partisan split overlaps with the religious divide as a clear majority of the non-Orthodox side with the Democrats, while a majority of the Orthodox side with the Republicans. Indeed, just like the Orthodox, Jewish Republicans are more emotionally attached to Israel than Jewish Democrats, as is illustrated in Table 6.6.[33]

To sum up, while a large majority of American Jews are attached to Israel, there are significant gaps in the level of attachment. The Orthodox, the affiliated, the in-married, Republicans, and older Jews are all more attached to Israel than nonreligious, intermarried, unaffiliated, Democrats, and younger Jews,

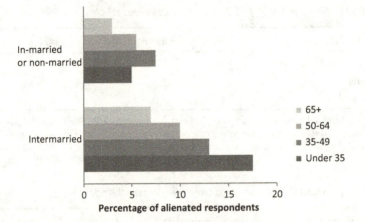

FIGURE 6.2. Alienation from Israel: In-Married and Intermarried, 2007 (From Cohen and Kelman, *Beyond Distancing*, p. 15. Reprinted with permission from Steven M. Cohen and Andrea and Charles Bronfman Philanthropies.)

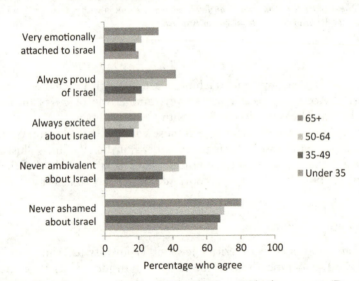

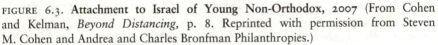

FIGURE 6.3. Attachment to Israel of Young Non-Orthodox, 2007 (From Cohen and Kelman, *Beyond Distancing*, p. 8. Reprinted with permission from Steven M. Cohen and Andrea and Charles Bronfman Philanthropies.)

respectively. To a significant extent this divide mirrors a wider polarization, as younger non-Orthodox Jews are much more likely to be unaffiliated and intermarried, while the Orthodox are the most likely to be in-married and affiliated. In both cases, the first group retains a strong sense of Jewish

TABLE 6.6. *Party Identification and Attachment to Israel, 2013 (%)*

	Very/Somewhat Attached	Not very/Not attached
GOP	84	15
DEM	65	35

Data from Pew Research Center[34]

peoplehood, which includes a strong sense of commitment to Jews worldwide, especially in Israel. In contrast, the second group has a weaker sense of Jewish peoplehood, a more individualistic Jewish identity, and consequently this group feels less obligated to Jews outside America, including Israel. According to some, this attachment gap signals that American Jews are gradually distancing themselves from Israel. This issue is addressed below.

ARE AMERICAN JEWS GROWING MORE DISTANT FROM ISRAEL?

The Distancing Thesis

Since the latter half of the 1980s many observers have claimed that American Jews are growing more distant from Israel. According to Steven Cohen and Ari Kelman,[35] distancing from Israel is related to generational change in the nature of American Jewish identity. In the past, American Jewish support for Israel was underwritten by the sense of belonging to a common people summed up in the old United Jewish Appeal slogan: "We Are One." Consequently it is no surprise that the younger generation of non-Orthodox Jews – which is more individualistic and less inclined to feel a strong sense of ethnically based Jewish peoplehood – is also less attached to Israel than older generations.[36]

This generational change in identity, it is argued, has been reinforced by a shift in generational experiences of Israel. The generations that grew up at the time of the Holocaust and the founding of the State, along with those whose defining experiences were the Six Day War and the Yom Kippur War, share an image of an embattled heroic peace-seeking Israel, a democratic and progressive David surrounded and mortally threatened by a malevolent and fanatical Goliath – the Arabs. In other words, the three factors that underlay the transformation of Zionism into the American Jewish consensus – a strong sense of Jewish peoplehood, a high level of threat perception, and an image of Israel as an expression of their liberal values – remained in place. In contrast, for those who came to maturity in the 1980s and after, things are different. Their defining experiences regarding Israel include both Lebanon Wars (1982, 2006) and both Palestinian intifadas (1987–1991, 2000–2005). These conflicts were perceived by many as morally and politically complex with Israel viewed as the stronger party, no longer under existential threat. In this vein, the founding editor of the Jewish magazine *Moment*, Leonard Fein, and a former editor of the *New Republic*, Peter Beinart, have argued that young liberal Jews have been turned off Israel due to the rise of the religious Right in Israel, hawkish Israeli policies towards the Palestinians, and the supposedly noncritical positions adopted towards these issues by the American Jewish establishment.[37]

Evidence for Distancing

In 1981 more than 80 percent of American Jews felt that Israel's destruction would be a personal tragedy; in 2007 just under two-thirds felt this way, while the number who disagreed almost trebled from about 10 percent to 28 percent. Moreover in 2007, less than half of Jews under the age of thirty-five felt that Israel's destruction would be a personal tragedy, compared to more than three-quarters of the over-65s (see Figure 6.4).[38] These numbers are reinforced by evidence from focus groups conducted in 2002 and reported in *Israel in the Age of Eminem*, which concluded that young Jewish adults' "association with Israel is frighteningly weak and ill-defined."[39]

In addition, polls consistently indicate that a majority of American Jews think Israelis are too nationalistic and militaristic.[40] Following the First Lebanon War, in 1983 surveys showed that nearly half of American Jews and American Jewish leaders were often troubled by Israeli government policies related to the Arab-Israeli conflict.[41] Similarly in 2005, another poll revealed that a majority is sometimes disturbed by Israeli policies; almost half is sometimes ashamed by those policies, and 39 percent are sometimes "alienated" by Israeli policies.[42] In 2010 there was a large gap in the responses of younger and older Jews to the flotilla incident, in which nine people died when Israel sought to prevent pro-Palestinian activists from breaking its naval blockade of Gaza. Among the over-60s, the incident made almost a third feel more attached to Israel and only 4 percent less attached. In contrast, among the 18- to 29-year-olds, 16 percent felt more attached and 16 percent less attached.[43] Meanwhile,

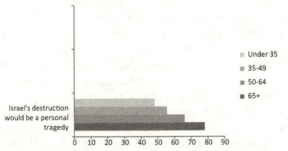

FIGURE 6.4. **Young Non-Orthodox – Percentage Agreeing That "the Destruction of Israel Would Be a Personal Tragedy"** (From Cohen and Kelman, *Beyond Distancing*, p. 9. Reprinted with permission from Steven M. Cohen Andrea and Charles Bronfman Philanthropies.)

focus groups conducted in 2009 indicated that many Reform Jews find Israel's policies towards liberal Jewish movements alienating.[44]

Trends in Jewish philanthropy have also been interpreted as indicating distancing.[45] In the 1990s, the community shifted its financial resources away from Israel, investing the majority of its money inside the U.S. Whereas in 1967, more than three-quarters of the federations' UJA campaign was earmarked for Israel; the proportion dropped to less than 50 percent in 1990 and to about a quarter in 2004.[46] At the same time, it is also more difficult to mobilize American Jews as a whole than in the past.[47] Membership in the largest Zionist organization, Hadassah, has fallen by 20 percent in recent decades from 385,000 to around 300,000. In 1987 the organized Jewish community succeeded in mobilizing an estimated 250,000 people to attend a rally in Washington, DC, in support of the right of Soviet Jewry to immigrate to Israel.[48] By contrast, in April 2002, more than a year after the start of the second intifada and at the height of the wave of suicide terror outrages, they managed to bring only a crowd of 50,000–100,000 to Washington for a rally in support of Israel.[49]

Evidence for Continued Attachment

On the other hand, there is strong evidence that American Jews continue to be strongly attached to Israel. According to the annual AJC surveys of American Jewish opinion, in the first decade of the twenty-first century nearly 75 percent consistently felt that caring about Israel (see Figure 6.5) was an important part of their being Jewish, and about the same percentage felt close or very close to Israel.[50] Moreover, an extensive 2010 survey found that in contrast to the focus groups reported in *Israel in the Age of Eminem*, American Jewish college students were very attached to Israel and their attitudes to Israel were closer to those of their parents than to non-Jewish students their age.[51]

Second, the expression of American Jewish attachment to Israel has always ebbed and flowed. It has always peaked in times of crisis and war: 1947–1948, 1967, and 1973. Yes, in the 1990s with the peace process underway, the American Jewish community did shift some of its resources and attention away from Israel. However, the collapse of the Oslo process, coupled with a massive wave of suicide terrorist attacks against Israelis, generated massive American Jewish solidarity with Israel. Given the sense of crisis, Israel became, once again, more central to the American Jewish agenda. Solidarity with Israel was evident at the 2001 AIPAC conference, which set new records for attendance and money raised for Israel.[52] AIPAC's membership soared from 55,000 to 100,000. Survey evidence indicated that 10 percent of Jews became more involved with Israel, 20 percent among the under-35s.[53] Attendance at the annual Salute to Israel Parade, which had been declining, shot up to record levels, with more than 100,000 participating and many more cheering from the sidelines.[54] During the Second Lebanon War in 2006, when Hezbollah

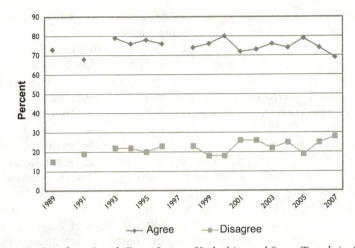

FIGURE 6.5. **Caring about Israel** (From Sasson, Kadushin, and Saxe, *Trends in American Jewish Attachment to Israel*, p. 12. Reprinted with permission from Theodore Sasson and the Cohen Center for Modern Jewish Studies.)

launched thousands of rockets against targets in northern Israel, the United Jewish Communities (UJC) pledged $350 million in emergency aid, and the annual General Assembly of the UJC shifted its agenda to focus on Israel.[55]

Third, the decline of large top-down, centralized organizations that directed fundraising and political advocacy has been compensated for by increased bottom-up direct engagement with Israel. Alongside the mainstream organizations, a spate of private organizations have sprung up that are playing a major role in advocacy, such as the Israel Project, Stand with Us, Israel 21C, the David Project, and Honest Reporting. Meanwhile, many more American Jews visit Israel and get their information about the country direct from English-language Israeli sources available over the Internet. American Jews have also developed direct transnational political ties with ideologically kin organizations in Israel, including direct philanthropic donations. For example, far-right parties in Israel have extensive ties with the ZOA, while American Friends of Peace Now and Meretz USA have extensive ties with their Israel counterparts.[56]

In parallel, the decline of Israel-based philanthropy via centralized communal organizations does not mean less money is being donated to Israel. In fact, this decline has been compensated for, as Jews increasingly give directly to projects and organizations in Israel.[57] Between 1990 and 2000, such donations increased by 400 percent, totaling more than $2 billion. Between 2001 and 2006 they increased by a further two-thirds. In 2008, the Israeli nonprofit sector collected an estimated $1.5 billion in contributions from foreign donors and foundations, most of it from American Jews.[58]

Fourth, increased criticism of Israeli policies does not necessarily indicate distancing. The Orthodox, who were most vociferous in criticism of left-wing

Israeli governments, were also the sector that felt closest to Israel.[59] On the other side of the religious spectrum, the Reform movement has become more Zionist. In 1978 Rabbi Eric Yoffie established the Association of Reform Zionists of America, and in 1997 the movement's Miami Platform determined that *aliyah* (immigration to Israel) is a very important means of fulfilling Jewish identity. Yoffie was President of the Union for Reform Judaism (1996–2012), and a strident critic of Israeli settlements. Thus, increased public criticism of Israeli policies does not represent distancing, but rather the replacement of a heroic idealized image of Israel with a more sober and mature form of engagement.[60]

Fifth, 80–90 percent consistently assert that Israelis are peace loving and democratic.[61] Despite the anguished response to the flotilla incident from some liberal Jewish commentators,[62] American Jews overwhelmingly blamed pro-Palestinian activists. For the overwhelming majority, including young Jews, the incident did not affect their feelings of attachment to Israel.[63] The American Jewish mainstream wishes Israel to continue to be both a Jewish and democratic state; this indicates a closeness to Israel, since maintaining this balance is the core consensual value of Jewish Israelis. The mainstream supports Israel as a homeland and safe haven for Jews. They support its maintaining a Jewish majority by encouraging Jewish immigration, preserving the Law of Return, and retaining national symbols that represent the Jewish majority. At the same time, they aspire to maximize Israel's liberal democratic character, and here there are criticisms of Israel, especially on the issue of religion and state.[64] This is nothing new; after all, a foundation of Brandeis's American Zionism was that Zion should be shaped by liberal values.

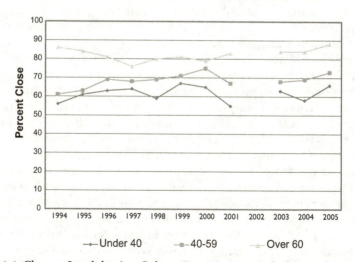

FIGURE 6.6. **Close to Israel, by Age Cohort** (From Sasson, Kadushin, and Saxe, *Trends in American Jewish Attachment to Israel*, p. 15. Reprinted with permission from Theodore Sasson and the Cohen Center for Modern Jewish Studies.)

Finally, according to Theodore Sasson and others,[65] the fact that older American Jews are far more attached to Israel than the under-35s does not indicate a generational decline in attachment. Rather it is related to life-cycle factors – as people get older, their outlook changes. Yes, surveys from the 1970s onward have indicated a consistent divide between the old and the young,[66] but the levels of attachment for each age cohort have remained stable (see Figure 6.6). If there was a process of distancing, one would expect the level of attachment of older generations to decline over time, yet this has not occurred. This seems to indicate the importance of life-cycle factors, like marriage and having children, on attachment to Israel. In this vein, analysis of AJC surveys from 2000 to 2005 indicated that among the non-Orthodox aged 18–39, those married with children were twice as likely to feel very close to Israel than the unmarried or childless married; the latter group were also 50 percent more likely to feel distant from Israel.[67]

Counteracting Distancing: The Rise of Orthodoxy and Increased Travel to Israel

Overall, American Jews are not distancing from Israel. There has been a process of generational decline in Israel attachment primarily among the non-Orthodox, the unaffiliated, and especially the intermarried, which derives from a decline in the sense of Jewish peoplehood. However, this generational decline is being offset by the growing proportion of young Jews who are Orthodox and the impact of the massive increase in travel to Israel among the young non-Orthodox. This is so even after controlling for self-selection by the level of Jewish involvement. The travel effect (see Table 6.7) has been driven by Birthright Israel (aka *Taglit*), which brought more than 200,000 young American Jews to Israel as part of a peer group trip in the first decade of the twenty-first century. In 2012 alone, 45,000 young American Jews completed the online registration process.[68] Birthright participants were 23 percent more likely than nonparticipants to report feeling "very much" connected to Israel, and 40 percent of participants made a return trip to Israel.[69] Return visits are significant, because for those who visited Israel twice, the age-related gap in Israel attachment disappears altogether.[70] Travel to Israel also increases the likelihood of taking Israel's side in the conflict, for example, regarding the flotilla incident (see Table 6.8).[71]

In fact, at the end of the first decade of the twenty-first century, there are signs of an increased connection with Israel among American Jewish leaders. Thus, among young adults in leadership positions in the Jewish community, 56 percent are alumni of long-term Israel programs, whereas only 30 percent of older leaders spent four months or longer in Israel. Similarly the proportion of young leaders who described their facility with Hebrew as excellent or good was twice as large as among older leaders (48 versus 21 percent).[72] Clearly, then, there are political consequences to the demographics of Israel attachment. These are explored below.

TABLE 6.7. *Travel to Israel and Attachment to Israel among Under-35 Non-Orthodox Jews, 2007 (%)*

	High	Low
Never visited Israel	19	42
One trip	34	17
Two or more trips	52	9

Data from Synovate, Inc.[73]

TABLE 6.8. *Travel to Israel and Blame for 2010 Flotilla Incident (%)*

	Blamed Pro-Palestinian Activists	Didn't Know Whom to Blame
Never visited Israel	53	37
Visited Israel	70	22

Data from Knowledge Networks (KN)[74]

POLITICAL CONSEQUENCES

The Jewish Vote

One way in which Jewish attachment to Israel has traditionally had a political impact is in presidential elections. Although American Jews make up perhaps 4 percent of the national electorate, their electoral significance, especially in presidential elections, is magnified for three reasons. First, their voter turnout is much higher than the American average. Second, they are geographically concentrated in more populous states that counts for more in the Electoral College system. Third, the Jewish vote is important in what are often considered to be swing states.[75] In ideological terms, Jews are the most liberal of all religious groups in America, more liberal than even the religiously unaffiliated. In the first decade of the twenty-first century, around 45 percent identified as liberal while about a fifth identified as conservative, roughly the opposite of the responses among the general public.[76] In parallel, Jews are also more strongly supportive of the Democratic Party than any other religious group. More than half of American Jews identify with the Democrats, less than a fifth with the Republicans.[77] That leaves a swing factor of up to 30 percent in the Jewish vote, and the Israel factor has been a key influence on this swing vote, notably in 1972, 1980, and 1992.[78] What effect will the shifts identified above in the demographics of Israel attachment have on the "Israel swing factor"?

In 2008, surveys determined that for more than half of American Jews, Israel was important or very important in determining their voting intensions in the presidential election. However, Israel ranked only eighth out of fifteen issues in importance as a presidential election consideration for Jews as a whole, with only 15 percent choosing Israel as one of their top three issues. Given that Obama's pro-Israel credentials were a campaign issue, it is significant than only 15 percent, as opposed to the maximum swing of 30 percent, thought that Israel was an issue. In that same 2008 survey, the over-65s were nearly twice as likely to consider Israel as a key issue as the under-35.[79] The fact that the older Jews view Israel as a more important issue may indicate that the Israel swing factor is in decline, especially as younger Jewish voters identify with the Democrats more than their parents and grandparents.[80]

There appeared to be some evidence of this in 2008. In the wake of doubts expressed about Obama's pro-Israel credentials, he tried to reassure American Jews by visiting Israel and declaring himself a friend of Israel. But he did less than previous candidates; notably, he did not promise to move the American embassy to Jerusalem. The Obama campaign was also willing to make critical comments about the Likud and AIPAC – stating that neither defined what it means to be pro-Israel[81] – that were bound to offend some Israel supporters. Evidently, Obama calculated that he did not need to please all of those who rank the Israel factor highly, as many would vote Republican anyway. Indeed, it is likely that a large part of the 20 percent Jewish swing to Obama was to do with the economy and the selection of Sarah Palin as the Republican candidate for vice president, which American Jews did not like because of her conservatism on domestic issues, despite her strong support for Israel.[82]

On the other hand, a survey conducted for the National Jewish Democratic Council found that a candidate's support for Israel can create a potential 42-point swing in the vote.[83] Still, only brazen disregard for the pro-Israel sentiments of most American Jews could exact such a political price. For as both the director of the Republican Jewish Coalition, Matt Brooks, and the acting director of the National Jewish Democratic Council, Aaron Keyak, admitted in 2013,[84] Israel is primarily a threshold issue for American Jews. In other words, so long as a candidate is viewed as sufficiently pro-Israel (even if the candidate is not viewed as the most pro-Israel), the bulk of the Jewish electorate will decide their vote based on other issues.

Nonetheless, the Israel factor does appear to have retained influence. Thus, the 2010 AJC survey indicated growing Jewish concern with President Obama's handling of U.S.-Israeli relations, with an almost even split on the question. In parallel, for the first time, Jewish support for Obama fell by *more* than the national average. By mid-2012, Obama's standing on U.S.-Israel relations had largely recovered. Nonetheless, the Israel factor did seem to impact on the Jewish vote, though not in a way that was important in determining the overall result. Thus, between the 2008 and 2012 elections, Obama's share of the popular vote fell by 2 percent, while his share of the Jewish vote fell by 5–9 percent.[85]

There are also some indications that the Israel factor may actually increase in importance. First, Birthright participants are much more likely to consider

Israel an important issue in a presidential election. Second, there are the Orthodox, who are growing demographically. In 2008, 80 percent of the Orthodox under thirty-five viewed Israel as a top issue affecting their vote.[86] Since 2004 a majority of the Orthodox have voted for the Republican candidate in presidential elections. To some extent the swing to the Republicans is part of a broader trend in which conservative religious groups have come to increasingly identify with the Republicans. However, this is by no means the whole story. In congressional and local elections, where foreign policy is much less of an issue, the Orthodox often vote Democrat. Moreover, Orthodox disapproval of Obama's handling of U.S.-Israeli relations in 2010–2011 was more than 25 percentage points higher than among Americans Jews in general. This suggests that the Orthodox swing away from the Democrats in presidential elections has a lot to do with the perception that the Republican candidate is better for Israel.[87]

Pro-Israel Advocacy

Aside from voting, American Jewish attachment to Israel also has a political impact by serving as a recruiting sergeant for pro-Israel advocacy and lobbying. The declining interest of the younger generation in mainstream Jewish organizations and mass demonstrations could indicate a weakening of the foundations of pro-Israel activism. AIPAC itself is not too concerned even if fewer Jews overall can be mobilized, since its membership is larger than ever and it believes that its large core of supporters is what counts politically.[88] "Politics," as one leading professional working in a pro-Israel advocacy organization, told me, "is about those who turn up." In any case, there are indications that since the onset of the second intifada, the number of pro-Israel activists has actually risen, along with an expansion in the number of start-up pro-Israel advocacy organizations. On top of this, there is the impact over the last decade of increased travel to Israel. Thus, participants in a Birthright trip, subsequent to their return, were two to three times more likely than nonparticipants to be involved in Israel-related activities on campus.[89]

Pro-Israel activism is not simply a function of American Jewish attachment to Israel. It is also affected by Israeli actions and policies toward American Jewry. Israeli actions have at times discouraged non-Orthodox Jews from getting involved in Israel advocacy because of the State's approach to non-Orthodox streams of Judaism. Thus, at the height of the "Who is a Jew" controversy in 1988, leading American Jewish organizations, including Hadassah, threatened to stop pro-Israel lobbying unless the Israeli government reversed its position on the issue. If Israeli governments give in to their Ultra-Orthodox coalition partners on issues related to "Who is a Jew," this could have serious political consequences, reducing the willingness of non-Orthodox American Jews to be politically active on behalf of Israel. Since the Ultra-Orthodox are the fastest-growing sector of Israeli society, this issue could become more contentious in the future. Pro-Israel activism is also affected by American Jewish attitudes toward the Arab-Israeli conflict and peace process. This is examined in detail in the next chapter.

CONCLUSION

From the 1980s onward, the declining fear of anti-Semitism, the growing strength of the State of Israel, and challenges to the image of Israel as a bastion of liberal values have led American Jews to become far more willing to criticize Israeli actions publicly. However, none of these changes in of themselves decreased attachment to Israel. In contrast, the decline in the sense of Jewish peoplehood did decrease attachment to Israel. Still, this decline has not been uniform. Older, more Orthodox, and affiliated Jews tend to retain a stronger sense of Jewish peoplehood and a great sense of attachment to Israel. Intermarried Jews and younger non-Orthodox Jews have a weaker sense of Jewish peoplehood and attachment to Israel. However, this distancing trend among the non-Orthodox has been offset by the growth of Orthodoxy and by increased visits of the young American Jews to Israel through the Birthright Israel program. Overall, American Jews are not distancing themselves from Israel. Yet even as American Jewish attachment has been sustained, the nature of that attachment has changed. In turn, this has changed the way in which the community relates to the Arab-Israeli conflict, which is the focus of the next chapter.

7

American Jews and the Peace Process:
Divided We Stand?

AIPAC's great success derives from its capacity to define what it means to be pro-Israel.

—Liz Shrayer, AIPAC political director, 1983–1994[1]

AIPAC doesn't speak for the entire Jewish community.

—Joseph Biden, vice presidential nominee, 2008[2]

INTRODUCTION

For many years American Jewry stood united behind Israel in its struggle against the Arab states and the PLO. This unity found institutional expression in the pro-Israel lobby spearheaded by AIPAC. However, in the wake of the first intifada, vociferous debate over Israeli policy stirred within the community, and in 2008, amid much fanfare and controversy, a new dovish pro-Israel lobby was established: J Street. It challenged the dominant approach of AIPAC and the mainstream and claimed to represent a large slice of American Jewish opinion. This seemed to signal unprecedented Jewish divisions over the Arab-Israeli conflict. On the other hand, the collapse of the peace process in 2000 was blamed on the Arab side by the overwhelming majority of American Jews. Subsequently, AIPAC's annual conference set new records for attendance and fund-raising.[3] Renowned academics John Mearsheimer and Stephen Walt claimed that the pro-Israel lobby was all-powerful.[4]

This apparent contradiction begs the following questions: Is American Jewry increasingly divided over the peace process? What changes have taken place in their approach to the conflict? And what are the political implications of these changes? This chapter answers these questions in two parts. The first part deals with American Jewish attitudes towards the conflict. The second part deals with the approach of the organized Jewish community.

AMERICAN JEWISH OPINION AND DISCOURSE OVER THE PEACE PROCESS

In general, American Jews have supported peace negotiations between Israel and its neighbors. In the 1970s and 1980s they were generally more willing than Israelis, *in principle*, to support territorial compromise in the context of a peace treaty and security for Israel.[5] Yet paradoxically most thought Israeli policies *in practice* were about right.[6] Whatever their preferences, the bulk of American Jews did not take a strong stand on these issues. As Charles Liebman explained, "Because Israel is a symbol, its particular policies are not very important to American Jews."[7] Since the late 1980s this situation has gradually changed. Whereas in the 1980s approximately a third reported having no opinion in response to survey questions about the future of the West Bank and Gaza, since the early 1990s that figure has fallen to about 10 percent.[8]

Preferences on the Core Issues: Palestinian Statehood, Settlements, and Jerusalem

The American Jewish Committee (AJC) has been conducting an annual survey of American Jewish opinion for many years.[9] They have consistently asked questions regarding three of the main substantive issues of the peace process: Palestinian statehood, settlements, and Jerusalem. The answers to these questions are summarized in Table 7.1. Between 1993 and 2010, a majority consistently opposed handing over part of Jerusalem to the Palestinians, but a significant minority was willing to do so, with the number rising from 30 percent in 1993 to 44 percent in 2001, in the wake of Israel's willingness to divide the city during peace talks, before falling back again when the peace process collapsed.[10] Nonetheless, a majority has generally supported the creation of a Palestinian state "in the current context," though a large minority has been opposed;[11] after Hamas took control of Gaza, support for a Palestinian state eroded.[12] On settlements, a majority have consistently expressed a willingness to withdraw from some settlements, though at least a third has been consistently unwilling to dismantle any settlements. An extensive 2013 survey by Pew indicates the prevalence of negative attitudes toward the settlements, with a plurality believing that settlements hurt Israeli security.[13]

When asked in polls conducted by dovish Jewish organizations if they would support the creation of a Palestinian state and withdrawal from settlements in the context of a permanent agreement that guaranteed Israel's peace and security, support for a Palestinian state rose to 80–90 percent,[14] and a plurality supported withdrawal from *most* settlements, though opposition to a divided

TABLE 7.1. *American Jewish Opinion on the Peace Process, 1993–2010 (%)*
1. *In current situation, do you favor or oppose the **establishment of a Palestinian state?***

	favor	oppose
2007–2010	48	43
2000–2006	55	39
1998–1999	43	48
1993–1994	55	32

2. *In the framework of a permanent peace with the Palestinians, should Israel be willing to compromise on the **status of Jerusalem** as a united city under Israeli jurisdiction?*

	Yes	No
2007–2010	36	59
1999–2006	40	54
1993–1998	33	61

3. *As part of a permanent settlement with the Palestinians, should Israel be willing to dismantle all, some, or none of the **Jewish settlements in the West Bank?***

	All	Some	None
2009–2010	8	54	35
2000–2005	12	53	33
1995–1999	5	52	40

Data from American Jewish Committee's annual surveys of American Jewish Opinion[15]

Jerusalem remained, when it was addressed as a stand-alone issue.[16] Still, when asked about a *package* similar to the Clinton Parameters for a permanent agreement including the division of Jerusalem, three-quarters endorsed it.[17]

How can the difference between this apparently dovish consensus and the divisions apparent in the AJC polls be explained? Since the 1980s there was always a large gap between what American Jews were prepared to agree to immediately and what they were prepared to agree to in the context of a peace agreement that guaranteed Israeli security. The consensus in favor of a Palestinian state and withdrawal from many settlements holds so long as American Jews really believe that genuine peace and security will ensue for Israel. So the key question is whether they think there is a partner for peace.

TABLE 7.2. *"The Goal of the Arabs Is Not the Return of Occupied Territories But Rather the Destruction of Israel"*

	Agree (%)	Disagree (%)
2001–2010	77	19
1994–1995	53	39
1993	42	50

Data from American Jewish Committee annual surveys of American Jewish Opinion[18]

In this regard, during periods of conflict negative beliefs about Arab intentions increased and the willingness for compromise declined.[19] This effect was most noticeable after the 1991 Gulf War, during the course of which the PLO sided with Iraq, whose SCUD missiles struck at Israel. Since the collapse of the peace process in 2000, American Jews have become more skeptical about the chances of reaching a permanent peace, with the proportion of those distrusting Arab intentions rising to about three-quarters throughout the first decade of the new millennium. (See Table 7.2.)

Even when the centrist Israeli government led by Ehud Olmert was negotiating with the Palestinian leader Mahmoud Abbas in 2007, more than half thought that the negotiations would not lead to peace, compared to just a third who were more optimistic.[20] Overall, there was a strong correlation between those who believed that the goal of the Arabs was the return of territories rather than the destruction of Israel, (about a fifth of those surveyed by the AJC) and those that were more willing to support Israeli compromises.[21] This strongly suggests that a major factor inhibiting many American Jews from supporting compromises *in practice* that they support in theory is a lack of faith in Arab intentions.

Attitudes to Israeli Policy: Right and Left

In 1993, immediately following the signing of the Oslo Accords, 84 percent of American Jews supported Oslo, and only 9 percent opposed.[22] There were two main reasons for the extremely high level of support. First of all, Americans Jews had previously favored negotiating with the PLO if it recognized Israel and abandoned terrorism; this the PLO formally did in the Oslo Accords. Second, the Accords were initiated by the Israeli government, headed by the military hero of the Six Day War and former ambassador to the U.S., Yitzhak Rabin, without external pressure; this, too, served to widen support. The importance of an action being taken freely by the Israeli government was evident again in 2005, when 62 percent supported the Disengagement from Gaza, which included the evacuation of all eight thousand settlers and all the settlements there; only 23 percent were opposed.[23] In contrast, when the initiative for compromise on settlements came from the U.S. administration, the position of the Jewish public was more equivocal and divided. Thus, a March 2009 poll sponsored by J Street indicated that 60 percent opposed expanding West Bank settlements.[24] However, in a September 2009 AJC poll, only 40 percent supported Obama's call for a settlement freeze, with 51 percent opposed.[25]

In general, Labor has been more popular than Likud.[26] Approximately 60 percent of American Jews preferred Labor in the 1996 elections, and a larger majority preferred Barak over Netanyahu in the 1999 elections.[27] Still, about 60 percent consistently had a favorable view of Netanyahu as prime minister and thought he was handling the peace process well. In contrast, in 1997 only 24 percent had a favorable view of Arafat. In March 1999, 43 percent thought Netanyahu was not doing enough to implement the Wye Agreements, but 88 percent thought that the Palestinian Authority was not doing enough.[28] In other words, even if the majority of American Jews would not have voted for Netanyahu and harbored criticisms of his policies, he retained their support. Indeed, when Netanyahu returned to power in 2009, 60 percent of American Jews felt warmth for him, only 1 percent less than received by the leader of the center-left opposition, Tzippi Livni.[29]

Again, part of the reason for this situation lies in American Jews' understanding of who is to blame for the collapse of the peace process in 2000. The unprecedented concessions offered by Barak on the one hand and Arafat's rejection of those compromises and role in fanning violence during the second intifada on the other hand led American Jews to unequivocally blame the Palestinians for the collapse of the peace process. Thus, in the 2002 AJC survey, 80 percent thought that the Palestinians were responsible for the violence.[30] A similar proportion approved of Operation Cast Lead against Hamas in Gaza while holding Hamas responsible for the violence. Against this backdrop, in 2010, 91 percent thought that Israel was doing more to bring peace than the Palestinians.[31] Still, when the focus of attention shifted to negotiations between the center-right Netanyahu government and the relatively moderate Abbas, attitudes shifted somewhat. Thus in 2013, a plurality of American Jews did not think that the Netanyahu government was making a sincere effort to make peace. However, even then, over three times as many thought that the Israeli government was sincere as compared to the Palestinian leadership.[32]

Criticism and Pressure

AJC polls demonstrate that in principle, a majority of between half and two-thirds consistently believe that American Jews should support the policy of the elected government of Israel regardless of an individual's view. On the other hand, a similar majority has consistently supported the right to criticize Israeli policy.[33] Evidently the American Jewish public respects the right to freedom of speech and dissent while continuing to identify with the approach of the mainstream pro-Israel lobby. This conclusion is reinforced by the fact that from

1992 to 2008, 66 to 83 percent of American Jews thought that the U.S. should support Israel over the Palestinians.[34]

Then there is the vexed issue of U.S. pressure on Israel to promote the peace process. Traditionally, American Jews opposed such pressure.[35] However, a 1998 AJC poll showed them almost evenly divided on the issue, while an *Israel Policy Forum* survey demonstrated that three-quarters were in favor of pressure on *both* sides.[36] Polls conducted by J Street (2008–2010) also showed that more than 70 percent were willing to support pressure on both sides to help achieve peace. Taken together, these polls demonstrate that American Jews remained more or less evenly divided on the *theoretical* question of whether the U.S. should publicly criticize or pressure Israel – *assuming* it was Israel that was blocking a peace agreement from being reached.[37]

However, these results overstate the willingness to pressure Israel *in practice* because, as noted above, American Jews overwhelmingly believed that the Arab side has been the main block on peace. Thus, by margins of 60 to 28 percent and 48 to 14 percent, a large majority thought that *in practice* the U.S. should generally support the Israeli government position.[38] In any case, there is only majority support for pressure when it is applied on both sides by a president who is viewed as sympathetic to Israel, and only if there is perceived to be a real chance for advancing peace.

AMERICAN JEWISH ATTITUDES: DISSECTING DEMOGRAPHIC DISTINCTIONS

The Orthodox are consistently far more hawkish than any other demographic. Indeed, Orthodoxy is by far the most significant variable determining opinion to the peace process.[39] About two-thirds of the Orthodox were unwilling to compromise on Jerusalem, settlements, or a Palestinian state, compared to about a quarter of Conservative, Reform, and "Just Jews."[40] Over half of the Orthodox opposed the 2005 Disengagement from Gaza, while two-thirds of the non-Orthodox supported it.[41] These differences among the Jewish public were reflected in the positions of the respective movements' rabbis.[42]

Political ideology also plays a major role in explaining divisions of opinion. Analysis of the AJC surveys from 2000 to 2005 demonstrates that liberals were twice as likely as conservatives to support a Palestinian state and compromise on Jerusalem and settlements.[43] Similarly, in a 2010 survey, 62 percent of conservatives opposed dismantling any settlements, compared to a third of moderates and 13 percent of the liberals.[44] To a significant degree, religious Orthodoxy and political conservatism reinforce each other, since the Orthodox are much more likely to be politically conservative than the non-Orthodox. The same overlap exists regarding party identification. Thus, while a plurality of Jewish Republicans thought that settlements helps Israeli security, a majority of Jewish Democrats thought that settlements hurt Israeli security (see Table 7.3).[45]

TABLE 7.3. *Settlements and Israeli Security, 2013 (%)*

	Helps	Hurts	Makes No Difference
All Jews	17	44	29
Orthodox	34	16	39
Conservative	23	36	30
Reform	23	50	26
No denomination	13	48	31

Data from Pew Research Center[46]

This opinion divide was also reflected in focus groups conducted in 2008.[47] In these discussions three discourses were apparent: center, Left, and Right. Notwithstanding increasing polarization at the margins, the overwhelmingly dominant discourse was that of the center. The centrists were deeply affected by the collapse of the peace process in 2000. As they viewed it, the Palestinians were offered everything but walked away from the deal. For centrists the main problem was the lack of a partner on the Palestinian/Arab side. They did not view this as inevitable, but as a function of political choices made by the Palestinian leadership and the promotion of vitriolic anti-Israel themes in Palestinian educational institutions and more widely in their discourse, including the depiction of Jews in anti-Semitic terms and the production of school maps that do not show Israel. With the collapse of the Oslo process, discussion of historical and religious rights had been marginalized; the issue of Israeli security and whether any peace agreement would be secure and lasting became the primary focus of concern. There remained a willingness to make major territorial concessions in principle, but the main issue was whether the Palestinian side was really prepared to accept and honor a peace deal; on this the mainstream was skeptical. Consequently, while they would have liked to see the U.S. engaged in mediating the conflict, that view was balanced by a simultaneous desire for the U.S. to be supportive of Israel against her enemies. These mainstream themes were clearly dominant in the Reform, Conservative, and unaffiliated groups.

Meanwhile, the left-wing discourse was prevalent among members of Reconstructionist synagogues, college students, and members of Jewish peace organizations. They placed a much greater degree of blame on Israel both for the conflict in general and for the collapse of the peace process in 2000. They emphasized that Israel must immediately withdraw from the West Bank in order to protect its Jewish majority and democratic character. Several speakers contended that, as a consequence of the occupation, Israel does not presently qualify as a democracy.[48] For some, like Peter Beinart, this critique is part of a broader call for American Jews to not automatically support any Israeli government, but rather to take sides inside Israel by supporting liberals against the Right. Beinart views this call as in the tradition of Brandeis's American

Zionism, which emphasized that support for Zionism was as much to do with progressive liberal values, as with a sense of Jewish peoplehood. Beinart and others also tend to think that the mainstream discourse exaggerates the level of security threat Israel faces.[49] These types of views were likely to be the dominant voice in the left-wing Jewish periodical *Tikkun*, run by Michael Lerner. Another major source informing this outlook is the liberal Israeli newspaper *Haaretz*, which has had an online English language edition since the late 1990s. While anti-/post-Zionism is marginal among identifying Jews, it has been much discussed within the community, due to Jewish intellectuals promoting this stance in mainstream publications. One notable example is Tony Judt's article "Israel: The Alternative," which appeared in the *New York Review of Books*. It called the very idea of a Jewish state anachronistic, while calling for the dissolution of the Zionist enterprise.[50]

Finally, there is the right-wing discourse, to which the Orthodox are primarily drawn. The hallmark of this discourse was its utter rejection of the possibility of reaching a secure peace settlement with the Palestinians under any terms. As one participant put it, "I see very little difference between the Palestinians' attitude toward Jews and Israel, and Hitler's attitude."[51] Such a hawkish outlook is predominant. The *Jewish Press* strongly opposed the Oslo process in the 1990s; one article compared the Rabin government to a "Judenrat" handing over Jews to be killed by Arafat.[52] Many Orthodox Jews' opposition was informed by their belief that was wrong to cede territory for national and religious reasons. Many have spent a gap year in Israel studying in religious seminaries run by the followers of Rabbi Abraham Kook, who form the ideological backbone of the settler movement in Israel.[53] Still, since 2000, the arguments presented by the Orthodox in focus groups were grounded less on these claims and more on the perception that the idea of peace was a dangerous illusion.[54]

Resolving the Unity/Disunity Paradox

In one sense then, American Jews are deeply divided about the conflict. They have divergent perspectives regarding the degree of compromise Israel should make in principle and the degree to which the U.S. should pressure Israel to achieve peace. These differences are informed primarily by political ideology and religious Orthodoxy, and they are reflected in vigorous debate about these issues in the media, and increasingly within Jewish organizational life, as we will see in the next section. However, in a deeper sense there is still a large mainstream consensus regarding the conflict. Ideologically, American Jews remain very strongly committed to the Zionist idea of Israel as a Jewish and democratic state. On this, there is no difference between the denominations. More than 90 percent of Orthodox, Conservative, and Reform Jews back the idea that the Palestinians should recognize Israel as a Jewish state in a final peace agreement.[55] While on the strategic level, the Palestinians are viewed as overwhelmingly responsible for the lack of peace. Crucially, were American Jews to believe that a partner for peace existed that would ensure that Israel obtained true peace and security, then there would be consensual support for the establishment of a Palestinian state and the removal of a great many settlements. These underlying elements of consensus significantly constrain the intensity of ideological divisions.

THE ORGANIZED JEWISH COMMUNITY AND THE PEACE PROCESS, 1973–2000: FROM CONSENSUS TO PLURALISM

In the interwar period, American Jewry's lobbying efforts for Zionism were hampered by internal divisions. However, by the 1950s a more coordinated, centralized structure emerged as support for Israel became part of a cross-communal consensus. There are now several large mainstream American Jewish organizations that lobby for Israel: notably, the AJC, the Anti-Defamation League (ADL), the Jewish Council of Public Affairs (JCPA), the Conference of Presidents of Major American Jewish Organizations, and AIPAC. JCPA and the Conference of Presidents are umbrella organizations that operate on the basis of consensus. AIPAC is the most important pro-Israel organization; unlike the others, its agenda is solely focused on Israel. It has one hundred thousand dues-paying members and holds an annual policy conference that has often draws half the members of Congress.

Until the late 1980s the dominant approach within the organized Jewish community was one of consensual solidarity. Widespread support for Israel was channeled via large, centralized, communal institutions that focused on securing foreign aid and preventing pressure on Israel. The approach entailed the acceptance of Israeli political leadership through an internal communal consensus that presented a unified public line in support of Israeli policies in public. Internal disagreements and criticisms of Israeli policy were aired only in private. As ADL head Abe Foxman put it, "Israeli democracy should decide; American Jews should support."[56] The norm of consensual solidarity was evident when the right-wing Likud first came to power in Israel in 1977. At that time, a delegation of the top American Jewish leaders visited Israel. All the delegates opposed the construction of settlements promoted by Likud, but no one spoke out.[57] However, by the 1990s a shift was taking place in American Jewry's approach to Israel in the context of the peace process away from a centrally mediated, unified, consensual, deferential approach toward a more direct, polarized, pluralistic, assertive approach. American Jewish solidarity with Israel remains strong, but by the 1990s it was shifting from consensual solidarity to a more pluralistic form of solidarity.

The norms of consensual solidarity were first challenged in 1973 with the formation of *Breira* (Hebrew for "choice"). Though avowedly Zionist, it bucked the Israeli consensus at the time by publicly supporting the creation of a Palestinian state. It also challenged the taboo on criticizing Israeli policy publicly. Breira quickly disappeared, but other organizations such as New Jewish Agenda and Americans for Peace Now were formed that adopted similar positions, though all of this occurred at the periphery of the organized community.[58]

The first major incident affecting the mainstream occurred during the 1982 Lebanon War, when established American Jewish leaders expressed public criticism of Israeli policy. A more sustained assault on consensual solidarity followed the outbreak of the first intifada in December 1987. The leaders of tens of Jewish organizations placed a newspaper advertisement informing Likud prime minister Yitzhak Shamir that while they continued to support Israel, they opposed his policies. Forceful attempts were made to pass antisettlement resolutions in the JCPA.[59] Seymour Reich, the outgoing chairman of the Presidents Conference, publicly condemned settlements.[60]

Things became especially heated in the wake of the George H. W. Bush administration's demand that Israel freeze settlement activity in return for a U.S. government guarantee on $10 billion of loans designed to facilitate the absorption of a million Jewish immigrants from the former Soviet Union. AIPAC and the other mainstream organizations, including those personally opposed to settlements, dutifully lobbied against the linkage. But after having failed, Shoshanna Cardin of the Presidents Conference publicly criticized the Israeli finance minister for stating that settlements were more important than loan guarantees, and even Abe Foxman criticized the Likud government for its lack of realism and its insensitivity to embarrassing American Jews.[61]

With the rise of the Labor party to power in 1992 and the onset of the Oslo process in 1993, the American Jewish debate over the peace process became far more vociferous. This involved not only criticism of Israeli policy from the Left and the Right, but it also involved lobbying the American government to adopt policies *opposed* by the Israeli government. Between 1993 and 1996, right-wing American Jewish organizations such as the ZOA, Americans for a Safe Israel, American Friends of Likud, and the Jewish Institute for National Security (JINSA) lobbied in the US *against* Israeli government policies. For example, in 1994 the ZOA successfully lobbied Congress to institute the Specter-Shelby Amendment regarding U.S. aid to the Palestinian Authority (PA). Both the Israeli government and AIPAC opposed the amendment.[62]

Subsequently, between 1996 and 1999 American Jewish liberal groups such as the newly formed Israel Policy Forum (IPF) and Americans for Peace Now (APN) gained influence with the Clinton administration, and they lobbied for U.S. pressure on the Netanyahu government to push forward the peace process. In the wake of the decision to construct the settlement of Har Homa in Jerusalem, even a mainstream representative umbrella organization, the National Jewish Community Relations Advisory Council (NJCRAC) passed a resolution urging the Israeli government to show "maximum restraint" on settlements by calling for a freeze and an end to housing subsidies in the settlements. Other mainstream Reform and Conservative leaders, as well as former leading figures within AIPAC and the Presidents Conference, also backed the administration's call for a settlement freeze.[63]

Explaining the Shift from Consensual to Pluralistic Solidarity

As is evident above, in the 1990s the conventional, centrally mediated, unified, consensual, and deferential approach eroded, as a more direct, diverse, and assertive approach became more prevalent. Organized American Jewry continued to show solidarity with Israel, but there was a shift from the norms of consensual solidarity to a more pluralistic form of solidarity. Four factors lay behind this change.

First, there was the influence of political and strategic changes in the Middle East. When the Arab world had been implacably opposed to Israel's existence, debate about what Israel should be willing to surrender for peace was largely mute, since there did not appear to be any realistic chance of peace in any case. However, as the peace process took off, it began to generate a debate about how serious these moves were and what price was worth paying. This debate started in Israel in earnest before it reached American Jewry, but eventually American Jews also became involved, having been influenced by the different positions adopted by Left and Right in Israel. As the Israeli debate polarized during the 1980s, it became easier for American Jews to disagree with Israeli government policy while remaining identified with significant groups in Israel itself. The willingness to break with the consensus was strongly reinforced in the 1990s when Israel reversed long-standing policies regarding the PLO and withdrawal from the Golan. For years Arafat had been compared to Hitler and the Golan declared to be of vital strategic importance. It was not so easy for many American Jews to turn on a dime and support diametrically opposite policies.

Second, there is the influence of globalization, especially the communications revolution. This magnified the effect of debate in Israel as American Jews became more able to easily access diverse Israeli opinions over the Internet.[64] Even before then, the increasing ability of the American media to broadcast on television images of Israeli military actions and the resultant civilian casualties during the First Lebanon War and, more important, the first intifada, supplied dovish critics of Likud policy with increased ammunition and legitimacy.[65]

Third, there is the impact of Israeli behavior toward American Jewry. The crises over "Who is a Jew" and the Pollard affair severely challenged the idealized image of the Israel that could do no wrong, and subsequently American Jews were less willing to accept Israel's political lead unquestioningly.[66]

Finally, there are the changes in nature of younger Jews' attachment to Israel, discussed in the previous chapter. Young non-Orthodox and nonestablishment leaders tend not to view Israel or American Jews as under serious threat, and consequently they do not identify with the established American Jewish defense organizations like AIPAC, the ADL, and the AJC, which embody the norm of consensual solidarity that arose in the wake of the Holocaust. Instead, those with progressive and/or expressive orientations seek to promote their values in Israel itself, and this involves taking sides in Israeli politics, notably concerning the peace process.[67]

INSTITUTIONAL POLARIZATION IN THE TWENTY-FIRST CENTURY: CAN THE CENTER HOLD?

Since the late 1980s centrifugal forces have been increasingly eroding the political and institutional coherence of the pro-Israel lobby. The question remains as to the extent of institutional polarization over Israel. In particular, three issues need to be addressed. First, is the norm of consensual solidarity weakening within the mainstream? Second, has the conventional lobby developed a tilt to the ideological right? And third, is the left-wing lobby drifting away from the center and the Zionist consensus toward post-Zionism?

The Weakening of Consensual Solidarity

The growth of ideological divisions over Israel has been institutionalized in the development of left- and right-wing pro-Israel lobbying organizations alongside the conventional mainstream organizations. On the Left there is Americans for Peace Now, founded in the 1980s; Israel Policy Forum, founded in the 1990s; and J Street, founded in 2008, which as of 2010 incorporates *Brit Tzedek v'Shalom*.[68]

Of these, J Street is the most important. Just eighteen months after its establishment, J Street's national conference drew more than 1,500 supporters and featured a keynote address from James Jones, the national security advisor, and a gala dinner attended by forty-four members of Congress. These organizations share the positions of the Zionist Left in Israel. They oppose Israel's occupation of the West Bank, favor a division of Jerusalem, and strongly support the establishment of a Palestinian state. They also favor strong U.S. diplomatic engagement to advance the peace process even if this involves pressure on the Israeli government. As one Brit Tzedek activist put it: "I distinguish between support for Israel and support for Israel's government."[69] Meanwhile, among the right-wing organizations are Americans for a Safe Israel, American Friends of Likud, JINSA, and, since the early 1990s, the ZOA.[70] They share the positions of the Israeli Right. As such they support settlements and Israel's control of the West Bank, and oppose the establishment of a Palestinian state, for a mixture of nationalist and security reasons. They tend to regard the Palestinians not as potential partners for peace but as implacable foes of Israel, and they are highly suspicious of U.S. diplomatic engagement in the peace process.

By publicly criticizing and lobbying against the Israeli government and by speaking and operating at cross-purposes to the conventional lobby, these ideological lobbies have eroded three central elements of consensual solidarity, namely, public support for the policy of the Israeli government, community consensus, and speaking with a unified voice. Since the 1990s, they have attracted increased attention and they play a significant role. Still it is important not to exaggerate their significance.[71] They are less popular, smaller, and less powerful than the mainstream organizations. Even according to a poll sponsored by J Street, a plurality of American Jews agreed that the established Jewish organizations represent their views on Israel.[72]

Moreover, the collapse of the Oslo process in 2000, coupled with a subsequent wave of suicide terrorist attacks against Israeli civilians, constrained the willingness to confront the Israeli government. As Rabbi Martin Wiener, president of the Central Conference of American Reform Rabbis (CCAR), admitted: "Many of us who supported the Oslo process in the past decade have to admit that Palestinians do not want peace."[73] Only fringe groups like those associated with *Tikkun* magazine adopted a decidedly different tact, sympathizing with the very small minority of Israeli Jews who refused to serve in the Israel Defense Forces.[74] Not surprisingly, representatives of the Right, such as the ZOA, opposed the Disengagement plan for a unilateral Israeli withdrawal from Gaza. However, they did not succeed in mobilizing a wide coalition against the policy. The Orthodox were muted in their response, in part because of the trauma induced by Rabin's assassination in 1995 and in part because Disengagement was initiated by Ariel Sharon and not the Left.[75] In addition, the American Jewish community was still able to demonstrate consensual solidarity with Israel during the 2006 Second Lebanon War, even though some had doubts about aspects of Israeli policy.

For the overwhelming majority, the consensus was summed up in a February 2008 plenum resolution of the Jewish Council of Public Affairs:

With regard to the issue of settlements generally, we recognize that within our own community there are divergent views ... At the same time, we are united in the belief that the root cause of the Israeli-Palestinian conflict is not Israeli settlements but the continued unwillingness of the Palestinian national leadership and most Arab states to accept the state of Israel as a permanent sovereign Jewish state in the Middle East within secure borders ... As the Israeli government enters negotiations on permanent status issues, the organized Jewish community should support those efforts, consistent with our longstanding tradition of supporting the efforts of Israel's government to achieve peace and security.[76]

Nonetheless, such expressions of solidarity did not represent a return to the 1970s. Some on the Israeli Left began to promote a narrative that placed the blame for the collapse of the Oslo process on both sides. This began to have an impact on liberals in the Diaspora, especially after the Labor party left Sharon's government in the autumn of 2003. Subsequently, the dovish Brit Zedek organization collected over ten thousand signatures in support for the Geneva draft permanent status agreement negotiated by Yossi Beilin and Yasir Abd Rabbo, which was vigorously opposed by Israeli prime minister Ariel Sharon.[77]

There were also increasing clashes between the mainstream and the left over more practical issues. Thus, there was disagreement over the question of U.S. aid to the PA. In 2006 AIPAC lobbied for legislation setting strict limits on aid to the PA so long as Hamas – which controlled Gaza – maintained its support for terrorism and refused to recognize Israel. Meanwhile, dovish Jewish groups argued for a softer version of the bill.[78] In 2007, AIPAC joined the doves in supporting aid to the PA, which annoyed some of its right-wing donors, who threatened to pull out of AIPAC while backing the ZOA campaign against aid.[79]

Not only had the divisions of the 1990s resurfaced, they actually intensified, becoming more deeply and widely ingrained. This was very apparent during the Gaza War in 2008–2009. While the mainstream lobby gave Israel very strong backing, dovish groups came out against the war from the outset, calling for an immediate cease-fire.[80] One day after the campaign began, J Street's campaigns director wrote that "while there is nothing 'right' in raining rockets on Israeli families or dispatching suicide bombers, there is nothing 'right' in punishing a million and a half already-suffering Gazans for the actions of the extremists among them ... Neither Israelis nor Palestinians have a monopoly on right or wrong."[81]

Meanwhile, on the Right, following the Disengagement, in December 2005 the Union of Orthodox Jewish Congregations (OU) passed a formal resolution giving its leadership the authority, for the first time, to take public stands on Israeli domestic policies and territorial integrity.[82] In 2007 the Ultra-Orthodox Agudath Yisrael of America passed a resolution stating that Israel should not surrender any part of Jerusalem to Palestinian sovereignty, and that America's government should not pressure it into doing so. This was the first time it took a public stance on the peace process. Subsequently, it joined with the OU and right-wing organizations in forming the Coalition for Jerusalem, which lobbied against the division of Jerusalem, which was then the policy of the Israeli government headed by Ehud Olmert.[83] In response the Union of Reform Judaism president, Eric Yoffie, declared, "If the Israeli right wing mobilizes its supporters in the U.S. against such an agreement, the Reform movement would respond in kind."[84] In fact, they had already taken some steps in this direction, having been publicly critical of Israeli policies regarding the separation barrier.[85] In 2009 the CCAR came out in support of Obama's call for a settlement freeze, declaring that settlements were "an obstacle to peace."[86] In 2012, the Reform movement came out against a congressional bid to close down the PLO office in Washington, which was supported by AIPAC.[87]

Tilting to the Right?

Perhaps more significant than these specific incidents is the sense among liberal Jewish organizations that the mainstream organizations tilt to the Right on Israel, and that this brings their claims to represent the American Jewish consensus into question. This issue was brought into sharp relief when the Conference of Presidents rejected J Street's application for membership in 2014. The Reform movement threatened that it might leave the Conference altogether over the issue. Other major players, such as JCPA and the Conservative movement, also called for reform of the Conference to make it more representative.[88]

Indeed, some claim that AIPAC and the Conference of Presidents do not strictly abide by the maxim of supporting the elected Israeli government.[89] As Rabbi Eric Yoffie noted with regard to the Conference of Presidents, "[It] has been much more outspoken and forceful in supporting governments of the right than those of the left. I feel strongly that during the Rabin and Barak years the conference simply did not demonstrate the same kind of energy and aggressive support for the policies of the Israeli government that it did during the Shamir and Netanyahu years."[90] Or as Dan Fleshler opined, "Their organizational cultures are most comfortable when they can take forceful stances against Israel's 'enemies' – e.g., Iran, Hamas, Hezbollah, and far left-wing critics of Israel. They tend to be less comfortable about enthusiastically supporting peace initiatives that require a certain amount of trust in Arab intentions or bold territorial compromises."[91] He later said, "It is not that they actively supported settlements, rather that they actively defended Likud governments, but were not actively supportive of the Oslo process."[92]

In the 1980s the Likud took a greater interest than Labor in the organized Jewish community, quietly supporting those more sympathetic to its approach, such as Malcolm Hoenlein, who became the executive director of the Conference of Presidents, to assume positions of power.[93] Moreover, within the Conference of Presidents, conservative groups outnumber the liberal ones; given that the Conference operates on the basis of consensus, this impedes the organization from taking forthright stands in favor of Israeli governments of the Left.[94]

AIPAC activists come in various ideological shades, but as Doug Bloomfield, a former AIPAC legislative director, explained, "AIPAC members tend to be more hard line and defensive when it comes to Israel's security than the mainstream of the American Jewish community."[95] A revealing example of this tendency was evident at AIPAC's 1993 annual policy conference:

When Israeli Ambassador, Itamar Rabinovich, told the 2,400 participants that not just Arabs but also Israel would have to make compromises for peace, only one delegate in the cavernous auditorium clapped. Sensing the awkward moment, Rabinovich recovered by saying: "If it is hard to applaud the concessions we have to make, let us applaud the concessions the Arabs will have to provide." The crowd roared.[96]

As the former AIPAC executive director Neil Sher remarked, "Getting AIPAC to support Oslo was like pulling teeth."[97] Former deputy foreign minister Yossi Beilin, an architect of the Oslo Accords, was also extremely critical of AIPAC on this score.[98]

Still, when Labor came to power in Israel in 1992 and Clinton took the White House in 1993, Steve Grossman, a Democrat and a moderate dove, was appointed chairman of AIPAC. AIPAC vice president Harvey Friedman was forced to resign after he declared that Prime Minister Rabin had chutzpah for suggesting that Israel might withdraw from the Golan, and after he made a derogatory reference to Yossi Beilin. AIPAC has always included the pursuit of peace in its talking points, and this sometimes became the focus of its lobbying efforts.[99] Thus, AIPAC assisted the Labor government by lobbying against ZOA initiatives to attack the Oslo process – for example, by opposing the Specter-Shelby Amendment and working to reverse initial congressional rejection of aid to the Palestinians following the Wye II Agreement between Barak and the PA. Also following Barak's victory in 1999, AIPAC dropped its opposition to a Palestinian state and – in response to requests from Jerusalem – did not criticize Clinton's use of the presidential veto regarding moving the U.S. embassy to Jerusalem.[100]

Despite this there are two issues about which the question of a rightward tilt remained pertinent in the first decade of the twenty-first century: the 2005 Disengagement from Gaza and the question of Jerusalem. With regard to the disengagement, although many mainstream organizations signed an Israel Policy Forum ad in the *New York Times* supporting Disengagement, AIPAC and the Conference of Presidents did not officially support it until a very late stage, and even then support was muted.[101] For a significant period, AIPAC did very little to drum up support for the plan in Congress.[102] However, AIPAC did strongly back the move at its 2005 Policy Conference, and it subsequently lobbied Congress for aid to help relocate the Gaza settlers. The delay in announcing support may have had something to do with uncertainty as to whether the plan would actually be implemented, given Sharon's defeat on the issue in the Likud referendum.[103] However, according to one participant in the discussion within the Conference of Presidents, even though a majority supported the plan, the situation deteriorated to a "critical point, threatening the unity of the organization."[104] Indeed, even after the measure gained the support of the Knesset, Foxman criticized the Conference of Presidents' support for Disengagement as "lukewarm and feeble."[105]

The challenge posed by the issue of Jerusalem has been more sustained and complicated. In 1995 Republican senator Robert Dole launched an initiative to move the American embassy to Jerusalem at the annual AIPAC conference. The Conference of Presidents supported the move in principle but was uncommitted to the specifics. The reason for its hesitation was that the Labor-led government opposed the move, fearing it could lead to the collapse of the peace process.[106] Given the Israeli position, the AJC and the National Jewish Community

Relations Advisory Council refused to back the Dole initiative.[107] The final version of the bill granted the president a waiver to postpone the move for six months on grounds of national security, which effectively neutralized it. This allowed everyone to support the bill. Indeed, as of 2014 the regular use of the waiver means that the American Embassy remains in Tel Aviv.

Matters reached a head again in 2000 when the Barak government proposed the division of Jerusalem at Camp David. Subsequently, mainstream Diaspora leaders, including Ronald Lauder, the chairman of the Conference of Presidents, took part in a large demonstration in Jerusalem to protest against such plans. Lauder claimed to have addressed the demonstration in a personal capacity but that was not how the Israeli government and some members of the Conference viewed the matter.[108] As a result, the organization banned its chairman from making further controversial statements.[109] Yet at the same time, Malcolm Hoenlein implicitly backed Lauder by arguing that Jerusalem was an issue on which the Jews worldwide should have a say. Similarly, in 2008 during the Annapolis negotiations, Abe Foxman argued that "since Jerusalem belongs to all the Jewish people, decisions about its future are not just an Israeli decision," but one that American Jews should have their say in, even if that meant opposing the policies of the Israeli government.[110] In adopting this position the ADL and the Conference of Presidents may have been, at least in part, attempting to counterbalance Arab and Muslim lobbying on Jerusalem. Muslim and Arab states see Jerusalem as an issue over which they should have a say – they do not view it as a purely Palestinian issue. Indeed, Egypt and Saudi Arabia actually worked to stiffen Palestinian opposition to compromise over Jerusalem in 2000.

This vague and intermittent right-wing tilt may become more pronounced. Ideological conservatives are 10 to 20 percent more likely than liberals to be among those with the *strongest* connection to Israel.[111] Many of these political conservatives identify with the Orthodox movement, which is the fastest growing segment of the community. They are already more politically mobilized for Israel per capita than other subgroups,[112] and much more hawkish regarding the peace process.

However, there is some intriguing counterevidence. It may be that most young Orthodox political activists will not adopt the stance of right-wing lobbying organizations in their political advocacy. In 2009, an internet survey of about 500 American Jewish, mostly Orthodox (about 60 percent), pro-Israel student activists and their friends was carried out.[113] Some of the results were unsurprising, such as the fact that conservative and reform students are more liberal and dovish than the Orthodox, right-wingers are more active than centrists, and the unaffiliated were largely apathetic in terms of Israel advocacy. However, some results concerning the Orthodox were very interesting. Seventy percent of the Orthodox surveyed defined themselves as centrists, compared to less than 15 percent who defined themselves as right-wing. Fifty-seven percent of the Orthodox agreed that ultimately Israel must find a way to end its occupation of the Palestinians; only 21 percent of the Orthodox disagreed. Although the survey was conducted by a student rather than a professional polling organization, the figures suggest that Orthodox pro-Israel *activists* are likely to abide by the old centrist norms of Israel advocacy.

Liberal Equivocation about Zionism?

Anti-Zionism has always existed among American Jews. But by the 1940s, it had become marginal. There remained prominent Jews who oppose the idea of a Jewish state, like Noam Chomsky, Naomi Klein, and Norman Finklestein, but Jewish anti-Zionist organizations like the American Council for Judaism shriveled into obscurity. In 1996, the anti-Zionist Jewish Voice for Peace was founded, but it remains on the fringe and is not considered a part of the organized Jewish community.[114] More significant are developments within avowedly Zionist left-wing organizations. Is their increasingly assertive stance against various Israeli government policies a heartfelt attempt to save Zionism and preserve the existence of a Jewish and democratic state? Or does it indicate an erosion in their commitment to Zionism, a blurring of the distinction between them and the anti/Post-Zionist Left?

The first thing to note is a blurring of the discourse – for example, in the writings of individuals such as Henry Seigman, the former head of the American Jewish Congress, and M. J. Rosenberg, who worked for the Israel Policy Forum and AIPAC. While they have not explicitly abandoned support for Israel as a Jewish state, the way they relate to the conflict sounds similar to the anti-Zionist postcolonial view. Thus, they put the overwhelming bulk of responsibility for resolving the conflict on Israel alone and frame the Israeli-Palestinian conflict in terms of the struggle against apartheid and for civil rights.[115] Their marginalization of both the role of political and religious extremism on the Palestinian side, and the threat posed to Israel by wider radical forces in the region, contrasts with the traditional dovish pro-Israel liberalism of people such as Leonard Fein and Michael Walzer, who also take a strong stand against the demonization of Israel by the anti-Zionist Far Left.[116] Then there is the left-wing journal *Tikkun*, founded by Michael Lerner. While Lerner himself is a self-proclaimed Zionist, the magazine gives a fair amount of space to anti-Zionist discourse. Lerner also supported the Presbyterian divestment campaign, which was inspired primarily by anti-Zionism and postcolonial ideas.

In the institutional arena, there is the case of the New Israel Fund (NIF) set up in the 1990s. NIF supports many causes dear to liberal Zionists, such as minority rights, social justice, and religious pluralism. However, it has also supported organizations whose agenda includes anti-Zionist campaigning that seeks to delegitimize the idea of a Jewish state. Indeed, while speaking to a Diaspora audience in the 1990s, the then director of the New Israel Fund, Avi Armoni, stated that the idea of a Jewish state was incompatible with the idea of a democratic state.[117]

Before he became the executive director of J Street, Jeremy Ben-Ami worked for the New Israel Fund. Ben-Ami himself identifies as a Zionist. His dovishness is driven by a sense that Israel must withdraw in order to preserve its Jewish identity and its democratic character before it is too late. He is utterly opposed to the so-called one-state solution which he refuses to even refer to as a solution.[118]

However, the organization and membership are more equivocal about Zionism that Ben-Ami. The board of J Street had a long debate about whether they should refer to themselves as a Zionist organization.[119] Reports of the first J Street conference seemed to indicate a generational divide; older participants were more likely to declare themselves to be Zionists, while younger participants were more hesitant to do so and were more equivocal about the idea of two states for two peoples.[120] Indeed, J Street's university arm dropped the "pro-Israel" part of the organization's "pro-Israel, pro-peace" slogan.[121] Other incidents blurred the distinction between liberal Zionism and an anti-Zionist postcolonial outlook. One was J Street's response to the Gaza War, noted earlier in this chapter, which smacked of moral equivalence between Israel and Hamas. Significantly, Rabbi Eric Yoffie, a long-time liberal Zionist, lambasted the organization for this, declaring that J Street's statement was "morally deficient, profoundly out of touch with Jewish sentiment, and also appallingly naive."[122] J Street also implicitly endorsed Washington DC's J-Theater production of *7 Jewish Children*, a play comparing Israel's war with Hamas to the Nazi's treatment of the Jews, claiming it would stimulate "rigorous intellectual engagement."[123]

On the other hand, J Street threw out a poet from its first conference who had made comparisons between the Nazis and Israel, and it condemned the campaign to boycott Israel at the Toronto International Film Festival. Subsequently, the Israeli government ended its boycott of J Street.[124] Nonetheless, the controversies and the impression gained from speaking to J Street's student activists at their annual conference in 2013[125] and young nonestablishment American Jewish leaders[126] who identify with it, leads to a conclusion that beneath the surface, equivocation over what were articles of faith for liberal Zionists is a real phenomenon, even though it is not the prevailing orientation.

THE POLITICAL CONSEQUENCES OF PLURALISTIC SOLIDARITY

But what are the political implications of these changes? Wertheimer[127] is pessimistic – he characterizes the changes primarily in terms of fragmentation, a decline away from the golden era in which a united community promotes a shared agenda. Sasson[128] is sanguine – he interprets these changes as a sign of maturity; the decline of mass mobilization has been compensated for by greater direct involvement.

First it is important to assess the extent of the divisions. The plethora of groups on the Left and Right may weaken AIPAC and the Conference of

Presidents, but they lack the public support and financial clout of the mainstream.[129] The center no longer has the monopoly on lobbying, but it remains predominant. Still, the institutionalization of the ideological divide has had negative consequences for the leverage of the pro-Israel lobby as a whole. When centrist, left-, and right-wing organizations lobby at cross-purposes, they can cancel each other out. For example, when AIPAC sent out seven thousand delegates to lobby congressmen during its annual conference, the pro-Israel left and right lobbies sent their supporters out at the same time with messages that at least partially contradicted those of AIPAC.[130]

In a more general sense, overt ideological pluralism and political partisanship erode a key pillar of lobby power, which is based on the perception in Washington that supporting Israel confers political rewards, whereas failure to do so carries political costs. If politicians can credibly claim to support Israel by supporting contradictory policies, then there are in effect no clear political consequences either way. This seems to be part of the strategic thinking at J Street. In this vein, Jeremy Ben-Ami has challenged the Conference of Presidents' standing by referring to the organization's claim to speak for the entire Jewish community as "presumptuous."[131] This fits perfectly with what Ben-Ami identified as J Street's "number 1 agenda item," namely, "to do whatever we can in Congress to act as the president's blocking back." That is, their objective was to promote President Obama's Middle East policy by emphasizing splits within the pro-Israel lobby.[132] Important politicians grasped this. Thus, during the 2008 presidential election campaign the Democratic Party's vice presidential nominee, Joseph Biden, stated that AIPAC "doesn't speak for the entire Jewish community or for the State of Israel ... No one in AIPAC or any other organization can question my support of Israel."[133]

Against this background, the institutionalization of ideological divisions makes it very difficult to mobilize on issues on which there are deep divisions within the Jewish community, notably settlements. In 1991 the mainstream pro-Israel lobby organizations lobbied hard against the Bush administration's plan to link the granting of loan guarantees to Israel to a settlement freeze. In 2009 the mainstream lobby responded differently when the Obama administration called for a settlement freeze. The Netanyahu government initially opposed the idea, trying to limit its extent by seeking to exclude building related to "natural growth" and, when that was rejected, "normal life" in settlements. However, Netanyahu failed to garner the support of the mainstream lobby to fight on the issue of settlements. The administration worked with the mainstream and left-wing organizations to get them on board. While some of the mainstream lobby expressed concern about the tone of the administration's policy, none were prepared to publicly confront it over the issue itself. The fact that the Reform and Conservative movements were on board was crucial in shifting the balance within the mainstream. The result shocked the Netanyahu government, which then reluctantly accepted a ten-month settlement freeze.[134]

On the other hand, increased institutional and ideological pluralism has at least some positive effects for pro-Israel lobbying. The representation of different voices in various organizational frameworks allows a great number of Jews to feel at home inside the organized Jewish community.[135] As a student leader in a dovish organization put it: "A lot of students are very pro-Israel, but their sympathies lie with Labor or Meretz, not with Likud or the settlers. Brit Tzedek helps them find ways to express their Zionism and support for Israel."[136] Being a member of the organized community is an important determinant of political activism. Hence, even though there is a price to pay for greater pluralism, there is a potential political dividend to be reaped on consensual issues. Given the global nature of communications, political actors no longer have the luxury of varying their messaging when speaking to different groups without losing credibility. In such an environment, pluralism can be an advantage. For example on the consensual issue of countering boycotts, divestment, and sanctions (BDS) against Israel, dovish pro-Israel groups, with a record of working together with liberal churches on other issues, may be able to engage the churches in ways that mainstream organizations find difficult.[137]

CONCLUSION

A consistent majority of American Jews has been in favor of the creation of a Palestinian state, at least in theory. Nonetheless, there are significant differences of opinion on how to proceed in practice, as well as on specific issues like settlements and Jerusalem. However, since the collapse of the Oslo process in 2000, these differences of opinion have been constrained by the fact that a consistent majority has also perceived the Palestinians as mainly to blame for the failure to reach peace and for the violence. Yet, in institutional terms, ideological polarization among pro-Israel organizations has increased as American Jews have become less concerned with unity and less deferential toward the policies of the Israeli government. The center remains predominant, but its dominance has eroded significantly. These differences are clearly segmented, with the Orthodox being the most hawkish subgroup and non-Orthodox, nonestablishment young Jews being the most dovish group. This growing *divide over policy regarding the Arab-Israeli conflict* is driven both by changes in Israel and the Middle East and by generational and cultural changes in American Jewry itself, the same changes that undergird the growing *gap in attachment* to Israel that was identified in the previous chapter.

As a result, there has been a shift in American Jewry's approach to Israel away from a centrally mediated, unified, consensual, and deferential approach toward a more direct, polarized, and assertive approach. This is likely to make traditional pro-Israel lobbying more complex and difficult, though the mainstream lobby's position remains strong. Were the consensus to collapse regarding (a) the perception that Israel combines its Jewish identity with adherence to democratic principles, and (b) the perception that the Arab side is primarily responsible for the failure to achieve peace, then divisions would effectively nullify the organized Jewish community as an effective pro-Israel lobby. However, this is not the case, at least not at the time of writing. Critically, no major Jewish group advocates withholding U.S. aid to Israel in order to pressure it to change its policies.[138]

Conclusion

America's strong bonds with Israel are well known. This bond is unbreakable ...
But if we see this conflict only from one side or the other, then we will be blind to
the truth: The only resolution is for the aspirations of both sides to be met through
two states ... Hamas must put an end to violence, recognize past agreements,
recognize Israel's right to exist. At the same time ... the United States does not
accept the legitimacy of continued Israeli settlements. It is time for these settlements to stop.

—President Barack Obama, Cairo University, June 4, 2009[1]

In pursuit of a peace process, the United States today has exerted substantial
pressure on Israel while putting almost no pressure on the Palestinians and the
Arab world. We can encourage both parties in the conflict, but we must never
forget which one is our ally.

—Mitt Romney, AIPAC, October 2009[2]

Americans' identification with Israel is deeply rooted in American political
culture. Since the turn of the millennium, sympathy for Israel has grown to
new heights. At the same time the debate over how to handle the Arab-Israeli
conflict has become increasingly divisive, and these divisions increasingly line
up with the major political, ideological, and religious divides in America. This is
the "Israel paradox" in American political culture. The paradoxical growth of
both support for Israel and controversy surrounding its policies actually share
some common foundations. The consequences of widespread identification
with Israel are not confined to support for the Jewish state. Rather, identification with Israel means that what Israel does and what is done to Israel carries
with it an unusually high degree of symbolic meaning for Americans. Consequently, more is symbolically at stake in the Arab-Israeli conflict than in other
conflicts around the world.

Indeed, the Arab-Israeli conflict evokes such passionate debate precisely because it touches on core elements of American identity. Thus, for liberals, sympathy for Israel is rooted primarily in the American creed, specifically Israel's identity as a democracy. Because liberalism is at the core of that creed they expect Israel to live up to those values, and when Israeli policy toward the Palestinians is perceived as failing to do this, they are critical, much as they would be of U.S. policy in similar circumstances. On the other hand, while Conservatives also support Israel because it is a democracy, they give greater weight than liberals to the place of Israel in the ethno-religious dimension of American identity, and they are more skeptical of Israel's enemies' interest in/capability of becoming democratic; hence their support for Israel is more unwavering.

The strongest pro-Israel attitudes and the most virulent anti-Israel attitudes are not only a reflection of American identity per se, but also of attitudes toward the Jewish people as a collective. For American Jews attachment to Israel is especially strong, because of their sense of belonging to the Jewish people, whereas for evangelicals sympathy for Israel is especially strong because of the theological significance of the Jewish people. Equally, within the mainline Protestant churches, the "witness mentality" continues to inform a tendency to single out the Jewish people to be judged by standards different from other peoples'. This singling out is also apparent in the postcolonial approach to Israel. Indeed, according to Paul Berman,[3] such left-wing anti-Zionism is part of a long anti-Semitic tradition that casts Jewish peoplehood as standing in the way of some principle of *universal* justice and happiness.

At the same time, the increase in support for Israel and controversy surrounding the peace process is not only about the place of Israel and the Jewish people in the American imagination. It is also about the fact that 9/11 catapulted the Middle East to the center of Americans' practical concerns. Terrorism, radical Islam, the Iraq War, and the threat of a nuclear Iran have all served to maintain that focus. For the most part, this has led the American public to increasingly view Israel as an important strategic ally, with the Palestinians perceived as mainly to blame for the violence and lack of conflict resolution. In any case, with so much perceived to be at stake in the Middle East for America, it is not surprising that the Arab-Israeli conflict has become a major arena in which deep divisions over grand strategy are played out. In this vein, those who favor a more robust U.S. grand strategy, and who emphasize the divide between democratic and nondemocratic regimes, tend to favor Israel more strongly, while those who favor a more defensive grand strategy, and who tend to discount ideologies except for nationalism, tend to a more evenhanded or hostile approach to Israel. While this divide straddles both parties, increasingly, most Republicans tend to strongly favor a more robust approach, while Democrats are divided but lean toward a more defensive approach.

This hints at something important, namely that the surge in support for Israel is rooted in conceptions of American priorities and values. Consequently,

Republican views are not necessarily closer to the views of the mainstream Israeli public than the views of the Democrats. Ironically, Republicans were out of tune with the mainstream Israel public on some key issues in the first half of the 2000s, when many were "more Catholic than the Pope" (or in this case, the mainstream Israeli public and the Sharon/Kadima governments) on Palestinian statehood and settlements. Still, since the Second Lebanon War in 2006, when thousands of rockets, launched from areas where Israel had withdrawn, rained down on Israelis, Israeli public opinion has become more hawkish and reticent. In parallel, polls indicated that Israelis preferred George W. Bush's and Mitt Romney's approach to the region to that of Barack Obama.[4]

THE ISRAEL PARADOX AND WIDER CULTURAL TRENDS

While each of the political, ideological, and religious groups analyzed in this book has its own nuances, an overarching pattern is clear. First, in each case the underlying orientation is sympathy for Israel over the Palestinians. Second, the differences within each group are mutually reinforcing. Thus, evangelical Christians and Orthodox Jews are likely to hold conservative political views, prefer a hawkish strategy, and support the Republicans. All these groups are also more likely to believe that the U.S. should side with Israel and that the Palestinians are mainly to blame for the failure to achieve peace, while being equivocal about the creation of a Palestinian state and the construction of settlements. In contrast, non-Orthodox Jews and many mainline Christians are likely to hold liberal political views, prefer a dovish grand strategy, and support the Democrats.[5] These groups tend to oppose settlements and support the creation of a Palestinian state, as well as active American mediation, to achieve these ends. To be sure, the Left is more internally divided on policy to the conflict than the Right, but the basic division holds.

This coalescence into a single divide is symptomatic of the fact that Americans have become more ideologically polarized. And this situation finds expression in an increasingly partisan political environment in which the Republican base has become more conservative and the Democratic base more liberal. Indeed, the values gap between Republicans and Democrats has become greater than the gender, age, race, or class divides between them.[6] The fact that the partisan divide has grown across numerous issues strongly suggests that the growing divide over policy towards the Arab-Israeli conflict is part of this general process of partisan-ideological polarization in American politics.

This conclusion is reinforced by the fact the several key patterns associated with the "Israel paradox" fit in with global patterns of political culture charted by Ronald Inglehart and the World Values Survey (WVS). According to Inglehart, socioeconomic processes of modernization and postmodernization generate a universal process of cultural shift. As countries become wealthier and modernize their societies, they develop postmaterial values. Postmaterialists are concerned with individual meaning, minority rights, and multiculturalism; they are also dovish and relatively unconcerned by national security, while tending to find organized religion and nationalism unattractive. This cultural shift does not occur because individuals change their values; rather, it takes place through generational replacement as the more liberal postmaterial values of younger generations replace the more traditional materialist values of older generations. These postmaterial values increasingly come to define Left/liberal parties, while material/traditional values define the Right side of the spectrum. It is clear from the WVS and other surveys that these liberal values are increasingly prevalent among younger generations in America,[7] including among American Jews,[8] and that the Democratic Party base is increasingly made up of young people with liberal, postmaterial values. Despite the universal nature of postmodernization, political cultures across the world are not converging, but rather developing in parallel. This is because the traditional political culture of each country remains influential. Thus, despite postmodernization, Inglehart's cultural map shows that America remains distinct from Europe in that it retains more traditional values, as well as being more individualistic. America remains exceptional.

These general patterns fit the Israel paradox in two ways. First, it fits the finding that Americans remain more sympathetic to Israel than Europeans because of the nature of their respective political cultures. Attitudes exist in parallel, in that on both continents conservatives are more supportive of Israel than liberals. However, the resilience of national culture is demonstrated by virtue of the fact that American liberals remain more pro-Israel than European conservatives. Second, the growing gaps and divides *within* American political culture over the Arab-Israeli conflict is part of a general process of postmodernization in which younger generations come to adopt more liberal, postmaterial values. Younger liberals, including American Jews, are less drawn to traditional security- and nationalism-based arguments for Israel and more drawn to promoting peace with the Palestinians as well as with issues concerning the quality of Israeli democracy, including the way Israel treats its non-Jewish minorities. This explains why older Democrats are more sensitive to security threats to Israel than their younger counterparts. Clearly, this has political implications going forward.

CULTURAL TRENDS, SHIFTING ATTITUDES, AND THEIR POLITICAL IMPLICATIONS

One of the central findings of this book is that the underlying sympathy for Israel in America is incredibly resilient; intertwined as it is with the very foundations of American identity. In political terms this undergirds the special relationship, generating a willingness to support Israel's well-being, especially its security, on terms and in ways that the U.S. does not do for other countries. Even when crises in the relationship occur, the cultural foundations ensure that when the crisis subsides the relationship returns to the underlying norm of closeness.

Various factors point in the direction of this pro-Israel orientation becoming stronger. September 11, 2001, greatly enhanced the perception of Israel as a vital ally, while the demographic and political importance of Israel's strongest supporters, evangelicals, and Orthodox Jews has been growing. In contrast, the mainline church, the largest base of vociferous opposition to Israel, is declining in size and political significance. In parallel, the membership of AIPAC has increased, while the number of people attending AIPAC's annual policy conference has risen from about 500 in the early 1970s to 13,000 in 2013, including around half of the members of the Congress.

Yet there are several potential challenges to underlying sympathy for Israel. The first of these concerns American national identity itself. In his provocative book entitled, *Who Are We?*[9] Samuel Huntington argues that the American creed is under serious threat from globalization, multiculturalism, and their adoption by American elites. Huntington worries that because of this process, the mass immigration of Hispanics and Asians will not be acculturated into the American creed and that this would signal its decline. Given that support for Israel is closely tied to the creed, if Huntington is correct, this could signal a decline in sympathy for Israel.[10] One might even speculate that Hispanics may be relatively attracted to the postcolonialism, which has influence in Latin America in the form of dependency theory and the populist politics of leaders such as Hugo Chavez, who supported Iran while opposing Israel. Yet, while Hispanic sympathy for Israel is relatively low in America, the margin of sympathy over the Palestinians remains large, as they are among the groups least supportive of the Palestinians. Consequently, the growth of the Hispanic population will not pose a fundamental challenge to pro-Israel sympathy in the U.S.

Another social change of relevance is the decline in religious affiliation. In 1990 8.2 percent of Americans did not identify with any organized religious group; by 2012 this figure had more than doubled to about a fifth. This was mainly a result of generational replacement. America is also becoming less Christian. Eighty-six percent of American adults identified as Christians in 1990, 73 percent in 2012. Perhaps even more significant, for the first time, in 2012 fewer than half of Americans identified as Protestants.[11] This decline is of significance, because one of the main foundations of support for Israel is a widespread belief in the Bible. In contrast, the margin by which the religiously unaffiliated prefer Israel over the Palestinians is the narrowest of any ethnoreligious group in America. Yet even the unaffiliated prefer Israel over the Palestinians by more than a margin of 2–1. Given the contrast with secular Europeans who are generally more pro-Palestinian, this suggests that the pro-Israel orientation remains deeply embedded in American political culture. It may wane somewhat, but it will remain significant.

A further potential challenge could be a shift in American strategic culture. Americans who prefer a robust internationalist grand strategy tend to have more positive attitudes about Israel. At the end of the first decade of the twenty-first

century, Americans are increasingly inclined to support a strategy of retrenchment.[12] Yet Americans continue to view Israel as an ally in a struggle against
common enemies like radical Islamic terrorism and Iran, which do not look as if
they are going to disappear soon. Moreover, it is worth recalling that in the
early 1970s the Nixon administration had a strategy of retrenchment that
increased the strategic significance of strong, reliable allies like Israel.

What about changes in the Arab world? Sympathy for Israel has been
reinforced by negative perceptions of Muslim and Arab countries opposed to
Israel and the United States. Will the Arab Spring, with its promise of democratization, change attitudes? This is unlikely, because the benefactors of the Arab
Spring appear to be Islamists rather than secular democrats, and this only
serves to reinforce the sense of otherness Americans feel towards Arabs and
Muslims in the Middle East.

Another possibility is that a change in Arab states' policies and Palestinian
policies towards the U.S. and Israel may shift attitudes. In 1974, when Egypt
was still allied with the Soviet Union and was hostile to Israel, only 5 percent of
Americans viewed it favorably, whereas after President Sadat switched sides in
the Cold War and made peace with Israel, over 60 percent of Americans came
to view Egypt favorably.[13] Most Americans, including American Jews, consistently support the creation of a Palestinian state in the West Bank and Gaza if
the Palestinians demonstrate the will to live in peace with Israel. So if there is
perceived to be a real Arab partner for peace and if the Israeli leadership is
simultaneously viewed as not serious about peace, there will be public willingness to accept U.S. pressure on Israel.

However, the rise of Hamas and Hezbollah does not suggest such a scenario
is likely. More generally, Arab states and the Palestinians have been very
reluctant to follow in Sadat's footsteps. Even in the 1990s, Syria never made
a serious public peace gesture toward Israel, and it continued to support
terrorist groups opposed to the Oslo process. The Palestinians and Arab states
promote the demonization of Israel in international forums including the
United Nations, going beyond criticism of Israeli policies to questioning Israel's
right to exist, descending into anti-Semitism and into justifying terrorism as
"resistance."[14] Virulent anti-Israeli rhetoric and support for terrorism are good
for domestic legitimacy in the Arab world and elsewhere where postcolonialism
has resonance. But for the majority of Americans, such an approach continues
to reinforce the perception that the Arabs and Palestinians are not sincere about
peace with Israel.

Finally, changes within Israel might cause it to lose its status as the preferred
party. On numerous occasions the level of support for Israel among the general
public and American Jews has fallen in response to specific actions that were
viewed as inconsistent with democratic values or a genuine commitment to
peace. Examples include the dip in support for Israel following the Sabra and
Shatilla massacre in 1982 and the outbreak of the first intifada in December
1987. Yet, opinion bounced back quickly, so such events in the future would be

unlikely to yield a sustained realignment among the general public. However, they may well have a far more significant impact on Democrats, liberals, and young non-Orthodox Jews.

This raises the key political issue at the heart of the Israel paradox, namely whether higher levels of sympathy necessarily translate into higher levels of political support. Regarding Israeli security, the answer is yes. In the wake of 9/11, the rise of Hamas and Hezbollah, and the growing threat of a nuclear Iran, Israel has come to be viewed as one of America's closest allies. From this perspective, a victory for Israel against these enemies is a victory for the U.S., and a defeat for Israel would be a defeat for the U.S. This fusing of American and Israeli security in the public mind means that for the American public, presidential support for Israeli security serves as a kind of litmus test of presidential credibility on American security itself.[15]

Yet at the same time, the fact that the overwhelming bulk of the growth in support for Israel has been on the Right side of the political spectrum is also very significant. This means that a Republican administration is more likely to lean toward Israel and less likely to heavily pressure Israel in the context of the peace process than a Democratic administration. Even an Israeli government that vigorously pursued a peace agreement with the Palestinians recognized this. Thus, Israeli prime minister Ehud Olmert explained that a key reason why he pushed so hard for an agreement in the autumn of 2008 before George W. Bush left office was that he felt had the necessary support from the president to propose bold concessions without the fear of being undercut.[16]

This is all very well when the Republicans are in power, but, of course, this is not always the case. Democrats and liberals are very unlikely to follow their European counterparts and become pro-Palestinian, even as younger generations are less sympathetic toward Israel than older generations. However, those elements that are becoming increasingly central to the Democratic base – liberals, the religiously unaffiliated, and Hispanics – are among the least pro-Israel groups in America. Liberals in particular are increasingly critical of Israeli policies, and their support for Israel is increasingly influenced by Israel's willingness to advance the peace process. In addition, the idea that the U.S. should adopt an evenhanded approach toward the Arab-Israeli conflict is becoming increasingly strong among liberals. This trend is reinforced by trends within the Jewish community. Major organizations within the community – such as J Street, or the Reform and Conservative movements – are now willing to openly adopt positions at odds with the Israeli government on issues like settlements. Given that American Jews are predominantly liberal and support the Democratic Party, the overall consequence of this will be that a Democratic administration inclined to take an evenhanded approach to the conflict, including pressure on Israel, will face a less potent opposition. It will be able to credibly claim that it is pro-Israel, as it will have the backing of major pro-Israel organizations.

To sum up, identification with Israel remains deeply embedded in American political culture. Widespread sympathy for Israel, and the bipartisan norm of support for Israeli security that flows from this identification, have grown stronger. However, different interpretations of how to practically implement that norm as regards the peace process are coalescing along partisan and ideological lines. This has important political ramifications for Israel, because when the Democrats are in power, the Israeli government is likely to face an administration more inclined to be evenhanded while simultaneously being under greater pressure to demonstrate its willingness to make concessions. This was apparent during the first Obama administration. The political saliency of this will be affected by perceptions as to how serious Israel's Arab partners are about peace and by the prominence of other strategic challenges to regional stability that are not directly connected to the Arab-Israeli arena. But it still represents an important underlying shift.

The lesson for the State of Israel is that consensual support in America is more important than higher overall levels of support concentrated on one side of the political spectrum. In order to protect bipartisan support, Israel likely will be required to put forward policies that demonstrate its commitment to a two-state solution. That does *not* mean that Israel would have to give in to all Palestinian demands and dismantle all settlements tomorrow. There is more than sufficient bipartisan support that in any peace negotiations Israel's security requirements and concerns about the other side's commitment to peaceful coexistence would be understood very sympathetically, and it will continue to be possible to mobilize widespread support on these issues. This reality is reinforced by the inherent instability of the Middle East, which periodically deflects attention from the conflict, as the Arab Spring and the civil war in Syria have done. It is also reinforced by the tendency of the American public as a whole to focus on domestic economic issues. Nonetheless, the fact remains that the liberal and Democratic consensus opposes settlements, in any case. Further expansion of settlements and retreat from maintaining the possibility of a two-state solution will deepen divisions among Israel's friends and increase liberal and Democrat opposition to Israeli policies in ways that will have political consequences. It is an illusion for an Israeli government to think that over time it can retain bipartisan support in the U.S. and at the same time keep the settler movement happy.

As for Democratic administrations, while they have increased leverage over settlements, there remains significant domestic constraints on pressuring Israel on other issues *so long as* the Palestinians' and the Arab states' credibility on the question of peace remains so weak. In any case, the underlying cultural foundations of pro-Israel sentiment in America are so robust that the special relationship between Israel and the United States will remain virtually unbreakable.

Notes

INTRODUCTION

1. "Memorandum of Conversation, Palm Beach, Florida, December 27, 1962, 10 a.m.," in Nina J. Noring, ed., *Foreign Relations of the United States, 1961–1963, Volume 18: Near East 1962–1963* (Washington, DC: U.S. Government Printing Office, 1995), 280.

2. On Realism see William Wohlforth, "Realism and Foreign Policy," in Steve Smith, Amelia Hadfield, and Tim Dunne, eds., *Foreign Policy: Theories, Actors, Cases* (New York: Oxford University Press, 2008), 32–47.

3. A. F. K. Organski, *The $36 Billion Bargain: Strategy and Politics in U.S. Assistance to Israel* (New York: Columbia University Press, 1990).

4. Colin Dueck, *Reluctant Crusaders: Power, Culture, and Change in American Grand Strategy* (Princeton, NJ: Princeton University Press, 2006), 6; Peter Feaver, "What Is Grand Strategy and Why Do We Need It?" *Shadow Government* (blog), *Foreign Policy*, April 8, 2009, http://shadow.foreignpolicy.com/posts/2009/04/08/what_is_grand_strategy_and_why_do_we_need_it.

5. One particularly sophisticated work integrates subjective elements into both the domestic politics paradigm and the national interest paradigm, Abraham Ben-Zvi, *The United States and Israel: The Limits of the Special Relationship* (New York: Columbia University Press, 1993).

6. John J. Mearsheimer and Stephen M. Walt, *The Israel Lobby and U.S. Foreign Policy* (New York: Farrar, Straus and Giroux, 2007); George Ball and Douglas Ball, *The Passionate Attachment: America's Involvement with Israel, 1947 to the Present* (New York: W. W. Norton, 1992). For a more sober analysis of the pro-Israel lobby, see David Howard Goldberg, *Foreign Policy and Ethnic Interest Groups: American and Canadian Jews Lobby for Israel* (Westport, CT: Greenwood Press, 1990); Dan Fleshler, *Transforming America's Israel Lobby: The Limits of Its Power and the Potential for Change* (Washington, DC: Potomac Books, 2009).

7. Robert C. Lieberman, "The 'Israel Lobby' and American Politics," *Perspectives on Politics*, 7, no. 2 (2009): 235–257; Jonathan Rynhold, "Is the Pro-Israel Lobby a

Block on Reaching a Comprehensive Peace Settlement in the Middle East?" *Israel Studies Forum*, 25, no. 1 (2010): 29–49; Aaron David Miller, *The Much Too Promised Land: America's Elusive Search for Arab-Israeli Peace* (New York: Bantam Books, 2009), 75–125.

8. William Quandt, *Peace Process*, 3rd ed. (Washington, DC: Brookings Institution Press, 2005).

9. Mitchell Geoffrey Bard, *The Water's Edge and Beyond: Defining the Limits to Domestic Influence on United States Middle East Policy* (New Brunswick, NJ: Transaction, 1991).

10. Miller, *The Much Too Promised Land*, 95.

11. Fleshler, *Transforming America's Israel Lobby*, 36–43.

12. Kenneth D. Wald, *Religion and the Politics in the United States*, 4th ed. (Lanham, MD: Rowman and Littlefield, 2003), 152.

13. Miller, *The Much Too Promised Land*, 86.

14. Gideon Rose, "Neoclassical Realism and Theories of Foreign Policy," *World Politics* 51, no. 1 (1998): 144–172; Colin Dueck, *Hard Line: The Republican Party and U.S. Foreign Policy since World War II* (Princeton, NJ: Princeton University Press, 2010); Dueck, *Reluctant Crusaders*.

15. John S. Duffield, "Political Culture and State Behavior: Why Germany Confounds Neorealism," *International Organization* 53, no. 4 (1999): 770–772; Valerie M. Hudson, ed., *Culture and Foreign Policy* (Boulder, CO: Lynne Rienner, 1997); Juliet Kaarbo, "Foreign Policy Analysis in the Twenty-First Century: Back to Comparison, Forward to Identity and Ideas," *International Studies Review* 5, no. 2 (2003): 156–163.

16. Ronald L. Jepperson, Alexander Wendt, and Peter J. Katzenstein, "Norms, Identity, and Culture in National Security," in Peter J. Katzenstein, ed., *The Culture of National Security: Norms and Identity in World Politics* (New York: Columbia University Press, 1996), 33–75; Emmanuel Adler, "Seizing the Middle Ground: Constructivism in World Politics," *European Journal of International Relations* 3, no. 3 (1997): 319–363; Jutta Weldes, "Constructing National Interests," *European Journal of International Relations* 2, no. 3 (1996): 275–318.

17. Michael N. Barnett, "Identity and Alliances in the Middle East," in Katzenstein, ed., *The Culture of National Security*, 400–447.

18. Michelle Mart, *Eye on Israel: How America Came to View Israel as an Ally* (Albany, NY: State University of New York Press, 2006); Elizabeth Stephens, *US Policy towards Israel: The Role of Political Culture in Defining the "Special Relationship"* (Eastbourne, UK: Sussex Academic Press, 2008); Camille Mansour, *Beyond Alliance: Israel and U.S. Foreign Policy*, trans. James A. Cohen (New York: Columbia University Press, 1994); Michael B. Oren, *Power, Faith, and Fantasy: America in the Middle East, 1776 to the Present* (New York: W. W. Norton, 2007); Peter Grose, *Israel in the Mind of America* (New York: Knopf, 1983), 4–5; Moshe Davis, *America and the Holy Land* (Westport, CT: Praeger, 1995), 13–19, 135–145; Eytan Gilboa, *American Public Opinion toward Israel and the Arab-Israeli Conflict* (Lexington, MA: Lexington Books, 1987).

19. On the importance of cultural change in influencing foreign policy change see Jonathan Rynhold, "Cultural Shift and Foreign Policy Change: Israel and the

Making of the Oslo Accords," *Cooperation and Conflict* 42, no. 4 (2007); Jonathan Rynhold, "The German Question in Central and Eastern Europe and the Long Peace in Europe after 1945: An Integrated Theoretical Explanation," *Review of International Studies* 37, no. 1 (2010): 249–275; Thomas Berger, "Norms, Identity, and National Security in Germany and Japan," in Katzenstein, ed., *The Culture of National Security*, 317–356.

20. A norm "describe[s] collective expectations for the proper behavior of actors with a given identity… Norms thus either define (or constitute) identities or prescribe (or regulate) behavior." Peter Katzenstein, "Introduction," in Katzenstein, ed., *The Culture of National Security*, 5.

21. David Sills and Robert King Merton, eds., *International Encyclopedia of the Social Sciences* (New York: Macmillan, 1968), 218.

22. "The concept of identity … refers to the image of individuality and distinctiveness ('selfhood') held and projected by an actor and form (and modified over time), in part through relations with significant others." Ronald Jepperson, Alexander Wendt, and Peter Katzenstein, "Norms, Identity, and Culture in National Security" 59. "Identity … depicts ideologies of collective distinctiveness and purpose, which are enacted domestically and projected internationally." Katzenstein, "Introduction," in Katzenstein, ed. *The Culture of National Security*, 5.

23. An ideology can be defined as a set of interrelated, coherent, and more or less systematic ideas that provide a basis for political action. Ideologies are both descriptive and prescriptive. They contain normative beliefs and principles that inform end goals. They also contain certain beliefs pertaining to causality – what is possible and not possible – that inform instrumental values (that is, the preferred means for obtaining the end goals). See Andrew Heywood, *Political Ideologies: An Introduction*, 2nd ed. (New York: St. Martin's Press, 1998), 1–11.

24. Gabriel A. Almond and Sidney Verba, *The Civic Culture: Political Attitudes and Democracy in Five Nations* (Princeton, NJ: Princeton University Press, 1963).

25. Brian Girvin, "Change and Continuity in Liberal Democratic Political Culture," in John Gibbens, ed., *Contemporary Political Culture: Politics in a Postmodern Age* (London: Sage, 1989).

26. For a discussion of the different approaches see Stephen Welch, *The Concept of Political Culture* (New York: St. Martin's Press, 1993); Michael Brint, *A Genealogy of Political Culture* (Boulder, CO: Westview Press, 1991).

27. Robert M. Entman, *Projections of Power: Framing News, Public Opinion, and U.S. Foreign Policy* (Chicago: University of Chicago Press, 2004), 5.

28. B. Dan Wood, *The Myth of Presidential Representation* (Cambridge: Cambridge University Press, 2009).

29. Author interviews with Peter Beinart, 2011, and with a congressional staffer, 2013.

1. LIKE U.S.: AMERICAN IDENTIFICATION WITH ISRAEL

1. Quoted in Peter Golden, *Quiet Diplomat: A Biography of Max M. Fisher* (New York: Cornwell Books, 1992), 424.

2. Walter Russell Mead, "The New Israel and the Old: Why Gentile Americans Back the Jewish State," *Foreign Affairs* 87, no. 4 (2008): 29.

3. Anatol Lieven, *America, Right or Wrong: An Anatomy of American Nationalism* (New York: Oxford University Press, 2004); Henry R. Nau, *At Home Abroad:*

Identity and Power in American Foreign Policy (Ithaca, NY: Cornell University Press, 2002).

4. Anthony D. Smith, *The Ethnic Origins of Nations* (Oxford: Blackwell, 1988).

5. Walter Russell Mead, "The Jacksonian Tradition," *National Interest* 58 (Winter 1999–2000).

6. U.S. Census Bureau, http://quickfacts.census.gov/qfd/states/00000.html; "Religious Landscape Survey," Pew Forum for Religion and Public Life, February 2008, http://religions.pewforum.org/reports#.

7. Mead, "The Jacksonian Tradition."

8. Quoted in Seymour Martin Lipset, *American Exceptionalism: A Double-Edged Sword* (New York: W. W. Norton, 1997), 31.

9. Ibid.

10. Lieven, *America, Right or Wrong*, 49; Jeffrey Jones, "Americans See U.S. as Exceptional," Gallup, December 22, 2010, http://www.gallup.com/poll/145358/Americans-Exceptional-Doubt-Obama.aspx.

11. Colin Dueck, *Reluctant Crusaders: Power, Culture, and Change in American Grand Strategy* (Princeton, NJ: Princeton University Press, 2006), 22.

12. Christopher Coker, *Reflections on American Foreign Policy since 1945* (London: Pinter, 1989).

13. Moshe Davis, *America and the Holy Land* (Westport, CT: Praeger, 1995), 13–19, 135–145; Shalom Goldman, *God's Sacred Tongue: Hebrew and the American Imagination* (Chapel Hill, NC: University of North Carolina Press, 2004).

14. Daniel Elazar, *Covenant and Constitutionalism: The Great Frontier and the Matrix of Federal Democracy* (New Brunswick, NJ: Transaction, 1998); Kenneth D. Wald and Alison Calhoun-Brown, *Religion and Politics in the United States*, 5th ed. (Lanham, MD: Rowman and Littlefield, 2007), 43–45.

15. Peter Grose, *Israel in the Mind of America* (New York: Knopf, 1983), 5.

16. Bruce Feiler, "Moses, the Patron Saint of Washington," *Washington Post*, October 18, 2009.

17. Conrad Cherry, ed., *God's New Israel: Religious Interpretations of American Destiny* (Englewood Cliffs, NJ: Prentice Hall, 1971), 65.

18. Cited in Jonathan Sacks, *The Home We Build Together: Recreating Society* (London: Continuum, 2009), 156.

19. Quoted in Ron Kurtus, "Bill Clinton's Second Inaugural Address in 1997," Ron Kurtus' School for Champions, http://www.school-for-champions.com/speeches/clinton_second_inaugural.htm.

20. Davis, *America and the Holy Land*, 25–26.

21. Ibid., 64.

22. Clark Clifford with Richard Holbrooke, *Counsel to the President: A Memoir* (New York: Random House, 1991), 7–8.

23. Davis, *America and the Holy Land*, 31.

24. Paul Merkley, *American Presidents, Religion, and Israel: The Heirs of Cyrus* (Westport, CT: Praeger, 2004).

25. Bill Clinton, *My Life* (London: Hutchinson, 2004), 353.

26. Ronald R. Stockton, "Christian Zionism: Prophecy and Public Opinion," *Middle East Journal* 41, no. 2 (1987): 253; John Green, "The American Public and Sympathy for Israel: Present and Future," *Journal of Ecumenical Studies* 44,

no. 1 (2009); Jeffrey Jones, "In U.S., 3 in 10 Say They Take the Bible Literally," Gallup, July 8, 2011; Lydia Saad, "Holy Land, or Just Ancient?" Gallup, July 29, 2003, http://www.gallup.com/poll/8941/Holy-Land-Just-Ancient.aspx.

27. Paul Charles Merkley, *The Politics of Christian Zionism, 1891–1948* (London: Frank Cass, 1998), 55; Yaakov Ariel, *On Behalf of Israel: American Fundamentalist Attitudes toward Jews, Judaism, and Zionism, 1865–1945* (Brooklyn, NY: Carlson, 1991), 77.

28. Green, "The American Public and Sympathy for Israel"; Stephan Spector, *Evangelicals and Israel: The Story of American Christian Zionism* (New York: Oxford University Press, 2009), 186–187; Jones, "In U.S., 3 in 10 Say They Take the Bible Literally."

29. James Guth and William Kenan Jr., "Religious Factors and American Public Support for Israel: 1992–2008," (paper presented at the annual meeting of the American Political Science Association, Seattle, WA, September 1–4, 2011).

30. Michael Oren, *Power, Faith, and Fantasy: America in the Middle East, 1776 to the Present* (New York: W. W. Norton, 2007), 278–282; Yaakov Ariel, "An American Initiative for a Jewish State: William Blackstone and the Petition of 1891," *Studies in Zionism* 10, no. 2 (1989): 125–137.

31. D.B. Robertson, ed., *Love and Justice: Selections from the Shorter Writings of Reinhold Niebuhr* (Louisville, KY: Westminster/John Knox Press, 1957), 133–142.

32. Golden, *Quiet Diplomat*, 424.

33. Michelle Mart, "Eleanor Roosevelt, Liberalism, and Israel," *Shofar: An Interdisciplinary Journal of Jewish Studies* 24, no. 3 (2006): 75.

34. Benny Morris, *Righteous Victims: A History of the Zionist-Arab Conflict, 1881–1999* (London: John Murray, 2000), 178.

35. Ibid.

36. "Harry Truman," National Cold War Exhibition, Royal Air Force Museum, http://www.nationalcoldwarexhibition.org/the-cold-war/biographies/harry-truman/.

37. "Survey: Optimism Reigns, Technology Plays Key Role," Pew Research Center for the People and the Press, October 24, 1999, http://www.people-press.org/1999/10/24/optimism-reigns-technology-plays-key-role/.

38. U.S. Department of State, "Vice President Biden's Speech at Tel Aviv University," IIP Digital, March 11, 2010,http://iipdigital.usembassy.gov/st/english/texttrans/2010/03/20100311123835eaifaso.9307062.html#axzz39BpiUsXk. (Emphasis added.)

39. Mart, "Eleanor Roosevelt, Liberalism, and Israel," 75.

40. Author interview with a high-ranking Taiwanese official on visit to Taiwan, 2002.

41. Melissa Radler, "Poll Shows Americans Back Israel in Intifada," *Jerusalem Post*, March 14, 2001; The Israel Project Election Day Survey, November 4, 2008, http://www.theisraelproject.org/atf/cf/%7B84DC5887-741E-4056-8D91-A389164BC94E%7D/081620%20TIP%20ELECTION%20NIGHT%20FOR%20RELEASE.PPT#1.

42. Green, "The American Public and Sympathy for Israel"; "Modest Backing for Israel in Gaza Crisis," Pew Research Center for the People and the Press, January 13, 2009, http://people-press.org:80/report/482/israel-hamas-conflict.

43. Jerome A. Chanes, "Antisemitism and Jewish Security in AmericaToday," in Jerome A. Chanes, ed., *Antisemitism in America Today: Outspoken Experts Explode the Myths* (New York: Birch Lane Press, 1995), 14.

44. Edward Linenthal, *American Sacred Space* (Bloomington, IN: Indiana University Press, 1995), 222–224.

45. Eyal Naveh, "Unconventional 'Christian Zionist': The Theologian Reinhold Nie-
    buhr and His Attitude toward the Jewish National Movement," *Studies in Zionism*
    11, no. 2 (1990) Mart, "Eleanor Roosevelt, Liberalism, and Israel," 66.

46. Ronald Reagan, *An American Life* (London: Hutchison, 1990), 410. On Truman
    and Johnson see Elizabeth Stephens, *U.S. Policy towards Israel: The Role of
    Political Culture in Defining the "Special Relationship"* (Brighton, UK: Sussex
    Academic Press, 2006), 89; Lenny Ben-David, 'Lyndon Johnson – A Friend in
    Deed,' *Jerusalem Post*, September 10, 2008.

47. John McCain, "Why Israel," *Reader's Digest*, December 2003, 126–127.
    (Emphasis added.)

48. "Public Opinion toward Foreign Aid," Jewish Virtual Library, http://www.jewish-
    virtuallibrary.org/jsource/US-Israel/poaid.html; see also CNN Poll, August 2–3,
    2006; CNN/*USA Today*/Gallup Poll, September 14–15, 2001; "Most Americans
    Favor End to U.S. Foreign Aid to Middle East, Except Israel,' Rasmussen Reports,
    February 25, 2011, http://www.rasmussenreports.com/public_content/politics/
    current_events/israel_the_middle_east/most_americans_favor_end_to_u_s_foreign_
    aid_to_middle_east_except_israel.

49. "Global Views 2006," Chicago Council on Foreign Relations, U.S. Public Topline
    Report, October 2006, http://www.thechicagocouncil.org/UserFiles/File/POS_Top-
    line%20Reports/POS%202006/2006%20US%20Topline.pdf.

50. "Goal of Libyan Operation Less Clear to Public: Top Middle East Priority:
    Preventing Terrorism," Pew Research Center for the People and the Press, April
    5, 2011, http://www.people-press.org/2011/04/05/goal-of-libyan-operation-less-
    clear-to-public.

51. A. F. K. Organski, *The $36 Billion Bargain: Strategy and Politics in U.S. Assistance
    to Israel* (New York: Columbia University Press, 1990), 40–42.

52. Ronald Reagan, "Recognizing the Israeli Asset," *Washington Post*, August 15,
    1979.

53. For the Harris, *USA Today*, and Rasmussen polls, see "Reliable Ally Polls," Jewish
    Virtual Library, http://www.jewishvirtuallibrary.org/jsource/US-Israel/poally.html;
    see also "Americans Have Very Different Attitudes to Different Countries in, or near
    the Middle East," The Harris Poll, November 20, 2009, http://www.harrisinteractive.
    com/vault/Harris-Interactive-Poll-Research-Middle-East-Allies-2009-11.pdf; "Egypt,
    Kuwait Top the List of Countries in the Middle East That Americans Think of
    as Friendly," The Harris Poll, November 10, 2010, http://www.harrisinteractive.
    com/NewsRoom/HarrisPolls/tabid/447/ctl/ReadCustom%20Default/mid/1508/
    ArticleId/619/Default.aspx.

54. "Worldviews 2002: American Public Opinion and Foreign Policy," The Chicago
    Council on Global Affairs, http://www.thechicagocouncil.org/UserFiles/File/
    POS_Topline%20Reports/POS%202002/2002_US_Report.pdf.

55. *Constrained Internationalism: Adapting to New Realities: Results of a 2010
    National Survey of Public Opinion*, (Chicago: The Chicago Council on Global
    Affairs, 2010), http://www.thechicagocouncil.org/UserFiles/File/POS_Topline%
    20Reports/POS%202010/Global%20Views%202010.pdf; Jeffrey Jones, "In U.S.,
    6 in 10 View Iran as Critical Threat to U.S. Interests," Gallup, February 16, 2010,
    http://www.gallup.com/poll/125996/View-Iran-Critical-Threat-Interests.aspx?
    CSTS=alert. On perceptions of the threat from Islamist extremist groups, see

"More See America's Loss of Global Respect as Major Problem," Pew Research Center for the People and the Press, June 16, 2008, http://people-press.org/2008/06/16/more-see-americas-loss-of-global-respect-as-major-problem/; "U.S. Seen as Less Important, China as More Powerful," Pew Research Center for the People and the Press, December 3, 2009, http://people-press.org/2009/12/03/us-seen-as-less-important-china-as-more-powerful/.

56. "Americans Continue to Rate Iran as Greatest U.S. Enemy"; "Americans Continue to Tilt Pro-Israel," Gallup, http://www.gallup.com/poll/153092/Americans-Continue-Tilt-Pro-Israel.aspx.

57. Elizabeth Mendes, "Americans Continue to Tilt Pro-Israel: More view Israel Favorably than the Palestinian Authority or Iran," Gallup, March 2, 2012, http://www.gallup.com/poll/153092/Americans-Continue-Tilt-Pro-Israel.aspx.

58. U.S. Department of State, "State Sponsors of Terrorism Overview," April 30, 2007, http://www.state.gov/s/ct/rls/crt/2006/82736.htm.

59. Lydia Saad, "Canada Remains Americans' Most Favored Nation," Gallup, February 19, 2009, http://www.gallup.com/poll/115258/canada-remains-americans-favored-nation.aspx; "Country Ratings," Gallup, http://www.gallup.com/poll/1624/Perceptions-Foreign-Countries.aspx; see also Harris polls on states regarded as unfriendly or enemies from the 1990s until 2006, which are available at "American Opinion on National Allies," Jewish Virtual Library, http://www.jewishvirtuallibrary.org/jsource/US-Israel/poally.html; Jeffrey Jones, "Americans Continue to Rate Iran as Greatest U.S. Enemy: North Korea, China Tie for Second; Mentions of Iraq Down Significantly," Gallup, February 18, 2011, http://www.gallup.com/poll/146165/americans-continue-rate-iran-greatest-enemy.aspx.

60. Oren, *Power, Faith, and Fantasy.*

61. Eytan Gilboa, *American Public Opinion toward Israel and the Arab-Israeli Conflict* (Lexington, MA: Lexington Books, 1987), 306–307.

62. "Unfavorable Views of Both Jews and Muslims on the Increase in Europe," Pew Research Global Attitudes Project, September 17, 2008, http://www.pewglobal.org/2008/09/17/unfavorable-views-of-jews-and-muslims-on-the-increase-in-europe/; "Muslim-Western Tensions Persist," Pew Research Global Attitudes Project, July 21, 2011, http://www.pewglobal.org/files/2011/07/Pew-Global-Attitudes-Muslim-Western-Relations-FINAL-FOR-PRINT-July-21-2011.pdf.

63. "Diminished Public Appetite for Military Force and Mideast Oil: Five Years Later," Pew Research Center for the People and the Press, September 6, 2006, http://people-press.org/report/288/diminished-public-appetite-for-military-force-and-mideast-oil.

64. "Views of Islam Remain Sharply Divided: Plurality Sees Islam as More Likely to Encourage Violence," Pew Research and Public Life Project, September 9, 2004, http://www.pewforum.org/2004/09/09/views-of-islam-remain-sharply-divided/; "Public Expresses Mixed Views of Islam, Mormonism," Pew Research and Public Life Project, September 25, 2007, http://www.pewforum.org/2007/09/26/public-expresses-mixed-views-of-islam-mormonism/.

65. Frank Newport, "Complex But Hopeful Pattern of American Attitudes toward Muslims: Little Change in Opinions since 2002 Survey," Gallup, March 23, 2006, http://www.gallup.com/poll/22021/complex-hopeful-pattern-american-attitudes-toward-muslims.aspx.

66. Anthony Cordesman and Khalid R. Al-Rodhan, *The Changing Dynamics of Energy in the Middle East* (Westport, CT: Praeger Security International, 2006), 120, 125; Arab Human Development Reports, http://www.arab-hdr.org/.

67. Cited in Kenneth Pollack, *A Path Out of the Dessert: A Grand Strategy for America in the Middle East* (New York: Random House, 2008), 33, 102.

68. Robert Weisbrod and Richard Kazarian, *Israel in the Black American Perspective* (Westport, CT: Greenwood Press, 1985); Melani McAlister, *Epic Encounters: Culture, Media, and U.S. Interests in the Middle East, 1945–2000* (Berkeley: University of California Press, 2001), 84–115.

69. Quoted in Richard T. Hughes, *Myths America Lives By* (Urbana, IL: University of Illinois Press, 2003), 11.

70. Martin Luther King Jr., "I Have a Dream," speech delivered at the March on Washington, DC, August 28, 1963, Historic Documents, UShistory.org, http://www.ushistory.org/documents/i-have-a-dream.htm.

71. Quoted in Seymour Martin Lipset, "The Socialism of Fools: The Left, the Jews, and Israel," *Encounter*, 33, no. 6 (1969): 24.

72. Arnold Forster, "American Radicals and Israel," in Robert S. Wistrich, ed., *The Left against Zion: Communism, Israel and the Middle East* (London: Vallentine Mitchell, 1979), 221–225.

73. Robert Ruby, "A Six-Day War: Its Aftermath in American Public Opinion," Pew Forum on Religion and Public Life, May 30, 2007, http://pewresearch.org/pubs/491/six-day-war; Gilboa, *American Public Opinion toward Israel*, 20–21.

74. Mitchell Bard, "Public Opinion toward Israel," Jewish Virtual Library, http://www.jewishvirtuallibrary.org/jsource/US-Israel/American_attitudes_toward_Israel.html; "Gallup Polls on American Sympathy oward Israel and the Arabs/Palestinians," Jewish Virtual Library, http://www.jewishvirtuallibrary.org/jsource/US-Israel/gallup.html.

75. Gilboa, *American Public Opinion toward Israel*, 181–201; Gallup polls from 1994 to 2002, cited in "American Attitudes toward Yasser Arafat," Jewish Virtual Library, http://www.jewishvirtuallibrary.org/jsource/US-Israel/arafatpo.html.

76. Ruby, "A Six-Day War"; Gilboa, *American Public Opinion toward Israel*, 181–183.

77. Ruby, "A Six-Day War."

78. Jodie Allen and Alec Tyson, "The U.S. Public's Pro-Israel History," Pew Research Center, July 19, 2006, http://www.pewresearch.org/pubs/39/the-us-publics-pro-israel-history.

79. Lydia Saad, "Support for Israel in U.S. at 63%, Near Record High," Gallup, February 24, 2010, http://www.gallup.com/poll/126155/Support-Israel-Near-Record-High.aspx?CSTS=alert.

80. Ibid.

81. Lydia Saad, "Americans' Support for Israel Unchanged Since Gaza Conflict: Most Americans Sympathize with Israel, View It Favorably," Gallup, March 3, 2009, http://www.gallup.com/poll/116308/Americans-Support-Israel-Unchanged-Gaza-Conflict.aspx.

82. See several NBC/*Wall Street Journal* polls taken between July and December 1991 and several Harris polls taken in 1997 and 1998, available at "American Public Opinion Polls: Attitudes toward the Peace Process (1991–1999)," Jewish Virtual Library, http://www.jewishvirtuallibrary.org/jsource/US-Israel/popeace1.html.

83. Polls available at PollingReport.com, http://www.pollingreport.com/israel3. htm; and "American Public Opinion Polls: Attitudes toward the Peace Process (2000–2002)," Jewish Virtual Library, http://www.jewishvirtuallibrary.org/ jsource/US-Israel/popeace2.html.

84. "Modest Backing for Israel in Gaza Crisis." Pew Research Center for the People and the Press, January 13, 2009,http://www.people-press.org/2009/01/13/modest-backing-for-israel-in-gaza-crisis/.

85. TIP Public Opinion Strategies, September 9, 11, 12, 2010. See "New Poll Finds Strong Support of Israel among Americans," The Israel Project, http://www.kintera. org/site/apps/nlnet/content3.aspx?c=ewJXKcOUJllaG&b=7717029&ct=11142797#. VAYuX8VdWSo.

86. Over the rest of the decade, support for a Palestinian state fell back to 51 percent, while opposition increased to 29 percent. Lydia Saad, "Americans Remain Skeptical about Middle East Peace," Gallup, June 4, 2009, http://www.gallup.com/poll/ 120728/americans-remain-skeptical-middle-east-peace.aspx.

87. Polls available at "American Public Opinion Polls: Views on Palestinian Statehood," Jewish Virtual Library, http://www.jewishvirtuallibrary.org/jsource/US-Israel/popalhome.html.

88. "The ADL 2005 Survey of American Attitudes Toward Israel and the Middle East," Anti-Defamation League, http://archive.adl.org/israel/us_israel_200503_ files/frame.html; see also the 2007, 2009, and 2011 surveys by the ADL, available at http://www.jewishvirtuallibrary.org/jsource/US-Israel/popalhome.html.

89. PIPA survey, May 8, 2002, cited in "American Public Opinion Polls: Attitudes toward the Peace Process (2000–2002)"; *Constrained Internationalism.*

90. Louis Harris, "Pro-Israel Support Still Strong," The Harris Survey, September 22, 1991; Kurt Holden, "Public Opinion: Clinton's Tilt toward Israel Losing Public Opinion Support," *Washington Report on Middle East Affairs* (June–July 1997), 50–54; see also numerous polls available at "American Public Opinion Polls: Attitudes Regarding Jerusalem," Jewish Virtual Library, http://www.jewishvirtual-library.org/jsource/US-Israel/pousjeru.html; see also polls conducted by Harris in 2002, available at PollingReport.com, http://www.pollingreport.com/israel2.htm; see also the poll conducted by Greenberg Quinlin Rosner Research for the Israel Project in December 2010.

91. Middle East Gallup Polls, http://www.gallup.com/poll/1639/middle-east.aspx; "American Polls: American Attitudes toward the Peace Process," Jewish Virtual Library, http://www.jewishvirtuallibrary.org/jsource/US-Israel/popeace.html; *Constrained Internationalism.*

92. Guth and Kenan, "Religious Factors and American Public Support for Israel: 1992–2008."

93. Polls available at PollingReport.com, http://www.pollingreport.com/israel3.htm.

94. "Modest Backing for Israel in Gaza Crisis."

95. Benjamin Phillips, Eszter Lengyel, and Leonard Saxe, *American Attitudes toward Israel* (Waltham, MA: Brandeis University, Cohen Center for Modern Jewish Studies, 2002), 64.

96. *USA Today*, August 1991, *Time/CNN*, August 1991, *Wall Street Journal/NBC News*, April 5–7, 2002; *Newsweek* polls from 2001 and 2002, all cited in "American Polls: American Attitudes toward the Peace Process."

97. Gallup polls 2007, 2008, 2013, available at "Middle East," Gallup, http://www.gallup.com/poll/1639/middle-east.aspx; Lydia Saad, "Americans Favor More Pressure on Palestinians than Israelis," Gallup, March 18, 2013, http://www.gallup.com/poll/161405/americans-favor-pressure-palestinians-israelis.aspx.

98. The data for the U.S. is available by clicking on the "View methodology, full question results, and trend data" link at http://www.gallup.com/poll152735/Americans-Give-Record-High-Ratings-Several-Allies.aspx. The 2011 data from the UK and France is taken from surveys by Greenberg Rosner Quinlin Research for the Israel Project: "Opinions on Israeli-Palestinian Peace Talks in UK/France conducted April 2011," http://www.theisraelproject.org/site/apps/nlnet/content2.aspx?c=hsJPKoPIJpH&b=689705&ct=9357717 (no longer available). The data for Spain in 2010 is taken from a DYM Institute survey undertaken for Casa Sefarad Israel, http://www.sefarad-israel.es/otros550125_inf_rev%207-9.pdf (no longer available). The data for Europe 2002–2007 comes from surveys conducting for the Anti-Defamation League available in "Attitudes toward Jews, Israel and the Palestinian-Israeli conflict in Ten European Countries," April 2004, http://archive.adl.org/anti_semitism/european_attitudes_april_2004.pdf.

99. "Despite Their Wide Differences, Many Israelis and Palestinians Want Bigger Role for Obama in Resolving Conflict," Pew Research Global Attitudes Project, May 9, 2013, http://www.pewglobal.org/2013/05/09/despite-their-wide-differences-many-israelis-and-palestinians-want-bigger-role-for-obama-in-resolving-conflict/; "Americans and Europeans Differ Widely on Foreign Policy Issues," Pew Research Global Attitudes Project, April 17, 2002, http://www.pewglobal.org/2002/04/17/americans-and-europeans-differ-widely-on-foreign-policy-issues/; "America's Image Slips, But Allies Share U.S. Concerns over Iran, Hamas," Pew Research Global Attitudes Project, June 13, 2006, http://www.pewglobal.org/reports/display.php?ReportID=252; "Ideological Gaps over Israel on Both Sides of Atlantic," Pew Research Global Attitudes Project.

100. Penn Schoen Berland and First International Resources, January 25 and February 17, 2001, available at "American Public Opinion Polls: Attitudes toward the Peace Process (2000–2002)"; "American Attitudes toward the Middle East," Anti-Defamation League, December 2003, http://www.adl.org/Israel/am_attitudes_2003/am_attitudes_2003.pdf.

101. "Modest Backing for Israel in Gaza Crisis."

102. Yougov Poll for the *Daily Telegraph*, July 24–26, 2006, http://d25d2506sfb94s.cloudfront.net/today_uk_import/YG-Archives-pol-dTel-ConflictLebanon-060728.pdf; Yougov Poll for the *Jewish Chronicle*, January 28–29, 2009 .

103. "'American Attitudes toward the Middle East," Anti-Defamation League, October 2009, http://www.adl.org/Israel/poll_israel2009/poll_israel2009.pdf.

104. Populus Polls in the UK opinion, 2010 (unpublished poll).

105. On opinion in the UK and France, see polls by Greenberg Quinlin Rosner for the Israel Project: "As Israeli PM Ariel Sharon Heads to France, Polls Show that Europeans and Americans Support Israel's Plan to Withdraw from Gaza and Parts of West Bank," June 17–21 2005, and May 2010 (unpublished poll), http://www.theisraelproject.org/site/apps/nlnet/content2.aspx?

c=hsJPKoPIJpH&b=5708939&ct=7791679; "New European Polling Shows Huge Drop in Support for Palestinians," June 6, 2006, http://www.theisraelproject.org/site/apps/nlnet/content2.aspx?c=hsJPKoPIJpH&b=5708939&ct=7791659; "British Attitudes toward Israel and the Palestinians," May 2010 (unpublished); see also "Ten Years of British Attitudes toward the Middle East Conflict," Populus Polling Report, August 2010 (unpublished).

106. "Transatlantic Trends 2011," German Marshall Fund, http://www.gmfus.org/publications_/TT/TT2011_final_web.pdf.

107. Eurobarometer Survey, conducted by Taylor Nelson Sofres / EOS Gallup Europe, October 8–16 2003; "'American Attitudes toward the Middle East," Anti-Defamation League, December 2003.

108. "The American-Western European Values Gap: American Exceptionalism Subsides," Pew Research Global Attitudes Project, November 17, 2011, http://www.pewglobal.org/2011/11/17/the-american-western-european-values-gap/; Peter Ford, "What Place for God in Europe?" *Christian Science Monitor*, February 22, 2005.

109. Gertrude Himmelfarb, *The People of the Book: Philosemitism in England from Cromwell to Churchill* (New York: Encounter, 2011), chapter 5; Barbara Tuchman, *Bible and Sword: England and Palestine from the Bronze Age to Balfour* (New York: New York University Press, 1956).

110. On Polish attitudes see "Unfavorable Views of Both Jews and Muslims on the Increase in Europe," Pew Research Global Attitudes Project; "Worldviews 2002 European Public Opinion and Foreign Policy," Chicago Council on Global Affairs, 10, http://www.thechicagocouncil.org/UserFiles/File/POS_Topline%20Reports/POS%202002/2002_Europe_Report.pdf.; "Ideological Gaps over Israel on Both Sides of Atlantic," Pew Research Global Attitudes Project, January 29, 2009, http://pewresearch.org/pubs/1097/america-europe-ideological-gaps-over-israel.

111. Anatol Lieven, *America, Right or Wrong: An Anatomy of American Nationalism* (New York: Oxford University Press, 2004), 19; Lipset, *American Exceptionalism*, 51.

112. "Two Decades after the Wall's Fall," Pew Research Global Attitudes Project, November 2, 2009, 58, http://www.pewglobal.org/files/2009/11/Pew-Global-Attitudes-2009-Pulse-of-Europe-Report-Nov-2-1030am-NOT-EMBARGOED.pdf

113. "Transatlantic Trends 2011."

114. On Holocaust remembrance in Europe see Elisabeth Kuebler, "Holocaust Remembrance in the Council of Europe: Deplorable Victims and Evil Ideologies without Perpetrators," *Jewish Political Studies Review* 22, no. 3–4 (Fall 2010). On the way the Holocaust is interpreted in Europe to inform an anti-Israeli position, see Alain Finkielkraut, "The Religion of Humanity and the Sin of the Jews," *Azure* 21 (Summer 2005).

115. See polls conducted by the Anti-Defamation League: "Attitudes toward Jews in Twelve European Countries," May 2005, http://www.adl.org/anti_semitism/european_attitudes_may_2005.pdf; "Attitudes toward Jews and the Middle East in Six European Countries," July 2007, http://www.adl.org/anti_semitism/European_Attitudes_Survey_July_2007.pdf; "Attitudes toward Jews and the Middle East in Five European Countries," May 2007, http://www.adl.org/anti_semitism/European_Attitudes_Survey_May_2007.pdf; "Attitudes toward Jews in Seven European Countries," February 2009, http://www.adl.org/Public%20ADL%20Anti-Semitism%20Presentation%20February%202009%20_3_.pdf;

Marttila Strategies, "A Survey Of American Attitudes toward Jews in America," October 2011, http://www.adl.org/anti_semitism_domestic/ADL-2011-Anti-Semitism_Presentation.pdf.

116. Lipset, *American Exceptionalism*, 35, 81–88; Russell Dalton, *Citizen Politics: Public Opinion and Political Parties in Advanced Industrial Democracies*, 5th ed. (Washington, DC: CQ Press, 2008), 85, 116. On the relative liberalism of the American Left vis-à-vis Europe, see Paul Berman, *A Tale of Two Utopias: The Political Journey of the Generation of 1968* (New York: W. W. Norton, 1996), 49–52.

117. Mark Visser et al., "Support for Radical Left Ideologies in Europe," *European Journal of Political Research* 53, no. 3 (August 2014): 541–558.

118. Jonathan Rynhold and Jonathan Spyer, "British Policy in the Arab-Israeli Arena, 1973–2004," *British Journal of Middle Eastern Studies* 34, no. 2 (2007).

119. "Unfavorable Views of Both Jews and Muslims on the Increase in Europe," Pew Research Global Attitudes Project.

120. Edward H. Kaplan and Charles A. Small, "Anti-Israel Sentiment Predicts Anti-Semitism in Europe," *Journal of Conflict Resolution*, 50, no. 4 (2006): 548–561.

121. Rynhold and Spyer, "British Policy in the Arab-Israeli Arena"; José María Aznar, "Support Israel: If It Goes Down, We All Go Down," *Times* (London), June 17, 2010; Natasha Mozgovaya, "Focus U.S.A. / Can the West Stay Strong If Israel Is Weakened?' *Haaretz*, September 15, 2010.

122. "Ideological Gaps over Israel on Both Sides of Atlantic," Pew Research Global Attitudes Project. For similar results with regard to the UK and Spain, see Simon Sarkar, "British Public Divided over Middle East Conflict," Gallup, May 14, 2002, http://www.gallup.com/poll/6013/British-Public-Divided-Over-Middle-East-Conflict. aspx; Casa Sefarad Israel, http://sefarad-israel.es/otros550125_inf_rev%207-9.pdf (no longer available).

123. Colin Shindler, *Israel and the European Left: Between Solidarity and Delegitimization* (New York: Continuum, 2012); Robert S. Wistrich, ed., *The Left against Zion: Communism, Israel and the Middle East* (London: Vallentine Mitchell, 1979), 1–12; Ben Cohen, "The Persistence of Anti-Semitism on the British Left," *Jewish Political Studies Review* 16, no. 3–4 (2004).

124. Bashir Abu-Manneh, "Israel in the U.S. Empire," in Elleke Boehmer and Stephen Morton, eds., *Terror and the Postcolonial: A Concise Companion* (Oxford: Wiley-Blackwell, 2010), 226–252; Noam Chomsky, "The Israel Lobby?" *ZNet* (March 28, 2006), http://www.zcomm.org/znetarticle/the-israel-lobby-by-noam-chomsky; Efraim Sicher, "The Image of Israel and Postcolonial Discourse in the Early 21st Century: A View from Britain," *Israel Studies* 16, no. 1 (2011).

125. Irfan Khawaja, "Essentialism, Consistency and Islam: A Critique of Edward Said's *Orientalism*," *Israel Affairs* 13, no. 4 (2007) Ronald Niezen, "Postcolonialism and the Utopian Imagination," *Israel Affairs* 13, no. 4 (2007).

126. Robert S. Wistrich, "Left-Wing Anti-Zionism in Western Societies," in Robert S. Wistrich, ed., *Anti-Zionism and Antisemitism in the Contemporary World* (London: Macmillan, 1990), 48.

127. Joel Schalit, *Israel vs. Utopia* (New York: Akashic Books, 2009), 29–31, 62–63; Ernest Sternberg, "Purifying the World: What the New Radical Ideology Stands For," *Orbis* 54, no. 1 (2010): 61–86.

128. For revealing comments on this issue, see an interview with Norman Finklestein, "Arguing the BDS Case," Imperial College, London, February 9, 2012, http://www.youtube.com/watch?v=iggdO7C70P8, also at http://www.youtube.com/watch?v=M7RWb24VKhA&feature=related.

129. On the Far Left and the boycott movement in the UK, see Jonathan Rynhold, "The Meaning of the UK Campaign for an Academic Boycott of Israel," *MERIA Journal*, 14, no. 2 (2010), http://www.gloria-center.org/2010/06/rynhold-2010-06-04/.

130. Emanuele Ottolenghi, "Making Sense of European Anti-Semitism," *Human Rights Review* 8, no. 2 (2007): 104–126; Alvin H. Rosenfeld, *Anti-Zionism in Great Britain and Beyond: A "Respectable" Anti-Semitism?* (New York: American Jewish Committee, 2004), 7–13; Robert S. Wistrich, "Cruel Britannia," *Azure* 21 (Summer 2005); Mitchell Cohen, "Anti-Semitism and the Left That Doesn't Learn," *Dissent*, Winter 2008, http://www.dissentmagazine.org/article/?article=972.

131. Winston Pickett, "Nasty or Nazi? The Use of Anti-Semitic Topoi by the Left-Liberal Media," in Paul Iganski and Barry Kosmin, eds., *A New Antisemitism? Debating Judeophobia in 21st-Century Britain* (London: Profile Books, 2003).

132. Paul Berman, "Bigotry in Print. Crowds Chant Murder. Something's Changed," *Forward*, May 24, 2002, http://www.chicagopeacenow.org/rr-22.html (no longer available).

133. He also declared the Jewish nation as "the root of evil" while later speaking about Jewish control over the U.S. government. Herb Keinon, "Greece Repudiates Theodorakis' Anti-Semitism," *Jerusalem Post*, November 14, 2003; Ari Shavit, "The Jewish Problem, According to Theodorakis," *Haaretz*, August 27, 2004.

134. Eytan Gilboa, "Public Diplomacy: The Missing Component in Israel's Diplomacy," *Israel Affairs* 12, no. 4 (2006). More generally, in the first years of the second intifada, the Greek media regularly portrayed Israel as a "Nazi" state, in Dina Porat and Roni Stauber, eds., *Antisemitism Worldwide 2003/4* (Tel Aviv: Tel Aviv University, 2005), 7, http://www.tau.ac.il/Anti-Semitism/asw2003-4/general analysis.htm.

135. "Working Definition of Antisemitism," European Forum on Antisemitism, http://www.european-forum-on-antisemitism.org/working-definition-of-antisemitism/english/.

136. *Report of the All-Party Parliamentary Inquiry into Anti-Semitism*, All-Party Parliamentary Group against Anti-Semitism, September 2006, http://antisemitism.org.uk/wp-content/uploads/All-Party-Parliamentary-Inquiry-into-Antisemitism-REPORT.pdf.

137. This is independent research carried out by the author. In the UK there only five national broadsheet newspapers, so they are self-selecting. In the United States, the first four U.S. publications are generally regarded as the leading broadsheets. The *Chicago Tribune* was selected as the fifth source because it had a high circulation and a significant number of articles relating to the Israeli-Palestinian conflict.

138. For supporting evidence see a comparison of the *Guardian* and the *New York Times* reports on the Israeli-Palestinian conflict in Eric Heinze and Rosa Freedman, "Public Awareness of Human Rights: Distortions in the Mass Media,' *International Journal of Human Rights*, 14, no. 4 (2010): 491–523; see also Colin

Shindler, "Reading *The Guardian*: Jews, Israel-Palestine and the Origins of Irritation," in Tudor Parfitt and Yulia Egorova, eds., *Jews, Muslims, and Mass Media:
Mediating the "Other"* (London: RoutledgeCurzon, 2003), 157–177.

139. Pascal Bruckner, *The Tyranny of Guilt: An Essay on Western Masochism*, trans.
Steven Rendall (Princeton, NJ: Princeton University Press, 2010); Nick Cohen,
What's Left: How Liberals Lost Their Way (London: Fourth Estate, 2007); see
also Bernard-Henri Lévy, "The Task of the Jews," *American Interest* (September–
October 2008).

140. Even Sartre argued that he could not condemn Palestinian terrorist attacks against
Israelis, as they were part of a struggle that was similar to that which the Algerian
independence movement had been fighting against France; see Jonathan Judaken,
"Sartre at 100: Revisiting His Interventions in the Arab-Israeli Conflict," *Antisemitism International* 3–4 (2006). A more detailed survey of the differences between
the liberal and postcolonial Left discourse is presented in chapter 3.

141. Andrew Anthony, *The Fall Out: How a Guilty Liberal Lost His Innocence*
(London: Jonathan Cape, 2007); Bruckner, *The Tyranny of Guilt*.

142. "Unfavorable Views of Both Jews and Muslims on the Increase in Europe," Pew
Research Global Attitudes Project; "Muslim-Western Tensions Persist," Pew
Research Global Attitudes Project, July 21, 2011, http://www.pewglobal.
org/files/2011/07/Pew-Global-Attitudes-Muslim-Western-Relations-FINAL-FOR-
PRINT-July-21-2011.pdf.

143. "Muslim Americans: Middle Class and Mostly Mainstream," Pew Research
Center, May 22, 2007, http://www.pewresearch.org/pubs/483/muslim-americans;
"How Many Muslims Are in the U.S. and the Rest of the World?" Religious
Tolerance.org, http://www.religioustolerance.org/isl_numb.htm.

2. REPUBLICANS, CONSERVATIVES, AND THE RIGHT

1. George Will, "The End of Our Holiday from History," *Washington Post*, September
12, 2001, A27.

2. Lydia Saad, "Support for Israel in U.S. at 63%, Near Record High," Gallup, February
24, 2010, http://www.gallup.com/poll/126155/Support-Israel-Near-Record-High.
aspx?CSTS=alert.

3. Frank Newport and Joseph Carroll, "Republicans and Religious Americans Most
Sympathetic to Israel," Gallup, March 27, 2006; "Modest Backing for Israel in Gaza
Crisis," Pew Research Center for the People and the Press, January 13, 2009, http://
people-press.org:80/report/482/israel-hamas-conflict.

4. Lydia Saad, "Conservatives Continue to Outnumber Moderates in 2010," Gallup,
December 16, 2010, http://www.gallup.com/poll/145271/conservatives-continue-
outnumber-moderates-2010.aspx.

5. Saad, "Conservatives Continue to Outnumber Moderates in 2010."

6. "The 2005 Political Typology," Pew Research Center for the People and the Press,
May 10, 2005, http://people-press.org/files/legacy-pdf/242.pdf.

7. Saad, "Conservatives Continue to Outnumber Moderates in 2010."

8. "Independents Take Center Stage in Obama Era: Trends in Political Values
and Core Attitudes: 1987–2009," Pew Research Center for the People and the Press,

May 21, 2009, http://people-press.org/2009/05/21/independents-take-center-stage-in-obama-era/.

9. Jeet Heer, "When Conservatives Loved the Palestinians," *Sans Everything* (blog), February 25, 2008, http://sanseverything.wordpress.com/2008/02/25/when-conservatives-loved-the-palestinians/. On conservatives' attitudes toward Israel prior to 1967, see also Jeet Heer, "Goldberg's 'Fascism' and the Real Thing," *Sans Everything* (blog), December 20, 2007, http://sanseverything.wordpress.com/2007/12/20/goldbergs-fascism-and-the-real-thing/; George Nash, "Forgotten Godfathers: Premature Jewish Conservatives and the Rise of *National Review*," *American Jewish History*, 87, no. 2–3 (1999); Franklin Foer, "Once Again, America First," *New York Times*, October 10, 2004.

10. This is explained more fully below and in a later chapter on the mainline Protestant church.

11. Joseph Scotchie, ed., *The Paleoconservatives: New Voices of the Old Right* (New Brunswick, NJ: Transaction, 1999); Paul Gottfried, "Paleoconservatism," in Bruce Frohnen, Jeremy Beer, and Jeffrey O. Nelson, eds., *American Conservatism: An Encyclopedia* (Wilmington, DE: ISI Books, 2006).

12. Pat Buchanan, "The Sun Could Be Setting on the American Empire," *San Jose Mercury News*, February 17, 1999, 6B.

13. Quoted in Justin Raimondo, "Now Entering Imperium," *American Conservative*, October 7, 2002.

14. Stephen M. Walt, "In the National Interest: A New Grand Strategy for American Foreign Policy," *Boston Review*, February 1, 2005; Zbigniew Brzezinski and Brent Scowcroft, *America and the World: Conversations on the Future of American Foreign Policy* (New York: Basic Books, 2008), 351.

15. James Mann, *Rise of the Vulcans: The History of Bush's War Cabinet* (London: Penguin Books, 2004), 43–44, 53.

16. Foer, "Once Again, America First."

17. Patrick J. Buchanan, "Islamo-fascism?", Patrick J. Buchanan – Official Website, September 1, 2006, http://buchanan.org/blog/pjb-islamo-fascism-75; Pat Buchanan, syndicated column, September 19, 1989, quoted in "Patrick Buchanan, in His Own Words," FAIR, February 26, 1996, http://www.fair.org/press-releace/pat-buchanan-in-his-own-words/.

18. Quoted in James L. Baughman, *Henry Luce and the Rise of the American News Media* (Baltimore, MD: Johns Hopkins University Press, 2001), 135.

19. Stephen M. Walt, *Taming American Power: The Global Response to U.S. Primacy* (New York: Norton, 2005); Patrick Buchanan, *A Republic, Not an Empire: Reclaiming America's Destiny* (Washington, DC: Regnery, 1999).

20. Libertarians and paleoconservatives were more isolationist than the Realists, as they advocated withdrawing from Europe and NATO altogether, unlike the Realists.

21. Leon T. Hadar, "What Green Peril," *Foreign Affairs* 72, no. 2 (Spring 1993).

22. Pat Buchanan, "Let's Make Iran Our New Friend," *San Jose Mercury News*, January 14, 1998, 6B.

23. Daniel Pipes, "Looking Back on the Middle East: James A. Baker III," *Middle East Quarterly* (September 1994); Michael Desch, "Ominous Precedent," *American Conservative*, May 5, 2003; Christopher Layne, "Balancing Act," *American Conservative*, September 10, 2007.

24. Brzezinski and Scowcroft, *America and the World*; Coalition for a Realistic Foreign Policy, "The Perils of Occupation", statement, October 28, 2004, http://www.realisticforeignpolicy.org/downloads/perils_of_occupation_1004.pdf.

25. Doug Bandow, "Israel's Democracy Dilemma," *American Conservative*, November 3 2003; John J. Mearsheimer and Stephen M. Walt, *The Israel Lobby: and U.S. Foreign Policy* (New York: Farrar, Straus and Giroux, 2007), 86–87; Taki, "Not So Clean Break," *American Conservative*, September 11, 2006; Patrick J. Buchanan, "The Persecution of the Palestinians," *American Conservative*, June 5, 2006; George Szamuely, "Thomas Friedman, Dean of Liberal Imperialism," *American Conservative*, December 2, 2002; John J. Mearsheimer, "Saving Israel from Itself," *American Conservative*, May 18, 2009.

26. "Ron Paul Courageously Speaks the Truth," video, Fox News, May 16, 2007, available on YouTube, http://www.youtube.com/watch?v=G7d_e9lrcZ8.

27. Stephen M. Walt, "Taming American Power," *Foreign Affairs*, 84, no. 5 (2005). Libertarians advocated a wholesale American military withdrawal from the region; see Leon T. Hadar, *Quagmire: America in the Middle East* (Washington, DC: Cato Institute, 1992); Leon Hadar, *Sandstorm: Policy Failure in the Middle East* (New York: Palgrave Macmillan, 2005).

28. Pat Buchanan, "Let's Make Iran Our New Friend"; Brzezinski and Scowcroft, *America and the World*, 57–59, 77–78; Seth Colter Walls, "Bush 41 Adviser Scowcroft Says He'd Tell Israel to 'Calm Down' on Iran Strike," *Huffington Post*, July 22, 2008, http://www.huffingtonpost.com/2008/07/22/mccain-adviser-scowcroft_n_114379.html; "U.S. Presidential Hopeful Ron Paul: 'Friendship' Is Best Way to Deal with Iran," *Haaretz*, November 6, 2011.

29. Brendan O'Neill, "Burdening Israel," *American Conservative*, March 9, 2009; Philip Weiss, "Mondoweiss, Chapter One," *American Conservative*, June 4, 2007; Philip Weiss, "Freeman's Fight," *American Conservative*, March 23, 2009; Philip Weiss, "Looking into the Lobby," *American Conservative*, June 30, 2008; Philip Weiss, "The Long Fuse to the Iraq War," *American Conservative* January 28, 2008; Philip Weiss, "Honest Broker," *American Conservative*, February 26, 2007.

30. Brzezinski and Scowcroft, *America and the World*, 87 (emphasis added); Mearsheimer and Walt, *The Israel Lobby*.

31. Scott McConnell, "America's New Nationalism," *American Conservative*, March 14, 2005; Leon Hadar, "Bad For You Too?" *American Conservative*, November 7, 2005; Patrick J. Buchanan, "Whose War?" *American Conservative*, March 24, 2003; Layne, "Balancing Act."

32. Dennis Ross and David Makovsky, *Myths, Illusions and Peace: Finding a New Direction for America in the Middle East* (New York: Viking, 2009).

33. For example, Patrick J. Buchanan, "Foreign Aid: Ever with Us," Patrick J. Buchanan – Official Website, December 21, 1994, http://buchanan.org/blog/foreign-aid-ever-with-us-166; Ivan Eland, "Israel and the United States," in Srdja Trifkovic, ed., *Peace in the Promised Land: A Realist Scenario* (Rockford IL: Chronicles Press, 2006). Andrew Sullivan, "Giving Up on Israel?" *Atlantic*, http://andrewsullivan.theatlantic.com/the_daily_dish/2010/12/giving-up-on-israel.html; Leon T. Hadar, "Let the Locals Fix the Israeli-Palestinian Conflict," Cato Institute, June 21, 2001, http://www.cato.org/publications/commentary/let-locals-fix-israelipalestinian-conflict.

34. Steven L. Spiegel, *The Other Arab-Israeli Conflict: Making America's Middle East Policy, from Truman to Reagan* (Chicago: University of Chicago Press, 1986), 16–49.

35. Abraham Ben-Zvi, *Decade of Transition: Eisenhower, Kennedy, and the Origins of the American-Israeli Alliance* (New York: Columbia University Press, 1998), 28, 45–53.

36. Mearsheimer and Walt, *The Israel Lobby*, 58–77.

37. Caspar Weinberger, "Let a Muslim Army Occupy Iraq,' *Middle East Quarterly* 6, no. 3 (September 1999), 73–81; Brent Scowcroft, "The Tools for Peace," *Washington Post*, May 17, 2002, A29; Coalition for a Realistic Foreign Policy, "Ending the Israeli-Palestinian Stalemate," January 1, 2005, http://www.realisticforeign-policy.org/archives/2005/01/ending_the_isra.php; Patrick J. Buchanan, "Israel's Isolation ... and Ours." Patrick J. Buchanan – Official Website, March 29, 2004, http://buchanan.org/blog/pjb-israels-isolation-and-ours-589; Brent Scowcroft, "Beyond Lebanon: This Is the Time for a U.S.-Led Comprehensive Settlement," *Washington Post*, July 30, 2006; B07; James Baker et al., *The Iraq Study Group Report* (New York: Vintage Books, 2006), 7; Brzezinski and Scowcroft, *America and the World*, pp, 64, 87, 104; Mearsheimer and Walt, *The Israel Lobby*, 58–77, 335–255.

38. Brzezinski and Scowcroft, *America and the World*, 85.

39. Mearsheimer and Walt, *The Israel Lobby*, 226, 381 note 38.

40. Brzezinski and Scowcroft, *America and the World*, 19, 80–92; Mearsheimer and Walt, *The Israel Lobby*; Patrick J. Buchanan, "The Prisoner of Sharon," Patrick J. Buchanan – Official Website, April 5, 2002, http://buchanan.org/blog/pjb-the-prisoner-of-sharon-438.

41. Hadar, "Let the Locals Fix the Israeli-Palestinian Conflict"; Leon Hadar, "The Real Lesson of the Oslo Accord: 'Localize' the Arab-Israeli Conflict," Foreign Policy Briefing, No. 31, Cato Institute, May 9, 1994, http://www.cato.org/publica-tions/foreign-policy-briefing/real-lesson-oslo-accord-localize-arabisraeli-conflict; Srdja Trifkovic, "An Exercise in Futility," *Chronicles*, September 3, 2010.

42. Mearsheimer and Walt, *The Israel Lobby*, 64–65.

43. Scott McConnell, "Divided and Conquered," *American Conservative*, July 3, 2006.

44. *CNN Capital Gang*, transcript, CNN.com, November 24, 2001, http://transcripts.cnn.com/TRANSCRIPTS/0111/24/cg.00.html.

45. Anders Strindberg, "Forgotten Christians," *American Conservative*, May 24, 2004.

46. Scott McConnell, "Divided and Conquered," *American Conservative*, July 3, 2006.

47. Michael Oren, *Power, Faith, and Fantasy: America in the Middle East, 1776 to the Present* (New York: W. W. Norton, 2007), 218, 289, 367–368, 424; Robert D. Kaplan, *The Arabists: The Romance of an American Elite* (New York: Free Press, 1995).

48. Barry Rubin, *Secrets of State: The State Department and the Struggle over U.S. Foreign Policy* (New York: Oxford University Press, 1987), 136, 247.

49. Ed Lasky, "Baker's ISG: Shilling for the Saudis," American Thinker, December 19, 2006, http://www.americanthinker.com/2006/12/personnel_is_policy_the_case_o.html.

50. Edward H. Crane and William A. Niskanen, "Upholding Liberty in America," *Financial Times*, June 24, 2003; Andrew Sullivan, "A False Premise", *Atlantic*, February 5, 2009, http://www.theatlantic.com/daily-dish/archive/2009/02/-a-false-premise/205994/.

51. William F. Buckley, "In Search of Anti-Semitism," *National Review*, December 30, 1991; Susanne Klingenstein, "It's Splendid When the Town Whore Gets Religion and Joins the Church: The Rise of the Jewish Neoconservatives as Observed by the Paleoconservatives in the 1980s," *Shofar: An Interdisciplinary Journal of Jewish Studies* 21, no. 3 (2003): 83–98; Ilana Mercer, "Libertarians Who Loathe Israel," *WND*, August 13, 2003, http://www.wnd.com/news/article.asp?ARTICLE_ID=34057; Ron Kampeas, "Jewish Conservatives Push Back against Paul Surge," *JTA*, December 27, 2011.

52. Patrick J. Buchanan, "A Phony Crisis – and a Real One," *WND*, July 15, 2008, http://www.wnd.com/index.php?pageId=69665.

53. Stephen Sniegoski, *The Transparent Cabal: The Neoconservative Agenda, War in the Middle East, and the National Interest of Israel* (Norfolk, VA: Enigma Editions, 2008).

54. Pat Buchanan, *The McLaughlin Group*, June 15, 1990, quoted in "Pat Buchanan on American Jews and the Pro-Israel Lobby," Anti-Defamation League, http://www.adl.org/special_reports/buchanan_own_words/buchanan_intro.asp; Andrew Sullivan, "Israel Derangement Syndrome II" *Atlantic*, June 4, 2010, http://theatlantic.com/daily-dish/archive/2010/06/israel-derangement-syndrome-ii/186259/.

55. Gary Dorrien, *Imperial Designs: Neoconservatism and the New Pax Americana* (London: Routledge, 2004), 22–25; Mearsheimer and Walt, *The Israel Lobby*; on Pat Buchanan, see *The McLaughlin Group*, August 26, 1990, and *The McLaughlin Group*, June 15, 1990 (both quoted in "Pat Buchanan on American Jews and the Pro-Israel Lobby").

56. Malcolm Kerr, *The Arab Cold War: Gamal Abd al-Nasir and His Rivals, 1958–1970* (Oxford: Oxford University Press, 1971).

57. National Security Council Meeting, August 7, 1958, quoted in Ben-Zvi, *Decade of Transition*, 81.

58. Abraham Ben-Zvi, *The American Approach to Superpower Collaboration in the Middle East, 1973–1986*, (Boulder, CO: Westview Press, 1986).

59. "Middle East Breakthrough," *National Review*, October 4, 1993, 16; "Look over Jordan," *National Review*, August 15, 1994, 18.

60. William F. Buckley Jr. "The End of Arafat," *National Review*, December 31, 2001, 50.

61. On populist nationalism and American strategy and foreign policy, see Walter Russell Mead, *Special Providence: American Foreign Policy and How It Changed the World* (New York: Routledge, 2002); Walter Russell Mead, "The New Israel and the Old: Why Gentile Americans Back the Jewish State," *Foreign Affairs* 87, no. 4 (July–August 2008); Mann, *Rise of the Vulcans*, 58–73, 125.

62. Walter Russell Mead. "The Tea Party and American Foreign Policy," *Foreign Affairs* 90, no. 2 (March–April 2011); "Strong on Defense and Israel, Tough on China: Tea Party and Foreign Policy," Pew Research Center for the People and the Press, October 7, 2011 http://www.people-press.org/2011/10/07/strong-on-defense-and-israel-tough-on-china/.

63. Henry Nau, "Conservative Internationalism," *Policy Review* 150 (August–September 2008), 3–45.

64. Jacob Heilbrunn, *They Knew They Were Right: The Rise of the Neocons* (New York: Anchor, 2009); Benjamin Balint, *Running Commentary: The Contentious Magazine That Transformed the Jewish Left into the Neoconservative Right* (New York: Public Affairs, 2010); Gary J. Dorrien, *The Neoconservative Mind: Politics, Culture, and the War of Ideology* (Philadelphia: Temple University Press, 1993).

65. Heilbrunn, *They Knew They Were Right*, 12, 44–47, 95, 114–115; Douglas J. Feith, *War and Decision: Inside the Pentagon at the Dawn of the War on Terrorism* (New York: HarperCollins, 2008).

66. Mann, *Rise of the Vulcans*, 27–29, 74–75

67. Mann, *Rise of the Vulcans*, 130–135, 210–215; Heilbrunn, *They Knew They Were Right*, 173–177, 201.

68. Mann, *Rise of the Vulcans*, 198–199; 235–236; Thomas Ricks, "Holding Their Ground," *Washington Post*, December 23, 2003.

69. Nathan Abrams, *Norman Podhoretz and Commentary Magazine: The Rise and Fall of the Neocons* (New York: Continuum, 2010), 5.

70. Fawaz Gerges, *America and Political Islam: Clash of Cultures or Clash of Interests?* (Cambridge: Cambridge University Press, 1999), 55, 70.

71. Dorrien, *Imperial Designs*, 181; author interview with Danielle Pletka, vice president of Foreign and Defense Policy Studies, American Enterprise Institute, 2013.

72. Norman Podhoretz, *World War IV: The Long Struggle against Islamofascism*, (New York: Doubleday, 2007).

73. This subsection draws heavily on Walter Russell Mead, *Special Providence*.

74. Mitt Romney, "10/19/09 – 2009 AIPAC National Summit" (speech, AIPAC National Summit, October 19, 2009), Mitt Romney Central, http://mittromney-central.com/speeches/2009-speeches/101909-2009-aipac-national-summit/.

75. George Will, "Netanyahu: Promises to Keep," *Washington Post*, June 23, 1996, C07; Victor Davis Hanson, "Islamic Fascism 101," *National Review Online*, September 25, 2006, http://www.nationalreview.com/articles/218799/islamic-fascism-101/victor-davis-hanson.

76. Heilbrunn, *They Knew They Were Right*, 80, 129, 140; Eugene Rostow, "The American Stake in Israel," *Commentary*, April 1977, 32–46; George Will, "Stalin's Lingering Traces," *Washington Post*, August 8, 1991, A19.

77. *A Clean Break: A New Strategy for Securing the Realm* (Washington, DC: Institute for Advanced Strategic and Political Studies, 1996).

78. Elliot Abrams, "Israel and the Peace Process," in Robert Kagan and William Kristol, eds., *Present Dangers: Crisis and Opportunity in American Foreign and Defense Policy* (San Francisco: Encounter, 2000), 221–240.

79. Saad, "Support for Israel in U.S. at 63%, Near Record High."

80. Jeffrey Goldberg, "McCain on Israel, Iran and the Holocaust," *Atlantic*, May 30, 2008, http://www.theatlantic.com/international/archive/2008/05/mccain-on-israel-iran-and-the-holocaust/8346/.

81. Romney, "10/19/09 – 2009 AIPAC National Summit."

82. Author interview with Noam Neusner, White House Liaison to the Jewish Community during the George W. Bush administration, 2013.

83. William Safire, "Israel's Shame," *New York Times*, December 23, 1999, 29.
84. For example, see Norman Podhoretz, "Israel – with Grandchildren," *Commentary*, December 1995, 38–48; Douglas Feith, "Land for No Peace," *Commentary*, June 1994, 32–37.
85. Susan A. Glenn, "The Vogue of Jewish Self-Hatred in Post–World War II America", *Jewish Social Studies* 12, no. 3 (2006): 95–136; Balint, *Running* Commentary: *The Contentious Magazine*, 26, 36–38, 47, 84, 115, 214;.
86. Author interview with Elliot Abrams, 2013; author interview with Shoshana Bryen, director of the Jewish Institute for National Security and later of the Jewish Policy Center, 2013.
87. "Goal of Libyan Occupation Less Clear to Public," Pew Research Center for the People and the Press, April 5, 2011, http://www.people-press.org/2011/04/05/goal-of-libyan-operation-less-clear-to-public/.
88. Ralph Z. Hallow, "Evangelical Faith Drives Palin's Pro-Israel View," *Washington Times*, September 4, 2008, http://www.washingtontimes.com/news/2008/sep/04/palins-evangelical-faith-drives-pro-israel-view/?page=all.
89. Rachel Weiner, "Rick Perry's Israel Appeal," *Washington Post*, September 20, 2011.
90. "Address of U.S. President George Bush to the Knesset", May 15, 2008," The Knesset, http://www.knesset.gov.il/description/eng/doc/speech_bush_2008_eng.htm.
91. "Public Expresses Mixed Views of Islam, Mormonism," Pew Research Religion, and Public Life Project, September 25, 2007, http://pewforum.org/surveys/religionviews07/.
92. Jeremy D. Mayer, "Christian Fundamentalists and Public Opinion toward the Middle East: Israel's New Best Friends?" *Social Science Quarterly*, 85, no. 3 (2004): 695–712.
93. "Rick Santorum: 'There Are No Palestinians,'" *Israel Hayom*, January 4, 2012.
94. Associated Press, "Republican Huckabee Supports Israeli Settlements," Ynetnews.com, August 17, 2009, http://www.ynetnews.com/articles/0,7340,L-3763241,00.html; Dan Murphy, "Sarah Palin Urges Israel Settlement Expansion, Attacks Barack Obama," *Christian Science Monitor*, November 18, 2009, http://www.csmonitor.com/World/Global-News/2009/1118/sarah-palin-urges-israel-settlement-expansion-attacks-barack-obama.
95. James M. Inhofe, "America's Stake in Israel's War on Terrorism" (speech, U.S. Senate, December 4, 2001), http://www.inhofe.senate.gov/newsroom/speech/americas-stake-in-israels-war-on-terrorism.
96. Dick Armey, *Hardball with Chris Matthews*, CNBC, May 1, 2002.
97. Romney, "10/19/09 – 2009 AIPAC National Summit."
98. Midge Decter, "Neocon Memoir," *American Jewish History*, 87, no. 2–3 (1999); Heilbrunn, *They Knew They Were Right*, 94, 151.
99. *A Clean Break*.
100. For details see Jonathan Rynhold and Dov Waxman, "Ideological Change and Israel's Disengagement from Gaza," *Political Science Quarterly*, 123, no. 1 (2008).
101. Charles Krauthammer, "Bibi's Endgame: Behind the Sound and Fury of the High-Stakes Peace Talks," *Weekly Standard*, June 8, 1998, 22.
102. Peter Berkowitz, "Good Fences Make Good Neighbors," *Weekly Standard*, March 1, 2004; Peter Berkowitz, "Israel after Sharon ... and Palestine after

Fatah," *Weekly Standard*, February 6, 2006; Tom Rose, "No Greater Israel: No New Middle East. What's Next?" *Weekly Standard*, November 6, 2000, 19.

103. David Pryce-Jones, "Fantasy Time," *National Review*, May 6, 2002, 20–24.

104. Ron Kampeas, "Wolfowitz Backs Peace Petition," *JTA*, November 3, 2003; Ron Kampeas, "'Virtual' Accord Gaining Real Support Ahead of Backers' Washington Visit," *JTA*, December 2, 2003.

105. Norman Podhoretz, "America and Israel: An Ominous Change," *Commentary*, January 1992, 21; David Bar-Illan, "Why a Palestinian State Is Still a Mortal Threat," *Commentary*, November 1993, 27–32; Yuval Steinitz, "When the Palestinian Army Invades the Heart of Israel," *Commentary*, December 1999, 39–43; Feith, "Land for No Peace"; Yigal Carmon, "The Story behind the Handshake," *Commentary*, March 1994, 25–31; Douglas Feith, "Wye and the Road to War," *Commentary*, January 1999, 43–47.

106. Abrams, "Israel and the Peace Process"; Dorrien, *Imperial Designs*, 197; Pryce-Jones, "Fantasy Time"; Hillel Halkin, "Intifada II: Israel's Nightmare," *Commentary*, December 2000, 44–48.

107. William Safire, "Across the River," *New York Times*, December 14, 1998, 31; Elliott Abrams and Michael Singh, "Spoilers: The End of the Peace Process," *World Affairs* 172, no. 2 (Fall 2009), http://www.worldaffairsjournal.org/article/spoilers-end-peace-process; Hillel Halkin, "Beyond the Geneva Accord," *Commentary*, January 2004, 21–28.

108. William Safire, "If I Forget Thee...," *New York Times*, September 30, 1996, 17; William Safire, "Now the Hard Part," *New York Times*, October 26, 1998, 21.

109. For readership figures both in print and electronic editions, see "The State of the News Media 2001," Pew Research Center's Project for Excellence in Journalism, http://stateofthemedia.org/2011/magazines-essay/; "The State of the News Media 2010: Opinion Magazines," Pew Research Center's Project for Excellence in Journalism, http://stateofthemedia.org/2010/magazines-summary-essay/opinion-magazines/; "*The American Conservative*," Wikipedia, http://en.wikipedia.org/wiki/The_American_Conservative. For *Commentary*'s official figures, see the magazine's December edition for any given year; for example, p. 68 for 1995, p. 72 for 2000, p. 82 for 2005; see also "*Commentary* (magazine)," Wikipedia, http://en.wikipedia.org/wiki/Commentary_(magazine); Peter Steinfels, "All in the Mespoche," *Democracy: A Journal of Ideas* 17 (Summer 2010), http://www.democracyjournal.org/17/6762.php?page=all.

110. Other important conservative columnists like the *Washington Post*'s Charles Krauthammer also wrote consistently on this topic. But unlike Safire and Will, Krauthammer also wrote extensively for the *Weekly Standard*, so his views are already covered there.

111. "Middle East Breakthrough?" *National Review*, September 20, 1993, 22; "Dealing with the Enemy," *National Review*, October 4, 1993, 70–72; "Middle East Breakthrough," *National Review*, October 4, 1993, 16.

112. Jonathan Silvers, "The Synagogue Militant," *National Review*, December 11, 1995, 36–37; "Massacre in Hebron," *National Review*, March 21, 1994, 14–17; "Books in Brief – *Zealots for Zion: Inside Israel's West Bank*," *National Review*, January 18, 1993, 58.

113. "After Hebron," *National Review*, February 10, 1997, 19; "Hebron Hangups," *National Review*, January 27, 1997; Peter Rodman, "Fearful Summitry," *National Review*, October 28, 1996, 58–59.

114. "Last Tango in Damascus," *National Review*, May 20, 1996, 16; David Bar-Illan, "Rain of Terror," *National Review*, March 6, 1995, 26; Rael Jean Isaac, "Israel Unarmed," *National Review*, April 22, 1996, 26–29; "Declaration of War," *National Review*, March 25, 1996, 21; David Pryce-Jones, "Birth of a Nation: The Perils of Palestinian Statehood," *National Review*, May 31, 1999, 22–24.

115. David Klinghoffer, "Book of Books," *National Review*, October 23, 2000; Chandler Burr, "Zionist Crackup," *National Review*, August 14, 2000, 60–61.

116. Bill Press and Pat Buchanan, "What Should the U.S. Position Be on a Palestinian State?" *Crossfire*, CNN, May 7, 1998; Bill Press and Pat Buchanan, "Mideast Diplomacy Dance between Palestine and Israel," *Crossfire*, CNN, January 20, 1998.

117. Charles Krauthammer, "Israel Is Taken In by Arafat's Deadly Zero-Sum Game," *Chicago Tribune*, May 20, 1994; Abrams, "Israel and the Peace Process"; Podhoretz, "A Statement on the Peace Process," *Commentary*, April 1993, 19; William Safire, "Responding to Terror," *New York Times*, January 26, 1995, 21.

118. David Bar-Illan, "The Wages of Oslo," *Commentary*, May 1996, 23–30; Dore Gold, "Where Is the Peace Process Going?" *Commentary*, August 1995, 38–43; Charles Krauthammer, "Why Bibi Won," *Weekly Standard*, June 17, 1996, 29; David Bar-Illan, "What Arafat Is Up To," *Weekly Standard*, March 18, 1996, 14; Daniel Pipes and Alexander Stillman, "Two-Faced Yasir," *Weekly Standard*, September 25, 1995, 10.

119. Krauthammer, "Israel Is Taken In by Arafat's Deadly Zero-Sum Game"; Abrams, "Israel and the Peace Process."

120. For example, George Will, "Land for a Liar's Promises," *Washington Post*, March 27, 1997, A27; George Will, "A Peace with Considerable Risks," *Washington Post*, September 9, 1993, A21; George Will, "No Partners for Peace," *Washington Post*, October 22, 2000, B07.

121. Safire, "Responding to Terror"; David Bar-Illan, "A Vote for Realism," *Weekly Standard*, June 10, 1996, 18; Krauthammer, "Why Bibi Won"; Feith, "Land for No Peace."

122. Elliott Abrams, "Seize the Moment, by Richard Nixon," *Commentary*, March 1992, 62; Charles Krauthammer, "Under a Thatched Roof, with Warren Christopher," *Weekly Standard*, May 6. 1996; "Clinton's Feckless Foreign Policy," editorial, *Weekly Standard*, May 25, 1998, 11; William Safire, "The Phantom Alliance," *New York Times*, February 4, 1999, 27; Norman Podhoretz, "A Statement on the Peace Process"; Feith, "Land for No Peace."

123. William Safire, "Not Arafat's Fault?" *New York Times*, July 30, 2001, 17; William Safire, "Arafat's 'War Process,'" *New York Times*, November 20, 2000, 27; David Pryce-Jones, "Arafat's Moment of Truth: It's Now or Never," *National Review*, August 28, 2000, 26–27; Daniel Pipes, "Land for What? How the Peace Process Brought Israel to the Brink of War," *American Spectator*, March 2001, 12–14; Tom Rose, "Arafat's War," *Weekly Standard*, October 23, 2000, 20; Charles Krauthammer, "Arafat's War," *Weekly Standard*, September 3, 2001, 25; Robert Kagan and William Kristol, "A Green Light for Israel," *Weekly*

Standard, September 3, 2001, 9; "The Middle East: The Wages of No," *National Review*, March 5, 2001, 17; Efraim Karsh, "Israel's War," *Commentary*, April 2002, 23–28; William Safire, "Arafat's Implausible Denials," *New York Times*, January 10, 2002, 27; Michael Oren, "Does the U.S. Finally Understand Israel?" *Commentary*, July–August 2002, 33–37; David Pryce-Jones, "The New Cold War," *National Review*, November 5, 2001, 38–41; Jay Nordlinger, "In Israel, Part IV," *National Review Online*, September 16, 2004.

124. "The Future Is Now," *National Review*, April 22, 2002, 15; David Pryce-Jones, "Priests of Killing," *National Review*, April 22, 2002, 19–20; "No Propitiation," *National Review*, April 8, 2002, 15–16; "Lost," *National Review*, May 6, 2002, 14–15; Jay Nordlinger, "'Two girls,' the Prez and 'I:' Peres over Paris," *National Review Online*, April 8, 2002; Jonah Goldberg, "Moral Styrofoam," *National Review Online*, April 8, 2002; Editors, "The Future Is Now," *National Review Online*, April 5, 2002; Michael Ledeen, "Gulled," *National Review Online*, April 3, 2002; "Letter from the Project for the New American Century," *National Review Online*, April 3, 2002; Victor Davis Hanson, "The 1930s, Again," *National Review Online*, March 25, 2002; Editors, "No Propitiation," *National Review Online*, March 25, 2002; William Safire, "Hamas vs. Abbas," *New York Times*, May 1, 2003, 35; William Safire, "Man of Peace," *New York Times*, May 6, 2002, 21.

125. David Brooks, "Keeping It Simple," *Daily Standard*; Tom Rose, "A New Regime for the Palestinians? The Sharansky Plan Gains Traction," *Weekly Standard*, May 20, 2002, 17; William Kristol, "Bush's Speech," *Daily Standard*, June 25, 2002.

126. Will, "The End of Our Holiday from History"; Ramesh Ponnuru, "Blame America First...or Israel – Whichever," *National Review*, October 15, 2001, 30–32; David Pryce-Jones, "Why They Hate Us," *National Review*, October 1, 2001, 8; Jay Nordlinger, "Thanks for the MEMRI (.org)," *National Review*, May 6, 2002, 33–35; Victor Davis Hanson, "And Then They Came after Us," *National Review Online*, July 22, 2005.

127. Victor Davis Hanson, "Why Support Israel?" *National Review*, February 4, 2002; David Brooks "A Season of Cynicism," *Daily Standard*, April 1, 2002; Fred Barnes, "Bush Stands with Israel: And against the State Department," *Weekly Standard*, April 29, 2002, 12; Robert Kagan and William Kristol, "Back on Track?" *Weekly Standard*, April 29, 2002, 9; William Safire, "Our 'Relentless' Liberation," *New York Times*, October 8, 2001, 17; George Will, "A Plan for Arafat," *Washington Post*, December 4, 2001, A25; Norman Podhoretz, "World War IV: How It Started, What It Means, and Why We Have to Win," *Commentary*, September 2004, 17–54; Michael Ledeen, "Books in Review: The War That Never Ended," *American Spectator*, July–August 2002, 72–73.

128. Krauthammer, "Bibi's Endgame."

129. David Brooks, "Keeping It Simple," *The Daily Standard*, June 25, 2002; Krauthammer, "Arafat's War"; George Will, "A War and Then a Wall," *Washington Post*, August 17, 2001, A23.

130. William Safire, "Win Some, Lose Some," *New York Times*, January 24, 2005, 17; Norman Podhoretz, "Bush, Sharon, My Daughter, and Me," *Commentary*, April 2005, 38–49.

131. Halkin, "Beyond the Geneva Accord"; Hillel Halkin, "Does Sharon Have a Plan?" *Commentary*, June 2004, 17–22.

132. Hillel Halkin, "Israel's New Reality," *Commentary*, October 2006, 21–27.

133. Dan Darling, "Hezbollah's Arsenal; It's More Lethal Than Everyone Thought," *Weekly Standard*, July 31, 2006; Fred Barnes, "Letting Israel Be Israel; Bush's Consistent Approach to War and Peace in the Middle East," *Weekly Standard*, July 31, 2006; Philip Klein, "Let Israel Stay the Course," *American Spectator Online*, August 7, 2006; R. Emmett Tyrrell Jr. "Cool under Pressure," *American Spectator Online*, August 3, 2006; Jed Babbin, "Israel as George Bush," *American Spectator Online*, July 31, 2006; Jed Babbin, "Endgame Conservatives, Chapter Two," *American Spectator Online*, July 17, 2006.

134. "Dead Letter," *National Review*, September 11, 2006, 14–15; David Pryce-Jones, "You Call That a War?" *National Review*, September 11, 2006. 17–18; "Losing in Lebanon," *National Review*, August 28, 2006, 14, 16.

135. Reuel Marc Gerecht, "The Return of Weakness; President Obama Means Well. iran Doesn't," *Weekly Standard*, April 6, 2009; Elliott Abrams, "Bibi Speaks; Netanyahu Endorses a Demilitarized Palestinian State – Rejects Obama's Call for a Settlement Freeze," *Weekly Standard*, June 14, 2009.

136. Editors, "Praying for Handshakes and Empty Words," *National Review Online*, November 27, 2007; Lee Smith, "The Price of Annapolis: Lebanese Democracy," *Daily Standard*, November 30, 2007.

137. Clifford May, "The Battle of Gaza," *National Review Online*, January 22, 2009; Andrew McCarthy, "Breaking the Will of the Palestinians," *National Review Online*, January 6, 2009; Mona Charen, "What Good Can Come of This?" *National Review Online*, January 6, 2009; Clifford May, "Peace Processing 101," *National Review Online*, February 19, 2009; Victor Davis Hanson, "The Gaza Rules," *National Review Online*, January 3, 2009.

138. The Mideast: Clinton's Dreamscape," *National Review*, July 31, 2000, 12; "The Middle East: Dancing at Camp David," *National Review*, August 14, 2000, 16–17.

139. Buckley, "The End of Arafat."

140. William F. Buckley Jr., "Sharon's Contribution," *National Review*, May 6, 2002, 55; William F. Buckley Jr., "Did the Israelis Do It?" *National Review Online*, May 3, 2002.

141. William F. Buckley Jr., "The Bush Initiative," *National Review*, July 29, 2002, 54–55; William F. Buckley Jr., "Palestine: Essays in Democracy," *National Review*, September 2, 2002, 50.

142. William F. Buckley Jr., "Where Do We Go from Here?" *National Review*, November 6, 2000, 71; William F. Buckley Jr., "Israeli/Arab Primer," *National Review*, January 22, 2001, 59; William F. Buckley Jr., "Mare's-Nest in Durban," *National Review Online*, September 4, 2001; William F. Buckley Jr., "The War Parties at Work," *National Review*, August 28, 2001; William F. Buckley Jr., "Road Map for Israel," *National Review*, May 19, 2003, 66–67.

143. "Palestinian Suicide," *National Review*, September 3, 2001, 14–15. For an opposing view that took a positive view of the Jewish settler presence, see David Klinghoffer, "No Place for Mortals," *National Review*, February 5, 2001, 53–55.

144. "Road Map to Chaos," *National Review*, October 13, 2003, 63.

145. David Pryce-Jones, "Unsettled Settlers," *National Review*, August 29, 2005, 26–27; "A Leader's Courage," *National Review*, January 30, 2006, 17.

146. Jay Nordlinger, "All the Gaps Are Bridgeable," *National Review*, June 8, 2009, 26–27; Jay Nordlinger, "Davos in the Desert, Part III," *National Review Online*, May 20, 2009; Jay Nordlinger, "Sharm El Sheikh Journal, Part II," *National Review Online*, May 20, 2008; Jay Nordlinger, "Tzipi, Bibi and Co.," *National Review Online*, February 24, 2009.

147. Pat Buchanan, "Israel's Remaining Options … and Ours," Townhall.com, December 5, 2011, http://townhall.com/columnists/PatBuchanan/2001/12/05/ israels_remaining_optionsand_ours/page/full/; Scott McConnell, "A Friend's Lament," *American Conservative*, May 24, 2004; Michael Desch, "The Peace That Failed," *American Conservative*, November 8, 2004.

148. Buchanan, "The Prisoner of Sharon"; Patrick J. Buchanan, "Palestinians Are Winning," *WND*, April 2, 2002, http://www.wnd.com/2002/04/13362/.

149. Christopher Layne, "Balancing Act," *American Conservative*, September 10, 2007.

150. Buchanan, "The Prisoner of Sharon."

151. Buchanan, "Israel's Isolation…and Ours."

152. Patrick Buchanan, "Mideast Peace an Illusion?" Patrick J. Buchanan – Official Website, October 20, 2001, http://buchanan.org/blog/pjb-mideast-peace-an-illusion-395; Patrick J. Buchanan, "Peace Plan for the Holy Land," *WND*, December 27, 2001, http://www.wnd.com/2001/12/12174/.

153. Buchanan, "Islamo-fascism?"; see also Brzezinski and Scowcroft, *America and the World*, 84–85; Adam Kushner, "A Return to Realism," *Newsweek International*, January 26, 2009; "Report: U.S. Officials Urge Obama to Engage Hamas," *Haaretz*, March 26, 2009.

154. Philip Weiss, "The Long Fuse to the Iraq War," *American Conservative*, January 28, 2008; John Mearsheimer, "Saving Israel from Itself," *American Conservative*, May 18, 2009; Andrew Bacevich, "Middle East Paradigm Shift," *American Conservative*, August 1, 2005.

155. Philip Weiss, "Looking into the Lobby," *American Conservative*, June 30, 2008.

156. Buchanan, "Whose War?"

157. Ibid.; Philip Weiss, "Mondoweiss, Chapter One," *American Conservative*, June 4, 2007; Justin Raimondo, "AIPAC on Trial," *American Conservative*, May 7, 2007.

158. Mearsheimer and Walt, *The Israel Lobby*.

159. "In Shift from Bush Era, More Conservatives Say 'Come Home, America,'" Pew Research Center for the People and the Press, June 16, 2011, http://www.people-press.org/2011/06/16/in-shift-from-bush-era-more-conservatives-say-come-home-america/.

160. "U.S. Seen as Less Important, China as More Powerful," Pew Research Center for the People and the Press, December 3, 2009, http://people-press.org/2009/12/03/ us-seen-as-less-important-china-as-more-powerful/.

161. *Constrained Internationalism: Adapting to New Realities: Results of a 2010 National Survey of American Public Opinion* (Chicago: The Chicago Council on Global Affairs, 2010), 78, http://www.thechicagocouncil.org/UserFiles/File/POS_T-opline%20Reports/POS%202010/Global%20Views%202010.pdf; "Beyond Red

vs. Blue: Political Typology," Pew Research Center for the People and the Press, May 4, 2011, http://people-press.org/files/legacy-pdf/Beyond-Red-vs-Blue-The-Political-Typology.pdf; "Views of Middle East Unchanged by Recent Events." Pew Research Center for the People and the Press, June 10, 2011, http://www.people-press.org/2011/06/10/views-of-middle-east-unchanged-by-recent-events/.

162. "Independents Take Center Stage in Obama Era."

163. "Continuing Divide in Views of Islam and Violence," Pew Research Center for the People and the Press, March 9, 2011, http://www.people-press.org/2011/03/09/continuing-divide-in-views-of-islam-and-violence/, http://www.people-press.org/2002/03/20/part-2-views-of-islam-and-religion-in-the-world/; "Public Expresses Mixed Views of Islam, Mormonism."

164. "More See America's Loss of Global Respect as Major Problem," Pew Research Center for the People and the Press, June 16, 2008, http://people-press.org/2008/06/16/more-see-americas-loss-of-global-respect-as-major-problem/; "U.S. Seen as Less Important, China as More Powerful."

165. "Americans Closely Divided over Israel's Gaza Attacks", Rasmussen Reports, December 31, 2008, http://www.rasmussenreports.com/public_content/politics/current_events/israel_the_middle_east/americans_closely_divided_over_israel_s_gaza_attacks.

166. Survey conducted in December 2010 by Public Opinion Strategies and Greenberg, Quinlin, Rosner Research for the Israel Project.

167. Eytan Gilboa, *American Public Opinion toward Israel and the Arab-Israeli Conflict* (Lexington, MA: Lexington Books, 1987), 294; Nimrod Novik, *The United States and Israel: Domestic Determinants of a Changing U.S. Commitment* (Boulder, CO: Westview Press, 1986), 21; "Modest Backing for Israel in Gaza Crisis"; *America's Place in the World 2009*, Pew Research Center for the People and the Press, December 2009, 37, http://people-press.org/files/legacy-pdf/569.pdf; "Ideological Gaps over Israel on Both Sides of Atlantic," Pew Research Global Attitudes Project, January 29, 2009, http://pewresearch.org/pubs/1097/america-europe-ideological-gaps-over-israel.

168. Saad, "Support for Israel in U.S. at 63%, Near Record High."

169. David W. Moore, "Americans Skeptical Either Side in Palestinian-Israeli Conflict Wants Peace," Gallup, June 11, 2002, http://www.gallup.com/poll/6193/Americans-Skeptical-Either-Side-PalestinianIsraeli-Conflict-Wants-Peace.aspx.

170. See the survey of registered voters conducted by Public Opinion Strategies for the Israel Project, April 5–7, 2011, http://www.theisraelproject.org/atf/cf/%7B84dc5887-741e-4056-8d91-a389164bc94e%7D/042011_US_NATIONAL_CHARTS.PDF. Independents' opinion was in the middle, but closer to the Democrats.

171. Jeffrey M. Jones, "Americans Continue to Be Pessimistic About Middle East Peace," Gallup, March 13, 2007, http://www.gallup.com/poll/26860/americans-continue-pessimistic-about-middle-east-peace.aspx.

172. However, when the question was phrased so that Israeli control was linked to Israel "keeping all the Christian, Muslim, and Jewish holy sites open and safe for all faiths," the position of Democrats reversed, with over half supporting complete Israeli control and just over a quarter favoring division. See the survey of

registered voters conducted by Public Opinion Strategies for the Israel Project, December 12–14, 2010.

173. Jeffrey M. Jones, "Nearly Half of Americans Favor Independent Palestinian State" Gallup, June 3, 2002, http://www.gallup.com/poll/6115/Nearly-Half-Americans-Favor-Independent-Palestinian-State.aspx; Lydia Saad, "Americans Remain Skeptical about Middle East Peace," Gallup, June 4, 2009, http://www.gallup.com/poll/120728/americans-remain-skeptical-middle-east-peace.aspx.

174. *The Doha Debates: Should the U.S. "Get Tough with Israel,"* Zogby International, April 2009, http://www.aaiusa.org/page/-/Polls/ArabAmericanOpinion/DohaDebates_2009.pdf.

175. Moore, "Americans Skeptical Either Side in Palestinian-Israeli Conflict Wants Peace." A similar divide was already apparent on this issue in April 2002; see "Questions and Answers about American Public Opinion and the Middle East," Gallup, April 10, 2002, http://www.gallup.com/poll/5596/questions-answers-about-american-public-opinion-middle-east.aspx.

176. "American Attitudes Hold Steady in Face of Foreign Crises," Pew Research Center for the People and the Press, August 17, 2006, http://people-press.org/2006/08/17/american-attitudes-hold-steady-in-face-of-foreign-crises/; "Modest Backing for Israel in Gaza Crisis."

177. "Most Americans Favor End to U.S. Foreign Aid to Middle East, Except Israel," Rasmussen Reports, February 25, 2011, http://www.rasmussenreports.com/public_content/politics/current_events/israel_the_middle_east/most_americans_favor_end_to_u_s_foreign_aid_to_middle_east_except_israel.

178. Jonathan Rynhold, "The U.S. and the Middle East Peace Process: Conflict Management vs. Conflict Resolution," in Efraim Inbar and Eytan Gilboa, eds., *U.S.-Israeli Relations in a New Era* (London: Routledge, 2009), 140–157.

179. Author interview with Danielle Pletka, 2013. Pletka authored the MEPFA while serving as an advisor to Helms as a senior staff member on the Senate Committee on Foreign Relations (1992–2002).

180. Elizabeth A. Oldmixon, Beth A. Rosenson, and Kenneth D. Wald, "Conflict over Israel: The Role of Religion, Race, Party, and Ideology in the U.S. House of Representatives, 1997–2002," *Terrorism and Political Violence*, 17, no. 3 (2005): 407–426. In the Senate, Republicans were more supportive of Israel throughout the 1990s; see Beth A. Rosenson, Elizabeth A. Oldmixon, and Kenneth D. Wald, "U.S. Senators' Support for Israel Examined through Sponsorship/Cosponsorship Decisions, 1993–2002: The Influence of Elite and Constituent Factors," *Foreign Policy Analysis*, 5, no. 1 (2009): 73–91.

181. Author interview with Lara Friedman, director of Policy and Government Relations, Americans for Peace Now, 2013.

182. Jonathan Rynhold, "Behind the Rhetoric: President Bush and U.S. Policy on the Israeli-Palestinian Conflict," *American Diplomacy*, 10, no. 4 (2005); Robert O. Freedman, "George W. Bush, Barack Obama, and the Arab-Israeli Conflict from 2001 to 2011," in Robert O. Freedman, ed., *Israel and the United States: Six Decades of U.S.-Israeli Relations* (Boulder, CO: Westview Press, 2012); Elliot Abrams, *Tested by Zion: The Bush Administration and the Israeli-Palestinian Conflict* (Cambridge: Cambridge University Press, 2013), chapter 2.

183. George W. Bush, *Decision Points* (New York: Crown, 2010), 400.

184. "In Shift from Bush Era, More Conservatives Say 'Come Home, America.'"
185. Ron Kampeas, "Republicans 'Starting from Zero' Aid Proposal Startles Pro-Israel Community," *JTA*, November 15, 2011.
186. Natasha Mozgovaya, "ADL Bid for U.S. Bipartisan Support for Israel Faces Staunch Resistance," *Haaretz*, October 25, 2011.

3. DEMOCRATS, LIBERALS, AND THE LEFT

1. Thomas L. Friedman, "Arafat's War," *New York Times*, October 13, 2000, 33.
2. Jimmy Carter, *Palestine: Peace Not Apartheid* (New York: Simon and Schuster, 2006), 208–209.
3. Charles A. Kupchan and Peter L. Trubowitz, "Dead Center: The Demise of Liberal Internationalism in the United States," *International Security*, 32, no. 2 (2007): 7–44; Peter Beinart, "When Politics No Longer Stops at the Water's Edge: Partisan Polarization and Foreign Policy," in Pietro S. Nivola and David W. Brady, eds., *Red and Blue Nation? Vol. 2: Consequences and Correction of America's Polarized Politics* (Washington, DC: Brookings Institution Press, 2008), 151–167.
4. Jack Snyder, Robert Y. Shapiro, and Yaeli Bloch-Elkon, "Free Hand Abroad, Divide and Rule at Home," *World Politics*, 61, no. 1 (2009): 155–187.
5. Lydia Saad, "Conservatives Continue to Outnumber Moderates in 2010," Gallup, December 16, 2010, http://www.gallup.com/poll/145271/conservatives-continue-outnumber-moderates-2010.aspx.
6. "Millennials in Adulthood: Millennials Less Conservative Than Older Generations," Pew Research Social and Demographic Trends, March 5, 2014, http://www.pewsocialtrends.org/2014/03/07/millennials-in-adulthood/sdt-next-america-03-07-2014-1-06/; 'The Millennials: Confident. Connected. Open to Change' Pew Research Social and Demographic Trends, February 24, 2010, http://pewsocial-trends.org/2010/02/24/millennials-confident-connected-open-to-change/.
7. Jeffrey Jones, "Liberal Self-Identification Edges Up to New High in 2013: Fifteen-Percentage-Point Conservative Advantage Ties As Smallest to Date," Gallup, January 10, 2014, http://www.gallup.com/poll/166787/liberal-self-identifica-tion-edges-new-high-2013.aspx.
8. Jones, "Liberal Self-Identification Edges Up to New High in 2013."
9. "Independents Take Center Stage in Obama Era: Trends in Political Values and Core Attitudes: 1987–2009," Pew Research Center for the People and the Press, May 21, 2009, http://people-press.org/2009/05/21/independents-take-center-stage-in-obama-era/'; "'Nones' on the Rise," Pew Research Religion and Public Life Project, October 9, 2012, http://www.pewforum.org/unaffiliated/nones-on-the-rise.aspx.
10. For example, see Thomas L. Friedman, *From Beirut to Jerusalem* (New York: Farrar, Straus and Giroux, 1989); and Richard Cohen, "Shamir Is Wrong," *Washington Post*, September 27, 1991, A29.
11. Interview with Dennis Ross, December 2012. He termed his approach liberal on domestic issues and centrist on foreign policy.
12. Peter Beinart, *The Good Fight: Why Liberals – and Only Liberals – Can Win the War on Terror and Make America Great Again* (New York: HarperCollins, 2006), 4–6.

13. Dennis Ross, *Statecraft: And How to Restore America's Standing in the World* (New York: Farrar, Straus, and Giroux, 2007), 3–28.

14. "Address by President Bill Clinton to the UN General Assembly, September 26, 1994," U.S. Department of State, http://www.state.gov/p/io/potusunga/207377.htm.

15. William A. Galston, "Incomplete Victory: The Rise of the New Democrats," in Peter Berkowitz, ed., *Varieties of Progressivism in America* (Stanford, CA: Hoover Institute Press, 2004).

16. Beinart, *The Good Fight*, 173; Ross, *Statecraft*.

17. Dennis Ross and David Makovsky, *Myths, Illusions and Peace: Finding a New Direction for America in the Middle East* (New York: Viking, 2009), 6, 20; Kenneth M. Pollack, *A Path out of the Desert: A Grand Strategy for America in the Middle East* (New York: Random House, 2008), chapter 5.

18. Michael Walzer, "Five Questions about Terrorism," *Dissent*, Winter 2002.

19. Paul Berman, *Terror and Liberalism* (New York: W. W. Norton, 2004), 121–153.

20. Author interview with Dennis Ross.

21. Ross and Makovsky, *Myths, Illusions and Peace*; Pollack, *A Path out of the Desert*; Thomas Friedman, "Order vs. Disorder," *New York Times*, July 21, 2006, 19; Jeffrey Goldberg, "The Great Atlantic Israel-Iran Debate," *Atlantic*, August 27, 2010.

22. Pollack, *A Path out of the Desert*; Ross, *Statecraft*, 295.

23. Ross and Makovsky, *Myths, Illusions and Peace*; Pollack, *A Path out of the Desert*.

24. Ross, *Statecraft*, 228.

25. Interview with David Makovsky, June 2012.

26. Richard Cohen, "Israel's Answer to Arafat," *Washington Post*, February 8, 2001, A23; Eugene Goodheart, "A Non-Zionist Reflects on the Israeli-Palestinian Conflict," *Dissent*, Summer 2007.

27. William Quandt, *Peace Process*, 3rd ed. (Washington, DC: Brookings Institution Press, 2005), 293–295; Dennis Ross, "Taking Stock," *National Interest* 73 (Fall 2003); Hilary Leila Krieger, "Ross: Now's Not Prime Time for Peace Deal," *Jerusalem Post*, February 7, 2012.

28. The Institute is a leading think tank on Middle East policy. It is pro-Israel but nonpartisan.

29. Interview with David Makovsky, June 2013.

30. Gerald Sorin, *Irving Howe: A Life of Passionate Dissent* (New York: New York University Press, 2003), 224–226.

31. Ross and Makovsky, *Myths, Illusions and Peace*, 278; Goodheart, "A Non-Zionist Reflects on the Israeli-Palestinian Conflict"; Gershom Gorenberg, "Burning Gush," *New Republic*, April 18, 1994, 21; Leon Wieseltier, "Letting Go," *New Republic*, October 4, 1993, 27–29; Jeffrey Goldberg, "Israel's Self-Delegitimization Movement," *Atlantic*, December 23, 2010; Richard Cohen, "Settlements That Settle Nothing," *Washington Post*, June 15, 2004, A23; Friedman, *From Beirut to Jerusalem*; Richard Cohen, "Whose Israel Shall It Be?" *Washington Post*, February 24, 2009, A13.

32. Richard Cohen, "Apartheid? Not Israel," *Washington Post*, March 2, 2010, A15.

33. Richard Cohen, "Bowing to Historical Forces," *Washington Post*, September 3, 1993, A25; Thomas Friedman, "The New Math," *New York Times*, January 15,

2003, 21; Jeffrey Goldberg, "Is Israel America's Ultimate Ally?" *Atlantic*, April 26, 2011.

34. Mitchell Cohen, "Anti-Semitism and the Left That Doesn't Learn," *Dissent*, Winter 2008; Richard Cohen, "Why Boycott Israel?" *Washington Post*, April 24, 2007, A2; Thomas Friedman, "Campus Hypocrisy," *New York Times*, October 16, 2002, 23; Leon Wieseltier, "At the Window," *New Republic*, March 27, 2009, 48; Richard Cohen, "Zionism: Refuge, Not Racism," *Washington Post*, September 6, 2001, A23; Thomas Friedman, "The Gridlock Gang," *New York Times*, February 26, 2003, 25; Jeffrey Goldberg, "The New Israel Fund, Dipping Its Toe into the BDS Swamp," *Atlantic*, November 17, 2010.

35. Kupchan and Trubowitz, "Dead Center"; Robert Y. Shapiro and Yaeli Bloch-Elkon, "Foreign Policy, Meet the People," *National Interest* 97 (September–October 2008), 37–42; Beinart, "When Politics No Longer Stops at the Water's Edge."

36. On the influence of Realists in the Obama administration, see James Mann, *The Obamians: The Struggle inside the White House to Redefine American Power* (New York: Viking 2012), 156–167.

37. Colin Dueck, *Reluctant Crusaders: Power, Culture and Change in American Grand Strategy* (Princeton, NJ: Princeton University Press, 2006); G. John Ikenberry, "An Agenda for Liberal International Renewal," in Michele A. Flourney and Shawn Brimley, eds., *Finding Our Way: Debating American Grand Strategy* (Washington, DC: Center for a New American Security: 2008), 43–60; G. John Ikenberry et al., *The Crisis of American Foreign Policy: Wilsonianism in the Twenty-First Century* (Princeton, NJ: Princeton University Press, 2009); Henry Nau, *Conservative Internationalism: Armed Diplomacy under Jefferson, Polk, Truman, and Reagan* (Princeton, NJ: Princeton University Press, 2013), chapter 2.

38. Peter Beinart, *The Icarus Syndrome: A History of American Hubris* (New York: Harper, 2010).

39. G. John Ikenberry and Anne-Marie Slaughter, *Forging a World of Liberty under Law: U.S. National Security in the 21st Century: Final Report of the Princeton Project on National Security* (Princeton, NJ: Woodrow Wilson School of Public and International Affairs, 2006).

40. Beinart, "When Politics No Longer Stops at the Water's Edge."

41. Ikenberry and Slaughter, *Forging a World of Liberty under Law*.

42. Ikenberry, "An Agenda for Liberal International Renewal."

43. Dana H. Allin and Steven Simon, "America's Predicament," *Survival*, 46, no. 4 (2004): 7–30; Dan Kurtzer and Scott Lasensky, *Negotiating Arab-Israeli Peace: American Leadership in the Middle East* (Washington, DC: United States Institute of Peace, 2008), 8; Daniel Levy, "Political Islam 101," *American Prospect*, March 2009, 33; Marc Lynch, "Veiled Truths," *Foreign Affairs* 89, no. 4 (July–August 2010).

44. Bruce O. Riedel, *The Search for Al Qaeda: Its Leadership, Ideology, and Future* (Washington, DC: Brookings Institution Press, 2008).

45. Michael Lind, "American Strategy Project – Grand Strategy No. 1," New America Foundation, March 13, 2003, http://newamerica.net/publications/policy/american_strategy_project_grand_strategy_no_1.

46. Zbigniew Brzezinski and Brent Scowcroft, *America and the World* (New York: Basic Books, 2008), 21–29.

47. Shibley Telhami et al., "Middle Eastern Views of the United States: What Do the Trends Indicate?" *Middle East Policy* 13, no. 3 (2006); Brzezinski and Scowcroft, *America and the World*, 19.

48. Mara Rudman and Brian Katulis, "U.S. Must Lead for Middle East Progress," *Washington Post*, May 28, 2007; Brian Katulis, Marc Lynch, and Robert C. Adler, "Window of Opportunity for a Two-State Solution: Policy Recommendations to the Obama Administration on the Israeli-Palestinian Front," Center for American Progress, July 2009; Riedel, *The Search for Al Qaeda*; Robert Reich, "How to Be Tough on Terrorism," *American Prospect*, November 2001, 48; Daniel Levy, "Fork in the Road Map," *American Prospect*, July 2005, 19; Robert Malley and Hussein Agha, "A Durable Middle East Peace," *American Prospect*, November 2003, 55; Daniel Levy "Political Islam 101."

49. Kurtzer and Lasensky, *Negotiating Arab-Israeli Peace*, 78.

50. Samuel Berger and James A. Baker III, foreword to *Pathways to Peace: America and the Arab-Israeli Conflict*, edited by Daniel C. Kurtzer (New York: Palgrave Macmillan, 2012), vii–xii.

51. Katulis, Lynch, and Adler, "Window of Opportunity for a Two-State Solution."

52. Author interview, January 2013.

53. Dana H. Allin and Steven Simon, "The Moral Psychology of US Support for Israel," *Survival*, 45, no. 3 (2003): 123–144; John Judis, "The Real Foreign-Policy Debate," *American Prospect*, May 2002, 10; Brzezinski and Scowcroft, *America and the World*, 80–81.

54. Rudman and Katulis, "U.S. Must Lead for Middle East Progress;" Daniel C. Kurtzer, "American Policy, Strategy, and Tactics," in Kurtzer, ed., *Pathways to Peace*, 196.

55. Malley and Agha, "A Durable Middle East Peace,", 55.

56. Katulis, Lynch, and Adler, "Window of Opportunity for a Two-State Solution."

57. Ibid.; Helena Cobban, "Who Is the Real Hamas?" *Salon*, March 2, 2006; Daniel Levy and Amjad Atallah, "A Path to Peace," *American Prospect*, March 2010, 13; Henry Siegman, "Hamas: The Last Chance for Peace?" *New York Review of Books*, April 27, 2006; Zbigniew Brzezinski et al., "Failure Risks Devastating Consequences," *New York Review of Books*, November 8, 2007.

58. Ernest Sternberg, "Purifying the World: What the New Radical Ideology Stands For," *Orbis*, 54 no. 1 (2010): 61–86; Jeffrey C. Isaac, "The Poverty of Progressivism and the Tragedy of Civil Society," in Peter Berkowitz, ed., *Varieties of Progressivism in America* (Stanford, CA: Hoover Institution Press, 2004).

59. Justus Doenecke, "Non-Interventionism of the Left: The Keep America Out of the War Congress, 1938–41," *Journal of Contemporary History*, 12, no. 2 (1977): 221–236; Robert Johnson, *The Peace Progressives and American Foreign Relations* (Cambridge: Harvard University Press, 1995).

60. Beinart, *The Good Fight*, 33–53.

61. Robert Young, *Postcolonialism: An Historical Introduction* (Oxford: Blackwell, 2003), 6

62. See Young, *Postcolonialism*, chapter 26.

63. Naomi Klein, "Terror's Greatest Recruitment Tool," *Nation*, August 29, 2005; Peter Beinart, *The Good Fight*, 171; Simon Cottee, "The Culture of Denial: Islamic Terrorism and the Delinquent Left," *Journal of Human Rights*, 4, no. 1 (2005):

119–135; Paul Hollander, ed., *Understanding Anti-Americanism: It's Origins and Impact at Home and Abroad* (Chicago: Ivan R. Dee, 2004), 24–27; Noam Chomsky, "The New War against Terror," transcript, October 18, 2001, http://www.zmag.org/ GlobalWatch/chomskymit.htm (no longer available); Tony Smith, "Wilsonianism after Iraq," in Ikenberry et al., *The Crisis of American Foreign Policy: Wilsonianism in the Twenty-First Century*.

64. Fern Oppenheim, "The Segmentation Study of the American Market, Fourth Quarter 2010," conducted by the Brand Israel Group and the Conference of Presidents of Major American Jewish Organizations.

65. Irfan Khawaja, "Essentialism, Consistency and Islam: A Critique of Edward Said's *Orientalism*," *Israel Affairs* 13, no. 4 (2007); Ronald Niezen, "Postcolonialism and the Utopian Imagination," *Israel Affairs*, 13, no. 4 (2007).

66. Robert Wistrich, "Anti-Semitism and Multiculturalism: The Uneasy Connection," Hebrew University of Jerusalem, Vidal Sassoon International Center for the Study of Antisemitism, http://sicsa.huji.ac.il/pprobert.pdf.

67. Arnold Forster, "American Radicals and Israel" in Robert S. Wistrich, ed., *The Left against Zion: Communism, Israel, and the Middle East* (London: Vallentine Mitchell, 1979), 221–225; Noam Chomsky, *Peace in the Middle East? Reflections on Justice and Nationhood* (New York: Vintage Books, 1974), 17, 28, 119; Michael Neumann, *The Case against Israel* (Petrolia, CA: CounterPunch, 2005), 7, 13, 61–62, 89, 161; Joel Kovel and Jeff Halper, letters to the editors, in "Israel's Radical Left; Henry James's Conservatism," *Azure* 42 (2010), http://www.azure.org.il/include/print.php?id=557.

68. Author interview with Stuart Eizenstat, July 2013, regarding the development of Jimmy Carter's view of the conflict; John B. Judis, *Genesis: Truman, American Jews, and the Origins of the Arab/Israeli Conflict* (New York: Farrar, Straus and Giroux, 2014). One particularly vitriolic work is Max Blumenthal, *Goliath: Life and Loathing in Greater Israel* (New York: Nation Books, 2013).

69. George McGovern, *The Essential America: Our Founders and the Liberal Tradition* (New York: Simon and Schuster, 2004), 22–23; Tony Judt, "The Rootless Cosmopolitan," *Nation*, July 19, 2004, 29; Carter, *Palestine*, 17–28, 208–209; Naomi Klein, "Israel: Boycott, Divest, Sanction," naomiklein.org, January 7, 2009, http://www.naomiklein.org/articles/2009/01/israel-boycott-divest-sanction; Sara Roy, "Apartheid, Israeli-Style," *Nation*, July 26, 1993; Sternberg, "Purifying the World."

70. Phyllis Bennis, "Death Blow to the Peace Talks," *Nation*, March 1, 1993, 264–267; "The US and the Mideast," *Nation*, April 8, 2002; "Mideast Mirage?" *Nation*, March 7, 2005; Henry Siegman, "A Last Chance at Middle East Peace?" *Nation*, January 12, 2009.

71. Eric Alterman, "AIPAC's Back (Oy Vay!)," *Nation*, July 29, 1996, 24; Philip Weiss, "Israel Lobby Watch," *Nation*, September 18, 2006; Alexander Cockburn, "Israel on the Slide: Who's to Blame?" *Nation*, September 11, 2006; Michael Massing, "The Israel Lobby," *Nation*, June 10, 2002; Judis, *Genesis*.

72. Stephen Morris, "Whitewashing Dictatorship in Communist Vietnam and Cambodia," in Peter Collier and David Horowitz, eds., *The Anti-Chomsky Reader* (San Francisco: Encounter Books, 2004), 1–29.

73. Gerald Steinberg, "Soft Powers Play Hardball: NGOs Wage War against Israel," *Israel Affairs*, 12 no. 4 (2006): 748–768.

74. Robert L. Bernstein, "Rights Watchdog, Lost in the Mideast," *New York Times*, October 19, 2009.

75. *Hardball with Chris Matthews*, transcript for January 31, 2006, broadcast, updated February 2, 2006, NBC News, http://www.msnbc.msn.com/id/11145182/.

76. Carter, *Palestine*, 59–62, 74–80, 98–104.

77. "Noam Chomsky on Israel, the U.S. and Palestine," *Socialist Worker*, March 24, 2001; Richard Falk, "Slouching toward a Palestinian Holocaust," Transnational Foundation for Peace and Future Research, June 29, 2007, http://www.oldsite. transnational.org/Area_MiddleEast/ 2007/Falk_PalestineGenocide.html; Elhanan Yakira, *Post-Zionism, Post-Holocaust: Three Essays on Denial, Forgetting, and the Delegitimation of Israel* (Cambridge: Cambridge University Press, 2010), 37–45.

78. The *Daily Kos* is a discussion forum for activists interested in influencing the Democratic Party. It ranks as the tenth most popular political website in overall traffic, with over a million unique visitors per month. See Adam Levick, "Anti-Israelism and Anti-Semitism in Progressive U.S. Blogs/News Websites: Influential and Poorly Monitored," *Post-Holocaust and Anti-Semitism* 92 (January 2010). On Far Left anti-Semitism in America, see Stephen H. Norwood, *Antisemitism and the American Far Left* (Cambridge: Cambridge University Press, 2013).

79. Martin Kramer, *Ivory Towers on Sand: The Failure of Middle Eastern Studies in America* (Washington, DC: Washington Institute for Near East Policy, 2001), chapter 3.

80. Richard Falk, "Trusting Khomeini," *New York Times*, February 16, 1979, A27.

81. "Judith Butler on Hamas, Hezbollah and the Israel Lobby (2006)," Radical Archives, March 28, 2010, http://radicalarchives.org/2010/03/28/jbutler-on-hamas-hezbollah-israel-lobby/. Ely Karmon, "Hizballah and the Anitglobalization Movement: A New Coalition?" Policywatch 949, Washington Institute, January 27, 2005, http://www.washingtoninstitute.org/policy-analysis/view/hizballah-and-the-anitglo-balization-movement-a-new-coalition.

82. On the size of the readership of these publications see Katerina-Eva Matsa, Tom Rosenstiel, and Paul Moore, "The State of the News Media 2011," Pew Research Center's Project for Excellence in Journalism, http://stateofthemedia. org/2011/magazines-essay/; "About Us," *American Prospect*, http://prospect.org/ cs/about_tap/our_mission; "About the *Review*," *New York Review of Books*, http://www.nybooks.com/about/; Daniel Treiman, "As the Left Says No to War, a Journal's Editor Dissents," *Jewish Daily Forward*, January 31, 2003, http://www. forward.com/articles/9243/.

83. Richard Cohen, "...And the Rise of the Zealots," *Washington Post*, November 6, 1995, A25; Thomas L. Friedman, "Foreign Affairs: Mona and Maya, Yitzhak and Yasir," *New York Times*, October 15, 1995, 15.

84. Leon Wieseltier, "Letting Go"; Michael Walzer, "On the Road," *New Republic*, October 4, 1993, 22–26; Michael Kinsley, "TRB: Arafat and Hitler," *New Republic*, October 11, 1993, 6; Leon Wieseltier, "Peace and Illusion," *New Republic*, March 25, 1996, 12; Thomas L. Friedman, "Foreign Affairs: It's Time to Separate," *New York Times*, January 29, 1995, 15; Richard Cohen, "Tokens of Their

Courage," *Washington Post*, March 11, 1996, A19; Thomas L. Friedman, "Foreign Affairs: Who Are You?" *New York Times*, March 6, 1996, 21.

85. Martin Peretz, "The Bomb's Diameters," *New Republic*, December 17, 2001, 46.
86. "Shepherdstown Blues," *New Republic*, January 17, 2000, 9.
87. Thomas L. Friedman, "Foreign Affairs: Bibi and Gennadi," *New York Times*, May 29, 1996, 19.
88. Thomas Friedman, "Foreign Affairs: Waiting for the Wild Card," *New York Times*, May 12, 1996, 13.
89. Jonathan Frankel, "Netanyahu's Second Year: Farce and Tragedy," *Dissent*, Fall 1997, 16–22.
90. Richard Cohen, "Time for Some Tough Love," *Washington Post*, October 9, 1997, A23; Thomas L. Friedman, "Foreign Affairs: A Dangerous Peace," *New York Times*, January 12, 1999, 19
91. Thomas L. Friedman, "Foreign Affairs: In Defense of Peace," *New York Times*, September 24, 1995, 13; Richard Cohen, "Speak Out!" *Washington Post*, February 24, 1988, A25; Leon Wieseltier, "Gog, Magog, Agog," *New Republic*, May 15, 1995, 46.
92. Richard Cohen, "Wrong About Netanyahu," *Washington Post*, January 16, 1997, A21; Thomas L. Friedman, "Foreign Affairs: What Hebron Tells Us," *New York Times*, January 15, 1997, 19.
93. Richard Cohen, "Mrs. Arafat's Allegations," *Washington Post*, November 18, 1999, A41; Richard Cohen, "Arafat: On the Way to a Police State?" *Washington Post*, January 4, 1996, A25; Thomas L. Friedman, "Foreign Affairs: The Arab Burden," *New York Times*, November 20, 1996, 25; Thomas L. Friedman, "Foreign Affairs: The Twilight Zone," *New York Times*, June 25, 1995, 15; Thomas L. Friedman, "Foreign Affairs: To Tell the Truth," *New York Times*, April 20, 2001, 19.
94. "Chancing Peace," *Nation*, September 27, 1993, 303; Christopher Hitchens, Minority Report (column on the mutual recognition agreement between Israel and the Palestine Liberation Organization), *Nation*, October 11, 1993, 379; James Zogby, "Palestine, Yes!" *Nation*, October 25, 1993, 449.
95. Edward Said, "Arafat's Deal," *Nation*, September 20, 1993, 269–270; Alexander Cockburn, "Beat the Devil," *Nation*, October 4, 1993.
96. Edward Said, "For Palestinian Independence: Rally and Resist," *Nation*, February 14, 1994, 190; Edward Said, "The Mirage of Peace," *Nation*, October 16, 1995, 413.
97. "Piecemeal Peace," *Nation*, October 16, 1995 407.
98. "The Wye Accords," *Nation*, November 16, 1998, 3.
99. Richard Cohen, "Don't Forget Jerusalem," *Washington Post*, April 20, 2010, A15.
100. Thomas L. Friedman, "Foreign Affairs: Arafat's War," *New York Times*, October 13, 2000, 33; David Samuels, "In a Ruined Country: How Yasir Arafat Destroyed Palestine," *Atlantic*, September 2005, http://www.theatlantic.com/magazine/print/2005/09/in-a-ruined-country/4167/.
101. Michael Walzer, "The Four Wars of Israel/Palestine," *Dissent*, Fall 2002; Dennis Ross, "The Missing Peace Disabused," *New Republic*, August 7, 2000, 8; Benny Morris, "The Rejection," *New Republic*, April 21, 2003-April 28, 2003, Leon

Wieseltier, "After Peace," *New Republic*, April 15, 2002, 19; Richard Cohen, "Israel's Answer to Arafat," *Washington Post*, February 8, 2001, A23; Thomas L. Friedman, "Foreign Affairs: The New Mideast Paradigm," *New York Times*, March 6, 2001, 21.

102. Thomas L. Friedman, "Foreign Affairs: Empty Deeds, Ugly Words," *New York Times*, May 11, 2001, 35; Richard Cohen, "The Ugly Arab Press," *Washington Post*, March 13, 2001, A21; Richard Cohen, "The Pope's Silence," *Washington Post*, May 8, 2001, A23; Thomas L. Friedman, "The Hidden Victims," *New York Times*, May 1, 2002, 25.

103. Walter Laqueur, "A Failure of Intelligence," *Atlantic*, March 2002, 127–130.

104. Thomas L. Friedman, "Foreign Affairs: It's Freedom, Stupid," *New York Times*, October 9, 2001, 25.

105. Richard Cohen, "Stop Using Children," *Washington Post*, March 30, 2004, A19; James Bennet, "Beyond Belief," *Atlantic*, March 2009, 12; Thomas L. Friedman, "On the Eve of Madness," *New York Times*, July 28, 2006, 29.

106. Richard Cohen, "Truth Massacred," *Washington Post*, August 6, 2002, A15.

107. Leonard Fein, "Reflections of a Sometime Israel Lobbyist," *Dissent*, Spring 2008; Michael Walzer, "The Four Wars of Israel/Palestine," *Dissent*, Fall 2002; Leon Wieseltier, "The Children of Qana," *New Republic*, August 14, 2006–August 21, 2006, 38; "How Bad Was Jenin?" *Atlantic*, July–August 2003, 38.

108. Richard Cohen, "Palestinian State of Nature," *Washington Post*, September 13, 2005, A27; Thomas L. Friedman, "Foreign Affairs: The New Mideast Paradigm," *New York Times*, March 6, 2001, 21.

109. "It Happened Here," *New Republic*, September 24, 2001, 10; Dennis Ross, "Squeeze Play," *New Republic*, April 23, 2007, 18; Richard Cohen, "Extremists Don't Give an Inch," *Washington Post*, September 20, 2001, A35; Thomas L. Friedman, "Foreign Affairs: World War III," *New York Times*, September 13, 2001, 27.

110. Thomas L. Friedman, "The Intifada Is Over," *New York Times*, December 5, 2001, 29.

111. Richard Cohen, "Two Brands of Terror," *Washington Post*, August 21, 2003, A23.

112. Richard Cohen, "Build a Fence," *Washington Post*, April 16, 2002, A19; Thomas L. Friedman, "The Wailing Wall?" *New York Times*, September 7, 2003, 13; Abigail Cutler. "Security Fences," *Atlantic*, March 2005, 40.

113. Richard Cohen, "Time to Take Control," *Washington Post*, August 16, 2001, A25; Richard Cohen, "Arafat's Alibi," *Washington Post*, May 9, 2002, A31; Thomas L. Friedman, "A Foul Wind," *New York Times*, March 10, 2002, 19.

114. Leon Wieseltier, "After Peace," *New Republic*, April 15, 2002, 19; Richard Cohen, "A 'Traitor' for Peace," *Washington Post*, December 9, 2003 A27; Thomas L. Friedman, "An Intriguing Signal from the Saudi Crown Prince," *New York Times*, February 17, 2002, 11.

115. "Exit Strategy," *New Republic*, May 3, 2004, 7; Leon Wieseltier, "Unsettled," *New Republic*, January 23, 2006, 34; Thomas L. Friedman, "A Hole in the Heart," *New York Times*, October 28, 2004, 29.

116. Thomas L. Friedman, "Arabs, It's Your Move," *New York Times*, February 12, 2004, 37.

117. Michael Walzer, "Israel at 60 Essay," Americans for Peace Now, May 6, 2008; Richard Cohen, "From Algiers to Jerusalem." *Washington Post*, April 2, 2002, A15; Richard Cohen, "Following the Sharon Way," *Washington Post*, January 10, 2006, A15.

118. Michael Walzer "War Fair," *New Republic*, July 31, 2006, 15; Richard Cohen, "A Conflict Hamas Caused," *Washington Post*, January 6, 2009, A13; Thomas L. Friedman, "The Kidnapping of Democracy," *New York Times*, July 14, 2006, 19; Jeffrey Goldberg, "Unforgiven," *Atlantic*, May 2008, 32–51; Jeffrey Goldberg, "Nizar Rayyan of Hamas on God's Hatred of Jews," *Atlantic*, January 2, 2009; Richard Cohen, "Mideast Echoes Of 1938," *Washington Post*, August 22, 2006, A15.

119. Thomas L. Friedman, "The Morning after the Morning After," *New York Times*, August 11, 2006, 15; Dennis Ross, "Roll Back," *New Republic*, July 31, 2006, 17.

120. Walzer, "War Fair"; Wieseltier, "The Children of Qana."

121. Richard Cohen, "Mideast Echoes of 1938," *Washington Post*, August 22, 2006, A15

122. Friedman, "The Gridlock Gang."

123. Thomas L. Friedman, "Not So Smart," *New York Times*, July 19, 2006, 21. Thomas L. Friedman, "The Mideast's Ground Zero," *New York Times*, January 7, 2009, 27

124. Michael Walzer, "Response to Jerome Slater: The Lebanon War," *Dissent*, Winter 2007; Martin Peretz, "Who Lost Gaza?" *New Republic*, July 2, 2007, 3; Cohen, "A Conflict Hamas Caused"; Thomas L. Friedman, "Let Hamas Sink or Swim on Its Own," *New York Times*, February 17, 2006, 23.

125. Richard Cohen, "Hamas's Bloody Hands," *Washington Post*, April 21, 2009, A23; Thomas L. Friedman, "Time for Radical Pragmatism," *New York Times*, June 4, 2008, 25.

126. Thomas L. Friedman, "Beyond The Banks," *New York Times*, February 8, 2009, 10; Thomas L. Friedman, "Green Shoots In Palestine II," *New York Times*, August 9, 2009, 8; Jeffrey Goldberg and Hussein Ibish, "Good News From The Middle East (Really)," *New York Times*, January 25, 2011.

127. Richard Cohen, "Whose Israel Shall It Be?" *Washington Post*, February 24, 2009, A13; Jeffrey Goldberg, "The Lieberman Disaster," *Atlantic*, March 17, 2009.

128. Thomas L. Friedman, "Reality Check," *New York Times*, December 12, 2010, 8; Jeffrey Goldberg. "How Iran Could Save The Middle East," *Atlantic*, July–August 2009, 66–68.

129. Leon Wieseltier, "At the Window," *New Republic*, March 27, 2009, 48; Richard Cohen, "Conscience Hits a Wall in the West Bank," *Washington Post*, April 13, 2010, A17.

130. Benjamin Schwarz, "Will Israel Live to 100?" *Atlantic*, May 2005, 29–30, 32; Jeffrey Goldberg, "Goldblog vs. Peter Beinart, Part I," *Atlantic*, May 18, 2010.

131. Robert Jensen, "Occupation Blues (Book Review)," *Nation*, January 6, 2003; Edward Said, "The End Of Oslo," *Nation*, October 30, 2000; "Bitter Facts in the Mideast," *Nation*, November 6, 2000; Christopher Hitchens, "National Security?" *Nation*, December 31, 2001; Neve Gordon, "Israel: Into the Abyss," *Nation*, September 17, 2001; Naomi Klein "Israel: Boycott, Divest, Sanction"; Judith Butler, "You Will Not Be Alone," *The Nation*, April 13, 2010.

132. Alexander Cockburn, "Sharon or Arafat: Which Is the Sponsor of Terror?" *Nation*, December 24, 2001; Richard Falk, "Ending the Death Dance," *Nation*, April 29, 2002; "Sharon's Bulldozers," *Nation*, May 6, 2002.

133. Meredith Tax, "Not in Our Name," *Nation*, June 4, 2001, p.7; "Reaping The Whirlwind," *Nation*, December 24, 2001.

134. Editors, "In Fact ... with Friends Like These...," *Nation*, November 21, 2005.

135. Roane Carey and Adam Shatz, "Pastrami and Champagne," *Nation*, May 10, 2004; Richard Falk, "Gaza Illusions," *Nation*, August 25, 2005.

136. "Lawless in Gaza," *Nation*, July 14, 2006.

137. "Too High a Price," *Nation*, July 14, 2006.

138. Robert Schneer, "Gaza Clouds Obama's Prospects," *Nation*, December 31, 2008; Roane Carey, "Misreading Gaza," *Nation*, January 7, 2009; Richard Falk, "Israel's War Crimes," *Nation*, December 29, 2008; "Toward Peace in Gaza," *Nation*, January 7, 2009.

139. Sasha Polakow-Suransky, "Who Killed Camp David?" *American Prospect*, October 2004, 44; Avishai Margalit, "The Middle East: Snakes and Ladders," *New York Review of Books*, May 17, 2001; Flore de Preneuf, "Clock Running Out on Clinton's Mideast Legacy," *Salon*, January 3, 2001; Ben Barber, "Dragged Back into the Fight," *Salon*, April 19, 2001; Henry Siegman, "Partners for War," *New York Review of Books*, January 16, 2003; John Judis, "Bush Doesn't Want to Push Peace," *American Prospect*, March 11, 2002, 10.

140. Amos Elon, "Israelis and Palestinians: What Went Wrong?" *New York Review of Books*, December 19, 2002; Gary Kamiya, "How Yasser Arafat will go down in history," *Salon*, November 11, 2004; Gershom Gorenberg, "Spontaneous Fission," *American Prospect*, June 17, 2002, 15; Henry Siegman, "Israel: The Threat from Within," *New York Review of Books*, February 26, 2004.

141. Robert Malley and Hussein Agha, "Camp David: The Tragedy of Errors," *New York Review of Books*, August 9, 2001.

142. Aaron David Miller, *The Much Too Promised Land: American Elusive Search for Arab-Israeli Peace* (New York: Bantam Books, 2008).

143. Flore de Preneuf and Daryl Lindsey, "I Hope He Will Be Better Than His Father," *Salon*, January 4, 2001; Flore de Preneuf, "Israel's Apartheid," *Salon*, November 3, 2000; Michael Adams, "The Fraud of American 'Peacemaking,'" *Salon*, January 4, 2001.

144. Flore de Preneuf, "The Children's War," *Salon*, October 17, 2000.

145. Flore de Preneuf, "Palestinian Rioters Hail Bin Laden," *Salon*, October 8, 2001; Flore de Preneuf, "Rejoicing in the Streets of Jenin," *Salon*, September 11, 2001.

146. Suzy Hansen, "Why Terrorism works," *Salon*, September 12, 2002; Asla Aydintasbas, "Saving Arafat, Again," *Salon*, April 16, 2002; Mark Follman, "After Arafat," *Salon*, November 11, 2004; Flore de Preneuf, "Living with Terrorism," *Salon*, September 13, 2001.

147. Michelle Goldberg, "Intolerance on the Left," *Salon*, February 12, 2003; Dennis Fox, "The Shame of the Pro-Palestinian Left," *Salon*, May 14, 2002.

148. Gershom Gorenberg, "Road Map to Grand Apartheid?" *American Prospect*, July–August, 2003, 15; John Judis, "The Road to Aqaba," *American Prospect*, July–August 2003, 12; Henry Siegman, "Sharon's Phony War," *New York Review of Books*, December 18, 2003.

149. Paul Starr, "Peace by Other Means," *American Prospect*, May 6, 2002, 2; Anthony Lewis, "Is There a Solution?" *New York Review of Books*, April 25, 2002; Ferry Biedermann, "Exiling Peace," *Salon*, April 4, 2002; Gary Kamiya, "Last Exit before Armageddon," *Salon*, March 31, 2002; Paul Wachter, "Amid Chaos, an Olive Branch," *Salon*, March 28, 2002.

150. For example, see Aluf Benn, "The End of the Affair," *Salon*, August 18, 2005.

151. Tony Judt, "Israel: The Alternative," *New York Review of Books*, October 23, 2003.

152. Julie Flint, "The Fallout from Qana," *Salon*, July 31, 2006; Mitch Prothero, "The 'Hiding among Civilians' Myth," *Salon*, July 28, 2006; Juan Cole, "Israel's Maximal Option," *Salon*, July 19, 2006.

153. Sidney Blumenthal, "Israel's Debacle, Courtesy of Bush," *Salon*, August 17, 2006; Glenn Greenwald, "Neoconservatives Can't Dig Their Way out of This Hole," *Salon*, August 7, 2006; Laura Rozen, "Bush's Diplomacy Allergy," *Salon*, July 25, 2006; Tim Grieve, "The Lessons That Haven't Been Learned," *Salon*, July 19, 2006; Mitchell Prothero, "Lebanon Pays for Hezbollah's Sins," *Salon*, July 14, 2006; Gary Kamiya, "Leave the Muslim World Alone," *Salon*, July 17, 2007; Glenn Greenwald, "Krauthammer's Plan to Deny Palestinians Gas and Electricity," *Salon*, June 22, 2007.

154. Kathleen Haley, "We Need to Talk to Them," *Salon*, February 25, 2006; Cobban, "Who Is the Real Hamas?"; Juan Cole, "How Do You Like Your Democracy Now, Mr. Bush?" *Salon*, January 27, 2006; Gary Kamiya, "Bush's Delusions Die in Gaza," *Salon*, January 29, 2008; Levy and Atallah, "A Path to Peace"; Henry Siegman, "Hamas: The Last Chance for Peace?"; Brzezinski et al., "Failure Risks Devastating Consequences," Richard Cohen, "Eyeless in Gaza," *New York Review of Books*, February 12, 2009.

155. Gary Kamiya, "The Israel Rules," *Salon*, January 6, 2009.

156. John Judis, "Some Mideast Realism, Please," *American Prospect*, January 13, 2003, 8; Robert Dreyfuss, "Tinker, Banker, Neocon, Spy," *American Prospect*, November 18, 2002, 28; John Judis, "Two Steps Backward," *American Prospect*, August 12, 2002, 10; Michael Lind, "From Fantasy to Fiasco," *American Prospect*, April 2008, 37; Michael Massing, "Deal Breakers," *American Prospect*, March 11, 2002, 18; Daniel Levy, "Is It Good for the Jews?" *American Prospect*, July–August 2006, 33; Laura Rozen and Jason Vest, "Cloak and Swagger," *American Prospect*, November 2004, 21; Max Blumenthal, "Born-Again for Sharon," *Salon*, November 1, 2004; Jason Boyett, "Apocalypse Soon," *Salon*, August 7, 2006; Michelle Goldberg, "Antichrist Politics," *Salon*, May 24, 2002; Juan Cole, "The New McCarthyism," *Salon*, April 22, 2005; Gary Kamiya, "Can American Jews Unplug the Israel Lobby?" *Salon*, March 20, 2007; Glenn Greenwald, "Exploiting Religious Divisions for Political Gain," *Salon*, August 8, 2006; Glenn Greenwald, "New Poll Reveals How Unrepresentative Neocon Jewish Groups Are," *Salon*, December 12, 2007; Glenn Greenwald, "Some Hateful, Radical Ministers – White Evangelicals – Are Acceptable," *Salon*, February 28, 2008.

157. Peter Beinart, "The Failure of the American Jewish Establishment," *New York Review of Books*, June 10. 2010.

158. John Judis, "The Real Foreign-Policy Debate," *American Prospect*, May 6, 2002, 10; Bruce Ackerman and Todd Gitlin, "We Answer to the Name of Liberals," *American Prospect*, November 2006, 24.

159. "The American Public: Opinions and Values in a 51%–48% Nation," Pew Research Center for the People and the Press, January 20, 2005, http://www.pewresearch.org/files/old-assets/trends/trends2005-public.pdf.

160. "Beyond Red vs. Blue: Political Typology," Pew Research Center for the People and the Press, May 4, 2011, http://people-press.org/files/legacy-pdf/Beyond-Red-vs-Blue-The-Political-Typology.pdf; "Beyond Red vs. Blue," Pew Research Center for the People and the Press, May 10, 2005, http://www.people-press.org/2005/05/10/beyond-red-vs-blue/; Pew Research Center, spreadsheet, 2005 poll.

161. "Independents Take Center Stage in Obama Era: Trends in Political Values and Core Attitudes: 1987–2009," Pew Research Center for the People and the Press, May 21, 2009, http://people-press.org/2009/05/21/independents-take-center-stage-in-obama-era/.

162. *Constrained Internationalism: Adapting to New Realities: Results of a 2010 National Survey of American Public Opinion* (Chicago: Chicago Council on Global Affairs, 2010), 78, http://www.thechicagocouncil.org/UserFiles/File/POS_Topline%20Reports/POS%202010/Global%20Views%202010.pdf.

163. "U.S. Seen as Less Important, China as More Powerful," Pew Research Center for the People and the Press, December 3, 2009, http://people-press.org/2009/12/03/us-seen-as-less-important-china-as-more-powerful/.

164. "U.S. Seen as Less Important, China as More Powerful."

165. "Continuing Divide in Views of Islam and Violence," Pew Research Center for the People and the Press, March 9, 2011, http://www.people-press.org/2011/03/09/continuing-divide-in-views-of-islam-and-violence/; "Part 2: Views of Islam and Religion in the World," Pew Research Center for the People and the Press, March 20, 2002, http://www.people-press.org/2002/03/20/part-2-views-of-islam-and-religion-in-the-world/;
"Public Expresses Mixed Views of Islam, Mormonism", Pew Research Religion and Public Life Project, September 25, 2007, http://pewforum.org/Public-Expresses-Mixed-Views-of-Islam-Mormonism.aspx.

166. Newport and Carroll, "Republicans and Religious Americans Most Sympathetic to Israel."

167. "Modest Backing For Israel in Gaza Crisis".

168. "Foreign Policy Views: Afghanistan, Iran, Israel," Pew Research Center for the People and the Press, March 15, 2012, http://www.people-press.org/files/legacy-pdf/03-15-12%20Foreign%20Policy%20Release.pdf.

169. Ibid.; "War Support Slips, Fewer Expect a Successful Outcome," Pew Research Center for the People and the Press, February 15, 2007, http://www.people-press.org/2007/02/15/war-support-slips-fewer-expect-a-successful-outcome/.

170. "More See America's Loss of Global Respect as Major Problem," Pew Research Center for the People and the Press, June 16, 2008, http://people-press.org/2008/06/16/more-see-americas-loss-of-global-respect-as-major-problem/; "U.S. Seen as Less Important, China as More Powerful."

171. Eytan Gilboa, *American Public Opinion toward Israel and the Arab-Israeli Conflict* (Lexington, MA: Lexington Books, 1987), 294; "Modest Backing for Israel in Gaza Crisis," Pew Research Center for the People and the Press, January 13, 2009, http://www.people-press.org/2009/01/13/modest-backing-for-israel-in-gaza-crisis/; Lydia Saad, "Support for Israel in U.S. at 63%, Near Record High:

Near-Record-Low 30% Optimistic about Arab-Israeli Peace," Gallup, February 24, 2010, http://www.gallup.com/poll/126155/support-israel-near-record-high. aspx.

172. Lydia Saad, "Recent Middle East Violence Costs Israel Some U.S. Public Support" Gallup, March 15, 2002, http://www.gallup.com/poll/5476/recent-middle-east-violence-costs-israel-some-us-public-support.aspx; "Modest Backing for Israel in Gaza Crisis"; "America's Place in the World 2009," Pew Research Center for the People and the Press, December 2009, http://people-press.org/reports/pdf/569. pdf.

173. Saad, "Recent Middle East Violence Costs Israel Some Public Support."

174. Jeffrey M. Jones, "Nearly Half of Americans Favor Independent Palestinian State," Gallup, June 3, 2002, http://www.gallup.com/poll/6115/Nearly-Half-Americans-Favor-Independent-Palestinian-State.aspx; Lydia Saad, "Americans Remain Skeptical about Middle East Peace," Gallup, June 4, 2009, http://www.gallup.com/poll/120728/americans-remain-skeptical-middle-east-peace.aspx.

175. However, when the question was phrased so that Israeli control was linked to Israel "keeping all the Christian, Muslim and Jewish holy sites open and safe for all faiths," the position of Democrats reversed, with over half supporting complete Israeli control and just over a quarter favoring division. See the survey of registered voters conducted by Public Opinion Strategies for the Israel Project, December 12–14, 2010.

176. Zogby International, *The Doha Debates: Should the U.S. 'Get Tough with Israel,"* Arab American Institute, April 2009, http://www.aaiusa.org/page/-/Polls/ArabAmericanOpinion/DohaDebates_2009.pdf.

177. David W. Moore, "Americans Skeptical Either Side in Palestinian-Israeli Conflict Wants Peace: Four in Ten Say United States Supports Israel 'Too Much,'" Gallup, June 11, 2002, http://www.gallup.com/poll/6193/Americans-Skeptical-Either-Side-PalestinianIsraeli-Conflict-Wants-Peace.aspx.

178. "American Attitudes Hold Steady in Face of Foreign Crises," Pew Research Center for the People and the Press, August 17, 2006, http://people-press.org/2006/08/17/american-attitudes-hold-steady-in-face-of-foreign-crises/; "Modest Backing for Israel in Gaza Crisis."

179. "American Attitudes Hold Steady in Face of Foreign Crises." Independents were positioned roughly midway between Republicans and Democrats.

180. "Modest Backing for Israel in Gaza Crisis."

181. Moore, "Americans Skeptical Either Side in Palestinian-Israeli Conflict Wants Peace"; "Questions and Answers about American Public Opinion and the Middle East" Gallup, April 10, 2002, http://www.gallup.com/poll/5596/questions-answers-about-american-public-opinion-middle-east.aspx.

182. "American Attitudes Hold Steady in Face of Foreign Crises."

183. "Modest Backing For Israel in Gaza Crisis."

184. "American Attitudes Hold Steady in Face of Foreign Crises"; "Modest Backing for Israel in Gaza Crisis."

185. Jones, "Americans Continue to Be Pessimistic About Middle East Peace."

186. Unpublished documents commissioned by a pro-Israeli organization. Greenberg, Quinlan Rosner Research for the Israel Project April 20, 2010.

187. Martin Indyk, *Innocents Abroad: An Intimate Account of American Peace Diplomacy in the Middle East* (New York: Simon and Schuster, 2009).

188. David Makovsky, *Making Peace with the PLO: Policy and Politics in the Rabin Government* (Boulder, CO: Westview Press, 1995), 144.

189. Makovsky, *Making Peace with the PLO*.

190. Jonathan Rynhold, *Israeli Political Culture in Israel's Relations with the United States over the Palestinian Question, 1981–1996* (Ph.D submitted in the Department of International Relations, London School of Economics and Political Science, 1998), chapter 7.

191. "US-Israel Memorandum of Agreement," James Martin Center for Nonproliferation Studies, October 31, 1998, http://cns.miis.edu/wmdme/isrl_moa.htm.

192. Jonathan Rynhold, "Making Sense of Tragedy: Barak, the Israeli Left and the Oslo Peace Process," *Israel Studies Forum*, 19, no. 1 (2003).

193. Dennis Ross, *The Missing Peace: The Inside Story of the Fight for Middle East Peace* (New York: Farrar, Straus and Giroux, 2005), 801–805.

194. Indyk was a senior official during the Clinton Administration serving as ambassador to Israel and as senior director of Near East and South Asian Affairs at the United States National Security Council.

195. Ibid.; Martin Indyk, *Innocents Abroad*.

196. "Remarks By the President on a New Beginning Cairo University", White House, June 4, 2009, www.whitehouse.gov/the_press_office/Remarks-by-the-President-at-Cairo-University-6-04-09/.

197. This "evenhanded" perspective was also apparent in the only reference he made to the Arab-Israeli conflict in his 2006 book, *The Audacity of Hope*; see Peter Beinart, *The Crisis of Zionism* (New York: Times Books/Henry Holt, 2012), 90.

198. Ron Kampeas, "Obama Gets Jewish Support on Peace Push," *JTA*, July 13, 2009, http://www.jta.org/news/article/2009/07/13/1006510/obama-gets-jewish-support-on-peace-push-questions-about-style.

199. Robert O. Freedman, "George W. Bush, Barack Obama, and the Arab-Israeli Conflict from 2001 to 2011," in Robert O Freedman, ed., *Israel and the United States: Six Decades of U.S.-Israeli Relations* (Boulder, CO: Westview, 2012).

200. Beinart, *The Crisis of Zionism*, 126.

201. Ibid., 129.

202. See Obama interview with Joe Klein in "It Always Takes Longer Than You Think,", *Time*, February 1, 2010.

203. "Dennis Ross Departs," *Jewish Week*, November 15, 2011; Beinart, *The Crisis of Zionism*, 130–148.

204. Freedman, "George W. Bush, Barack Obama, and the Arab-Israeli Conflict from 2001 to 2011."

205. Cited in Hilary Leila Krieger, "Forcing the Peace," *Jerusalem Post*, April 30, 2010.

206. "Remarks by the President on the Middle East and North Africa" (State Department, Washington DC), White House, May 19, 2011, http://www.whitehouse.gov/the-press-office/2011/05/19/remarks-president-middle-east-and-north-africa.

207. On the debate inside the administration between the approach of Ross, Mitchell, and the "quartet of staffers" over presenting a U.S. plan and the Palestinian move at the UN, see Beinart, *The Crisis of Zionism*, 146–148.

208. Elizabeth A. Oldmixon, Beth A. Rosenson, and Kenneth D. Wald, "Conflict over Israel: The Role of Religion, Race, Party, and Ideology in the U.S. House of Representatives, 1997–2002," *Terrorism and Political Violence*, 17, no. 3 (2005), 407–426. In the Senate, Republicans were more supportive of Israel throughout the 1990s; see Beth A. Rosenson, Elizabeth A. Oldmixon, and Kenneth D. Wald, "U.S. Senators' Support for Israel Examined through Sponsorship/Cosponsorship Decisions, 1993–2002: The Influence of Elite and Constituent Factors," *Foreign Policy Analysis*, 5, no. 1 (2009): 73–91.

209. Glenn Kessler and Howard Schneider, "U.S. Urges Israel to End Expansion," *Washington Post*, May 24, 2009.

210. Caroline Glick, "Column One: Republicans, Democrats and Israel," *Jerusalem Post*, April 30, 2010, http://www.jpost.com/Opinion/Editorials/Article.aspx?id=174345.

211. David Nather, "Reid's Pro-Israel Message to Obama," *Congressional Quarterly*, June 15, 2009; U.S. House of Representatives, Committee on Foreign Affairs Democrats, "Berman Calls on Abbas to Accept Netanyahu Proposal for Unconditional Peace Talks,"http://www.democrats.foreignaffairs.house.gov/press_display.asp?id=632; "US delegates blame Palestinians for no peace talks," Agence France-Presse, August 13, 2009.

212. Herb Keinon, "Hoyer: E. J'lem not same as W. Bank," *Jerusalem Post*, August 11, 2009; "Schumer: Obama's 'Counter-Productive' Israel Policy 'Has to Stop," *Politico*, April 23, 2010; http://www.politico.com/blogs/bensmith/0410/Schumer_Obamas_Counterproductive_Israel_policy_has_to_stop.html; Ben Smith, "Criticism on Israel move builds on Hill," *Politico*, April 22, 2010.

213. Lahav Harkov, "Senators Stress Value of US-Israel Ties," *Jerusalem Post*, April 14, 2010.

214. Natasha Mozgovaya, "US House opposes unilateral declaration of Palestinian state," *Haaretz*, December 6, 2010.

215. "Faith on the Hill—The Religious Composition of the 112th Congress," Pew Research Religion and Public Life Project, January 5, 2011, http://www.pewforum.org/2011/01/05/faith-on-the-hill-the-religious-composition-of-the-112th-congress/.

216. Scott Wilson, "Democrats Restore to Party Platform Language on Jerusalem," *Washington Post*, September 5, 2012; interview with person on the Democratic Convention conference floor at the time.

217. Mark Hugo Lopez and Susan Minushkin, "2008 National Survey of Latinos: Hispanic Voter Attitudes," Pew Research Hispanic Trends Project, July 24. 2008, http://www.pewhispanic.org/2008/07/24/2008-national-survey-of-latinos-hispanic-voter-attitudes/; Mark Hugo Lopez, "Latinos and the 2010 Elections: Strong Support for Democrats; Weak Voter Motivation," Pew Research Hispanic Trends Project, October 5, 2010, http://www.pewhispanic.org/2010/10/05/latinos-and-the-2010-elections-strong-support-for-democrats-weak-voter-motivation/.

218. Lopez and Minushkin, "2008 National Survey of Latinos"; Mark Hugo Lopez, "The Latino Vote in the 2010 Elections," Pew Research Hispanic Trends Project, March 11, 2010. http://www.pewhispanic.org/2010/11/03/the-latino-vote-in-the-2010-elections.

219. Frank Newport and Joseph Carroll, "Just How Democratic Is the Jewish Population in America Today?" Gallup, September 16, 2002, http://www.gallup.com/

poll/6799/just-how-democratic-jewish-population-america-today.aspx; Frank Newport, "Mormons Most Conservative Major Religious Group in U.S.," Gallup, January 11, 2010, http://www.gallup.com/poll/125021/Mormons-Conservative-Major-Religious-Group.aspx; "Trends in Political Values and Core Attitudes: 1987–2007," Pew Research Center for the People and the Press, March 22, 2007, 8. http://people-press.org/files/legacy-pdf/312.pdf.

220. "Independents Take Center Stage in Obama Era: Trends in Political Values and Core Attitudes: 1987–2009", Pew Research Center for the People and the Press, May 21, 2009, http://people-press.org/2009/05/21/independents-take-center-stage-in-obama-era/.

221. James L. Guth and William R. Kenan Jr., "Religious Factors and American Public Support for Israel: 1992–2008" (paper presented at the annual meeting of the American Political Science Association, Seattle, WA, September 1–4, 2011).

222. Green, "The American Public and Sympathy for Israel." Similar results were obtained in a 2009 poll during the Gaza War; see "Modest Backing for Israel in Gaza Crisis."

223. "The Generation Gap and the 2012 Election," Pew Research Center for the People and the Press, November 3, 2011, http://www.people-press.org/2011/11/03/the-generation-gap-and-the-2012-election-3/?src=prc-headline; "Independents Take Center Stage in Obama Era."

224. John C. Green, "The American Public and Sympathy for Israel: Present and Future," *Journal of Ecumenical Studies*, 44, no. 1 (2009): 107–121. See also Benjamin Phillips, Eszter Lengyel, and Leonard Saxe, *American Attitudes toward Israel*. (Waltham, MA: Brandeis University, Cohen Center for Modern Jewish Studies, 2002), 41, 105–106, and figures 15, 54; Frank Newport and Joseph Carroll, "Republicans and Religious Americans Most Sympathetic to Israel," Gallup, March 27, 2006, http://www.gallup.com/poll/22063/republicans-religious-americans-most-sympathetic-israel.aspx; Lydia Saad, "In U.S., Canada Places First in Image Contest; Iran Last," Gallup, February 19, 2010, http://www.gallup.com/poll/126116/Canada-Places-First-Image-Contest-Iran-Last.aspx.

225. "Goal of Libyan Operation Less Clear to Public," Pew Research Center for the People and the Press, April 5, 2011, http://www.people-press.org/2011/04/05/goal-of-libyan-operation-less-clear-to-public/.

226. Author interview with Peter Beinart.

227. Author interview with Matthew Yglesias; Spencer Ackerman, "That Liberal Zionism Question Again (Illiberal Israel Edition)," Attackerman, May 23, 2010, http://attackerman.firedoglake.com/2010/05/23/that-liberal-zionism-question-again-illiberal-israel-edition/; Josh Marshall, "Doing Israel No Favors," *Talking Points Memo*, June 9, 2009, http://talkingpointsmemo.com/edblog/doing-israel-no-favors.

228. Matthew Yglesias, "The Duty to Do the Right Thing," ThinkProgress, May 19, 2010, http://thinkprogress.org/yglesias/2010/05/19/197286/the-duty-to-do-the-right-thing/; Spencer Ackerman, "Has Jeffrey Goldberg Actually Read Anything Trita Parsi Wrote?" Attackerman, November 2, 2009, http://attackerman.firedoglake.com/2009/11/02/has-jeffrey-goldberg-actually-read-anything-trita-parsi-wrote/.

229. Josh Marshall, "A Number of Readers," *Talking Points Memo*, March 14, 2003; Matthew Yglesias, "A Palestinian Partner," ThinkProgress, June 11, 2010, http://thinkprogress.org/yglesias/2010/06/11/197533/a-palestinian-partner/; Matthew Yglesias, "Most Arabs Ready for Peace," ThinkProgress, August 6, 2010, http://thinkprogress.org/yglesias/2010/08/06/198145/most-arabs-ready-for-peace/.

230. Josh Marshall, "Two Points Further On," *Talking Points Memo*, April 15, 2002.

231. Josh Marshall, "Hubris," *Talking Points Memo*, February 3, 2011, http://talkingpointsmemo.com/edblog/hubris; Josh Marshall, "I Didn't Go To," *Talking Points Memo*, April 15, 2002, http://talkingpointsmemo.com/edblog/–99727; Spencer Ackerman, "Somewhere, Khaled Meshal Is Laughing," Attackerman, November 1, 2009, http://attackerman.firedoglake.com/2009/11/01/somewhere-khaled-meshal-is-laughing/.

232. Spencer Ackerman, "Peace Is Possible," Attackerman, December 30, 2008, http://attackerman.firedoglake.com/2008/12/30/peace-is-possible/.

233. Ezra Klein, "Can't Take the Politics out of Politics," *American Prospect*, December 30, 2008, http://prospect.org/article/cant-take-politics-out-politics.

234. Ezra Klein, "Israel, Wrong," *American Prospect*, December 28, 2008. http://prospect.org/article/israel-wrong.

235. Spencer Ackerman, "This Is Starting to Get Dangerous for Us," Attackerman, March 12, 2010, http://attackerman.firedoglake.com/2010/03/12/this-is-starting-to-get-dangerous-for-us/; Matthew Yglesias "Lazare on *The Israel Lobby*," *Atlantic*, October 19, 2007, http://www.theatlantic.com/politics/archive/2007/10/lazare-on-em-the-israel-lobby-em/43347/; Ezra Klein, "Crazy Ravings from a Madman," *American Prospect*, December 28, 2008, http://prospect.org/article/crazy-ravings-madman.

236. Matthew Yglesias, "Palestinian Unity Deal Shouldn't Preclude American Action on Israeli-Palestinian Conflict," ThinkProgress, May 18, 2011, http://thinkprogress.org/yglesias/2011/05/18/201029/palestinian-unity-deal-shouldnt-preclude-american-action-on-israeli-palestinian-conflict/; Matthew Yglesias, "Low Standards," *Atlantic*, July 29, 2008, http://www.theatlantic.com/politics/archive/2008/07/low-standards/49525/.

237. Ezra Klein, "Focusing on the Settlements," *American Prospect*, February 12, 2009, http://prospect.org/article/focusing-settlements.

238. "Beyond Red vs. Blue," May 10, 2005.

239. Gilboa, *American Public Opinion toward Israel*, 282–284.

240. Oppenheim, "The Segmentation Study of the American Market, Fourth Quarter 2010."

241. Frank Luntz, *America 2020* (The Israel Project, June 2005).

242. *Public Opinion Strategies Survey of US College Students*, October 28–November 8, 2011, conducted for the Israel Project and the American-Israeli Cooperative Enterprise.

243. Phillips, Lengyel, and Saxe, *American Attitudes toward Israel*, 41, 105–106, figures 15, 54; Oppenheim, "The Segmentation Study of the American Market."

244. *Public Opinion Strategies Survey of US College Students*.

245. See, for example, Ronald Inglehart, *Modernization and Postmodernization: Cultural, Economic, and Political Change in 43 Societies* (Princeton, NJ: Princeton University Press, 1997).

246. "Obama Advisor Samantha Power Calls for Invasion of Israel," 2002 video, YouTube, http://www.youtube.com/watch?v=oFdt6fjdHQw; "Samantha Power on U.S. Foreign Policy," Harvard University, John F. Kennedy School of Government, May 30, 2007, http://web.archive.org/web/20070813072047/http://www.ksg.harvard.edu/ksgnews/KSGInsight/power.html.

247. Luntz, *America 2020*.

248. See Matthew Yglesias's blog posts for 2002; for example, "So the Saudi Plan," February 27, 2002 http://yglesias.blogspot.co.il/2002_02_24_archive.html; "It's Been a While Since," April 11, 2002, http://yglesias.blogspot.co.il/2002_04_07_ archive.html.

249. Author interview with Matthew Yglesias.

250. Author interview, 2013.

251. *Public Opinion Strategies*, May 2010 survey for the Israel Project.

252. "After Boston, Little Change in Views of Islam and Violence," Pew Research Center for the People and the Press, May 7, 2013, http://www.people-press.org/2013/05/07/after-boston-little-change-in-views-of-islam-and-violence/.

253. "Foreign Policy Views: Afghanistan, Iran, Israel."

254. "Public Takes Strong Stance Against Iran's Nuclear Program" Pew Research Center for the People and the Press, February 15, 2012, http://www.people-press.org/files/legacy-pdf/02-15-12%20Foreign%20Policy%20release.pdf.

255. "Pro-Israel margin" refers to the difference between sympathy levels for Israel and the Palestinians. Calculations are based on figures presented in David Moore, "Republicans, Conservatives More Supportive of Israelis Than Democrats, Liberals: Pattern Has Persisted for At Least the Past Decade," Gallup, April 17, 2002, http://www.gallup.com/poll/5836/Republicans-Conservatives-More-Supportive-Israelis-than-Democrats-Liberals.aspx; Newport and Carroll, "Republicans and Religious Americans Most Sympathetic to Israel"; "Modest Backing for Israel in Gaza Crisis"; Lydia Saad, "Americans Maintain Broad Support for Israel," Gallup, February 28, 2011, http://www.gallup.com/poll/146408/americans-maintain-broad-support-israel.aspx.

256. Jones, "Nearly Half of Americans Favor Independent Palestinian State"; Saad, "Americans Remain Skeptical about Middle East Peace."

4. EVANGELICALS AND CHRISTIAN ZIONISM

1. *Moral Majority Report*, March 14, 1980. Quoted in Colin Shindler, "Likud and the Christian Dispensationalists," *Israel Studies* 5, no. 1 (2000), and in Jerry Falwell, *Listen, America!* (New York: Bantam Books, 1980).

2. Gershon Gorenberg, *The End of Days: Fundamentalism and the Struggle for the Temple Mount* (Oxford: Oxford University Press, 2000).

3. David Brog, *Standing with Israel* (Lake Mary, FL: FrontLine, 2006).

4. Stephen Spector, *Evangelicals and Israel: The Story of American Christian Zionism* (Oxford: Oxford University Press, 2009), 43–45; Gary Dorrien, "Evangelical Ironies: Theology, Politics and Israel," in Alan Mittleman, Byron Johnson, and Nancy Isserman, eds., *Uneasy Allies? Evangelical and Jewish Relations* (Lanham, MD: Lexington Books, 2007), 103–126; Gerald McDermott, "Evangelicals and Israel," in Mittleman, Johnson, and Isserman, eds., *Uneasy Allies?* 129–132.

5. George M. Marsden, *Understanding Fundamentalism and Evangelicalism* (Grand Rapids, MI: Eerdmans, 1991), 1–5; McDermott, "Evangelicals and Israel."

6. Paul Boyer, *When Time Shall Be No More: Prophecy Belief in Modern American Culture* (Cambridge: Belknap Press, 1992), 93; Ernest R. Sandeen, *The Roots of Fundamentalism: British and American Millenarianism, 1800–1930* (Chicago: University of Chicago Press, 1970). About half the contributors to "The Fundamentals" were premillennialists; see Malise Ruthven, *Fundamentalism: The Search for Meaning* (Oxford: Oxford University Press, 2005), 10–14.

7. "U.S. Religious Landscape Survey," Pew Forum on Religion and Public Life, June 2008, http://religions.pewforum.org/pdf/report2-religious-landscape-study-full.pdf.

8. Walter Russell Mead, "The New Israel and the Old: Why Gentile Americans Back the Jewish State," *Foreign Affairs* 87, no. 4 (July–August 2008).

9. John C. Green, "The American Religious Landscape and Political Attitudes: A Baseline for 2004," University of Akron, Ray C. Bliss Institute of Applied Politics, no date, https://www.uakron.edu/bliss/research/archives/2004/Religious_-Landscape_2004.pdf; "U.S. Religious Landscape Survey," June 2008.

10. John Micklethwait and Adrian Wooldrige, *God Is Back: How the Global Revival of Faith Is Changing the World* (London: Penguin Press, 2009), 52.

11. Dinesh D'Souza, *Jerry Falwell: Before the Millennium: A Critical Biography* (Chicago: Regnery, 1984), 10.

12. "Trends in Party Identification of Religious Groups," Pew Research Religion and Public Life Project, February 2, 2012, http://www.pewforum.org/2012/02/02/trends-in-party-identification-of-religious-groups-affiliation/.

13. Spector, *Evangelicals and Israel*, 3.

14. Barbara Tuchman, *Bible and Sword: England and Palestine from the Bronze Age to Balfour* (New York: Ballantine Books, 1984), 120–125; Yaakov Ariel, "An Unexpected Alliance: Christian Zionism and Its Historical Significance," *Modern Judaism* 26, no. 1 (2006); Peter Toon, ed., *Puritans, the Millennium and the Future of Israel: Puritan Eschatology, 1600 to 1660* (Cambridge: James Clarke, 1970), 23–26.

15. Timothy P. Weber, *On the Road to Armageddon: How Evangelicals Became Israel's Best Friend* (Grand Rapids, MI: Baker Academic, 2004), 20–25.

16. Ibid., 35–43.

17. Paul Charles Merkley, *The Politics Of Christian Zionism, 1891–1948* (London: Frank Cass, 1998).

18. Yaakov Ariel, *Philosemites or Antisemites? Evangelical Christian Attitudes toward Jews, Judaism, and the State of Israel* (Jerusalem: Hebrew University of Jerusalem, Vidal Sassoon International Center for the Study of Antisemitism, 2002), http://sicsa.huji.ac.il/20Ariel.htm.

19. L. Nelson Bell, "Unfolding Destiny," *Christianity Today*, July 21, 1967, 28.

20. *Washington Post*, March 23, 1981.

21. Weber, *On the Road to Armageddon*, 218–219.

22. Brog, *Standing with Israel*, 4

23. Zev Chafets, *Match Made in Heaven: American Jews, Christian Zionists, and One Man's Exploration of the Weird and Wonderful Judeo-Evangelical Alliance* (New York: HarperCollins, 2007), 73.

24. Paul Charles Merkley, *Christian Attitudes towards the State of Israel* (Montreal: McGill-Queens University Press, 2007), 172.

25. Ruth Sinai, "When Money Speaks Louder Than the Word," *Haaretz*, January 7, 2005; International Fellowship of Christians and Jews 2008 Annual Report, http://www.ifcj.org/ifcj-08/pdf/2008/2008-IFCJ-Annual-Report.pdf.

26. Uriel Heilman, "US Churches Pray for Israel," *Jerusalem Post*, October 18, 2004.

27. Sinai, "When Money Speaks Louder Than the Word"; Bill Broadway "Scripture Inspires Many Christians to Support Zionism Politically, Financially," *Washington Post*, March 27, 2004; Brog, *Standing with Israel*, 162; Victoria Clark, *Allies for Armageddon: The Rise of Christian Zionism* (New Haven, CT: Yale University Press, 2007), 231–232.

28. Jacob Berkman, "Jewish Agency Gives Evangelical Christians Powerful Seat at Table," *JTA*, December 30, 2007.

29. International Fellowship of Christians and Jews, Financial Summary, http://www.ifcj.org/site/PageNavigator/eng/about/financial_accountability/financial_statement/.

30. Chafets, *Match Made in Heaven*, 120–124.

31. Brog, *Standing with Israel*, 4.

32. Jerry Gordon, "What a 'Night to Honor Israel': The CUFI Washington Summit Dinner in DC," Israpundit, July 20, 2006; Wayne Slater, "Protecting Israel Is San Antonio Pastor John Hagee's Mission," *Dallas Morning News*, October 28, 2007, http://www.dallasnews.com/sharedcontent/dws/dn/religion/stories/102807dntex-hagee.37a2adf.html.

33. Jerry Falwell, "Our Citizenship as Americans," sermon, March 7, 1976, quoted in Warren L. Vinz, *Pulpit Politics: Faces of American Protestant Nationalism in the Twentieth Century* (Albany, NY: State University of New York Press, 1997), 181.

34. Jerry Falwell, "The Twenty-First Century and the End of the World," *Fundamentalist Journal*, May 1988, p. 10.

35. Pat Robertson, *The Collected Works of Pat Robertson: The New Millennium, the New World Order, the Secret Kingdom* (New York: Inspirational Press, 1994), 256–257.

36. John Hagee, *Final Dawn over Jerusalem* (Nashville: Thomas Nelson, 1998), 131.

37. "American Evangelicals and Israel," Pew Research Religion and Public Life Project, April 15, 2005 http://www.pewforum.org/2005/4/15/American-Evangelicals-and-Israel.aspx (though it is estimated that less than 20 percent of evangelicals believe in the specifics of Dispensationalism); Merkley, *Christian Attitudes towards the State of Israel*, 177, 189.

38. Cited in Brog, *Standing with Israel*, 78–79.

39. Bruce David Forbes, "How popular Are the *Left Behind* Books … and Why? A Discussion of Popular Culture," in Bruce David Forbes and Jeanne Halgren Kilde, eds., *Rapture, Revelation, and the End Times: Exploring the "Left Behind" Series* (New York: Palgrave Macmillan, 2004).

40. Brog, *Standing with Israel*, 69; Spector, *Evangelicals and Israel*, 23–25.

41. Falwell, *Listen, America!* 98.

42. Merill Simon, *Jerry Falwell and the Jews* (Middle Village, NY: Jonathan David, 1999), 64.

43. Ronald R. Stockton, "Christian Zionism: Prophecy and Public Opinion," *Middle East Journal* 41, no. 2 (1987): 253; John C. Green, "The American

Public and Sympathy for Israel: Present and Future," *Journal of Ecumenical Studies* 44, no. 1 (2009).

44. Merkley, *Christian Attitudes towards the State of Israel*, 169.

45. Brog, *Standing with Israel*, 78–79.

46. Clark, *Allies for Armageddon*, 26–27.

47. Corwin E. Smidt, "Religion and American Attitudes toward Islam and an Invasion of Iraq," *Sociology of Religion* 66, no. 3 (2005): 243–261; "American Evangelicals and Israel," Pew Research Religion and Public Life Project; "Religion and Politics: Contention and Consensus: Growing Number Says Islam Encourages Violence among Followers," Pew Research Center for the People and the Press, July 24, 2003, http://www.people-press.org/2003/07/24/religion-and-politics-contention-and-consensus/.

48. "Americans Struggle with Religion's Role at Home and Abroad," Pew Research Center for the People and the Press, March 20, 2002, http://www.people-press.org/2002/03/20/part-2-views-of-islam-and-religion-in-the-world/; "Views of Islam Remain Sharply Divided: Plurality Sees Islam as More Likely to Encourage Violence," Pew Research Religion and Public Life Project, September 9, 2004, http://www.pewforum.org/2004/09/09/views-of-islam-remain-sharply-divided/; "Public Expresses Mixed Views of Islam, Mormonism," Pew Research Religion and Public Life Project, September 26, 2007, http://www.pewforum.org/2007/09/26/public-expresses-mixed-views-of-islam-mormonism/.

49. Brog, *Standing with Israel*, 78–79.

50. Spector, *Evangelicals and Israel*, 32–33.

51. Brog, *Standing with Israel*, 66.

52. "Religion and Politics." *Pew Research Center for the People & the Press.*

53. Chafets, *Match Made in Heaven.*

54. James L. Guth, "Religious Leadership and Support for Israel: A Study of Clergy in Nineteen Denominations" (paper presented at the Annual Meeting of the Southern Political Science Association, New Orleans, January 2007).

55. Weber, *On the Road to Armageddon*, 225.

56. Grace Halsell, *Prophecy and Politics: Militant Evangelists on the Road to Nuclear War* (Westport, CT: Lawrence Hill, 1986), 106; Kendall Hamilton, Joseph Contreras, and Mark Dennis, "The Strange Case of Israel's Red Heifer," *Newsweek*, May 19, 1997; Yaakov S. Ariel, *On Behalf of Israel: American Fundamentalist Attitudes toward Jews, Judaism, and Zionism, 1865–1945* (Brooklyn, NY: Carlson, 1991), 204–205. Nadav Shragai, "Dreaming of a Third Temple," *Haaretz*, September 17, 1998.

57. Ariel, *Philosemites or Antisemites?*

58. "'Sen. Joe Lieberman Praises Pastor Who Said Holocaust Was God's Work," Reuters, July 23, 2008. For similar comments by other Christian Zionists see Brog, *Standing with Israel*, 80–87.

59. Spector, *Evangelicals and Israel*, 180, 190, 200.

60. Cited in Brog, *Standing with Israel*, 78–79.

61. James L. Guth and William R. Kenan Jr., "Religious Factors and American Public Support for Israel: 1992–2008" (paper presented at the annual meeting of the American Political Science Association, Seattle, WA, September 1–4, 2011). For a similar argument, see Timothy P. Weber, "American Evangelicals and Israel: A Complicated Alliance,: in Jonathan Frankel and Ezra Mendelsohn, eds., *The*

Protestant-Jewish Conundrum, Studies in Contemporary Jewry, vol. 24 (New York: Oxford University Press, 2010), 141–157.

62. "Religion and Politics"; see also Jody Baumgartner, Peter Francia, and Jonathan Morris, "A Clash of Civilizations? The Influence of Religion on Public Opinion of U.S. Foreign Policy in the Middle East," *Political Science Quarterly* 61, no. 2 (2008): 171–179; David W. Moore, "Protestant Tilt toward Israel Partially Explained by Biblical Connection," Gallup, April 29, 2002, http://www.gallup.com/poll/5893/Protestant-Tilt-Toward-Israel-Partially-Explained-Biblical-Connection.aspx; "American Evangelicals and Israel,"Pew Research Religion and Public Life Project; Green, "The American Public and Sympathy for Israel."

63. "Ideological Gaps over Israel on Both Sides of Atlantic," Pew Research Global Attitudes Project, January 29, 2009, http://www.pewglobal.org/2009/01/29/ideology-and-views-toward-the-middle-east-conflict/; "Modest Backing for Israel in Gaza Crisis," Pew Research Center for the People and the Press, January 13, 2009, http://www.people-press.org/2009/01/13/modest-backing-for-israel-in-gaza-crisis/1/.

64. "Ideological Gaps over Israel on Both Sides of Atlantic"; "Modest Backing for Israel in Gaza Crisis."

65. Jeremy D. Mayer, 'Christian Fundamentalists and Public Opinion toward the Middle East: Israel's New Best Friends?' *Social Science Quarterly* 85, no. 3 (2004): 695–712.

66. Ibid.

67. Todd Hertz, "The Evangelical View of Israel," *Christianity Today*, June 9, 2003; "Roadblocks and Voting Blocs: Today's Evangelicals Are Committed to Peace–Not Just Security–for Israel," *Christianity Today*, July 1, 2003.

68. Approximate figures based on "Ideological Gaps Over Israel on Both Sides of Atlantic"; "Modest Backing For Israel in Gaza Crisis."

69. Guth and Kenan, "Religious Factors and American Public Support for Israel: 1992–2008."

70. "Public Takes Strong Stance Against Iran's Nuclear Program," Pew Research Center for the People and the Press, February 15, 2012, http://www.people-press.org/files/legacy-pdf/02-15-12%20Foreign%20Policy%20release.pdf

71. "Goal of Libyan Operation Less Clear to Public: Top Middle East Priority: Preventing Terrorism," Pew Research Center for the People and the Press, April 5, 2011, http://www.people-press.org/2011/04/05/goal-of-libyan-operation-less-clear-to-public.

72. Guth and Kenan, "Religious Factors and American Public Support for Israel: 1992–2008.".

73. "Pat Robertson Interview on Road Map," *Jerusalem Post*, September 5, 2003.

74. *Proclamation of the Third International Christian Zionist Congress, 1996*, Affirmation 10, http://www.Christianactionforisrael.org/congress.html (no longer available); "American Evangelicals and Israel," Pew Research Religion and Public Life Project.

75. Spector, *Evangelicals and Israel*, 51–54.

76. Avram Goldstein, "Christian Coalition Rallies for Israel in Comeback Bid," *Washington Post*, October 12, 2002.

77. Shindler, "Likud and the Christian Dispensationalists"; Hal Lindsey, "Shades of Munich at Annapolis," *WND*, November 30, 2007, http://www.wnd.com/index. php?pageId=44808.

78. Ilan Chaim, "Anti–Road Map Book Mmakes 'NY Times' Best-Sellers List," *Jerusalem Post*, July 23, 2003.

79. John Hagee, *Jerusalem Countdown* (Lake Mary, FL: FrontLine, 2006), 26.

80. Daphna Berman, "'Don't Touch Jerusalem,' Evangelical Leader Warns Bush," *Jerusalem Post*, October 5, 2004; "Pat Robertson Interview on Road Map"; Eric Fingerhut, "Robertson Sees Armageddon in Jerusalem Struggle," *JTA*, February 3, 2009.

81. Pat Robertson, "Pat Answers Your Questions on Israel," *The 700 Club*, Christian Broadcasting Network, http://cbn.org/700club.

82. This sentence was originally part of a speech Hagee gave to the Israeli Knesset. But ultimately he refrained from saying it, though it remained in the written version. See Lily Galili, "Rapture – or Raptor," *Haaretz*, November 11, 2005.

83. Nathan Guttman, "Getting Tight with the Bible Belt," *Haaretz*, February 16, 2005; Lily Galili, 'National Union Tries to Rally American Right vs. Road Map," *Haaretz*, April 25, 2003; Spector, *Evangelicals and Israel*, 217.

84. Halsell, *Prophecy and Politics*, 168–177.

85. "Christians Differ over 'Road Map,'" Associated Press, July 25, 2003; Danielle Haas, "U.S. Christians Find Cause to Aid Israel/Evangelicals Financing Immigrants, Settlements," Chronicle Foreign Service, July 10, 2002; Aaron Hecht, "The Ariel-Evangelical Special Connection," *Jerusalem Post Christian Edition*, August 2007, 28–31; Ann Lordo, "Israeli Settlers Find Staunch Friends in Christians," *Baltimore Sun*, July 27, 1997; "About Us," International Christian Embassy Jerusalem, http://int.icej.org/about/about-us; "Life in the Settlements," *Word from Jerusalem*, May 2002, p7; International Christian Embassy, "Bulletproof Bus for Efrat" appeal, *Word from Jerusalem*, May 2002; Bridges for Peace, "New Life on the Farm," *Dispatch from Jerusalem*, January 2000, 5.

86. Sheera Frenkel, "American Christian Funding Flows to Jewish Settlers," *NPR*, June 12, 2009, http://www.npr.org/templates/story/story.php?storyId=105310088.

87. Jim Rutenberg, Mike Mcintire, and Ethan Bronner, "Tax-Exempt Funds Aid Settlements in West Bank," *New York Times*, July 5, 2010.

88. Sinai, "When Money Speaks Louder Than the Word."

89. Interview with Prof Gerald McDermott, March 30, 2011.

90. Quoted in Weber, "American Evangelicals and Israel: A Complicated Alliance," 141–157.

91. Ibid. Other leading evangelicals who take a moderate approach include Albert Mohler Jr., president of Southern Baptist Theological Seminary; and Craig Blaising, executive vice president and provost at Southwestern Baptist Theological Seminary. See Craig A. Blaising, "The Church and the Present State of Israel: A Progressive Dispensational View," Moore to the Point, May 1, 2002, http:// cdn1.russellmoore.com/documents/russellmoore/israel-church.pdf; Michael Foust, 'Mohler: Christians Should Support Israel, Yet Hold It Accountable," *Baptist Press*, April 25, 2002, http://www.bpnews.net/bpnews.asp?id=13230; "Prayer Is the Only Solution to Middle East Crisis," Come and See, May 9, 2002, http://www. comeandsee.com/view.php?sid=299.

92. Interview with Prof Gerald McDermott, March 30, 2011; see also the comments of Franklin Graham, president of the Billy Graham Evangelistic Association, in the *Charlotte Observer*, October 16, 2000.
93. Tom Strode, "Land: Evangelical Majority Supports Israel's Gaza Withdrawal," *Baptist Press*, September 26, 2005.
94. Spector, *Evangelicals and Israel*, 47, 167; Brog, *Standing with Israel*, p.162; Clark, *Allies for Armageddon*, 237–238.
95. Spector, *Evangelicals and Israel*, 175.
96. Ibid., 174.
97. Dexter Van Zile, "Mainline Churches Embrace Gary Burge's Harmful Mythology," CAMERA: Committee for Accuracy in Middle East Reporting in America, September 11, 2007, http://www.camera.org/index.asp?x_print=1&x_context=2&x_outlet=118&x_article=1371.
98. This is based on my own survey of all the articles on the conflict published in the magazine from 1993 to 2010. For examples of such articles, see Donald Neff, "Peace in Palestine," *Christianity Today*, October 4, 1993, 15; Jonathan Miles, "You Can't Get There from Here," *Christianity Today*, May 20, 1996, 66–67; Peri Stone, "Persecution Propaganda?" *Christianity Today*, July 13, 1998, 14–15; Calvin Shenk, "Jerusalem As Jesus Views It," *Christianity Today*, October 5, 1998, 44–46; Timothy Morgan, "Jerusalem's Living Stones," *Christianity Today*, May 20, 1996, 58–68; "Security versus Equality," *Christianity Today*, May 20, 1996, 60; Stan Guthrie, "Palestine's Christians Persist Despite Pressures," *Christianity Today*, October 1, 2001, 30; Elaine Ruth Fletcher, "Holy Land Roadblocks," *Christianity Today*, April 23, 2001, 22; Elaine Ruth Fletcher, "Between the Temple Mount and a Hard Place," *Christianity Today*, December 4, 2000, 66–68; Jonathan Kuttab, "The Peace Regress," *Christianity Today*, January 8, 2001, 66–70; Clarence H. Wagner Jr., "Between a Rock and a Holy Site," *Christianity Today*, February 5, 2001, 62–63; Jeremy Weber, "God in Gaza: Reconciliation Work Goes On Despite Worst Violence since 1967," *Christianity Today*, February 10, 2009, 13; Stan Guthrie, "Crackdown Hits Churches; Mideast Christians Torn over Tough Israeli Tactics at Churches," *Christianity Today*, May 21, 2002; "Roadblocks and Voting Blocs."
99. Yehiel Poupko, "Pro-Israel vs. Pro-Palestine: A Rabbi Hopes for a Better Conversation," *Christianity Today*, February 2008, 74; "Leveling the Investment Field: Why Has It Been So Hard for Organizations to Treat Israel Like Any Other State?" *Christianity Today*, August 2006; Kathleen Rutledge, "Assault on the Jewish People: New Presbyterian Policy on Israel Raise Hackles," *Christianity Today*, December 2004, 18; "What It Means to Love Israel: Beware Giving the Nation Too Much Theological Meaning and the Jews Too Little," *Christianity Today*, September 2007; Mark Harlan, "A Middle Way in the Middle East: A Third Theological Path through the Israeli-Palestinian Thicket," *Christianity Today*, April 1, 2003, 84; Trammel Madison, "Jesus and the Land," *Christianity Today*, May 2010, 62.
100. Weber, "American Evangelicals and Israel."
101. Shindler, "Likud and the Christian Dispensationalists"; Halsell, *Prophecy and Politics*, 178–179; Irvine H. Anderson, *Biblical Interpretation and Middle East Policy* (Gainesville, FL: University Press of Florida, 2005), 114–115.

102. Kyle M. Smith, *A Congruence of Interests: Christian Zionism And U.S. Policy toward Israel, 1977–1998* (paper submitted to the Graduate College of Bowling Green State University in partial fulfillment of the requirements for the Master of Arts, 2006).

103. Jonathan Rynhold, "Behind the Rhetoric: President Bush and U.S. Policy on the Israeli-Palestinian Conflict," *American Diplomacy* 10, no. 4 (2005): 1–23, http://www.unc.edu/depts/diplomat/item/2005/1012/rynh/rynhold_rhetoric.html.

104. Laurie Goldstein, "Evangelicals for Israel," *New York Times*, January 21, 1998.

105. Smith, *A Congruence of Interests*.

106. Elizabeth A. Oldmixon, Beth A. Rosenson, and Kenneth D. Wald, "Conflict over Israel: Religion, Race, Party, and Ideology in the U.S. House of Representatives, 1997–2002," *Terrorism and Political Violence* 17, no. 3 (2005): 407–426; Beth A. Rosenson, Elizabeth A. Oldmixon, and Kenneth D. Wald, "U.S. Senators' Support for Israel Examined through Sponsorship/Cosponsorship Decisions, 1993–2002: The Influence of Elite and Constituent Factors," *Foreign Policy Analysis* 5, no. 1 (2009): 73–91.

107. Lou Marano, "Christians Rally for Israel in Washington," United Press International, October 13, 2002.

108. Rosenson et al., "Conflict over Israel."

109. See, for example, Karen Armstrong, "Bush's Fondness for Fundamentalism is Courting Disaster," *Guardian* (London), July 31, 2006; Esther Kaplan, *With God on Their Side* (New York: New Press, 2004), 30; Deanne Stillman, "Onward Christian Soldiers," *Nation*, June 3, 2002.

110. "Address of U.S. President George Bush to the Knesset," The Knesset, May 15, 2008, http://www.knesset.gov.il/description/eng/doc/speech_bush_2008_eng.htm.

111. D. Michael Lindsay, *Faith in the Halls of Power* (Oxford: Oxford University Press, 2007), 51–52; Spector, *Evangelicals and Israel*, 206–209; David Aikman, *A Man of Faith: The Spiritual Journey of George W. Bush* (Nashville: W Publishing Group, 2004), 122–126.

112. "Christian Coalition of America Opposes Creation of a Palestinian State," press release, Christian Coalition of America, June 18, 2002, http://www.cc.org/becomeinformed/pressreleases061802.html (accessed September 27, 2005; no longer available).

113. George W. Bush, *Decision Points* (New York: Crown, 2010), 409–410.

114. Spector, *Evangelicals and Israel*, 249–253.

115. Rynhold, "Behind the Rhetoric."

116. Spector, *Evangelicals and Israel*, 229–239.

117. Ibid., 223–227.

118. Rynhold, "Behind the Rhetoric."

119. Spector, *Evangelicals and Israel*, 236.

120. Ibid., 218.

121. Melissa Radler, "U.S. Christians Call for 'Biblical Road Map,'" *Jerusalem Post*, May 1, 2003.

122. "Christians Differ over 'Road Map,'" Associated Press, July 25, 2003.

123. Gil Hoffman, "Elon Takes U.S. Heartland Anti-Disengagement Tour," *Jerusalem Post*, September 9, 2004.

124. Personal communication between the author and Ayalon.

125. Chafets, *Match Made in Heaven*, 67. See similar comments in Brog, *Standing with Israel*, 196; Simon, *Falwell and the Jews*, 63, 82.

126. Spector, *Evangelicals and Israel*, 173.

127. Yechiel Eckstein resigned from the board of *Voices United for Israel* because of its partisan pro-Likud posture. Sinai, "When Money Speaks Louder Than the Word."

128. John Hagee, "Why Christian Zionists Really Support Israel," *Jewish Daily Forward*, May 21, 2010.

129. Lawrence Grossman, "The Organized Jewish Community and Evangelical America," in Mittleman, Johnson, and Isserman, eds., *Uneasy Allies?* 49–72.

130. Clark, *Allies for Armageddon*, 249.

131. Green, "Evangelical Protestants and Jews," in Mittleman, Johnson, and Isserman, eds., *Uneasy Allies?*

132. Ethan Felson, "On the Road: The Jewish Community Relations Encounter with Evangelical Christians," in Alan Mittleman, Byron Johnson, and Nancy Isserman, eds., *Uneasy Allies?* 91–92.

133. Abraham Foxman, "Evangelical Support for Israel Is a Good Thing," *JTA*, July 16, 2002.

134. Carl Schrag, "American Jews and Evangelical Christians: Anatomy of a Changing Relationship" *Jewish Political Studies Review* 17, no. 1-2 (2005).

135. Shmuel Rosner, "Allying with Christian Zionists Is Bad for Israel," *Haaretz*, April 3, 2008.

136. In 2004, 30 percent of Americans defined themselves on the religious Left, 24 percent on the religious Right. The hard-core of each camp made up 12–15 percent of the electorate. See Lyman A. Kellstedt et al., "A Gentle Stream or a 'River Glorious'? The Religious Left in the 2004 Election," in David E. Campbell, ed., *A Matter of Faith: Religion in the 2004 Presidential Election* (Washington, DC: Brookings Institution Press, 2007), 232–256; John Green and Steven Waldman, "The Twelve Tribes of American Politics," Beliefnet, October 2004, http://www.beliefnet.com/News/Politics/2004/10/The-Twelve-Tribes-Of-American-Politics.aspx.

5. THE MAINLINE PROTESTANT CHURCH AND ANTI-ZIONISM

1. Presbyterian Church USA, http://www.pcusa.org/worldwide/israelpalestine/israel-palestineresolution.htm (no longer available).

2. On the characteristics of the mainline and the differences with evangelicals, see Kenneth D. Wald and Alison Calhoun-Brown, *Religion and Politics in the United States*, 5th ed. (Lanham MD: Rowman and Littlefield, 2007), 30.

3. "Religious Landscape Survey, Report 1: Religious Affiliation," Pew Research Religion and Public Life Project, http://religions.pewforum.org/reports; Eileen Lindner, ed., *Yearbook of American and Canadian Churches, 2006* (Nashville: Abingdon Press, 2006), 9–14.

4. 2004 NEP Exit Poll cited in Robert Jones and Daniel Cox, "Clergy Voices: Findings from the 2008 Mainline Protestant Clergy Voices Survey" (Washington, DC: Public Religion Research, 2009).

5. Lester Kurtz and Kelly Goran Fulton, "Love Your Enemies? Protestants and United States Foreign Policy," in Robert Wuthnow and John Evans, eds., *The Quiet Hand*

of God: Faith-Based Activism and the Public Role of Mainline Protestantism (Berkeley: University of California Press, 2002), 364.

6. Wuthnow and Evans, *The Quiet Hand of God*, 11–13; "U.S. Religious Landscape Survey: Religious Beliefs and Practices: Diverse and Politically Relevant," Pew Forum on Religion and Public Life, June 2008, http://religions.pewforum.org/pdf/report2-religious-landscape-study-full.pdf.

7. Clem Brooks and Jeff Manza, "A Great Divide? Religion and Political Change in U.S. National Elections, 1972–2000," *Sociological Quarterly* 45, no. 3 (2004): 421–450.

8. Laura R. Olson, "Whither the Religious Left? Religiopolitical Progressivism in Twenty-First-Century America," in J. Matthew Wilson, ed., *From Pews to Polling Places: Faith and Politics in the American Religious Mosaic* (Washington, DC: Georgetown University Press, 2007), 53–80.

9. Dieter T. Hessel, ed., *The Church's Public Role: Retrospect and Prospect* (Grand Rapids: Eerdmans, 1993), 21–38. On Liberation theology see Christopher Rowland, ed., *The Cambridge Companion to Liberation Theology* (Cambridge: Cambridge University Press, 1999).

10. Quoted in James Reichley, *Religion in American Public Life* (Washington, DC: Brookings Institution, 1985), 266.

11. Robert P. Jones and Daniel Cox, "Clergy Voices: Findings from the 2008 Mainline Protestant Clergy Voices Survey," Public Religion Research, March 2009, http://publicreligion.org/site/wp-content/uploads/2011/06/2008-Mainline-Protestant-Clergy-Voices-Survey-Report.pdf.

12. Reichley, *Religion in American Public Life*, 245–255, 341.

13. Jones and Cox, "Clergy Voices."

14. Pew Forum's "U.S. Religious Landscape Survey (June 2008) draws primarily on a new nationwide survey conducted from May 8 to August 13, 2007. See also "Trends in Party Identification of Religious Groups," Pew Research Religion and Public Life Project, February 2, 2012, http://www.pewforum.org/2012/02/02/trends-in-party-identification-of-religious-groups-affiliation/; John C. Green, "Religion and the 2004 Election: A Pre-Election Analysis," Pew Forum on Religion and Public Life, http://www.pewforum.org/files/2004/09/green-full1.pdf.

15. James Guth, "The Bush Administration, American Religious Politics, and Middle East Policy: The Evidence from National Surveys" (paper presented at the annual meeting of the American Political Science Association, Chicago, IL, September 2–5, 2004). In 2007, around 60 percent of white mainliners remained supportive of using preemptive force against terrorism, about the national average; see "U.S. Religious Landscape Survey" (June 2008).

16. "Ideological Gaps over Israel on Both Sides of Atlantic," Pew Research Global Attitudes Project, January 29, 2009, http://pewresearch.org/pubs/1097/america-europe-ideological-gaps-over-israel; America's Place in The World 2009, December 2009, *Pew Research Center For the People & the Press* http://people-press.org/files/legacy-pdf/569.pdf; "Modest Backing for Israel in Gaza Crisis," Pew Research Center for the People and the Press, January 13, 2009, http://www.people-press.org/2009/01/13/modest-backing-for-israel-in-gaza-crisis/1/.

17. "Ideological Gaps over Israel on Both Sides of Atlantic"; "Modest Backing For Israel in Gaza Crisis."

18. Guth and Kenan, "Religious Factors and American Public Support for Israel: 1992–2008."
19. "Goal of Libyan Operation Less Clear to Public: Top Middle East Priority: Preventing Terrorism," Pew Research Center for the People and the Press, April 5, 2011, http://www.people-press.org/2011/04/05/goal-of-libyan-operation-less-clear-to-public.
20. "Public Takes Strong Stance Against Iran's Nuclear Program," Pew Research Center for the People and the Press, February 15, 2012, http://www.people-press.org/files/legacy-pdf/02-15-12%20Foreign%20Policy%20release.pdf.
21. Presbyterian Church (USA) Research Services office, based on a November 2004 survey of 3,000 ministers, elders, members and specialized clergy known as the Presbyterian Panel. See Van Marter, "Poll: Most PC(USA) Members Unaware of GA Divestment Action."
22. Data from the National Survey of Religion and Politics – see James Guth and William Kenan Jr., "Religious Factors and American Public Support for Israel: 1992–2008" (paper presented at the annual meeting of the American Political Science Association, Seattle, WA, September 1–4, 2011); John C. Green, "The American Religious Landscape and Political Attitudes: A Baseline for 2004," University of Akron, Ray C. Bliss Institute of Applied Politics, , https://www.uakron.edu/bliss/research/archives/2004/Religious_Landscape_2004.pdf.
23. Jones and Cox, "Clergy Voices."
24. Joshua Trachtenberg, *The Devil and the Jews: The Medieval Conception of the Jew and Its Relation to Modern Anti-Semitism*, 2nd ed. (Philadelphia: Jewish Publication Society, 2002).
25. R. Kendall Soulen, *The God of Israel and Christian Theology* (Minneapolis: Fortress Press, 1996).
26. Hertzel Fishman, *American Protestantism and a Jewish State* (Detroit, MI: Wayne State University Press, 1973), 170, 175.
27. Ibid., 178.
28. *Christian Century*, May 3, 1933, 582–584, quoted in Fishman, *American Protestantism and a Jewish State*, 37.
29. Ibid.
30. Not including Sunday schools and theological centers. Robert Kaplan, *The Arabists: The Romance of an American Elite* (New York: Free Press, 1993), 18, 40.
31. George Antonius, *The Arab Awakening* (London: Hamish Hamilton, 1938), 42–43.
32. Haj Amin al-Husseini was appointed Mufti of Jerusalem in 1921. He was the most prominent Arab figure in Palestine during the Mandatory period. During World War II he collaborated with Nazi Germany, helping to recruit Bosnian Muslims for the Waffen-SS. See Barry Rubin and Wolfgang G. Schwanitz, *Nazis, Islamists, and the Making of the Modern Middle East* (New Haven, CT: Yale University Press, 2014).
33. Kaplan, *The Arabists*, 69–71.
34. Michael B. Oren, *Power, Faith, and Fantasy: America in the Middle East, 1776 to the Present* (New York: W. W. Norton, 2007), 423.
35. Carl Hermann Voss and David A. Rausch, "American Christians and Israel, 1948–1988," *American Jewish Archives* 40, no. 1 (1988).

36. Gary Dorrien, "Christian Realism: Niebuhr's Theology, Ethics, and Politics," in Daniel Rice, ed., *Reinhold Niebuhr Revisited: Engagement with an American Original* (Grand Rapids, MI: Eerdmans, 2009), 21–39.

37. Eyal Naveh, "Unconventional 'Christian Zionist': The Theologian Reinhold Niebuhr and His Attitude toward the Jewish National Movement," *Studies in Zionism* 11, no. 2 (1990).

38. Quoted in Fishman, *American Protestantism and a Jewish State*, 69.

39. D. B. Robertson, ed., *Love and Justice: Selections from the Shorter Writings of Reinhold Niebuhr* (Louisville, KY: Westminster/John Knox Press, 1957), 133–142.

40. Voss and Rausch, "American Christians and Israel, 1948–1988," 68.

41. National Council of Churches of Christ USA, "Middle East Policy Statement," November 6, 1980.

42. Duncan L. Clarke and Eric Flohr, "Christian Churches and the Palestine Question," *Journal of Palestine Studies* 21, no. 4 (1992): 67–79.

43. For example, James Wall, "The Other Jewish Lobby," *Christian Century*, July 15, 2008, 44; James Wall, "Unilateral Proposal," *Christian Century*, June 13, 2006; James Wall, "The Arms Deal," *Christian Century*, September 4, 2007; James Wall, "Impressions," *Christian Century*, September 5, 2006; Vernon Broyles, "Occupation Is the Issue: A Reply," *Christian Century*, February 8, 2005, 37–38; James Wall, "Brutal Blunder," *Christian Century*, May 4, 2004; James Wall, "Friends Like These," *Christian Century*, June 29, 2004, 45; James Wall, "In the Pressure Cooker," *Christian Century*, November 8, 2000, 1165; James Wall, "Preemptive Apologies," *Christian Century* April 12, 2000, 95; "A 'New Apartheid,'" *Christian Century*, December 20–27, 2000, 1329–1330; Jonathan Frerichs, "Apartheid in Israel/Palestine: Whose Land Is It?" *Christian Century*, July 17–30, 2002, 31. The same bias was apparent in the reports of the Presbyterian News Service; see Will Spotts, "Pride and Prejudice: The Presbyterian Divestment Story," September 28, 2005, http://www.c4rpme.org/bin/articles.cgi?Cat=churches&Subcat=presbyterian&ID=207 (no longer available).

44. For example, Yehiel Poupko, "Land Grant: Israel and the Promises of God," *Christian Century*, May 15, 2007, 21–25; James Hecht, "Precarious Vision: The U.S. Role in a Middle East Solution," *Christian Century*, November 15, 2005, 9; Marc Gopin, "A Failure to Communicate," *Christian Century*, 30 May 30, 2006, 8; Ira Youdovin, "Arguing about Israel: A Response to Donald Wagner," *Christian Century*, September 20, 2003, 48–49; Arnold Jacob Wolf, "Speaking Up for Israel," *Christian Century*, May 8–15, 2002, 9; Chris Herlinger, "Reckoning with Israel," *Christian Century*, May 22–29, 2002, 6; "U.S. Rabbis Urge Sharing Temple Mount," *Christian Century*, December 20–27, 2000, 1330; Aliza Becker, "To Israel and Back Again," *Christian Century*, February 27–March 6, 2002, 6; Warren Goldstein, "Blood and Rubble," *Christian Century*, August 22, 2006, 8.

45. "Under the Influence," *Christian Century*, April 18, 2006, 45; Yaakov Ariel, "On the Road to Armageddon," *Christian Century*, July 26, 2005; Ronald Goetz, "Property Rights: Israel and the Land," *Christian Century*, December 13, 2003, 34–37; "The Last Colonizer," *Christian Century*, August 15–22, 2001; Marc Ellis, "Holy Land Narratives of Lament and Hope," *Christian Century*, July 19–26, 2000, 762–764.

46. For example, James Wall, "The Unasked Question," *Christian Century*, March 25, 2008; James Wall, "Jerusalem Sprawl," Christian Century, April 19, 2005, 45; James Wall, "Israel's Non-Sacrifice," *Christian Century*, March 22, 2005, 44; James Wall, "In the Pressure Cooker," 1165; "A 'New Apartheid'"; James Wall, "The Missing Map," *Christian Century*, December 13, 2000, 1317; Rashid Khalidi, "Why the Peace Process Broke Down," *Christian Century*, November 22–29, 2000, 1206.

47. "After Israel Exits Gaza, Synagogues Destroyed," *Christian Century*, October 4, 2005, 16.

48. "Blockade," *Christian Century*, December 30, 2008, 8; "Disciples Latest to Critique Israeli Tactics," *Christian Century*, August 23, 2005, 10; "WCC: World Must Stop Holy Land Cycle of Violence," *Christian Century*, July 25, 2006; "Brutal Blunder."

49. James Wall, "Dance of Deception," *Christian Century*, August 9, 2005.

50. James Wall, "Friends Like These," *Christian Century*, June 29, 2004, 45.

51. Erik R. Nelson and Alan F. H. Wisdom, *Human Rights Advocacy in the Mainline Protestant Churches (2000–2003): A Critical Analysis* (Washington DC: Institute on Religion and Democracy, 2004).

52. Quoted in James Rudin, *A Jewish Guide to Interreligious Relations* (New York: American Jewish Committee, 2005), 24 (emphasis added). Many other mainline resolutions used similar language; see, for example, "Peace Depends on End to Israeli Occupation, Agency Says," United Methodist News Service, March 18, 2002, http://umns.umc.org/02/mar/111.htm (no longer available); "Barriers Do Not Bring Freedom," NCCCUSA Delegation to the Middle East Issues (statement), February 6, 2005, http://www.nccmiddleeast.blogspot.co.il/.

53. Rev. Clifton Kirkpatrick, letter to President Clinton, October 14, 2000, http://www.cmep.org/Statements/s31.htm (no longer available); "US Christian Ecumenical Delegation Calls for and Commits to Prayer for a Just Peace in the Middle East," World Council of Churches, December 12, 2000, http://www.wcc-coe.org/wcc/what/international/palestine/conflict13.html.

54. Presbyterian Church USA, http://www.pcusa.org/worldwide/israelpalestine/israel-palestineresolution.htm (no longer available).

55. For example, "Resolution on the Conflict in the Middle East," National Council of Churches, November 17, 2000, http://www.ncccusa.org/news/2000GA/mideastres.html; "National Council of Churches Delivers Pastoral Letter in Jerusalem," National Council of Churches, December 5, 2000, http://www.ncccusa.org/news/00news108.html; "Evangelical Lutheran Church of America (ELCA) Conference of Bishops Letter about Mideast Crisis," Evangelical Lutheran Church of America, October 12, 2000, http://www.elca.org/ob/mideast2.html (no longer available); PC (USA) Assembly "Resolution on Israel and Palestine: End the Occupation Now" 2003. http://www.pcusa.org/ga215/business/commbooks/comm12.pdf (no longer available).

56. See for example, "A Statement of the National Council of Churches USA and Church World Service on the Current Violence in the Middle East," in "Recalling When and Where Jesus Wept, NCC, CWS Call for an End to Mid East Violence," National Council of Churches, July 14, 2006, http://www.ncccusa.org/news/060714middleeast.html; "United Methodist General Board of Church and Society

Statement on the Current Violence in Israel, Gaza and Lebanon," Chruches for Middle East Peace, July 17, 2006, http://www.cmep.org/Statements/ 2006July17_UMC.htm (no longer available); John Dart, "Church Voice on War Measured, or Muffled?" *Christian Century*, September 5, 2006. For an in-depth analysis, see Dexter Van Zile, "Mainline Christian Churches Respond to Hamas and Hezbollah Aggression," CAMERA, July 27, 2006, http://www.camera.org/ index.asp?x_context=7&x_issue=61&x_article=1159.

57. Daniel Treiman, "Liberal Churches Slam Israel," *Jewish Daily Forward*, July 28, 2006.

58. http://memritv.org/Transcript.asp?P1=294 (no longer available).

59. "U.S. Church Leaders Criticized for Meeting with Hezbollah," Associated Press, December 3, 2005.

60. "A Resolution on Israel and Palestine: End the Occupation Now," Presbyterian Church USA, http://www.pcusa.org/ga215/business/commbooks/comm12.pdf (no longer available); Presbyterian Church USA, http://www.pcusa.org/worldwide/ israelpalestine/israelpalestineresolution.htm (no longer available).

61. Eugene Korn, "Divestment from Israel, the Liberal Churches, and Jewish Responses: A Strategic Analysis," *Post-Holocaust and Anti-Semitism* 52 (January 2007), http://jcpa.org/article/divestment-from-the-liberal-churches-and-jewish- responses-a-strategic-analysis/ (no longer available).

62. Ethan Felson, "On the Road: The Jewish Community Relations Encounter with Evangelical Christians" in Alan Mittleman, Byron Johnson, and Nancy Isserman, eds., *Uneasy Allies? Evangelical and Jewish Relations* (Lanham, MD: Lexington Books, 2006), 98.

63. Clarke and Flohr, "Christian Churches and the Palestine Question." Also among the NCC's members are Eastern Orthodox communions, including several churches whose membership is mainly Arab.

64. Nancy Gallagher, *Quakers in the Israeli-Palestinian Conflict: The Dilemmas of NGO Humanitarian Activism* (Cairo: American University in Cairo Press, 2007).

65. "Q and A: The Facts about Palestine and Israel," Quakers with a Concern for Palestine-Israel, http://www.quakerpi.org/QAction/QA-The-Facts-about-Palestine- Israel.pdf.

66. The other "peace church," the Mennonites, have also been active in the West Bank since 1948. See Alain Epp Weaver and Sonia K. Weaver, *Salt and Sign: Mennonite Central Committee in Palestine, 1949–1999* (Akron, PA: Mennonite Central Committee, 1999). The Mennonites are vociferously anti-Zionist – see Dexter Van Zile, "Key Mennonite Institutions against Israel," *Post-Holocaust and Anti-Semitism* 83 (2009), http://jcpa.org/article/key-mennonite-institutions- against-israel/.

67. Kenneth D. Wald et al., "Reclaiming Zion: How American Religious Groups View the Middle East" in Gabriel Sheffer, ed., *U.S.-Israeli Relations at the Crossroads* (London: Frank Cass, 1997), 156.

68. Ronald R. Stockton, "The Presbyterian Divestiture Vote and the Jewish Response," *Middle East Policy*, 12, no. 4 (2005).

69. Dexter Van Zile, "Sabeel's One-State Agenda," *Judeo-Christian Alliance Special Report*, 2005, http://www.judeo-christianalliance.org/index.php?option=com_- remository&Itemid=62&func=fileinfo&id=10 (no longer available); Manya A.

Brachear, "Event at Seminary Draws Fire," *Chicago Tribune*, October 9, 2005; Jeff Walton, "Sabeel Conference Links U.S. and Israel to 'Genocidal Theologies,'" *Juicy Ecumenism* (blog), Institute on Religion and Democracy, October 19, 2009, http://juicyecumenism.com/2009/10/19/sabeel-conference-links-u-s-and-israel-to-genocidal-theologies/; Hasdai Westbrook, "The Israel Divestment Debate," *Nation*, April 20, 2006, http://www.thenation.com/doc/20060508/westbrook.

70. Naim Stifan Ateek, *Justice and Only Justice: A Palestinian Theology of Liberation* (New York: Orbis Books, 1989), 166; "The Jerusalem Sabeel Document: Principles for a Just Peace in Palestine-Israel," Friends of Sabeel – North America: Voice of the Palestinian Christians, May 1, 2006, http://fosna.org/content/jerusalem-sabeel-document-principles-just-peace-palestine-israel.

71. Mark D. Tooley, "Liberation Theology in the Middle East," *Frontpagemag.com*, May 23, 2006, http://archive.frontpagemag.com/readArticle.aspx?ARTID=4322; Walton, "Sabeel Conference Links U.S. and Israel to 'Genocidal Theologies.'"

72. Michael Paulson, "Church Delegation Offers Mideast Peace Investment Plan," *Boston Globe*, July 2, 2005; James Besser, "Palestinian Nationalists Seen behind Divestment," *Jewish Week*, July 22, 2005;
John Adams, "PCUSA's Tack on Israel Parallels Liberation Group's," in The Layman Online, December 22, 2004, http://www.layman.org/majorissues0984/; Leslie Scanlon, "Palestinian Stories Open PC(USA) Training Event," The Presbyterian Outlook, February 14, 2005, http://pres-outlook.org/2005/02/palestinian-stories-open-pcusa-training-event/.

73. Adam Gregerman, "Old Wine in New Bottles: Liberation Theology and the Israeli-Palestinian Conflict," *Journal of Ecumenical Studies* 41, no. 3–4 (2004): 313–340.

74. Rosemary Radford Ruether, "The Occupation Must End," in Rosemary Radford Ruether and Marc Ellis, eds., *Beyond Occupation: American Jewish, Christian, and Palestinian Voices for Peace* (Boston: Beacon Press, 1990), 196.

75. Rosemary Radford Ruether, "False Messianism and Prophetic Consciousness," in Otto Maduro, ed., *Judaism, Christianity, and Liberation: An Agenda for Dialogue* (New York: Orbis Books, 1991), 89–91.

76. Walton, "Sabeel Conference Links U.S. and Israel to 'Genocidal Theologies.'"

77. Mark D. Tooley, "A Wildman against Israel," *Frontpagemag.com*, August 6, 2008, http://archive.frontpagemag.com/readArticle.aspx?ARTID=31919.

78. Paul Hollander, *Anti-Americanism: Critiques at Home and Abroad, 1965–1990* (New York: Oxford University Press, 1992), 83, 115–135, 225.

79. Sarah Posner, "Wright's Theology not 'New or Radical,'" *Salon*, May 3, 2008, http://www.salon.com/2008/05/03/black_church/.

80. Richard Cohen, "Obama's Farrakhan Test," *Washington Post*, January 15, 2008.

81. Robert McAfee Brown, "Christians in the West Must Confront the Middle East," in Ruether and Ellis, eds., *Beyond Occupation*, 138–154.

82. Dennis Hale, "Why the Left Abandoned Israel, Reclaiming Liberal Support for Israel" (speech delivered at Harvard University for the David Project, March 13, 2003); Richard Rubenstein, "Some Reflections on 'The Odd Couple': A Reply to Martin Marty," *Journal of Ecumenical Studies* 44, no. 1 (2009): 136–140.

83. Stephen R. Haynes, *Reluctant Witnesses: Jews and the Christian Imagination* (Louisville, KY: Westminster/John Knox Press 1995.), 8.

84. Ateek, *Justice and Only Justice*, 164; Dexter Van Zile, "Updating the Ancient Infrastructure of Christian Contempt: Sabeel," *Jewish Political Studies Review* 23, no. 1–2 (2011).

85. Adam Gregerman, "Old Wine in New Bottles: Liberation Theology and the Israeli-Palestinian Conflict," *Journal of Ecumenical Studies*, 41, no. 3–4 (2004): 313–340.

86. "Y.M.C.A. Free Palestine Campaign" East Jerusalem YMCA, 2004, http://www.ej-ymca.org/site/Display-Sub.cfm?Subld=7 (no longer available); Jean Zaru, "Jerusalem, 'Al-Quds,' in the Heart of Palestinian Christians," *Cornerstone* 15 (Spring 1999); Samia Costandi, "Resurrection in the Land of Resurrection," *Cornerstone* 21 (Spring 2001), http://www.sabeel.org/datadir/en-events/ev39/files/Issue%2021.pdf.

87. Naim Ateek, "The Zionist Ideology of Domination versus the Reign of God," AGW: A Globe of Witnesses, 2001. http://www.thewitness.org/agw/ateekkeynote.html.

88. Seth Gitell, "Liberal Church More 'Balanced' On Middle East," *New York Sun*, June 27, 2007, http://www.nysun.com/national/liberal-church-more-balanced-on-middle-east/57212/.

89. Interview with Ethan Felson. Richard Falk, Jeff Halper, Noam Chomsky, Uri Davis, and Joel Kovel have all spoken at Sabeel conferences; see Friends of Sabeel —North America: Voice of the Palestinian Christians, http://www.fosna.org/.

90. Rabbis for Human Rights, "Bad Waters: An Open Letter to the Presbyterian Church (USA)," July 26, 2004, http://jat-action.org/PCUSA_RabbisHuman-Rights.htm (accessed July 14, 2009; emphasis added).

91. Jerry Van Marter, "Poll: Most PC(USA) Members Unaware of GA Divestment Action," Presbyterian News Service, February 10, 2005, http://archive.wfn.org/2005/02/msg00083 (no longer available).

92. Zev Chafets, *Match Made in Heaven: American Jews, Christian Zionists, and One Man's Exploration of the Weird and Wonderful Judeo-Evangelical Alliance* (New York: HarperCollins, 2007), 83–88. Conservative mainliners also opposed divestment, though they were not politically active on the issue, as they were more concerned with other issues such as the ordination of gay clergy. Interview with Ethan Felson, March 2011.

93. Ronald R. Stockton, "Presbyterians, Jews, and Divestment: The Church Steps Back" (paper presented to the International Society for the Study of Reformed Communities), Princeton University, July 2006, http://www.calvin.edu/henry/ISSRC/Conferences/Papers/stockton06.pdf; Dexter Van Zile, "Mainline American Christian 'Peacemakers' against Israel," *Post-Holocaust and Anti-Semitism* 90 (November 2009).

94. Dexter Van Zile, "Updating the Ancient Infrastructure of Christian Contempt: Sabeel"; "The Kairos Palestine Document, Part II," Christians for Fair Witness on the Middle East, http://christianfairwitness.com/whatarethefacts/KairosPalestinianDocument2.pdf.

6. AMERICAN JEWISH ATTACHMENT TO ISRAEL

1. Frank Luntz, *Israel in the Age of Eminem: A Creative Brief for Israeli Messaging* (New York: Bronfman Philanthropies, 2003), 7, 14.

2. Charles Liebman, *The Ambivalent American Jew: Politics, Religion, and Family in American Jewish Life* (Philadelphia: Jewish Publication Society, 1973), 92.
3. Quoted in Samuel Halperin, *The Political World of American Zionism* (Silver Spring, MD: Information Dynamics, 1985), 76.
4. Naomi W. Cohen, *American Jews and the Zionist Idea* (New York: Ktav, 1975), 4–8, 62–71.
5. Jonathan Sarna, *American Judaism: A History* (New Haven, CT: Yale University Press, 2004), 254 (emphasis added).
6. Cohen, *American Jews and the Zionist Idea*, 62, 71; Halperin, *The Political World of American Zionism*, 136–165.
7. Sarna, *American Judaism*, 335–336.
8. Melvyn Urofsky, *We Are One! American Jewry and Israel* (Garden City, NY: Anchor Press, 1978), 238–242.
9. Ibid., 356–359.
10. Thomas L. Friedman, *From Beirut to Jerusalem* (New York: Farrar, Straus and Giroux, 1989), 454.
11. Daniel J. Elazar, *Community and Polity: The Organizational Dynamics of American Jewry* (Philadelphia: Jewish Publication Society, 1995), 107.
12. George E. Gruen, "The United States and Israel: Impact of the Lebanon War," in Milton Himmelfarb and David Singer, eds., *American Jewish Year Book*, vol. 84 (Philadelphia: Jewish Publication Society, 1983), 84–90.
13. Steven M. Cohen, *Ties and Tensions: An Update: The 1989 Survey of American Jewish Attitudes toward Israel and Israelis* (New York: American Jewish Committee, 1989); David Landau, *Who is a Jew? A Case Study of American Jewish Influence on Israeli Policy* (New York: American Jewish Committee, 1996); J. J. Goldberg, *Jewish Power: Inside the American Jewish Establishment* (Reading, MA: Addison-Wesley, 1996), 337–347; Colin Shindler, *Ploughshares into Swords? Israelis and Jews in the Shadow of the Intifada* (London: I. B. Taurus, 1991), 142–145.
14. Steven T. Rosenthal, *Irreconcilable Differences? The Waning of the American Jewish Love Affair with Israel* (Hanover, NH: University Press of New England, 2001); Nathan Gutman, "Israel Not High on Young U.S. Jews Agenda," *Haaretz*, June 1, 2003.
15. Ira Sheskin, "Four Questions about American Jewish Demography," *Jewish Political Studies Review* 20, no. 1–2 (Spring 2008); Leonard Saxe et al., *Reconsidering the Size and Characteristics of the American Jewish Population: New Estimates of a Larger and More Diverse Community* (Waltham, MA: Brandeis University, Steinhardt Social Research Institute, 2007); Chaim Waxman and Ruth Yaron, *The Jewish People Policy Planning Institute Annual Assessment, 2008, Executive Report*, no. 5, 18; Barry A. Kosmin, "The Changing Population Profile of American Jews, 1990–2008," (paper presented at the Fifteenth World Congress of Jewish Studies, Jerusalem, August 2009), http://www.jewishdata-bank.org/studies/downloadFile.cfm?FileID=3040; United Jewish Communities, *The National Jewish Population Survey 2000–01: Strength, Challenge and Diversity in the American Jewish Population* (New York: United Jewish Communities, 2003), 16–19, http://www.bjpa.org/Publications/downloadFile.cfm?FileID=7983.

16. Kosmin, "The Changing Population Profile of American Jews, 1990–2008"; Jonathon Ament, *American Jewish Religious Denominations* (New York: United Jewish Communities, 2005), http://www.jewishfederations.org/local_includes/downloads/7579.pdf.

17. Samuel C. Heilman, *Sliding to the Right: The Contest for the Future of American Jewish Orthodoxy* (Berkeley: University of California Press, 2006).

18. United Jewish Communities, *Strength, Challenge and Diversity*, 16–19; *A Portrait of Jewish Americans*, (Washington, DC: Pew Research Center, October 1, 2013), 35, http://www.pewforum.org/files/2013/10/jewish-american-full-report-for-web.pdf.

19. Steven M. Cohen, *A Tale of Two Jewries: The "Inconvenient Truth" for American Jews* (New York: Jewish Life Network/Steinhardt Foundation, November 2006).

20. United Jewish Communities, *The National Jewish Population Survey 2000–01*, 16–19.

21. Cited in Steven Cohen and Jack Wertheimer, "Whatever Happened to the Jewish People?" *Commentary*, June 2006, 33–37.

22. Steven M. Cohen and Arnold Eisen, *The Jew Within: Self, Family, and Community in America* (Bloomington, IN: Indiana University Press, 2000); Jack Wertheimer, *Generation of Change: How Leaders in Their Twenties and Thirties are Reshaping American Jewish Life* (Jerusalem: Avi Chai Foundation, 2010); Steven M. Cohen, *Profiling the Professionals: Who's Serving Our Communities? Jewish Communal Workers in North America: A Profile* (New York: New York University, Berman Jewish Policy Archive, Fall 2010), http://www.bjpa.org/Publications/downloadFile.cfm?FileID=7321.

23. Wertheimer, *Generation of Change*; Cohen, *Profiling the Professionals*.

24. Theodore Sasson, Charles Kadushin, and Leonard Saxe, *Trends in American Jewish Attachment to Israel: An Assessment of the "Distancing" Hypothesis* (Waltham, MA: Brandeis University, Cohen Center for Modern Jewish Studies, 2008), figures 1 and 2, 11–12.

25. Jonathon Ament, *Israel Connections and American Jews: Report Series on the National Jewish Population Survey 2000–01* (New York: New York University, Berman Jewish Policy Archive, August 2005), http://www.bjpa.org/Publications/details.cfm?PublicationID=2848.

26. *National Jewish Population Survey (NJPS) 1989–90* (New York: Council of Jewish Federations, 1990), http://www.jewishdatabank.org/studies/downloadFile.cfm?FileID=1462 (no longer available). The same picture emerges from the annual AJC surveys.

27. Ament, *Israel Connections and American Jews*.

28. Steven Cohen and Ari Kelman, *Beyond Distancing: Young Adult American Jews and Their Alienation from Israel* (New York: Bronfman Philanthropies, 2008).

29. Theodore Sasson et al., *Still Connected: American Jewish Attitudes about Israel* (Waltham, MA: Brandeis University, Cohen Center for Modern Jewish Studies, August 2010).

30. Ament asd, *Israel Connections and American Jews*; *National Jewish Population Survey (NJPS) 1989–90*.

31. Cohen and Kelman, *Beyond Distancing*.

32. Bethamie Horowitz, *Connections and Journeys: Assessing Critical Opportunities for Enhancing Jewish Identity* (New York: UJA–Federation of Jewish Philanthropies of

New York, 2000; revised 2003), http://www.levyinstitute.org/pubs/CP/AJP_conf_oct06_files/papers/Benthamie_Horowitz.pdf; Charles Kadushin, Shaul Kelner, and Leonard Saxe, *Being a Jewish Teenager in America: Trying to Make It* (Waltham, MA: Brandeis University, Cohen Center for Modern Jewish Studies, 2000).

33. Anna Greenberg and Kenneth D. Wald, "Still Liberal after All These Years? The Contemporary Political Behavior of American Jewry," in L. Sandy Maisel and Ira N. Forman, eds., *Jews in American Politics* (Lanham, MD: Rowman and Littlefield, 2001), 162–193; Lydia Saad, "U.S. Jews Lead Other Religious Groups in Support of Obama," Gallup, October 2, 2009, http://www.gallup.com/poll/123413/U.S.-Jews-Lead-Religious-Groups-Support-Obama.aspx; *A Portrait of Jewish Americans*, 96.

34. *A Portrait of Jewish Americans*, 96.

35. Cohen and Kelman, *Beyond Distancing*.

36. Cohen and Wertheimer, "Whatever Happened to the Jewish People?"; Cohen and Eisen, *The Jew Within*.

37. Peter Beinart, "The Failure of the American Jewish Establishment," *New York Review of Books*, June 10, 2010.

38. Benjamin Phillips, Eszter Lengyel, and Leonard Saxe. *American Attitudes toward Israel* (Waltham, MA: Brandeis University, Cohen Center for Modern Jewish Studies, 2002), 14; Cohen and Kelman, *Beyond Distancing*, 30. See other evidence from surveys cited in Cohen and Eisen, *The Jew Within*, 143; Cohen and Wertheimer, "Whatever Happened to the Jewish People?" 34.

39. Luntz, *Israel in the Age of Eminem*, 7, 14; author interview with Roger Bennett, vice president of Bronfman Philanthropies.

40. Phillips, Lengyel, and Saxe, *American Attitudes toward Israel*.

41. Surveys cited in Goldberg, *Jewish Power*, 216.

42. Steven M. Cohen, "Poll: Attachment of U.S. Jews to Israel Falls," *Jewish Daily Forward*, March 4, 2005.

43. Sasson et al., *Still Connected*, appendix B, 13.

44. Theodore Sasson, *The New Realism: American Jews' Views about Israel* (New York: American Jewish Committee, 2009).

45. Cohen and Wertheimer, "Whatever Happened to the Jewish People?" Steven M. Cohen and Gerald Bubis, *"Post-Zionist" Philanthropists: Emerging Attitudes of American Jewish Leaders toward Communal Allocations* (Jerusalem: Jerusalem Center for Public Affairs, 1998).

46. "American Jewish Contributions to Israel, 1948–2004," Jewish Virtual Library, http://www.jewishvirtuallibrary.org/jsource/US-Israel/ujatab.html (no longer available).

47. Sherry Israel, *Comprehensive Report on the 1995 CJP Demographic Study* (Boston: Combined Jewish Philanthropies, 1997); Luntz, *Israel in the Age of Eminem*.

48. Fred A. Lazin, *The Struggle for Soviet Jewry in American Politics: Israel versus the American Jewish Establishment* (Lanham, MD: Lexington Books, 2005), 226.

49. The figure of 100,000 is usually mentioned for this pro-Israel rally, but there is good reason to believe that the number was actually lower. See Jerry Tully, "The Numbers Game, Mideast-style," MSNBC, April 30, 2002, http://www.msnbc.msn.com/id/3071605/.

50. The annual AJC surveys of American Jewish opinion are available at http://www.ajc.org/site/c.ijITI2PHKoG/b.846741/k.8A33/Publications_Surveys/apps/nl/newsletter3.asp (accessed June 10, 2010). Similar results were obtained in the National Jewish Population Survey (NJPS) in 2000; see Ament, *Israel Connections and American Jews.*

51. Fern Oppenheim, "The Segmentation Study of the American Market, Fourth Quarter 2010," conducted by the Brand Israel Group and the Conference of Presidents of Major American Jewish Organizations.

52. Yossi Shain and Barry Bristman, "Diaspora, Kinship, and Loyalty: The Renewal of Jewish National Security," *International Affairs* 78, no. 1 (2002): 85.

53. Carl Schrag, *Ripples from the Matzav: Grassroots Responses of American Jewry to the Situation in Israel* (New York: American Jewish Committee, 2004).

54. Marissa Gross, "The Salute to Israel Parade," Jerusalem Center for Public Affairs, June 1, 2008, http://jcpa.org/article/the-salute-to-israel-parade/.

55. Lawrence Grossman, "Jewish Communal Affairs," in David Singer and Lawrence Grossman, eds., *American Jewish Year Book,* vol. 107 (New York: American Jewish Committee, 2007), 113; David Horovitz, "Editor's Notes: 'Mr. Reassurance' Sounds the Alarm," *Jerusalem Post,* November 3, 2006.

56. Theodore Sasson, "Mass Mobilization to Direct Engagement: American Jews' Changing Relationship to Israel," *Israel Studies* 15, no. 2 (2010): 173–195.

57. Amiram Barkat, "Reaping Their Fruits," *Haaretz,* March 6, 2005.

58. Sasson, "Mass Mobilization to Direct Engagement."

59. Chaim Waxman, "Israel in Orthodox Identity: The American Experience," in Danny Ben-Moshe and Zohar Segev, eds., *Israel, the Diaspora and Jewish Identity* (Brighton, UK: Sussex Academic Press, 2007), 52–61; Sasson, Kadushin, and Saxe, *Trends in American Jewish Attachment to Israel,* 13.

60. Jonathan Rynhold, "Israel's Foreign and Defence Policy and Diaspora Jewish Identity," in Ben-Moshe and Segev, eds., *Israel, the Diaspora, and Jewish Identity*; Sasson, *The New Realism.*

61. Sasson, *The New Realism,* 28–31.

62. Peter Beinart, "Israel's Indefensible Behavior," *Daily Beast,* June 21, 2010, http://www.thedailybeast.com/blogs-and-stories/2010-06-01/israel-flotilla-disaster-gaza-embargo-us-supporters-to-blame/; Eric Alterman, "Israel Agonists," *Nation,* June 21, 2010.

63. Sasson et al., *Still Connected.*

64. Cohen and Kelman, *Beyond Distancing*; Sasson, Kadushin, and Saxe, *Trends in American Jewish Attachment to Israel*; Sasson et al., *Still Connected.*

65. Sasson, Kadushin, and Saxe, *Trends in American Jewish Attachment to Israel*; Theodore Sasson et al., "Understanding Young Adult Attachment to Israel: Period, Lifecycle, and Generational Dynamics," *Contemporary Jewry,* 32, no. 1 (2012): 67–84.

66. Sasson, Kadushin, and Saxe, *Trends in American Jewish Attachment to Israel.*

67. Ukeles Associates, *Young Jewish Adults in the United States Today* (New York: American Jewish Committee, 2006), table 20, 81.

68. Theodore Sasson, *The New American Zionism* (New York: New York University Press, 2014), 104.

69. Leonard Saxe et al., *Generation Birthright Israel: The Impact of an Israel Experience on Jewish Identity and Choices* (Waltham, MA: Brandeis University, Cohen Center for Modern Jewish Studies, 2009).

70. Steven M. Cohen and Sam Abrams, "Israel off Their Minds: The Diminished Place of Israel in the Political Thinking of Young Jews," New York University, Berman Jewish Policy Archive, October 27, 2008, http://www.bjpa.org/Publications/details.cfm?PublicationID=207.

71. Sasson et al., *Still Connected*, appendix B, 13.

72. Sasson, *The New American Zionism*, 107.

73. Cohen and Kelman, *Beyond Distancing*, 17.

74. Sasson et al., *Still Connected*, appendix B, p. 13.

75. Sheskin, "Four Questions about American Jewish Demography"; Jeffrey Helmreich, "The Israel Swing Factor: How the American Jewish Vote Influences U.S. Elections," *Jerusalem Letter / Viewpoints* 446, January 15, 2001.

76. "U.S. Presidential Elections: Jewish Voting Record (1916–Present)," Jewish Virtual Library, http://www.jewishvirtuallibrary.org/jsource/US-Israel/jewvote.html; Mark S. Mellman, Aaron Strauss, and Kenneth D. Wald, *Jewish American Voting Behavior, 1972–2008: Just the Facts* (Washington, DC: Solomon Project, 2012).

77. Greenberg and Wald, "Still Liberal after All These Years?"; Saad, "U.S. Jews Lead Other Religious Groups in Support of Obama"; *A Portrait of Jewish Americans*.

78. Helmreich, "The Israel Swing Factor."

79. Steven M. Cohen, Sam Abrams, and Judith Veinstein, "American Jews and the 2008 Presidential Election: As Democratic and Liberal as Ever?" New York University, Berman Jewish Policy Archive, October 20, 2008, http://www.bjpa.org/Publications/details.cfm?PublicationID=2444; Cohen and Abrams, "Israel off Their Minds."

80. Mellman, Strauss, and Wald, *Jewish American Voting Behavior, 1972–2008: Just the Facts*.

81. Natasha Mozgovaya, "Biden: Israel's Decisions Must Be Made in Jerusalem, not DC," *Haaretz*, September 4, 2008; Ron Kampeas, "Obama: Don't Equate 'Pro-Israel' and 'Pro-Likud,'" *JTA*, February 24, 2008.

82. Eric Fingerhut, "Polls Show Obama Making Big Gains with Jewish Voters," *JTA*, October 24, 2008; Ron Kampeas, "Jews Looked Past Worries to Embrace Obama," *JTA*, November 5, 2008.

83. Michael Bloomfield and Mark Mellman, "Predicting Jewish Vote More Complicated," *Jewish Daily Forward*, November 18, 2011.

84. Author interviews, 2013.

85. "U.S. Presidential Elections: Jewish Voting Record (1916–Present)," Jewish Virtual Library, http://www.jewishvirtuallibrary.org/jsource/US-Israel/jewvote.html; Mellman, Strauss, and Wald, *Jewish American Voting Behavior, 1972–2008: Just the Facts*.

86. Cohen, Abrams, and Veinstein. "American Jews and the 2008 Presidential Election"; Cohen and Abrams, "Israel off Their Minds."

87. Mellman, Strauss, and Wald, *Jewish American Voting Behavior, 1972–2008: Just the Facts*; Hilary Leila Krieger, "Poll: McCain More Popular among Religious Than Secular Jews," *Jerusalem Post*, July 8, 2008; Cohen, Abrams, and Veinstein, "American Jews and the 2008 Presidential Election"; Lawrence Grossman, "Jewish Vote in Play," *JTA*, September 26, 2011; J. J. Goldberg, "Shhh: NY Times Reports on Orthodox GOP Vote," *Jewish Daily Forward*, November 25, 2102; author conversations with numerous Orthodox American Jews in New Jersey, Washington, DC, and Florida, 2012–2013.

88. Schrag, *Ripples from the Matzav.*
89. Leonard Saxe, Ted Sasson, and Shahar Hecht, *Taglit-Birthright Israel: Impact on Jewish Identity, Peoplehood and Connection to Israel* (Waltham, MA: Brandeis University, Cohen Center for Modern Jewish Studies, 2006).

7. AMERICAN JEWS AND THE PEACE PROCESS

1. Aaron David Miller, *The Much Too Promised Land: American Elusive Search for Arab-Israeli Peace* (New York: Bantam Books, 2009), 95.
2. Natasha Mozgovaya, "Biden: Israel's Decisions Must Be Made in Jerusalem, Not D.C.," *Haaretz,* September 4, 2008.
3. Yossi Shain and Barry Bristman, "'Diaspora, Kinship, and loyalty: The Renewal of Jewish National Security," *International Affairs* 78, no. 1 (2002): 85.
4. John J. Mearsheimer and Stephen M. Walt, *The Israel Lobby and U.S. Foreign Policy* (New York: Farrar, Straus and Giroux, 2007).
5. Steven M. Cohen, *Ties and Tensions: The 1986 Survey of American Jewish Attitudes toward Israel and Israelis* (New York: American Jewish Committee, 1987), 44.
6. Eytan Gilboa, *American Public Opinion toward Israel and the Arab-Israeli Conflict* (Lexington, MA: Lexington Books, 1987), 251–253.
7. Charles S. Liebman, *Pressure without Sanctions: The Influence of World Jewry on Israeli Policy* (Rutherford, NJ: Fairleigh Dickinson University Press, 1977), 202.
8. Theodore Sasson, "Mass Mobilization to Direct Engagement: American Jews' Changing Relationship to Israel," *Israel Studies* 15, no. 2 (2010): 173–195.
9. These polls are generally considered to be reliable, though they probably over-represent Jews who care about Israel. See Benjamin Phillips, Eszter Lengyel, and Leonard Saxe, *American Attitudes toward Israel* (Waltham, MA: Brandeis University, Cohen Center for Modern Jewish Studies, 2002); Joel Perlmann, *American Jewish Opinion about the Future of the West Bank: A Reanalysis of American Jewish Committee Surveys,* Working Paper no. 526 (Annandale-on-Hudson, NY: Bard College, Levy Economics Institute, December 2007).
10. Phillips et al., *American Attitudes toward Israel*; Perlmann, *American Jewish Opinion about the Future of the West Bank*; "2006 Annual Survey of American Jewish Opinion," AJC Global Jewish Advocacy, October 18, 2006, http://www.ajc.org/site/apps/nlnet/content3.aspx?c=70JILSPwFfJSG&b=8479755&ct=12483107; "2009 Annual Survey of American Jewish Opinion," Global Jewish Advocacy, October 1, 2009, http://www.ajc.org/site/apps/nlnet/content3.aspx?c=70JILSPwFfJSG&b=8479755&ct=12479167; "2010 Annual Survey of American Jewish Opinion," Global Jewish Advocacy, April 7, 2010, http://www.ajc.org/site/apps/nlnet/content3.aspx?c=70JILSPwFfJSG&b=8479755&ct=12478947.
11. The exception was the period 1996–1999, when the Netanyahu government was in power. See Phillips et al., *American Attitudes toward Israel.*
12. See the 2007, 2008, 2009 and 2010 AJC surveys at http://www.ajc.org.
13. *A Portrait of Jewish Americans* (Washington, DC: Pew Research Center, October 1, 2013), http://www.pewforum.org/files/2013/10/jewish-american-full-report-for-web.pdf.
14. Perlmann, *American Jewish Opinion about the Future of the West Bank.*
15. For details, see notes 9 and 10.

16. "Poll: U.S. Jews Overwhelmingly Support Israeli Gaza/West Bank Disengagement, Say Israel Should Depart Most Settlements to Secure Peace," Ameinu, April 11, 2005, http://www.ameinu.net/newsroom/press-release/poll-u-s-jews-overwhelm-ingly-support-israeli-gazawest-bank-disengagement-say-israel-should-depart-most-settlements-to-secure-peace/; Perlmann, *American Jewish Opinion about the Future of the West Bank*; "July 2008 Survey Results," *J Street Blog*, March 10, 2012, http://jstreet.org/blog/post/july-2008-survey-results_1.

17. "March 2009 Survey Results," *J Street Blog*, March 10, 2012, http://jstreet.org/blog/post/march-2009-survey-results; James Zogby, "Arab American and American Jews Agree on Path to Peace," Arab American Institute, August 4, 2003, http://www.aaiusa.org/dr-zogby/entry/w08040/.

18. For details, see notes 9 and 10.

19. Steven M. Cohen, *After the Gulf War: American Jews' Attitudes toward Israel: The 1991 National Survey of American Jews* (New York: American Jewish Committee, 1992).

20. "2007 Annual Survey of American Jewish Opinion," Global Jewish Advocacy, November 25, 2007, http://www.ajc.org/site/apps/nlnet/content3.aspx?c=7oJILSPwFfJSG&b=8479755&ct=12478843.

21. Perlmann, *American Jewish Opinion about the Future of the West Bank*.

22. Renae Cohen, *The Palestinian Autonomy Agreement and Israel-PLO Recognition: A Survey of American Jewish Opinion* (New York: American Jewish Committee, 1994).

23. "Poll: US Jews Overwhelmingly Support Israeli Gaza-West Bank Disengagement."

24. "March 2009 Survey Results."

25. "2009 Annual Survey of American Jewish Opinion."

26. This trend was already evident in the 1980s. Cohen, *Ties and Tensions*.

27. Poll cited in Ofira Seliktar, *Divided We Stand: American Jews, Israel, and the Peace Process* (Westport, CT: Praeger, 2002), 153.

28. Ibid., 158, 183.

29. "March 2009 Survey Results."

30. Phillips, Lengyel, and Saxe, *American Attitudes toward Israel*.

31. Eric Fingerhut, "Not Much Division in Community, According to ADL Poll," *JTA*, January 30, 2009, http://www.jta.org/2009/01/30/news-opinion/the-telegraph/not-much-division-in-community-according-to-adl-poll.

32. *A Portrait of Jewish Americans*, 89.

33. Phillips, Lengyel, and Saxe, *American Attitudes toward Israel*; Gilboa, *American Public Opinion toward Israel and the Arab-Israeli Conflict*, 258.

34. James Guth and William Kenan Jr., "Religious Factors and American Public Support for Israel: 1992–2008" (paper presented at the annual meeting of the American Political Science Association, Seattle, WA, September 1–4, 2011).

35. Gilboa, *American Public Opinion toward Israel and the Arab-Israeli Conflict*, 258.

36. Polls cited in Seliktar, *Divided We Stand*, 166; George Gruen, "Israel and the American Jewish Community," in Robert O. Freedman, ed., *Israel's First Fifty Years* (Gainesville, FL: University Press of Florida, 2000), 65, note 41.

37. "March 2009 Survey Results"; "March 2010 Survey Results," *J Street Blog*, March 10, 2012, http://jstreet.org/blog/post/march-2010-survey-results.

38. "Poll: U.S. Jews Overwhelmingly Support Israeli Gaza/West Bank Disengagement"; "July 2008 Survey Results."

39. This section is based on Perlmann, *American Jewish Opinion about the Future of the West Bank*. He used results from the 2000–2005 AJC surveys.

40. Differences between the non-Orthodox movements were almost negligible.

41. E. J. Kessler, "Orthodox Disagree with Other Jews on Gaza Pullout," *Jewish Daily Forward*, July 1, 2005.

42. Anand Sokhey, Paul Djupe, "Rabbi Engagement with the Peace Process in the Middle East," *Social Science Quarterly* 87, no. 4 (2006): 903–923; Theodore Sasson *The New Realism: American Jews Views about Israel* (New York: American Jewish Committee, 2009).

43. Perlmann, *American Jewish Opinion about the Future of the West Bank*.

44. Theodore Sasson et al., *Still Connected: American Jewish Attitudes about Israel* (Waltham, MA: Brandeis University, Cohen Center for Modern Jewish Studies, August 2010), table 11.

45. *A Portrait of Jewish Americans*, 91.

46. *A Portrait of Jewish Americans*.

47. Sasson, *The New Realism*, 15–16, 28–31.

48. Ibid.

49. Peter Beinart, "The Failure of the American Jewish Establishment," *New York Review of Books*, June 10, 2010; Jeffrey Goldberg, "Goldblog vs. Peter Beinart: Part II," *Atlantic*, May 18, 2010 http://www.theatlantic.com/national/archive/2010/05/goldblog-vs-peter-beinart-part-ii/56934/; Jeffrey Goldberg, "Goldblog vs. Peter Beinart: Part III" *Atlantic*, May 18, 2010, http://www.theatlantic.com/national/archive/2010/05/goldblog-vs-peter-beinart-part-iii-zionism-reloaded/57088/.

50. Tony Judt, "Israel: The Alternative," *New York Review of Books*, October 23, 2003, http://www.nybooks.com/articles/archives/2003/oct/23/israel-the-alternative/. See also Tony Kushner and Alisa Solomon, eds., *Wrestling with Zion: Progressive Jewish-American Responses to the Israeli-Palestinian Conflict* (New York: Grove Press, 2003); Alvin Rosenfeld, *"Progressive" Jewish Thought and the New Anti-Semitism* (New York: American Jewish Committee, 2006).

51. Sasson, *The New Realism*, p.13.

52. *Jewish Press*, September 15, 1995, 14; *Jewish Press*, October 6, 1993, 16; *Jerusalem Post*, September 6, 1995; *Jerusalem Report*, October 19, 1995, 38; *Yediot Aharonot*, September 11, 1995, 1.

53. Author interview with Nathan Diament, 2013.

54. Sasson, *The New Realism*, p.13.

55. Shmuel Rosner, "Reform Support 'Jewish State' More Than the Orthodox," *Rosner's Domain* (blog), *Jerusalem Post*, October 14, 2010, http://cgis.jpost.com/Blogs/rosner/entry/can_you_believe_it_reform (no longer available).

56. Glenn Frankel, *Beyond the Promised Land: Jews and Arabs on the Hard Road to a New Israel* (New York: Simon and Schuster, 1994), 222.

57. Dan Fleshler, *Transforming America's Israel Lobby: The Limits of Its Power and the Potential for Change* (Washington DC: Potomac Books, 2009), 115

58. Jack Wertheimer, "Breaking the Taboo: Critics of Israel and the American Jewish Establishment," in Allon Gal, ed., *Envisioning Israel: The Changing Ideals and Images of North American Jews* (Jerusalem: Hebrew University of Jerusalem, Magnes Press, 1996), 397–419.

59. Martin Raffel, "History of Israel Advocacy," in Alan Mittleman, Jonathan Sarna, and Robert Licht, eds., *Jewish Polity and American Civil Society: Communal Agencies and Religious Movements in the American Public Sphere* (New York: Rowman and Littlefield, 2002), 132.

60. *Jerusalem Post*, July 6, 1990; Lawrence Grossman, "Jewish Communal Affairs," in Ruth R. Seldin and David Singer, eds., *American Jewish Year Book*, vol. 92 (New York: American Jewish Committee, 1992), 245.

61. Jonathan Rynhold, "Labour, Likud, the 'Special Relationship,' and the Peace Process 1988–96," *Israel Affairs*, 3, no. 3–4 (1997): 239–262.

62. Seliktar, *Divided We Stand*, 137.

63. Ibid., 157; Fleshler, *Transforming America's Israel Lobby*, 107–110.

64. For example, during the Second Lebanon War over a quarter of young Jewish Americans consulted Israeli news sources, while the figure was more than 50 percent for those involved in Jewish student organizations. Leonard Saxe, Theodore Sasson, and Shahar Hecht, *Israel at War: The Impact of Peer-Oriented Israel Programs on Responses of American Jewish Young Adults* (Waltham, MA: Brandeis University, Cohen Center for Modern Jewish Studies, 2006), 5.

65. For a personal journalistic description of the impact of the Lebanon War and the intifada, see Thomas L. Friedman, *From Beirut to Jerusalem* (New York: Farrar, Straus and Giroux, 1989).

66. Yossi Shain, "Jewish Kinship at a Crossroads," *Political Science Quarterly* 117, no. 2 (2002): 279–309.

67. Jack Wertheimer, *Generation of Change: How Leaders in Their Twenties and Thirties Are Reshaping American Jewish Life* (Jerusalem: Avi Chai Foundation, 2010); Sasson, "Mass Mobilization to Direct Engagement."

68. Brit Tzedek claimed a network of 40,000 supporters, including more than 1,000 rabbis, though it later integrated into J Street. Dov Waxman, "The Israel Lobbies: A Survey of the Pro-Israel Community in the United States," *Israel Studies Forum* 25, no. 1 (2010).

69. Quoted in Carl Schrag, *Ripples from the Matzav: Grassroots Responses of American Jewry to the Situation in Israel* (New York: American Jewish Committee, 2004).

70. The ZOA claims thirty thousand dues-paying members. Waxman, "The Israel Lobbies."

71. Ibid.

72. This is according to polls conducted by the left-wing pro-Israel organization J Street, which is outside the conventional lobby. See "July 2008 Survey Results"; "March 2009 Survey Results."

73. Nathan Guttman, "The Waning American Jewish Liberal," *Haaretz*, April 3, 2002.

74. Shlomo Shamir, "The Silence of the Lambs," *Haaretz*, April 9, 2002.

75. Shlomo Shamir, "Is Right-Wing Influence Fading among U.S. Jews?" *Haaretz*, August 19, 2005; Yaakov Katz, "Battle over American Jewish Support," *Jerusalem Post*, March 15, 2005.

76. "Resolution on Israeli Palestinian Peace," http://tools.isovera.com/organizations/org/ResolutiononIsraeliPalestinianPeace-final.doc (no longer available).

77. Brit Tzedek v'Shalom, http://btvshalom.org/ (accessed October 11, 2004).

78. David Singer and Lawrence Grossman, eds., *American Jewish Yearbook*, vol. 107 (New York: American Jewish Committee, 2007); Nathan Guttman, "Washington: Splitting Hairs or Hair-Raising Splits?" *Jerusalem Post*, March 9, 2006.
79. Ron Kampeas, "AIPAC Stance Irks Donors," *JTA*, November 16, 2007, http://www.jta.org/2007/11/16/news-opinion/politics/aipac-stance-irks-donors.
80. Sasson, "Mass Mobilization to Direct Engagement," 178–179.
81. Quoted in James Traub, "The New Israel Lobby," *New York Times Magazine*, September 13, 2009; and in Eric Yoffie, "On Gaza, Sense, and Centrism," *Jewish Daily Forward*, January 9, 2009, http://www.forward.com/articles/14847/.
82. Lawrence Grossman, "Jewish Communal Affairs," in Singer and Grossman, eds., *American Jewish Year Book*, vol. 107, 113.
83. Anthony Weiss, "U.S. Ultra-Orthodox Group Breaks Mold by taking Stance on Peace Process," *Jewish Daily Forward*, December 2, 2007.
84. *Haaretz*, February 17, 2008.
85. Shlomo Shamir, "Bronfman: Jewish Leaders Creating Rift between Israel, U.S.," *Haaretz*, July 2004; Shlomo Shamir, "Reform Movement Rabbis Set to Condemn House Demolitions," *Haaretz*, June 24, 2004; "Reform Head Blasts Settlements," *Jerusalem Post*, November 13, 2003.
86. Matthew Wagner, "U.S. Reform Rabbis Urge Settlement Freeze," *Jerusalem Post*, June 15, 2009.
87. Ron Kampeas, "Reform, AIPAC Stake Out Opposing Positions on Penalizing Palestinians," *JTA*, January 3, 2013, http://www.jta.org/2013/01/03/news-opinion/politics/reform-aipac-stake-out-opposing-positions-on-penalizing-palestinians.
88. "Reform Jews Threaten to Leave Conference of Presidents," *JTA*, May 1, 2014; Nathan Guttman, "'Broken' Presidents Conference Faces Powerful Rebellion after J Street Debacle," *Jewish Daily Forward*, May 7, 2014.
89. Author interview with Yossi Beilin, 1998; Edward Tivnan, *The Lobby: Jewish Political Power and American Foreign Policy: A Collection of Essays* (New York: Simon and Schuster, 1987), 201–216; Michael Massing, "The Storm over the Israel Lobby," *New York Review of Books*, June 8, 2006.
90. Michael Massing, "Deal Breakers," *American Prospect*, March 11, 2002.
91. Fleshler, *Transforming America's Israel Lobby*, 64, 77.
92. Author interview with Dan Fleshler.
93. Rynhold, "Labour, Likud, the 'Special Relationship'"; J. J. Goldberg, *Jewish Power: Inside the American Jewish Establishment* (Reading, MA: Addison-Wesley, 1996), 218; Allison Hoffman, "King without a Crown," *Tablet Magazine*, May 10, 2010, http://www.tabletmag.com/news-and-politics/33176/king-without-a-crown.
94. Fleshler, *Transforming America's Israel Lobby*, 77–78.
95. E. J. Kessler, "Pro-Israel Activists Cheer," *Jewish Daily Forward*, March 10, 2006; Rynhold, "Labour, Likud, the 'Special Relationship.'"
96. *Jerusalem Post*, July 9, 1993.
97. Fleshler, *Transforming America's Israel Lobby*, 66.
98. Author interview with Yossi Beilin, 1998.
99. Fleshler, *Transforming America's Israel Lobby*, 67.
100. Seliktar, *Divided We Stand*, 137, 183, 185.

101. Ron Kampeas, "With Bush More Involved in Mideast, Group Finds Itself Back in the Center," *JTA*, June 2, 2005; Shmuel Rosner, "U.S. Jewish leadership Declares Support for Disengagement," *Haaretz*, August 17, 2005; Amiram Barkat, "U.S. Jewish Group's Stand on Pullout Attacked," *Haaretz*, February 17, 2005.

102. Author interview with Israeli official whose job involved liaising with AIPAC, 2006.

103. Ron Kampeas, "In Major Policy Shift, AIPAC Offers Strong Backing for Withdrawal Plan," *JTA*, May 24, 2005; Barkat, "U.S. Jewish Group's Stand on Pullout Attacked."

104. Shlomo Shamir, "U.S. Jewish Leaders Split over Public Support for Pullout," *Haaretz*, October 17, 2004.

105. Barkat, "U.S. Jewish Group's Stand on Pullout Attacked."

106. Rynhold, "Labour, Likud, the 'Special Relationship.'"

107. Marshall Breger, "Jerusalem Gambit," *National Review*, October 23, 1995, 41–45.

108. Shain, "Jewish Kinship at a Crossroads," 305; see also Anshel Pfeffer, "Reform Head behind Olmert on Jerusalem," *Haaretz*, February 17, 2008.

109. Michael Jordan, "President's Conference Sets Limits after Lauder's Jerusalem speech," *JTA*, February 1, 2001; Eli Wohlgelernter, "Avital Tells U.S. Jews to Stay Out of Israeli Politics," *Jerusalem Post*, January 5, 2001.

110. James Besser, "New Coalition to Fight Any Jerusalem Division," *The Jewish Week*, October 18, 2007; Anshel Pfeffer, "Reform Headlines up behind Olmert on Jerusalem," *Haaretz*, February 17, 2008.

111. Sasson et al., *Still Connected*, tables 2 and 3.

112. Schrag, *Ripples from the Matzav*.

113. Naava Shafner Posy, *Jewish American Activists: The Melting Pot for American, Israel and Jewish Identities* (seminar paper, Bar-Ilan University, Department of Political Science, Ramat Gan, 2010).

114. Waxman, "The Israel Lobbies."

115. Henry Siegman, "Imposing Middle East Peace," *Nation*, January 7, 2010; M. J. Rosenberg, "Lying about the Gaza Flotilla Disaster," *Huffington Post*, June 2, 2010, http://www.huffingtonpost.com/mj-rosenberg/lying-about-the-gaza-flot_b_597953.html.

116. Leonard Fein, "Reflections of a Sometime Israel Lobbyist," *Dissent*, Spring 2008; Michael Walzer, "The Four Wars of Israel/Palestine," *Dissent*, Fall 2002; Michael Walzer, "Response to Jerome Slater: The Lebanon War," *Dissent*, Winter 2007.

117. Dan Kosky, "New Israel Fund Should Not Fund Groups That Oppose Jewish State," *JTA*, July 27, 2009; see also "New Israel Fund," NGO Monitor, September 2, 2012, http://www.ngo-monitor.org/article/new_israel_fund. The Avi Armoni statement was personally witnessed by the author at a New Israel Fund event in London after the Rabin assassination; Professor Avi Ravistsky presented the alternative view, namely that the two are compatible.

118. Jeffrey Goldberg, "J Street's Ben-Ami On Zionism and Military Aid to Israel," *Atlantic*, October 23, 2009, http://jeffreygoldberg.theatlantic.com/archives/2009/10/j_streets_ben-ami_on_being_a_z.php#more.

119. Nathan Guttman, "J Street, Now a Player, Inches toward the Center," *Jewish Daily Forward*, November 6, 2009.

120. Eric Fingerhut, "J Street Confab Shows Generational Divide on Israel," *JTA*, October 27, 2009.

121. Hilary Krieger, "J Street Branch Drops Pro-Israel Slogan," *Jerusalem Post*, October 27, 2009.

122. Quoted in Traub, "The New Israel Lobby"; and in Yoffie, "On Gaza, Sense and Centrism."

123. Ari Roth, "J Street Letter of Support on Discussing 7JC," *Theater J Blog*, March 26, 2009, http://theaterjblogs.wordpress.com/2009/03/26/j-street-letter-of-support-on-discussing-7jc/.

124. Natasha Mozgovaya, "Israel Envoy Hosts J Street Chief in Bid to End Rift," *Haaretz*, April 16, 2010; Natasha Mozgovaya, "Poet Booted from J Street Meet for Comparing Guantanamo to Auschwitz," *Haaretz*, October 20, 2009; Eric Fingerhut, "J Street, B'nai B'rith Rip Toronto Film Festival Protests," *JTA*, September 9, 2009; Nathan Guttman, "From the Left: J Street Moves to Center on Iran Sanctions," *Jewish Daily Forward*, December 25, 2009.

125. Author interviews at the J Street U conference in Washington DC in 2013.

126. Wertheimer, *Generation of Change*.

127. Jack Wertheimer, "The Fragmentation of American Jewry and Its Leadership: Interview with Jack Wertheimer," *Changing Jewish Communities* 29 (February 6, 2008), available at http://jcpa.org/article/the-fragmentation-of-american-jewry-and-its-leadership/.

128. Sasson, *The New Realism*.

129. Waxman, "The Israel Lobbies."

130. Ron Kampeas, "Sitting between Bibi and Obama, AIPAC Criticized by Left and Right," *JTA*, May 7, 2009.

131. Hoffman, "King without a Crown." J Street subsequently applied to join the Conference.

132. Traub, "The New Israel Lobby."

133. Natasha Mozgovaya, "Biden: Israel's decisions must be made in Jerusalem, not DC.,"

134. Nathan Guttman, "Jewish Leaders Give Obama No Push-Back on Settlement Freeze," *Jewish Daily Forward*, July 24, 2009; Ron Kampeas, "At White House, US Jews Offer Little Resistance to Obama Policy on Settlements," *JTA*, July 13, 2009; Nathan Guttman, "Key U.S. Jews Wary of Netanyahu's Unbending Policy on Settlements," *Jewish Daily Forward*, June 3, 2009.

135. Author interview with Stuart Eizenstat, July 2013.

136. Schrag, "Ripples from the Matzav."

137. Paradoxically, the rise in these attacks on Israel's legitimacy has led to a rise in funding for more conservative pro-Israel groups. In turn, mainstream groups note that playing to the Right on these issues will raise more money, so they adjust their messages accordingly; interview with an official in a mainstream American Jewish organization, September 2008.

138. This was pointed out by David Saperstein, author interview, July 2013.

CONCLUSION

1. "Remarks by the President on a New Beginning" (Cairo University), White House, June 4, 2009, http://www.whitehouse.gov/the-press-office/remarks-president-cairo-university-6-04-09.
2. "Mitt Romney on Israel," Political Guide, September 3, 2012, http://www.thepoliticalguide.com/rep_bios.php?rep_id=64410102&category=views&id=201106131114008.
3. Michelle Sieff, "Gaza and After: An Interview with Paul Berman," *ZWORD*, March 2009, available at http://archive.today/19gnG.
4. "New BESA Center/ADL Poll: Attitudes of Israelis toward the U.S. Remain Strongly Positive," Anti-Defamation League, http://www.adl.org/PresRele/IslME_62/5517_62.htm (no longer available); Julian Pecquet, "Israelis Favor Romney over Obama by Wide Margin in Latest Poll," *Hill*, October 29, 2012, http://thehill.com/policy/international/264609-romney-polls-far-ahead-of-obama-in-israel.
5. The ideological polarization of American politics has been reinforced by congressional redistricting. See Jamie L. Carson et al., "'Redistricting and Party Polarization in the U.S. House of Representatives," *American Politics Research* 35, no. 6 (2007): 878–904.
6. "Partisan Polarization Surges in Bush, Obama Years: Trends in American Values: 1987–2012," Pew Research Center for the People and the Press, June 4, 2012, http://www.people-press.org/2012/06/04/partisan-polarization-surges-in-bush-obama-years/.
7. Ronald Inglehart, *Modernization and Postmodernization: Cultural, Economic, and Political Change in 43 Societies* (Princeton, NJ: Princeton University Press, 1997); Andrew Kohut and Bruce Stokes, *America against the World: How We Are Different and Why We Are Disliked* (New York: Henry Holt, 2006).
8. Steven M. Cohen and Arnold Eisen, *The Jew Within: Self, Family, and Community in America* (Bloomington, IN: Indiana University Press, 2000).
9. Samuel Huntington, *Who Are We? The Challenges to America's National Identity* (New York: Simon and Schuster, 2004).
10. Stuart Eizenstat identified this as a significant challenge. Author interview, July 2013.
11. "'Nones' on the Rise," Pew Research Religion and Public Life Project, October 9, 2012, http://www.pewforum.org/2012/10/09/nones-on-the-rise/; Barry Kosmin and Ariela Keysar, *American Religious Identification Survey 2008: Summary Report* (Hartford, CT: Trinity College, 2009).
12. "In Shift from Bush Era, More Conservatives Say 'Come Home, America,'" Pew Research Center for the People and the Press, June 16, 2011, http://www.people-press.org/2011/06/16/in-shift-from-bush-era-more-conservatives-say-come-home-america/.
13. A. F. K. Organski, *The $36 Billion Bargain: Strategy and Politics in U.S. Assistance to Israel* (New York: Columbia University Press, 1990), 247; Lydia Saad, "Americans' Support for Israel Unchanged since Gaza Conflict: Most Americans Sympathize with Israel, View It Favorably," Gallup, March 3, 2009, http://www.gallup.com/poll/116308/Americans-Support-Israel-Unchanged-Gaza-Conflict.aspx.

14. Kenneth S. Stern, *Antisemitism Today: How It Is the Same, How It Is Different, and How to Fight It* (New York: American Jewish Committee, 2006).

15. Jonathan Rynhold, "The Republican Primaries and the Israel Acid Test," *BESA Perspectives* (February 15, 2012). http://www.biu.ac.il/SOC/besa/docs/perspectives165.pdf.

16. Elliot Abrams, *Tested by Zion: The Bush Administration and the Israeli-Palestinian Conflict* (Cambridge: Cambridge University Press, 2013).

Bibliography

Abrams, Elliot. "Israel and the Peace Process." In Robert Kagan and William Kristol, eds., *Present Dangers: Crisis and Opportunity in American Foreign and Defense Policy*. San Francisco: Encounter, 2000, 221–240.

Tested by Zion: The Bush Administration and the Israeli-Palestinian Conflict. Cambridge: Cambridge University Press, 2013.

Abrams, Elliot and Michael Singh. "Spoilers: The End of the Peace Process." *World Affairs* 172, no. 2 (Fall 2009): 69–76. www.worldaffairsjournal.org/article/spoilers-end-peace-process.

Abrams, Nathan. *Norman Podhoretz and Commentary Magazine: The Rise and Fall of the Neocons*. New York: Continuum, 2010.

Abu-Manneh, Bashir. "Israel in the U.S. Empire." In Elleke Boehmer and Stephen Morton, eds., *Terror and the Postcolonial: A Concise Companion*. Oxford: Wiley-Blackwell, 2010, 226–252.

Adler, Emmanuel. "Seizing the Middle Ground: Constructivism in World Politics." *European Journal of International Relations* 3, no. 3 (1997): 319–363.

Aikman, David. *A Man of Faith: The Spiritual Journey of George W. Bush*. Nashville: W Publishing Group, 2004.

Allin, Dana H., and Steven Simon. "America's Predicament." *Survival* 46, no. 4 (2004): 7–30.

Almond, Gabriel A., and Sidney Verba. *The Civic Culture: Political Attitudes and Democracy in Five Nations*. Princeton, NJ: Princeton University Press, 1963.

Ament, Jonathon. *American Jewish Religious Denominations*. New York: United Jewish Communities, 2005. www.jewishfederations.org/local_includes/downloads/7579.pdf.

Israel Connections and American Jews: Report Series on the National Jewish Population Survey 2000–01. New York: New York University, Berman Jewish Policy Archive, August 2005. www.bjpa.org/Publications/details.cfm?PublicationID=2848.

J Street Blog. "March 2009 Survey Results." http://jstreet.org/blog/post/march-2009-survey-results.

"March 2010 Survey Results." http://jstreet.org/blog/post/march-2010-survey-results.

"July 2008 Survey Results." http://jstreet.org/blog/post/july-2008-survey-results_1.

Anderson, Irvine H. *Biblical Interpretation and Middle East Policy*. Gainesville: University Press of Florida, 2005.

Annual Surveys of American Jewish Opinion, 2007–2010. New York: American Jewish Global Jewish Advocacy. www.ajc.org/site/apps/nl/newsletter3.asp?c=7oJILSPwFfJ SG&b=8479755&rsCount=28&recordcount=10&page=2.

Anthony, Andrew. *The Fallout: How a Guilty Liberal Lost His Innocence*. London: Jonathan Cape, 2007.

Antonius, George. *The Arab Awakening*. London: Hamish Hamilton, 1938.

Ariel, Yaakov. "An American Initiative for a Jewish State: William Blackstone and the Petition of 1891." *Studies in Zionism* 10, no. 2 (1989): 125–137.

   On Behalf of Israel: American Fundamentalist Attitudes toward Jews, Judaism, and Zionism, 1865–1945. Brooklyn, NY: Carlson, 1991.

   Philosemites or Antisemites? Evangelical Christian Attitudes toward Jews, Judaism, and the State of Israel. Jerusalem: Hebrew University of Jerusalem, Vidal Sassoon International Center for the Study of Antisemitism, 2002. http://sicsa.huji.ac.il/ 20Ariel.htm.

   "An Unexpected Alliance: Christian Zionism and Its Historical Significance." *Modern Judaism* 26, no. 1 (2006): 74–100.

Ateek, Naim. *Justice and Only Justice: A Palestinian Theology of Liberation*. New York: Orbis Books, 1989.

   "The Zionist Ideology of Domination versus the Reign of God: The Ultimate Triumph of Justice and Love." Jerusalem: A Globe of Witnesses, 2001. www.thewitness.org/ agw/ateekkeynote.html.

Baker, James, Lee Hamilton, Lawrence S. Eagleburger, Vernon E. Jordan Jr., Edwin Meese III, Sandra Day O'Conner, Leon E. Panetta, William J. Perry, Charles S. Robb, and Alan K. Simpson. *The Iraq Study Group Report*. New York: Vintage Books, 2006.

Balint, Benjamin. *Running Commentary: The Contentious Magazine That Transformed the Jewish Left into the Neoconservative Right*. New York: Public Affairs, 2010.

Ball, George, and Douglas Ball. *The Passionate Attachment: America's Involvement with Israel, 1947 to the Present*. New York: W. W. Norton, 1992.

Bard, Mitchell. *The Water's Edge and Beyond: Defining the Limits to Domestic Influence on United States Middle East Policy*. New Brunswick, NJ: Transaction, 1991.

Barnett, Michael. "Ideology and Alliances in the Middle East." In Peter J. Katzenstein, ed., *The Culture of National Security: Norms and Identity in World Politics*. New York: Columbia University Press, 1996, 400–447.

Baughman, James L. *Henry Luce and the Rise of the American News Media*. Baltimore, MD: Johns Hopkins University Press, 2001.

Baumgartner, Jody, Peter Francia, and Jonathan Morris. "A Clash of Civilizations? The Influence of Religion on Public Opinion of U.S. Foreign Policy in the Middle East." *Political Science Quarterly* 61, no. 2 (2008): 171–179.

Beinart, Peter. *The Good Fight: Why Liberals – and Only Liberals – Can Win the War on Terror and Make America Great Again*. New York: HarperCollins, 2006.

   "When Politics No Longer Stops at the Water's Edge: Partisan Polarization and Foreign Policy." In Pietro S. Nivola and David W. Brady, eds., *Red and Blue Nation? Vol. 2: Consequences and Correction of America's Polarized Politics*. Washington, DC: Brookings Institution Press, 2008, 151–167.

The Icarus Syndrome: A History of American Hubris. New York: Harper, 2010.

The Crisis of Zionism. New York: Times Books/Henry Holt, 2012.

Ben-Zvi, Abraham. *The American Approach to Superpower Collaboration in the Middle East, 1973–1986.* Boulder: CO: Westview Press, 1986.

The United States and Israel: The Limits of the Special Relationship. New York: Columbia University Press, 1993.

Decade of Transition: Eisenhower, Kennedy, and the Origins of the American-Israeli Alliance. New York: Columbia University Press, 1998.

Berger, Sandy, and James Baker. Foreword to Daniel Kurtzer, ed., *Pathways to Peace: America and the Arab-Israeli Conflict.* New York: Palgrave Macmillan, 2012, vi–xiii.

Berger, Thomas. "Norms, Identity, and National Security in Germany and Japan." In Peter J. Katzenstein, ed., *The Culture of National Security: Norms and Identity in World Politics.* New York: Columbia University Press, 1996, 317–356.

Berman, Paul. *A Tale of Two Utopias: The Political Journey of the Generation of 1968.* New York: W. W. Norton, 1996.

Terror and Liberalism. New York: W. W. Norton, 2004.

Blumenthal, Max. *Goliath: Life and Loathing in Greater Israel.* New York: Nation Books, 2013.

Boyer, Paul. *When Time Shall Be No More: Prophecy Belief in Modern American Culture.* Cambridge: Belknap Press, 1992.

Brint, Michael. *A Genealogy of Political Culture.* Boulder, CO: Westview Press, 1991.

Brog, David. *Standing with Israel.* Lake Mary, FL: FrontLine, 2006.

Brooks, Clem, and Jeff Manza. "A Great Divide? Religion and Political Change in U.S. National Elections, 1972–2000." *Sociological Quarterly* 45, no. 3 (2004): 421–450.

Brown, Robert McAfee. "Christians in the West Must Confront the Middle East." In Rosemary Ruther and Marc Ellis, eds., *Beyond Occupation: American Jewish, Christian, and Palestinian Voices for Peace.* Boston: Beacon Press, 1990, 138–154.

Bruckner, Pascal. *The Tyranny of Guilt: An Essay on Western Masochism.* Princeton, NJ: Princeton University Press, 2010.

Brzezinski, Zbigniew, and Brent Scowcroft. *America and the World: Conversations on the Future of American Foreign Policy.* New York: Basic Books, 2008.

Buchanan, Patrick. *A Republic, Not an Empire: Reclaiming America's Destiny.* Washington, DC: Regnery, 1999.

Bush, George W. *Decision Points.* New York: Crown, 2010.

Carson, Jamie L., Michael H. Crespin, Charles J. Finocchiaro, and David W. Rohde. "Redistricting and Party Polarization in the U.S. House of Representatives." *American Politics Research* 35, no. 6 (2007): 878–904.

Carter, Jimmy. *Palestine: Peace Not Apartheid.* New York: Simon and Schuster, 2006.

Chafets, Zev. *Match Made in Heaven: American Jews, Christian Zionists, and One Man's Exploration of the Weird and Wonderful Judeo-Evangelical Alliance.* New York: Harper Collins, 2007.

Chanes, Jerome A. "Antisemitism and Jewish Security in America Today." In Jerome A. Chanes, ed., *Antisemitism in America Today: Outspoken Experts Explode the Myths.* New York: Birch Lane Press, 1995.

Cherry, Conrad. *God's New Israel: Religious Interpretations of American Destiny.* Englewood Cliffs, NJ: Prentice Hall, 1971.

Chomsky, Noam. *Peace in the Middle East? Reflections on Justice and Nationhood.* New York: Vintage Books, 1974.

"The Israel Lobby?" ZNet, March 28, 2006. www.zcomm.org/znetarticle/the-israel-lobby-by-noam-chomsky.

Clark, Victoria. *Allies for Armageddon: The Rise of Christian Zionism.* New Haven, CT: Yale University Press, 2007.

Clarke, Duncan L., and Eric Flohr. "Christian Churches and the Palestine Question." *Journal of Palestine Studies* 21, no. 4 (1992): 67–79.

A Clean Break: A New Strategy for Securing the Realm. Washington, DC: Institute for Advanced Strategic and Political Studies, 1996.

Clifford, Clark, with Richard Holbrooke. *Counsel to the President: A Memoir.* New York: Random House, 1991.

Clinton, Bill. *My Life.* London: Hutchinson 2004.

Cohen, Ben. "The Persistence of Anti-Semitism on the British Left." *Jewish Political Studies Review* 16, no. 3–4 (2004): 157–169.

Cohen, Mitchell. "Anti-Semitism and the Left That Doesn't Learn." *Dissent,* Winter 2008): 47–51. http://dissentmagazine.org/article/?article=972.

Cohen, Naomi W. *American Jews and the Zionist Idea.* New York: Ktav, 1975.

Cohen, Nick. *What's Left? How Liberals Lost Their Way.* London: Fourth Estate, 2007.

Cohen, Renae. *The Palestinian Autonomy Agreement and Israel-PLO Recognition: A Survey of American Jewish Opinion.* New York: American Jewish Committee, 1994.

Cohen, Steven M. *Ties and Tensions: The 1986 Survey of American Jewish Attitudes toward Israel and Israelis.* New York: American Jewish Committee, 1987.

Ties and Tensions: An Update: The 1989 Survey of American Jewish Attitudes toward Israel and Israelis. New York: American Jewish Committee, 1989.

After the Gulf War: American Jews' Attitudes toward Israel: The 1991 National Survey of American Jews. New York: American Jewish Committee, 1992.

A Tale of Two Jewries: The "Inconvenient Truth" for American Jews. New York: Jewish Life Network/Steinhardt Foundation, November 2006.

"*Profiling the Professionals: Who's Serving Our Communities?" Jewish Communal Workers in North America: A Profile.* New York: New York University, Berman Jewish Policy Archive, Fall 2010. www.bjpa.org/Publications/downloadFile.cfm?FileID=7321.

Cohen, Steven M. and Sam Abrams. *"Israel off their Minds: The Diminished Place of Israel in the Political Thinking of Young Jews. "* New York: New York University, Berman Jewish Policy Archive, October 27, 2008. www.bjpa.org/Publications/details.cfm?PublicationID=207.

Cohen, Steven M. and Gerald B. Bubis. "*Post Zionist" Philanthropists: Emerging Attitudes of American Jewish Leaders toward Communal Allocations'.* Jerusalem: Jerusalem Center for Public Affairs, 1998. http://research.policyarchive.org/9712.pdf.

Cohen, Steven M. and Arnold Eisen. *The Jew Within: Self, Family, and Community in America.* Bloomington, IN: Indiana University Press, 2000.

Cohen, Steven M. and Ari Kelman. *Beyond Distancing: Young Adult American Jews and Their Alienation from Israel.* New York: Bronfman Philanthropies, 2008.

Cohen, Steven M. and Jack Wertheimer. "Whatever Happened to the Jewish People?" *Commentary,* June 2006: 33–43.

Cohen, Steven M., Sam Abrams, and Judith Veinstein. *"American Jews and the 2008 Presidential Election: As Democratic and Liberal as Ever?"* New York: New York University, Berman Jewish Policy Archive, October 20, 2008. www.bjpa.org/Publications/details.cfm?PublicationID=2444.

Coker, Christopher. *Reflections on American Foreign Policy since 1945.* London: Pinter, 1989.

Cordesman, Anthony, and Khalid R. Al-Rodhan. *The Changing Dynamics of Energy in the Middle East.* Westport, CT: Praeger Security International, 2006.

Costandi, Samia. "Resurrection in the Land of Resurrection." *Cornerstone* 21 (Spring 2001).

Cottee, Simon. "The Culture of Denial: Islamic Terrorism and the Delinquent Left." *Journal of Human Rights* 4, no. 1 (2005): 119–135.

Dalton, Russell J. *Citizen Politics in Western Democracies: Public Opinion and Political Parties in the United States, Great Britain, West Germany, and France.* 5th ed. Washington, DC: CQ Press, 2008.

Davis, Moshe. *America and the Holy Land.* Westport, CT: Praeger, 1995.

Decter, Midge. "Neocon Memoir." *American Jewish History* 87, no. 2–3 (1999): 183–194.

Doenecke, Justus D. "Non-Interventionism of the Left: The Keep America out of the War Congress, 1938–41.' *Journal of Contemporary History* 12, no. 2 (1977): 221–236.

Dorrien, Gary J. *The Neoconservative Mind: Politics, Culture, and the War of Ideology.* Philadelphia: Temple University Press, 1993.
  Imperial Designs: Neoconservatism and the New Pax Americana. London: Routledge, 2004.
  "Evangelical Ironies: Theology, Politics and Israel." In Alan Mittleman, Byron Johnson, and Nancy Isserman, eds., *Uneasy Allies? Evangelical and Jewish Relations.* Lanham, MD: Lexington Books, 2007, 103–126.
  "Christian Realism: Niebuhr's Theology, Ethics, and Politics." In Daniel Rice, ed., *Reinhold Niebuhr Revisited: Engagement with an American Original.* Grand Rapids, MI: Eerdmans, 2009, 21–39.

D'Souza, Dinesh. *Jerry Falwell: Before the Millennium: A Critical Biography.* Chicago: Regnery, 1984.

Dueck, Colin. *Reluctant Crusaders: Power, Culture, and Change in American Grand Strategy.* Princeton, NJ: Princeton University Press, 2006.
  Hard Line: The Republican Party and U.S. Foreign Policy since World War II. Princeton, NJ: Princeton University Press, 2010.

Duffield, John S. "Political Culture and State Behavior: Why Germany Confounds Neorealism." *International Organization* 53, no. 4 (1999): 765–803.

Eland, Ivan. "Israel and the United States." In Srdja Trifkovic, ed., *Peace in the Promised Land: A Realist Scenario.* Rockford, IL: Chronicles Press, 2006.

Elazar, Daniel J. *Community and Polity: The Organizational Dynamics of American Jewry.* Philadelphia: Jewish Publication Society, 1995.
  Covenant and Constitutionalism: The Great Frontier and the Matrix of Federal Democracy. New Brunswick, NJ: Transaction, 1998.

Entman, Robert M. *Projections of Power: Framing News, Public Opinion, and U.S. Foreign Policy.* Chicago: University of Chicago Press, 2004.

Falwell, Jerry. *Listen, America!* New York: Bantam Books, 1980.

Feaver, Peter. "What Is Grand Strategy and Why Do We Need It?" Foreign Policy, April 8, 2009. http://shadow.foreignpolicy.com/posts/2009/04/08/what_is_grand_strategy_and_why_do_we_need_it.

Feith, Douglas J. *War and Decision: Inside the Pentagon at the Dawn of the War on Terrorism.* New York: HarperCollins, 2008.

Felson, Ethan. 'On the Road: The Jewish Community Relations Encounter with Evangelical Christians.' In Alan Mittleman, Byron Johnson, and Nancy Isserman, eds., *Uneasy Allies? Evangelical and Jewish Relations.* Lanham, MD: Lexington Books, 2006.

Finkielkraut, Alain. "The Religion of Humanity and the Sin of the Jews." *Azure* 21 (Summer 2005): 23–32.

Fishman, Hertzel. *American Protestantism and a Jewish State.* Detroit, MI: Wayne State University Press, 1973.

Fleshler, Dan. *Transforming America's Israel Lobby: The Limits of its Power and the Potential for Change.* Washington, DC: Potomac Books, 2009.

Forbes, Bruce David. "How popular Are the Left Behind Books...and Why? A Discussion of Popular Culture." In Bruce David Forbes and Jeanne Halgren Kilde, eds, *Rapture, Revelation, and the End Times: Exploring the "Left Behind" Series.* New York: Palgrave Macmillan, 2004, 5–32.

Forster, Arnold. "American Radicals and Israel." In Robert S. Wistrich, ed., *The Left against Zion: Communism, Israel, and the Middle East.* London: Vallentine Mitchell, 1979, 221–225.

Frankel, Glenn. *Beyond the Promised Land: Jews and Arabs on the Hard Road to a New Israel.* New York: Simon and Schuster, 1994.

Freedman, Robert O. "George W. Bush, Barack Obama and the Arab-Israeli Conflict From 2001 to 2011." In Robert O. Freedman, ed., *Israel and the United States: Six Decades of U.S.-Israeli Relations.* Boulder, CO: Westview Press, 2012, 36–78.

Friedman, Thomas L. *From Beirut to Jerusalem.* New York: Farrar, Straus and Giroux, 1989.

Gallagher, Nancy. *Quakers in the Israeli–Palestinian Conflict: The Dilemmas of NGO Humanitarian Activism.* Cairo: American University in Cairo Press, 2007.

Galston, William A. "Incomplete Victory: The Rise of the New Democrats." In Peter Berkowitz, ed., *Varieties of Progressivism in America.* Stanford, CA: Hoover Institute Press, 2004, 59–85.

Gerges, Fawaz. *America and Political Islam: Clash of Cultures or Clash of Interests?* Cambridge: Cambridge University Press, 1999.

Gilboa, Eytan. *American Public Opinion toward Israel and the Arab-Israeli Conflict.* Lexington, MA: Lexington Books, 1987.

"Public Diplomacy: The Missing Component in Israel's Diplomacy." *Israel Affairs* 12, no. 4 (2006): 715–747.

Girvin, Brian. "Change and Continuity in Liberal Democratic Political Culture." In John Gibbens, ed., *Contemporary Political Culture: Politics in a Postmodern Age.* London: Sage, 1989, 31–59.

Glenn, Susan A. "The Vogue of Jewish Self-Hatred in Post–World War II America." *Jewish Social Studies* 12, no. 3 (2006): 95–136.

Goldberg, David Howard. *Foreign Policy and Ethnic Interest Groups: American and Canadian Jews Lobby for Israel.* Westport, CT: Greenwood Press, 1990.

Goldberg, J. J. *Jewish Power: Inside the American Jewish Establishment*. Reading, MA: Addison-Wesley, 1996.

Golden, Peter. *Quiet Diplomat: A Biography of Max M. Fisher*. New York: Cornwell Books, 1992.

Goldman, Shalom. *God's Sacred Tongue: Hebrew and the American Imagination*. Chapel Hill, NC: University of North Carolina Press, 2004.

Gorenberg, Gershon. *The End of Days: Fundamentalism and the Struggle for the Temple Mount*. Oxford: Oxford University Press, 2000.

Gottfried, Paul. "Paleoconservatism." In Bruce Frohnen, Jeremy Beer, and Jeffrey O. Nelson, eds., *American Conservatism: An Encyclopedia*. Wilmington, DE: ISI Books, 2006.

Green, John. "The American Religious Landscape and Political Attitudes: A Baseline for 2004." Akron, OH: University of Akron, Ray C. Bliss Institute of Applied Politics, no date. www.uakron.edu/bliss/research/archives/2004/Religious_Landscape_2004.pdf.

"The American Public and Sympathy for Israel: Present and Future." *Journal of Ecumenical Studies* 44, no. 1 (2009): 107–121.

Green, John and Steven Waldman. "The Twelve Tribes of American Politics." Beliefnet, October 2004. www.beliefnet.com/News/Politics/2004/10/The-Twelve-Tribes-Of-American-Politics.aspx.

Greenberg, Anna, and Kenneth D. Wald. "Still Liberal after All These Years? The Contemporary Political Behavior of American Jewry." In L. Sandy Maisel and Ira N. Forman, eds., *Jews in American Politics*. Lanham, MD: Rowman and Littlefield, 2001.

Greenberg, Stanley, and Kate Monninger. *Messaging the Challenging Friendship: How to Address U.S.-Israel Relations with Mainstream Democrats*. Washington, DC: Greenberg Quinlan Rosner Research for the Israel Project, February 2011.

Gregerman, Adam. "Old Wine in New Bottles: Liberation Theology and the Israeli-Palestinian Conflict." *Journal of Ecumenical Studies* 41, no. 3–4 (2004): 313–340.

Grose, Peter. *Israel in the Mind of America*. New York: Knopf, 1983.

Gross, Marissa. "The Salute to Israel Parade." Jerusalem: Jerusalem Center for Public Affairs, June 1, 2008. http://jcpa.org/article/the-salute-to-Israel-parade/.

Grossman, Lawrence. "Jewish Communal Affairs." In David Singer and Ruth R. Seldin, eds., *American Jewish Year Book*, vol. 92. New York: American Jewish Committee, 1993, 238–260.

"Jewish Communal Affairs." In David Singer and Lawrence Grossman, eds., *American Jewish Year Book*, vol. 107. New York: American Jewish Committee, 2007, 111–132.

"The Organized Jewish Community and Evangelical America." In Alan Mittleman, Byron Johnson, and Nancy Isserman, eds., *Uneasy Allies? Evangelical and Jewish Relations*. Lanham, MD: Lexington Books, 2007, 49–72.

Gruen, George E. "The United States and Israel: Impact of the Lebanon War." In Milton Himmelfarb and David Singer, eds., *American Jewish Year Book*, vol. 84. Philadelphia: Jewish Publication Society, 1983, 73–103.

"Israel and the American Jewish Community." In Robert O. Freedman, ed., *Israel's First Fifty Years*. Gainesville, FL: University Press of Florida, 2000, 29–66.

Guth, James. *The Bush Administration, American Religious Politics and Middle East Policy*. Paper presented at the annual meeting of the American Political Science Association, Chicago, September 2, 2004.

Religious Leadership and Support for Israel: A Study of Clergy in Nineteen Denominations. Paper presented at the annual meeting of the Southern Political Science Association, New Orleans, January 2007.

Guth, James and William Kenan Jr. *Religious Factors and American Public Support for Israel: 1992–2008.* Paper presented at the annual meeting of the American Political Science Association, Seattle, WA, September 1–4, 2011.

Hadar, Leon T. *Quagmire: America in the Middle East.* Washington, DC: Cato Institute, 1992.

"What Green Peril." *Foreign Affairs* 72, no. 2 (Spring 1993): 27–42.

Sandstorm: Policy Failure in the Middle East. New York: Palgrave Macmillan, 2005.

Hagee, John. *Final Dawn over Jerusalem.* Nashville: Thomas Nelson, 1998.

Jerusalem Countdown. Lake Mary, FL: FrontLine, 2006.

Hale, Dennis. *Why the Left Abandoned Israel, Reclaiming Liberal Support for Israel.* Speech delivered at Harvard University for the David Project, March 13, 2003.

Halperin, Samuel. *The Political World of American Zionism.* Silver Spring, MD: Information Dynamics, 1985.

Halsell, Grace. *Prophecy and Politics: Militant Evangelists on the Road to Nuclear War.* Westport, CT: Lawrence Hill, 1986.

Haynes, Stephen R. *Reluctant Witnesses: Jews and the Christian Imagination.* Louisville, KY: Westminster/John Knox Press, 1995.

Heer, Jeet. "Goldberg's 'Fascism' and the Real Thing." Sans Everything (blog), December 20, 2007. http://sanseverything.wordpress.com/2007/12/20/goldbergs-fascism-and-the-real-thing/.

"When Conservatives Loved the Palestinians." Sans Everything (blog), February 25, 2008. http://sanseverything.wordpress.com/2008/02/25/when-conservatives-loved-the-palestinians/.

Heilbrunn, Jacob. *They Knew They Were Right: The Rise of the Neocons.* New York: Anchor, 2009.

Heilman, Samuel C. *Sliding to the Right: The Contest for the Future of American Jewish Orthodoxy.* Berkeley: University of California Press, 2006.

Heinze, Eric, and Rosa Freedman. "Public Awareness of Human Rights: Distortions in the Mass Media." *International Journal of Human Rights* 14, no. 4 (2006): 491–523.

Helmreich, Jeffrey S. "The Israel Swing Factor: How the American Jewish Vote Influences U.S. Elections." *Jerusalem Letter / Viewpoints*, 446 (January 15, 2001). http://research.policyarchive.org/18018.pdf.

Hessel, Dieter T., ed. *The Church's Public Role: Retrospect and Prospect.* Grand Rapids, MI: Eerdmans, 1993.

Heywood, Andrew. *Political Ideologies: An Introduction*, 2nd ed. New York: St Martin's Press, 1998.

Himmelfarb, Gertrude. *The People of the Book: Philosemitism in England from Cromwell to Churchill.* New York: Encounter, 2011.

Holden, Kurt. "Clinton's Tilt toward Israel Losing Public Opinion Support." *Washington Report on Middle East Affairs* 16, no. 1 (June–July 1997): 50–54.

Hollander, Paul. *Anti-Americanism: Critiques at Home and Abroad, 1965–1990.* New York: Oxford University Press, 1992.

Hollander, Paul. , ed. *Understanding Anti-Americanism: It's Origins and Impact at Home and Abroad.* Chicago: Ivan R. Dee, 2004.

Horowitz, Bethamie. *Connections and Journeys: Assessing Critical Opportunities for Enhancing Jewish Identity* New York: UJA–Federation of Jewish Philanthropies of New York, 2000, revised 2003. www.levyinstitute.org/pubs/CP/AJP_conf_octo6_files/papers/Benthamie_Horowitz.pdf.

Hudson, Valerie M., ed. *Culture and Foreign Policy.* Boulder, CO: Lynne Rienner, 1997.

Hughes, Richard T. *Myths America Lives By.* Urbana, IL: University of Illinois Press, 2003.

Huntington, Samuel. *Who Are We? The Challenges to America's National Identity.* New York: Simon and Schuster, 2004.

  ed. *The Church's Public Role: Retrospect and Prospect.* Grand Rapids, MI: W.B. Eerdmans, 1993.

Ikenberry, G. John. "An Agenda for Liberal International Renewal." In Michele A. Flourney and Shawn Brimley, eds. *Finding Our Way: Debating American Grand Strategy.* Washington, DC: Center for a New American Security, 2008, 43–60.

Ikenberry, G. John and Anne-Marie Slaughter. *Forging a World of Liberty under Law: U.S. National Security in the 21st Century: Final Report of the Princeton Project on National Security.* Princeton, NJ: Princeton University, Woodrow Wilson School of Public and International Affairs, 2006.

Ikenberry, G. John, Thomas Knock, Anne-Marie Slaughter, and Tony Smith. *The Crisis of American Foreign Policy: Wilsonianism in the Twenty-First Century.* Princeton, NJ: Princeton University Press, 2009.

Indyk, Martin. *Innocents Abroad: An Intimate Account of American Peace Diplomacy in the Middle East.* New York: Simon and Schuster, 2009.

Inglehart, Ronald. *Modernization and Postmodernization: Cultural, Economic, and Political Change in 43 Societies.* Princeton, NJ: Princeton University Press, 1997.

Isaac, Jeffrey C. "The Poverty of Progressivism and the Tragedy of Civil Society." In Peter Berkowitz, ed., *Varieties of Progressivism in America.* Stanford, CA: Hoover Institution Press, 2004, 145–188.

Israel, Sherry. *Comprehensive Report on the 1995 Demographic Study.* Boston: Combined Jewish Philanthropies, 1997.

Jepperson, Ronald L., Alexander Wendt, and Peter J. Katzenstein. "Norms, Identity, and Culture in National Security." In Peter J. Katzenstein, ed., *The Culture of National Security: Norms and Identity in World Politics.* New York: Columbia University Press, 1996, 33–75.

Johnson, Robert. *The Peace Progressives and American Foreign Relations.* Cambridge: Harvard University Press, 1995.

Jones, Robert, and Daniel Cox. *Clergy Voices: Findings from the 2008 Mainline Protestant Clergy Voices Survey.* Washington, DC: Public Religion Research, 2009.

Judaken, Jonathan. "Sartre at 100: Revisiting His Interventions in the Arab-Israeli Conflict." *Antisemitism International* 3–4 (2006): 94–102.

Judis, John B. *Genesis: Truman, American Jews, and the Origins of the Arab/Israeli Conflict.* New York: Farrar, Straus and Giroux, 2014.

Kaarbo, Juliet. "Foreign Policy Analysis in the Twenty-First Century: Back to Comparison, Forward to Identity and Ideas." *International Studies Review* 5, no. 2 (2003): 156–163.

Kadushin, Charles, Shaul Kelner, and Leonard Saxe. *Being a Jewish Teenager in America: Trying to Make It.* Waltham, MA: Brandeis University, Cohen Center for Modern Jewish Studies, 2000.

Kaplan, Edward, and Charles Small. "Anti-Israel Sentiment Predicts Anti-Semitism in Europe." *Journal of Conflict Resolution* 50, no. 4 (2006): 548–561.

Kaplan, Esther. *With God on Their Side: How Christian Fundamentalists Trampled Science, Policy, and Democracy in George Bush's White House.* New York: New Press, 2004.

Kaplan, Robert D. *The Arabists: The Romance of an American Elite.* New York: Free Press, 1995.

Karmon, Ely. "Hizballah and the Antiglobalization Movement: A New Coalition?" *Policywatch* 949, (January 27, 2005). www.washingtoninstitute.org/policy-analysis/view/hizballah-and-the-anitglobalization-movement-a-new-coalition.

Katulis, Brian, Marc Lynch, and Robert C. Adler. "Window of Opportunity for a Two-State Solution: Policy Recommendations to the Obama Administration on the Israeli-Palestinian Front." *Center for American Progress* (July 15, 2009). www.americanprogress.org/issues/security/report/2009/07/15/6412/window-of-opportunity-for-a-two-state-solution/.

Katzenstein, Peter J. "Introduction: Alternative Perspectives on National Security." In Peter J. Katzenstein, ed., *The Culture of National Security: Norms and Identity in World Politics.* New York: Columbia University Press, 1996, 1–32.

Kellstedt, Lyman A., Corwin E. Smidt, John C. Green, and James L. Guth. "A Gentle Stream or a 'River Glorious'? The Religious Left in the 2004 Election." In David E. Campbell, ed., *A Matter of Faith: Religion in the 2004 Presidential Election.* Washington DC: Brookings Institution Press, 2007, 232–256.

Kerr, Malcolm. *The Arab Cold War: Gamal Abd al-Nasir and His Rivals, 1958–1970.* Oxford: Oxford University Press, 1971.

Khawaja, Irfan. "Essentialism, Consistency and Islam: A Critique of Edward Said's *Orientalism.*" *Israel Affairs* 13, no. 4 (2007): 689–713.

Klingenstein, Susanne. "It's Splendid When the Town Whore Gets Religion and Joins the Church: The Rise of the Jewish Neoconservatives as Observed by the Paleoconservatives in the 1980s." *Shofar: An Interdisciplinary Journal of Jewish Studies* 21, no. 3 (2003): 83–98.

Kohut, Andrew, and Bruce Stokes. *America Against the World: How We Are Different and Why We Are Disliked.* New York: Henry Holt, 2006.

Korn, Eugene. "Divestment from Israel, the Liberal Churches, and Jewish Responses: A Strategic Analysis." *Post-Holocaust and Anti-Semitism* 52 (January 2007). http://jcpa.org/article/divestment-from-the-liberal-churches-and-jewish-responses-a-strategic-analysis/.

Kosmin, Barry A. "The Changing Population Profile of American Jews, 1990–2008." Paper presented at the Fifteenth World Congress of Jewish Studies, Jerusalem, August 2009. www.jewishdatabank.org/studies/downloadFile.cfm?FileID=3040.

Kosmin, Barry A. and Ariela Keysar. *American Religious Identification Survey 2008: Summary Report.* Hartford, CT: Trinity College, 2009.

Kramer, Martin. *Ivory Towers on Sand: The Failure of Middle Eastern Studies in America.* Washington, DC: Washington Institute for Near East Policy, 2001.

Kuebler, Elisabeth. "Holocaust Remembrance in the Council of Europe: Deplorable Victims and Evil Ideologies without Perpetrators." *Jewish Political Studies Review* 22, no. 3–4 (Fall 2010): 45–58.

Kupchan, Charles A., and Peter L. Trubowitz, "Dead Center: The Demise of Liberal Internationalism in the United States." *International Security* 32, no. 2 (2007): 7–44.

Kurtz, Lester, and Kelly Goran Fulton. "Love Your Enemies? Protestants and United States Foreign Policy." In Robert Wuthnow and John H. Evans, eds., *The Quiet Hand of God: Faith-Based Activism and the Public Role of Mainline Protestantism.* Berkeley: University of California Press, 2002, 364–380.

Kurtzer, Daniel. "American Policy, Strategy, and Tactics." In Daniel Kurtzer, ed., *Pathways to Peace: America and the Arab-Israeli Conflict.* New York: Palgrave Macmillan: 2012, vi–xii.

Kurtzer, Daniel and Scott Lasensky. *Negotiating Arab-Israeli Peace: American Leadership in the Middle East.* Washington, DC: United States Institute of Peace Press, 2008.

Kushner, Tony and Alisa Solomon, eds. *Wrestling with Zion: Progressive Jewish-American Responses to the Israeli-Palestinian Conflict.* New York: Grove Press, 2003.

Landau, David. *Who is a Jew? A Case Study of American Jewish Influence on Israeli Policy.* New York: American Jewish Committee, 1996.

Lazin, Fred A. *The Struggle for Soviet Jewry in American Politics: Israel versus the American Jewish Establishment.* Lanham, MD: Lexington Books, 2005.

Levick, Adam. "Anti-Israelism and Anti-Semitism in Progressive U.S. Blogs/News Websites: Influential and Poorly Monitored." *Post-Holocaust and Anti-Semitism* 92 (January 2010). http//jcpa.org/article/anti-israelism-and-anti-semitism-in-progressive-U-S-blogs-news/.

Lieberman, Robert C. "The 'Israel Lobby' and American Politics." *Perspectives on Politics* 7, no. 2 (2009): 235–257.

Liebman, Charles. *The Ambivalent American Jew: Politics, Religion, and Family in American Jewish Life.* Philadelphia: Jewish Publication Society, 1973.
    Pressure without Sanctions: The Influence of World Jewry on Israeli Policy. Rutherford, NJ: Fairleigh Dickinson University Press, 1977.

Lieven, Anatol. *America, Right or Wrong: An Anatomy of American Nationalism.* New York: Oxford University Press, 2004.

Lind, Michael. "American Strategy Project – Grand Strategy No. 1." New America Foundation (March 2003). http://asp.newamerica.net/publications/policy/american_strategy_project_grand_strategy_no_1.

Lindner, Eileen, ed. *Yearbook of American and Canadian Churches 2006.* Nashville: Abingdon Press, 2006.

Lindsay, D. Michael. *Faith in the Halls of Power: How Evangelicals Joined the American Elite.* Oxford: Oxford University Press, 2007.

Linenthal, Edward T. "Locating Holocaust Memory: The United States Holocaust Memorial Museum." In David Chidester and Edward T. Linenthal, eds., *American Sacred Space.* Bloomington, IN: Indiana University Press, 1995, 220–262.

Lipset, Seymour Martin. "The Socialism of Fools: The Left, the Jews, and Israel." *Encounter* 33, no. 6 (1969): 24–35.
    American Exceptionalism: A Double-Edged Sword. New York: W. W. Norton, 1997.

Luntz, Frank. *Israel in the Age of Eminem: A Creative Brief for Israeli Messaging.* New York: Bronfman Philanthropies, 2003.
    America 2020: How the Next Generation Views Israel. Washington, DC: The Israel Project, 2004.

McAlister, Melani. *Epic Encounters: Culture, Media, and U.S. Interests in the Middle East, 1945–2000*. Berkeley: University of California Press, 2001.

McDermott, Gerald. 'Evangelicals and Israel.' In Alan Mittleman, Byron Johnson, and Nancy Isserman, eds., *Uneasy Allies? Evangelical and Jewish Relations*. Lanham, MD: Lexington Books, 2007, 129–132.

McGovern, George. *The Essential America: Our Founders and the Liberal Tradition*. New York: Simon and Schuster, 2004.

Makovsky, David. *Making Peace with the PLO: Policy and Politics in the Rabin Government*. Boulder, CO: Westview Press, 1995.

Mann, James. *Rise of the Vulcans: The History of Bush's War Cabinet*. London: Penguin Books, 2004.

    The Obamians: The Struggle inside the White House to Redefine American Power. New York: Viking, 2012.

Mansour, Camille. *Beyond Alliance: Israel and U.S. Foreign Policy*. Translated from the French by James A. Cohen. New York: Columbia University Press, 1993.

Marsden, George M. *Understanding Fundamentalism and Evangelicalism*. Grand Rapids, MI: Eerdmans, 1991.

Mart, Michelle. *Eye on Israel: How America Came to View Israel as an Ally*. Albany, NY: State University of New York Press, 2006.

    "Eleanor Roosevelt, Liberalism, and Israel." *Shofar: An Interdisciplinary Journal of Jewish Studies* 24, no. 3 (2006): 58–89.

Mayer, Jeremy D. "Christian Fundamentalists and Public Opinion toward the Middle East: Israel's New Best Friends?" *Social Science Quarterly* 85, no. 3 (2004): 695–713.

Mead, Walter Russell. "The Jacksonian Tradition." *National Interest* 58 (Winter 1999–2000): 5–29.

    Special Providence: American Foreign Policy and How It Changed the World. New York: Routledge, 2002.

    '"The New Israel and the Old: Why Gentile Americans Back the Jewish State." *Foreign Affairs* 87, no. 4 (July–August 2008): 28–46.

    "The Tea Party and American Foreign Policy." *Foreign Affairs* 90, no. 2 (March–April 2011): 28–44.

Mearsheimer, John J., and Stephen M. Walt. *The Israel Lobby and U.S. Foreign Policy*. New York: Farrar, Straus and Giroux, 2007.

Mellman, Mark S., Aaron Strauss, and Kenneth D. Wald. *Jewish American Voting Behavior, 1972–2008: Just the Facts*. Washington, DC: Solomon Project, 2012.

Merkley, Paul Charles. *The Politics of Christian Zionism, 1891–1948*. London: Frank Cass, 1998.

    American Presidents, Religion, and Israel: The Heirs of Cyrus. Westport, CT: Praeger, 2004.

    Christian Attitudes towards the State of Israel. Montreal: McGill-Queens University Press, 2007.

Micklethwait, John, and Adrian Wooldridge. *God Is Back: How the Global Revival of Faith Is Changing the World*. London: Penguin Press, 2009.

Miller, Aaron David. *The Much Too Promised Land: America's Elusive Search for Arab-Israeli Peace*. New York: Bantam Books, 2009.

Morris, Benny. *Righteous Victims: A History of the Zionist-Arab Conflict, 1881–1999*. London: John Murray, 2000.

Morris, Stephen. "Whitewashing Dictatorship in Communist Vietnam and Cambodia." In Peter Collier and David Horowitz, eds., *The Anti-Chomsky Reader*. San Francisco: Encounter Books, 2004, 1–29.

Nash, George. "Forgotten Godfathers: Premature Jewish Conservatives and the Rise of *National Review*." *American Jewish History* 8, no. 2–3 (1999): 123–157.

Nau, Henry R. *At Home Abroad: Identity and Power in American Foreign Policy*. Ithaca, NY: Cornell University Press, 2002.

"Conservative Internationalism." *Policy Review* 150 (August–September 2008): 3–44.

Conservative Internationalism: Armed Diplomacy under Jefferson, Polk, Truman, and Reagan. Princeton, NJ: Princeton University Press, 2013.

Naveh, Eyal. "Unconventional 'Christian Zionist': The Theologian Reinhold Niebuhr and His Attitude toward the Jewish National Movement." *Studies in Zionism* 11, no. 2 (1990): 183–196.

Nelson, Erik R., and Alan F. H. Wisdom. *Human Rights Advocacy in the Mainline Protestant Churches (2000–2003): A Critical Analysis*. Washington DC: Institute on Religion and Democracy, 2004.

Neumann, Michael. *The Case against Israel*. Petrolia, CA: CounterPunch, 2005.

Niezen, Ronald. "Postcolonialism and the Utopian Imagination." *Israel Affairs* 13, no. 4 (2007): 714–729.

Norwood, Stephen H. *Antisemitism and the American Far Left*. Cambridge: Cambridge University Press, 2013.

Novik, Nimrod. *The United States and Israel: Domestic Determinants of a Changing U.S. Commitment*. Boulder, CO: Westview Press, 1986.

Oldmixon, Elizabeth A., Beth A. Rosenson, and Kenneth D. Wald. "Conflict over Israel: The Role of Religion, Race, Party, and Ideology in the U.S. House of Representatives, 1997–2002." *Terrorism and Political Violence* 17, no. 3 (2005): 407–426.

Olson, Laura R. 'Whither the Religious Left? Religiopolitical Progressivism in Twenty-First-Century America.' In J. Matthew Wilson, ed., *From Pews to Polling Places: Faith and Politics in the American Religious Mosaic*. Washington, DC: Georgetown University Press, 2007, 53–80.

Oppenheim, Fern. "*The Segmentation Study of the American Market, Fourth Quarter 2010*." New York: Brand Israel Group and the Conference of Presidents of Major American Jewish Organizations, 2010.

Oren, Michael B. *Power, Faith, and Fantasy: America in the Middle East, 1776 to the Present*. New York: W. W. Norton, 2007.

Organski, A. F. K. *The $36 Billion Bargain: Strategy and Politics in U.S. Assistance to Israel*. New York: Columbia University Press, 1990.

Ottolenghi, Emanuele. 'Making Sense of European Anti-Semitism.' *Human Rights Review* 8, no. 2 (2007): 104–126.

Perlmann, Joel. *American Jewish Opinion about the Future of the West Bank: A Reanalysis of American Jewish Committee Surveys*. Working Paper No. 526. Annandale-on-Hudson, NY: Bard College, Levy Economics Institute, December 2007.

Phillips, Benjamin, Eszter Lengyel, and Leonard Saxe. *American Attitudes toward Israel*. Waltham, MA: Brandeis University, Cohen Center for Modern Jewish Studies, 2002.

Pickett, Winston. "Nasty or Nazi? The Use of Anti-Semitic Topoi by the Left-Liberal Media." In Paul Iganski and Barry Kosmin, eds., *A New Antisemitism? Debating Judeophobia in 21st-Century Britain*. London: Profile Books, 2003, 149–166.

Pipes, Daniel. "Interview with James A. Baker III: Looking Back on the Middle East." *Middle East Quarterly* 1, no. 3 (September 1994): 83–86. Available at www.daniel-pipes.org/6304/looking-back-on-the-middle-east-james-a-baker.

Podhoretz, Norman. *World War IV: The Long Struggle against Islamofascism.* New York: Doubleday, 2007.

Pollack, Kenneth M. *A Path out of the Desert: A Grand Strategy for America in the Middle East.* New York: Random House, 2008.

Pye, Lucian W. 'Political Culture.' In David L. Sills and Robert King Merton, eds., *International Encyclopedia of the Social Sciences.* New York: Macmillan, 1968, 218.

Quandt, William. *Peace Process.* 3rd ed. Washington, DC: Brookings Institution Press, 2005.

Raffel, Martin. "History of Israel Advocacy." In Alan Mittleman, Jonathan Sarna, and Robert Licht, eds., *Jewish Polity and American Civil Society: Communal Agencies and Religious Movements in the American Public Sphere.* New York: Rowman and Littlefield, 2002, 103–179.

Reagan, Ronald. *An American Life.* London: Hutchison, 1990.

Reichley, James. *Religion in American Public Life.* Washington, DC: Brookings Institution, 1985.

Riedel, Bruce O. *The Search for Al Qaeda: Its Leadership, Ideology, and Future.* Washington, DC: Brookings Institution Press, 2008.

Robertson, D. B., ed. *Love and Justice: Selections from the Shorter Writings of Reinhold Niebuhr.* Louisville, KY: Westminster/John Knox Press, 1957.

Robertson, Pat. *The Collected Works of Pat Robertson: The New Millennium, the New World Order, the Secret Kingdom.* New York: Inspirational Press, 1994.

Rose, Gideon. "Neoclassical Realism and Theories of Foreign Policy." *World Politics* 51, no. 1 (1998): 144–172.

Rosenfeld, Alvin H. *Anti-Zionism in Great Britain and Beyond: A "Respectable" Anti-Semitism?* New York: American Jewish Committee, 2004.

   "Progressive" Jewish Thought and the New Anti-Semitism. New York: American Jewish Committee, 2006.

Rosenson, Beth A., Elizabeth A. Oldmixon, and Kenneth D. Wald. "U.S. Senators' Support for Israel Examined Through Sponsorship/Cosponsorship Decisions, 1993–2002: The Influence of Elite and Constituent Factors." *Foreign Policy Analysis* 5, no. 1 (2009): 73–91.

Rosenthal, Steven T. *Irreconcilable Differences? The Waning of the American Jewish Love Affair with Israel.* Hanover, NH: University Press of New England, 2001.

Ross, Dennis. "Taking Stock." *National Interest* 73 (Fall 2003): 11–21. http://nationalinterest.org/article/taking-stock-328.

   The Missing Peace: The Inside Story of the Fight for Middle East Peace. New York: Farrar, Straus and Giroux, 2005.

   Statecraft: And How to Restore America's Standing in the World. New York: Farrar, Straus and Giroux, 2007.

Ross, Dennis and David Makovsky. *Myths, Illusions and Peace: Finding a New Direction for America in the Middle East.* New York: Viking, 2009.

Rowland. Christopher, ed. *The Cambridge Companion to Liberation Theology.* Cambridge: Cambridge University Press, 1999.

Rubenstein, Richard. "Some Reflections on 'The Odd Couple': A Reply to Martin Marty." *Journal of Ecumenical Studies* 44, no. 1 (2009): 136–140.

Rubin, Barry. *Secrets of State: The State Department and the Struggle Over U.S. Foreign Policy*. New York: Oxford University Press, 1987.

Rudin, James. *A Jewish Guide to Interreligious Relations*. New York: American Jewish Committee 2005.

Ruether, Rosemary Radford. 'The Occupation Must End.' In Rosemary Radford Ruether and Marc Ellis, eds., *Beyond Occupation: American Jewish, Christian, and Palestinian Voices for Peace*. Boston: Beacon Press, 1990, 183–197.

"False Messianism and Prophetic Consciousness: Towards a Liberation Theology of Jewish-Christianity Solidarity." In Otto Maduro, ed., *Judaism, Christianity and Liberation: An Agenda for Dialogue*. New York: Orbis Books, 1991, 83–95.

Ruthven, Malise. *Fundamentalism: The Search for Meaning*. Oxford: Oxford University Press, 2005.

Rynhold, Jonathan. "Labour, Likud, the 'Special Relationship,' and the Peace Process, 1988–96." *Israel Affairs* 3, no. 3–4 (1997): 239–262.

Israeli Political Culture in Israel's Relations with the United States over the Palestinian Question, 1981–1996. PhD. diss., London School of Economics and Political Science, 1998.

"Making Sense of Tragedy: Barak, the Israeli Left and the Oslo Peace Process." *Israel Studies Forum* 19, no. 1 (2003): 9–33.

"Behind the Rhetoric: President Bush and U.S. Policy on the Israeli-Palestinian Conflict." *American Diplomacy* 10, no. 4 (2005): 1–23.

"Israeli Foreign and Defence Policy and Diaspora Jewish Identity." In Danny Ben-Moshe and Zohar Segev, eds., *Israel, the Diaspora, and Jewish Identity*. Brighton, UK: Sussex Academic Press, 2007, 144–157.

"Cultural Shift and Foreign Policy Change: Israel and the Making of the Oslo Accords." *Cooperation and Conflict* 42, no. 4 (2007): 419–440.

"The U.S. and the Middle East Peace Process: Conflict Management vs. Conflict Resolution." In Efraim Inbar and Eytan Gilboa, eds., *U.S.-Israeli Relations in a New Era: Issues and Challenges after 9/11*. London: Routledge, 2009, 140–157.

"The Meaning of the UK Campaign for an Academic Boycott of Israel." *MERIA Journal* 14, no. 2 (June 2010): 15–21. www.gloria-center.org/2010/06/rynhold-2010-06-04/.

"Is the Pro-Israel Lobby a Block on Reaching a Comprehensive Peace Settlement in the Middle East?" *Israel Studies Forum* 25, no. 1 (2010): 29–49.

"The German Question in Central and Eastern Europe and the Long Peace in Europe after 1945: An Integrated Theoretical Explanation." *Review of International Studies* 37, no. 1 (2010): 249–275.

'The Republican Primaries and the Israel Acid Test: The Israel Acid Test.' *BESA Perspectives* (February 15, 2012). www.biu.ac.il/SOC/besa/docs/perspectives165.pdf.

Rynhold, Jonathan and Jonathan Spyer. "British Policy in the Arab-Israeli Arena, 1973–2004." *British Journal of Middle Eastern Studies* 34, no. 2 (2007): 137–155.

Rynhold, Jonathan and Dov Waxman. "Ideological Change and Israel's Disengagement from Gaza." *Political Science Quarterly* 123, no. 1 (2008): 11–37.

Sacks, Jonathan. *The Home We Build Together: Recreating Society*. London: Continuum, 2009.

Sandeen, Ernest R. *The Roots of Fundamentalism: British and American Millenarianism, 1800–1930*. Chicago: University of Chicago Press, 1970.

Sarna, Jonathan. *American Judaism: A History*. New Haven, CT: Yale University Press, 2004.

Sasson, Theodore. *The New Realism: American Jews' Views about Israel*. New York: American Jewish Committee, 2009.

    'Mass Mobilization to Direct Engagement: American Jews' Changing Relationship to Israel.' *Israel Studies* 15, no. 2 (2010): 173–195.

    The New American Zionism. New York: New York University Press, 2014.

Sasson, Theodore, Charles Kadushin, and Leonard Saxe. *Trends in American Jewish Attachment to Israel: An Assessment of the "Distancing" Hypothesis*. Waltham, MA: Brandeis University, Cohen Center for Modern Jewish Studies, 2008.

Sasson, Theodore, Benjamin Phillips, Charles Kadushin, and Leonard Saxe. *Still Connected: American Jewish Attitudes about Israel*. Waltham, MA: Brandeis University, Cohen Center for Modern Jewish Studies, August 2010.

Sasson, Theodore, Benjamin Phillips, Graham Wright, Charles Kadushin, and Leonard Saxe. 'Understanding Young Adult Attachment to Israel: Period, Lifecycle, and Generational Dynamics' *Contemporary Jewry* 32, no. 1 (2012): 67–84.

Saxe, Leonard, Theodore Sasson, and Shahar Hecht. *Taglit-Birthright Israel: Impact on Jewish Identity, Peoplehood and Connection to Israel*. Waltham, MA: Brandeis University, Cohen Center for Modern Jewish Studies, 2006.

Saxe, Leonard, Benjamin Phillips, Theodore Sasson, Shahar Hecht, Michelle Shain, Graham Wright, and Charles Kadushin. *Generation Birthright Israel: The Impact of an Israel Experience on Jewish Identity and Choices*. Waltham, MA: Brandeis University, Cohen Center for Modern Jewish Studies, 2009.

    Israel at War: The Impact of Peer-Oriented Israel Programs on Responses of American Jewish Young Adults. Waltham, MA: Brandeis Univeristy, Cohen Center for Modern Jewish Studies, 2006.

Saxe, Leonard, Elizabeth Tighe, Benjamin Phillips, and Charles Kadishin. *Reconsidering the Size and Characteristics of the American Jewish Population: New Estimates of a Larger and More Diverse Community*. Waltham, MA: Brandeis University, Steinhardt Social Research Institute, 2007.

Schalit, Joel. *Israel vs. Utopia*. New York: Akashic Books, 2009.

Schrag, Carl. "American Jews and Evangelical Christians: Anatomy of a Changing Relationship." *Jewish Political Studies Review* 17, no. 1–2 (2005): 171–181.

    Ripples from the Matzav: Grassroots Responses of American Jewry to the Situation in Israel. New York: American Jewish Committee, 2004.

Scotchie, Joseph, ed. *The Paleoconservatives: New Voices of the Old Right*. New Brunswick, NJ: Transaction, 1999.

Seliktar, Ofira. *Divided We Stand: American Jews, Israel, and the Peace Process*. Westport, CT: Praeger, 2002.

Shafner Posy, Naava. *Jewish American Activists: The Melting Pot for American, Israel and Jewish Identities*, Seminar paper, Bar-Ilan University, Department of Political Science, Ramat Gan, 2010.

Shain, Yossi. "Jewish Kinship at a Crossroads: Lessons for Homelands and Diasporas." *Political Science Quarterly* 117, no. 2 (2002): 279–309.

Shain, Yossi and Barry Bristman. "Diaspora, Kinship, and Loyalty: The Renewal of Jewish National Security." *International Affairs* 78, no. 1 (2002): 69–95.

Shapiro, Robert Y., and Yaeli Bloch-Elkon. "Foreign Policy, Meet the People." *National Interest* 97 (September–October 2008): 37–42.

Shenhav, Shaul, Tamir Sheafer, and Itay Gabay. "Incoherent Narrator: Israeli Public Diplomacy during the Disengagement and the Elections in the Palestinian Authority." *Israel Studies* 15, no. 3 (2010): 143–162.

Sheskin, Ira. "Four Questions about American Jewish Demography." *Jewish Political Studies Review* 20, no. 1–2 (2008): 23–42.

Shindler, Colin. *Ploughshares into Swords? Israelis and Jews in the Shadow of the Intifada*. London: I. B. Taurus, 1991.

"Likud and the Christian Dispensationalists: A Symbolic Relationship." *Israel Studies* 5, no. 1 (2000): 153–182.

"Reading The Guardian: Jews, Israel-Palestine and the Origins of Irritation." In Tudor Parfitt and Yulia Egorova, eds., *Jews, Muslims and Mass Media: Mediating the "Other"*. London: RoutledgeCurzon, 2003, 157–177.

Israel and the European Left: Between Solidarity and Delegitimization. New York: Continuum, 2012.

Sicher, Efraim. "The Image of Israel and Postcolonial Discourse in the Early 21st Century: A View from Britain." *Israel Studies* 16, no. 1 (2011): 1–25.

Simon, Merill. *Jerry Falwell and the Jews*. Middle Village, NY: Jonathan David, 1999.

Smidt, Corwin. "Religion and American Attitudes toward Islam and an Invasion of Iraq." *Sociology of Religion* 66, no. 3 (2005): 243–261.

Smith, Anthony D. *The Ethnic Origins of Nations*. Oxford: Blackwell, 1988.

Smith, Kyle M. *A Congruence of Interests: Christian Zionism and U.S. Policy toward Israel, 1977–1998*. MA submission, Bowling Green State University, Graduate College, May 2006.

Smith, Tony. "Wilsonianism after Iraq: The End of Liberal Internationalism." In G. John Ikenberry, Thomas J. Knock, Anne-Marie Slaughter, and Tony Smith. *The Crisis of American Foreign Policy: Wilsonianism in the Twenty-first Century*. Princeton, NJ: Princeton University Press, 2009, 53–88.

Sniegoski, Stephen. *The Transparent Cabal: The Neoconservative Agenda, War in the Middle East, and the National Interest of Israel*. Norfolk, VA: Enigma Editions, 2008.

Snyder, Jack, Robert Y. Shapiro, and Yaeli Bloch-Elkon. "Free Hand Abroad, Divide and Rule at Home." *World Politics* 61, no. 1 (January 2009): 155–187.

Sokhey, Anand, and Paul Djupe. "Rabbi Engagement with the Peace Process in the Middle East." *Social Science Quarterly* 87, no. 4 (2006): 903–923.

Sorin, Gerald. *Irving Howe: A Life of Passionate Dissent*. New York: New York University Press, 2003.

Soulen, R. Kendall. *The God of Israel and Christian Theology*. Minneapolis: Fortress Press, 1996.

Spector, Stephan. *Evangelicals and Israel: The Story of American Christian Zionism*. New York: Oxford University Press, 2009.

Spiegel, Steven L. *The Other Arab-Israeli Conflict: Making America's Middle East Policy, from Truman to Reagan*. Chicago: University of Chicago Press, 1986.

Steinberg, Gerald. "Soft Powers Play Hardball: NGOs Wage War against Israel." *Israel Affairs* 12, no. 4 (2006): 748–768.

Steinfels, Peter. "All in the Mespoche." *Democracy: A Journal of Ideas* 17 (Summer 2010). www.democracyjournal.org/17/6762.php?page=all.

Stephens, Elizabeth. *U.S. Policy towards Israel: The Role of Political Culture in Defining the "Special Relationship."* Brighton, UK: Sussex Academic Press, 2006.

Stern, Kenneth S. *Antisemitism Today: How It Is the Same, How It Is Different, and How to Fight It.* New York: American Jewish Committee, 2006.

Sternberg, Ernest. "Purifying the World: What the New Radical Ideology Stands For." *Orbis* 54, no. 1 (2010): 61–86.

Stockton, Ronald R. "Christian Zionism: Prophecy and Public Opinion." *Middle East Journal* 41, no. 2 (1987): 234–253.

  "The Presbyterian Divestiture Vote and the Jewish Response." *Middle East Policy* 12, no. 4 (2005): 98–117.

Telhami, Shibley, Brian Katulis, Jon B. Alterman, and Milton Viorst. "Middle Eastern Views of the United States: What Do the Trends Indicate?" *Middle East Policy* 13, no. 3 (2006): 1–28.

Tivnan, Edward. *The Lobby: Jewish Political Power and American Foreign Policy: A Collection of Essays.* New York: Simon and Schuster, 1987.

Toon, Peter, ed. *Puritans, the Millennium and the Future of Israel: Puritan Eschatology, 1600 to 1660.* Cambridge: James Clarke, 1970.

Trachtenberg, Joshua. *The Devil and the Jews: The Medieval Conception of the Jew and Its Relation to Modern Anti-Semitism.* 2nd ed. Philadelphia: Jewish Publication Society, 2002.

Tuchman, Barbara. *Bible and Sword: England and Palestine from the Bronze Age to Balfour.* New York: New York University Press, 1956.

Ukeles Associates. *Young Jewish Adults in the United States Today.* New York: American Jewish Committee, 2006.

Urofsky, Melvyn. *We Are One! American Jewry and Israel.* Garden City, NY: Anchor Press, 1978.

Van Zile, Dexter. "Sabeel's One-State Agenda," *Judeo-Christian Alliance Special Report,* 2005. www.judeo-christianalliance.org/index.php?option=com_remository &Itemid= 62&func=fileinfo&id=10.

  "Key Mennonite Institutions against Israel." *Post-Holocaust and Anti-Semitism* 83 (2009). http://jcpa.org/article/key-mennonite-institutions-against-israel/.

  "Mainline American Christian 'Peacemakers' against Israel." *Post-Holocaust and Anti-Semitism* 90 (2009). http://jcpa.org/article/mainline-american-christian-peace-makers-against-israel/.

  "Updating the Ancient Infrastructure of Christian Contempt: Sabeel." *Jewish Political Studies Review* 23, no. 1–2 (2011): 7–37.

Vinz, Warren Lang. *Pulpit Politics: Faces of American Protestant Nationalism in the Twentieth Century.* Albany, NY: State University of New York Press, 1997.

Visser, Mark, Marcel Lubbers, Gerbert Kraaykamp, and Eva Jaspers. "Support for Radical Left Ideologies in Europe." *European Journal of Political Research* 53, no. 3 (August 2014), 541–558.

Voss, Carl Hermann and David A. Rausch. "American Christians and Israel, 1948–1988." *American Jewish Archives* 40, no. 1 (1988): 41–81.

Wald, Kenneth D., James L. Guth, Cleveland R. Fraser, John C. Green, Corwin E. Smidt, and Lyman A. Kellstedt. "Reclaiming Zion: How American Religious Groups View the Middle East." In Gabriel Sheffer, ed., *U.S.-Israeli Relations at the Crossroads*. London: Frank Cass, 1997. 147–168.

Wald, Kenneth D., and Alison Calhoun Brown. *Religion and Politics in the United States*. 4th ed. Lanham, MD: Rowman and Littlefield, 2003.

Walt, Stephen M. *Taming American Power: The Global Response to U.S. Primacy*. New York: Norton, 2005.

"In the National Interest: A Grand New Strategy for American Foreign Policy." *Boston Review* February 1, 2005. http://bostonreview.net/walt-national-interest.

"Taming American Power." *Foreign Affairs* 84, no. 5 (September–October 2005): 105–120.

Walton, Jeff. "Sabeel Conference Links U.S. and Israel to 'Genocidal Theologies.'" Institute on Religion and Democracy (October 19, 2009). http://juicyecumenism. com/2009/10/19/sabeel-conference-links-u-s-and-israel-to-genocidal-theologies/.

Waxman, Chaim. "Israel in Orthodox Identity: The American Experience." In Danny Ben-Moshe and Zohar Segev, eds., *Israel, the Diaspora and Jewish Identity*. Brighton, UK: Sussex Academic Press, 2007.

Waxman, Chaim and Ruth Yaron. *Annual Assessment, 2008*, Executive Report No. 5. Jerusalem: The Jewish People Policy Planning Institute, 2008 http://jppi.org.il/ uploads/Annual%20Assessment%202008.pdf.

Waxman, Dov. "The Israel Lobbies: A Survey of the Pro-Israel Community in the United States." *Israel Studies Forum* 25, no. 1 (2010): 5–28.

Weaver, Alain Epp, and Sonia K. Weaver. *Salt and Sign: Mennonite Central Committee in Palestine, 1949–1999*. Akron, PA: Mennonite Central Committee, 1999.

Weber, Timothy P. *On the Road to Armageddon: How Evangelicals Became Israel's Best Friend*. Grand Rapids, MI: Baker Academic, 2004.

"American Evangelicals and Israel: A Complicated Alliance." In Jonathan Frankel and Ezra Mendelsohn, eds., *The Protestant-Jewish Conundrum. Studies in Contemporary Jewry*, vol. 24. New York: Oxford University Press, 2010, 141–157.

Weinberger, Caspar. "Let a Muslim Army Occupy Iraq." *Middle East Quarterly* 6, no. 3 (September 1999): 73–81.

Weisbrod, Robert, and Richard Kazarian. *Israel in the Black American Perspective*. Westport, CT: Greenwood Press, 1985.

Welch, Stephen. *The Concept of Political Culture*. New York: St. Martin's Press, 1993.

Weldes, Jutta. "Constructing National Interests." *European Journal of International Relations* 2, no. 3 (1996): 275–318.

Wertheimer, Jack. "Breaking the Taboo: Critics of Israel and the American Jewish Establishment." In Allon Gal, ed., *Envisioning Israel: The Changing Ideals and Images of North American Jews*. Jerusalem: Hebrew University of Jerusalem, Magnes Press, 1996, 397–419.

"The Fragmentation of American Jewry and Its Leadership: Interview with Jack Wertheimer." *Changing Jewish Communities* 29 (February 6, 2008). Available at http://jcpa.org/article/the-fragmentation-of-american-jewry-and-its-lead-ership/.

Generation of Change: How Leaders in Their Twenties and Thirties Are Reshaping American Jewish Life. Jerusalem: Avi Chai Foundation, 2010.

Wistrich, Robert S., ed. *The Left against Zion: Communism, Israel and the Middle East*. London: Vallentine Mitchell, 1979.

"Left-Wing Anti-Zionism in Western Societies." In Robert S. Wistrich, ed., *Anti-Zionism and Antisemitism in the Contemporary World*. London, Macmillan, 1990, 46–52.

'Cruel Britannia.' *Azure* 21 (Summer 2005): 100–124.

"Anti-Semitism and Multiculturalism: The Uneasy Connection." Jerusalem: Hebrew University of Jerusalem, Vidal Sassoon International Center for the Study of Anti-semitism, (2006). http://sicsa.huji.ac.il/pprobert.pdf.

Wohlforth, William. "Realism and Foreign Policy." In Steve Smith, Amelia Hadfield and Tim Dunne, eds., *Foreign Policy: Theories, Actors, Cases*. Oxford: Oxford University Press, 2008, 32–47.

Wood, B. Dan. *The Myth of Presidential Representation*. Cambridge: Cambridge University Press, 2009.

Yakira, Elhanan. *Post-Zionism, Post-Holocaust: Three Essays on Denial, Forgetting, and the Delegitimation of Israel*. Cambridge: Cambridge University Press, 2010.

Young, Robert. *Postcolonialism: An Historical Introduction*. Oxford: Blackwell, 2003.

Zaru, Jean. "Jerusalem, 'Al-Quds,' in the Heart of Palestinian Christians." *Cornerstone* 15 (Spring 1999).

GALLUP

Jones, Jeffrey M. "Americans Felt Uneasy toward Arabs Even before September 11: Majority Supports Increased Security Measures Even for Arabs Who Are United States Citizens." *Gallup*, September 28, 2001. www.gallup.com/poll/4939/Ameri-cans-Felt-Uneasy-Toward-Arabs-Even-Before-September.aspx.

"Nearly Half of Americans Favor Independent Palestinian State: Views of Sharon, Arafat Growing More Negative over Time." *Gallup*, June 3, 2002. www.gallup.com/poll/6115/Nearly-Half-Americans-Favor-Independent-Palestinian-State.aspx.

"Americans Continue to Be Pessimistic about Middle East Peace: Divided on Whether U.S. Should Put More Pressure on Israelis or Palestinians." *Gallup*, March 13, 2007. www.gallup.com/poll/26860/americans-continue-pessimistic-about-middle-east-peace.aspx.

"In U.S., 6 in 10 View Iran as Critical Threat to U.S. Interests: International Terrorism Viewed as Top Threat to U.S." Gallup, February 16, 2010. www.gallup.com/poll/125996/View-Iran-Critical-Threat-Interests.aspx.

"Americans See U.S. as Exceptional; 37% Doubt Obama Does: Majority Believe U.S. at Risk of Losing Status as Greatest Country in the World." *Gallup*, December 22, 2010. www.gallup.com/poll/145358/Americans-Exceptional-Doubt-Obama.aspx.

"Americans Continue to Rate Iran as Greatest U.S. Enemy: North Korea, China Tie for Second; Mentions of Iraq Down Significantly." *Gallup*, February 18, 2011. www.gallup.com/poll/146165/Americans-Continue-Rate-Iran-Greatest-Enemy.aspx.

'In U.S., 3 in 10 Say They Take the Bible Literally: Plurality View Bible as Inspired Word of God But Say Not Everything In It Should Be Taken Literally." *Gallup*, July 8, 2011. www.gallup.com/poll/148427/Say-Bible-Literally.aspx.

"Liberal Self-Identification Edges Up to New High in 2013: Fifteen-Percentage-Point Conservative Advantage Ties as Smallest to Date." *Gallup*, January, 10 2014. www.gallup.com/poll/166787/liberal-self-identification-edges-new-high-2013.aspx.

Mendes, Elizabeth. "Americans Continue to Tilt Pro-Israel: More View Israel Favorably Than the Palestinian Authority or Iran." *Gallup*, March 2, 2012. www.gallup.com/poll/153092/Americans-Continue-Tilt-Pro-Israel.aspx.

Moore, David W. "Republicans, Conservatives More Supportive of Israelis Than Democrats, Liberals: Pattern Has Persisted for At Least the Past Decade." *Gallup*, April 17, 2002. www.gallup.com/poll/5836/Republicans-Conservatives-More-Supportive-Israelis-than-Democrats-Liberals.aspx.

"Protestant Tilt toward Israel Partially Explained by Biblical Connection: Catholic Support More Related to Pragmatic Concerns." *Gallup*, April, 29, 2002. www.gallup.com/poll/5893/Protestant-Tilt-Toward-Israel-Partially-Explained-Biblical-Connection.aspx.

"Americans Skeptical Either Side in Palestinian-Israeli Conflict Wants Peace: Four in Ten Say United States Supports Israel 'Too Much.'" *Gallup*, June 11, 2002. www.gallup.com/poll/6193/Americans-Skeptical-Either-Side-PalestinianIsraeli-Conflict-Wants-Peace.aspx.

Newport, Frank. 'Complex but Hopeful Pattern of American Attitudes toward Muslims: Little Change in Opinions since 2002 Survey." *Gallup*, March 23, 2006. www.gallup.com/poll/22021/Complex-Hopeful-Pattern-American-Attitudes-Toward-Muslims.aspx.

'Mormons Most Conservative Major Religious Group in U.S.: Six out of 10 Mormons are Politically Conservative." *Gallup*, January 11, 2010. www.gallup.com/poll/125021/Mormons-Conservative-Major-Religious-Group.aspx.

Moore, David W. and Joseph Carroll. "Just How Democratic Is the Jewish Population in America Today? About Half of Jewish Respondents are Democrats and One-Third Consider Themselves 'Liberal.'" *Gallup*, September 16, 2002. www.gallup.com/poll/6799/just-how-democratic-jewish-population-america-today.aspx.

"Republicans and Religious Americans Most Sympathetic to Israel." *Gallup*, March 27, 2006. www.gallup.com/poll/22063/republicans-religious-americans-most-sympathetic-israel.aspx.

Saad, Lydia. "Recent Middle East Violence Costs Israel Some U.S. Public Support: But Many Americans Remain Sympathetic to the Jewish State." *Gallup*, March 15, 2002. www.gallup.com/poll/5476/recent-middle-east-violence-costs-israel-some-us-public-support.aspx.

"Holy Land, or Just Ancient?" *Gallup*, July 29, 2003. www.gallup.com/poll/8941/Holy-Land-Just-Ancient.aspx.

"Canada Remains Americans' Most Favored Nation: Great Britain Nearly Ties Canada for Top Spot." *Gallup*, February 19, 2009. www.gallup.com/poll/115258/canada-remains-americans-favored-nation.aspx.

"Americans' Support for Israel Unchanged since Gaza Conflict: Most Americans Sympathize with Israel, View It Favorably." Gallup, March 3, 2009. www.gallup.com/poll/116308/Americans-Support-Israel-Unchanged-Gaza-Conflict.aspx.

"Americans Remain Skeptical About Middle East Peace: Just 32% Think Israel and Arabs Will Ever Live in Peace." *Gallup*, June 4, 2009. www.gallup.com/poll/120728/americans-remain-skeptical-middle-east-peace.aspx.

"U.S. Jews Lead Other Religious Groups in Support of Obama: Dip in Approval among Jews Similar to That among General Public." *Gallup*, October 2, 2009.

www.gallup.com/poll/123413/U.S.-Jews-Lead-Religious-Groups-Support-Obama.
aspx.

"In U.S., Canada Places First in Image Contest; Iran Last: Favorable Views of Russia, Palestinian Authority Up Slightly; Views of Iraq Down." *Gallup*, February 19, 2010. www.gallup.com/poll/126116/Canada-Places-First-Image-Contest-Iran-Last.aspx.

"Support for Israel in U.S. at 63%, Near Record High." *Gallup*, February 24, 2010. www.gallup.com/poll/126155/support-israel-near-record-high.aspx.

"Conservatives Continue to Outnumber Moderates in 2010." *Gallup*, December 16, 2010. www.gallup.com/poll/145271/conservatives-continue-outnumber-moderates-2010.aspx.

"Americans Maintain Broad Support for Israel: U.S. Adults nearly Four Times as Likely to Side with Israelis as with Palestinians." *Gallup*, February 28, 2011. www.gallup.com/poll/146408/americans-maintain-broad-support-israel.aspx.

"Americans Give Record-High Ratings to Several U.S. Allies: Iran has the Lowest Favorable Rating; China's Declines." Gallup, February 16, 2012. www.gallup.com/poll/152735/Americans-Give-Record-High-Ratings-Several-Allies.aspx.

"Americans Favor More Pressure on Palestinians Than Israelis: Generally Support a Palestinian State, But Don't See Conflict as Critical Threat to U.S." *Gallup*, March 18, 2013. www.gallup.com/poll/161405/americans-favor-pressure-palestinians-israelis.aspx.

"Country Ratings." *Gallup*. www.gallup.com/poll/1624/Perceptions-Foreign-Countries.aspx.

Sarkar, Simon. "British Public Divided over Middle East Conflict." *Gallup*, May 14, 2002. www.gallup.com/poll/6013/British-Public-Divided-Over-Middle-East-Conflict.aspx.

"Middle East" (poll, 1988–2013). *Gallup*. www.gallup.com/poll/1639/middle-east.aspx.

PEW RESEARCH CENTER

Allen, Jodie T., and Alec Tyson. "The U.S. Public's Pro-Israel History: In Mid-East Conflicts, Americans Consistently Side with Israel." *Pew Research Center*, July 19, 2006, http://pewresearch.org/pubs/39/the-us-publics-pro-israel-history.

Green, John. "Religion and the 2004 Election: A Pre-Election Analysis." September 9, 2004. *Pew Research Religion and Public Life Project*. www.pewforum.org/2004/09/09/religion-and-the-2004-election-a-pre-election-analysis/.

Lopez, Mark Hugo. 'Latinos and the 2010 Elections: Strong Support for Democrats; Weak Voter Motivation.' *Pew Research Hispanic Trends Project*, October 5, 2010. www.pewhispanic.org/2010/10/05/latinos-and-the-2010-elections-strong-support-for-democrats-weak-voter-motivation/.

Lopez, Marc Hugo, and Susan Minushkin. "2008 National Survey of Latinos: Hispanic Voter Attitudes." *Pew Hispanic Center*, July 24, 2008. http://pewhispanic.org/files/reports/90.pdf.

Ruby, Robert. "A Six-Day War: Its Aftermath in American Public Opinion." *Pew Research Religion and Public Life Project*, May 30, 2007. www.pewforum.org/2007/05/30/a-six-day-war-its-aftermath-in-american-public-opinion/.

Anonymous "Survey: Optimism Reigns, Technology Plays Key Role." *Pew Research Center for the People and the Press*, October 24, 1999. www.people-press.org/1999/10/24/optimism-reigns-technology-plays-key-role/.

"Americans Struggle with Religion's Role at Home and Abroad. Part 2: Views of Islam and Religion in the World." *Pew Research Center for the People and the Press*, March 20, 2002. www.people-press.org/2002/03/20/part-2-views-of-islam-and-religion-in-the-world/.

"Americans and Europeans Differ Widely on Foreign Policy Issues." *Pew Research Global Attitudes Project*, April 17, 2002. www.pewglobal.org/2002/04/17/americans-and-europeans-differ-widely-on-foreign-policy-issues/.

"Religion and Politics: Contention and Consensus: Growing Number Says Islam Encourages Violence among Followers." *Pew Research Center for the People and the Press*, July 24, 2003. www.people-press.org/2003/07/24/religion-and-politics-contention-and-consensus/.

"Views of Islam Remain Sharply Divided." *Pew Research Religion and Public Life Project*, September 9, 2004, www.pewforum.org/2004/09/09/views-of-islam-remain-sharply-divided/.

"Religious Landscape Survey." *Pew Research Religion and Public Life Project*. religions.pewforum.org/reports.

"The American Public: Opinion and Values in a 51%–48% Nation." *Pew Research Center for the People and the Press*, January 20, 2005. www.pewresearch.org/files/old-assets/trends/trends2005-public.pdf.

"'Trends 2005' by the Pew Research Center." *Pew Charitable Trusts*, January 25, 2005. www.pewtrusts.org/our_work_report_detail.aspx?id=23066.

"American Evangelicals and Israel." *Pew Research Religion and Public Life Project*, April, 15, 2005. www.pewforum.org/2005/04/15/american-evangelicals-and-israel/.

"Beyond Red vs. Blue: Republicans Divided About Role of Government – Democrats by Social and Personal Values." *Pew Research Center for the People and the Press*, May 10, 2005. www.people-press.org/2005/05/10/beyond-red-vs-blue/.

"America's Image Slips, But Allies Share U.S. Concerns over Iran, Hamas: No Global Warming Alarm in the U.S., China." *Pew Research Global Attitudes Project*, June 13, 2006. http://pewglobal.org/reports/display.php?ReportID=252.

"American Attitudes Hold Steady in Face of Foreign Crises: Strong Support for Israel – No Surge in Terror Concerns or Boost for Bush." *Pew Research Center for the People and the Press*, August 17, 2006, http://people-press.org/2006/08/17/american-attitudes-hold-steady-in-face-of-foreign-crises/.

"Diminished Public Appetite for Military Force and Mideast Oil: Five Years Later…" *Pew Research Center for the People and the Press*, September 6, 2006. http://people-press.org/report/288/diminished-public-appetite-for-military-force-and-mideast-oil.

"Trends in Political Values and Core Attitudes: 1987–2007: Political Landscape More Favorable to Democrats." *Pew Research Center for the People & the Press*, March 22, 2007. www.people-press.org/2007/03/22/trends-in-political-values-and-core-attitudes-1987-2007/.

"Muslim Americans: Middle Class and Mostly Mainstream." *Pew Research Center*, May 22, 2007. http://pewresearch.org/pubs/483/muslim-americans.

"Public Expresses Mixed Views of Islam, Mormonism." *Pew Research Religion and Public Life Project*, September 25, 2007. http://pewforum.org/Public-Expresses-Mixed-Views-of-Islam-Mormonism.aspx.

"Religious Landscape Survey: Religious Affiliation: Diverse and Dynamic," *Pew Research Religion & Public Life Project*, February 2008. http://religions.pewforum.org/reports#.

"U.S. Religious Landscape Survey: Religious Beliefs and Practices." *Pew Forum on Religion and Public Life*, June 2008. http://religions.pewforum.org/pdf/report2-religious-landscape-study-full.pdf.

"More See America's Loss of Global Respect as Major Problem: Majority of Republicans Say U.S. is Less Respected." *Pew Research Center for the People and the Press*, June 16, 2008. http://people-press.org/2008/06/16/more-see-americas-loss-of-global-respect-as-major-problem/.

"Unfavorable Views of Jews and Muslims on the Increase in Europe: Ethnocentric Attitudes Are on the Rise in Europe." *Pew Research Global Attitudes Project*, September 17, 2008. www.pewglobal.org/2008/09/17/unfavorable-views-of-jews-and-muslims-on-the-increase-in-europe/.

"Modest Backing For Israel in Gaza Crisis: No Desire for Greater U.S. Role in Resolving Conflict." *Pew Research Center for the People and the Press*, January 13, 2009. www.people-press.org/2009/01/13/modest-backing-for-israel-in-gaza-crisis/.

"Ideological Gaps over Israel on Both Sides of Atlantic." Pew Research Global *Attitudes Project*, January 29, 2009. http://pewresearch.org/pubs/1097/america-europe-ideological-gaps-over-israel.

"Independents Take Center Stage in Obama Era: Trends in Political Values and Core Attitudes: 1987–2009." *Pew Research Center for the People and the Press*, May 21, 2009. http://people-press.org/2009/05/21/independents-take-center-stage-in-obama-era/.

"America's Place in the World 2009: An Investigation of Public and Leadership Opinion about International Affairs." *Pew Research Center for the People and the Press*, December 2009. http://people-press.org/files/legacy-pdf/569.pdf.

"U.S. Seen as Less Important, China as More Powerful: Isolationist Sentiment Surges to Four-Decade High." *Pew Research Center for the People and the Press*, December 3, 2009. http://people-press.org/2009/12/03/us-seen-as-less-important-china-as-more-powerful/.

"Millennials: Confident. Connected. Open to Change." *Pew Research Social and Demographic Trends*, February 24, 2010. http://pewsocialtrends.org/2010/02/24/millennials-confident-connected-open-to-change/.

"Continuing Divide in Views of Islam and Violence." *Pew Research Center for the People and the Press*, March 9, 2011. www.people-press.org/2011/03/09/continuing-divide-in-views-of-islam-and-violence/.

"Goal of Libyan Operation Less Clear to Public: Top Middle East Priority: Preventing Terrorism." *Pew Research Center for the People and the Press*, April 5, 2011. www.people-press.org/2011/04/05/goal-of-libyan-operation-less-clear-to-public/.

"Beyond Red vs. Blue: The Political Typology." *Pew Research Center for the People and the Press*, May 4, 2011. www.people-press.org/2011/05/04/beyond-red-vs-blue-the-political-typology/.

"Views of Middle East Unchanged by Recent Events: Public Remains Wary of Global Engagement." *Pew Research Center for the People and the Press*, June 10, 2011. www.people-press.org/2011/06/10/views-of-middle-east-unchanged-by-recent-events/.

"In Shift from Bush Era, More Conservatives Say 'Come Home, America.'" *Pew Research Center for the People and the Press*, June 16, 2011. www.people-press.org/2011/06/16/in-shift-from-bush-era-more-conservatives-say-come-home-america/.

"Strong on Defense and Israel, Tough on China: Tea Party and Foreign Policy." *Pew Research Center for the People and the Press*, October 7, 2011. www.people-press.org/2011/10/07/strong-on-defense-and-israel-tough-on-china/?src=prc-headline.

"Common Concerns about Islamic Extremism: Muslim-Western Tensions Persist." *Pew Research Center Global Attitudes Project*, July 21, 2011. www.pewglobal.org/files/2011/07/Pew-Global-Attitudes-Muslim-Western-Relations-FINAL-FOR-PRINT-July-21-2011.pdf.

"The Generation Gap and the 2012 Election." *Pew Research Center for the People and the Press*, November 3, 2011. www.people-press.org/2011/11/03/the-generation-gap-and-the-2012-election-3/?src=prc-headline.

"The American–Western European Values Gap: American Exceptionalism Subsides." *Pew Research Global Attitudes Project*, November 17, 2011 (updated February 29, 2012). www.pewglobal.org/2011/11/17/the-american-western-european-values-gap/.

"Trends in Party Identification of Religious Groups: By Religious Affiliation." *Pew Research Religion and Political Life Project*, February 2, 2012. www.pewforum.org/Politics-and-Elections/Trends-in-Party-Identification-of-Religious-Groups-affiliation.aspx.

"Public Takes Strong Stance against Iran's Nuclear Program." *Pew Research Center for the People and the Press*, February 15, 2012. www.people-press.org/files/legacy-pdf/02-15-12%20Foreign%20Policy%20release.pdf.

"Little Support for U.S. Intervention in Syrian Conflict." *Pew Research Center for the People and the Press*, March 15, 2012. www.people-press.org/files/legacy-pdf/03-15-12%20Foreign%20Policy%20Release.pdf.

"Partisan Polarization Surges in Bush, Obama Years: Trends in American Values: 1987–2012." *Pew Research Center for the People and the Press*, June 4, 2012. www.people-press.org/2012/06/04/partisan-polarization-surges-in-bush-obama-years/.

"'Nones' on the Rise." *Pew Research Religion and Public Life Project*, October 9, 2012. www.pewforum.org/2012/10/09/nones-on-the-rise/.

"After Boston, Little Change in Views of Islam and Violence: 45% say Muslim Americans Face 'a Lot' of Discrimination." *Pew Research Center for the People and the Press*, May 7, 2013. www.people-press.org/2013/05/07/after-boston-little-change-in-views-of-islam-and-violence/.

"Despite Their Wide Differences, Many Israelis and Palestinians Want Bigger Role for Obama in Resolving Conflict: Survey Report." *Pew Research Global Research Project*, May 9, 2013. www.pewglobal.org/2013/05/09/despite-their-wide-differences-many-israelis-and-palestinians-want-bigger-role-for-obama-in-resolving-conflict/.

"A Portrait of Jewish Americans: Findings from a Pew Research Center Survey of U.S. Jews." *Pew Research Center Religion and Public Life Project*, October 1, 2013. www.pewforum.org/files/2013/10/jewish-american-full-report-for-web.pdf.

"Millennials in Adulthood: Millennials Less Conservative Than Older Generations." *Pew Research Social and Demographic Trends*, March 5, 2014. www.pewsocial-trends.org/2014/03/07/millennials-in-adulthood/sdt-next-america-03-07-2014-1-06/.

INTERVIEWS WITH AUTHOR

Elliot Abrams, National Security Council Senior Director for Democracy, Human Rights, and International Operations, 2001–2002; National Security Council Senior Director for Near East and North African Affairs, 2002–2005; Deputy National Security Advisor for Global Democracy, Strategy 2005–2008.

Carmiel Arbit, Assistant Director of Policy and Government Affairs, AIPAC.

Yossi Beilin, Deputy Foreign Minister of Israel, 1992–1995; Minister of Justice, 1999–2001.

Roger Bennett, Vice President, Bronfman Philanthropies.

Matt Brooks, Executive Director, Republican Jewish Coalition.

Shoshanna Bryen, Director of the Jewish Policy Center; former Director for Security Policy at Jewish Institute for National Security.

Steve Bayme, Director of Contemporary Jewish Life Dept., American Jewish Committee.

Peter Beinart, former editor of the *New Republic*.

Doug Bloomfield, former Legislative Director, AIPAC.

Jeremy Ben-Ami, Executive Director, J Street.

Eliot Cohen, Counselor to the United States Department of State, 2007–2009; former member of the Defense Policy Board Advisory Committee.

Nathan Diament, Executive Director of the Orthodox Union Advocacy Center.

Ambassador Stuart Eizenstadt, Chief Domestic Policy Advisor to President Carter; Deputy Secretary of the Treasury, 1999–2001.

Ethan Felson, Vice President and General Council, Jewish Council for Public Affairs.

Rabbi Steve Gutow, President and CEO, Jewish Council for Public Affairs.

Dan Fleshler, Board Member of Americans for Peace Now; Member of the J Street Advisory Council.

Marvin Feuer, Director of Policy and Government Affairs, AIPAC.

Lara Friedman, Director of Policy and Government Relations, Americans for Peace Now.

Brian Katulis, Senior Fellow, Center for American Progress.

Aaron Keyak, Interim Director, National Jewish Democratic Council, 2013.

Eugene Korn, Director of the Institute for Jewish-Christian Understanding and Cooperation; former Director of Interfaith Affairs for the Anti-Defamation League.

Rachel Lerner, Senior Vice President for Community Relations.

Ann Lewis, former Senior Advisor to Hillary Clinton; former Director of Communications and Counselor to President Bill Clinton.

Prof. Gerald McDermott, Professor of Religion, Roanoke College, Virginia; Teaching Pastor at St. John Lutheran Church.

David Makovsky, Director of the Washington Institute for Near East Policy Project on the Middle East Peace Process; Senior Advisor to the Special Middle East Envoy, U.S. State Department, 2013.

Dan Meryashin, Executive Vice President, B'nai B'rith.

Aaron Miller, former Senior Advisor for Arab-Israeli Negotiations and Deputy Special Middle East Coordinator for Arab-Israeli Negotiations in the U.S. State Department.

Noam Neusner, White House Liaison to the Jewish Community during the George W. Bush Administration.

Michael Oren, Israeli Ambassador to the United States, 2009–2013.

Emanuele Ottolenghi, Senior Fellow at the Foundation for the Defense of Democracies.

Danielle Pletka, Vice President for Foreign and Defense Policy Studies, American Enterprise Institute; former Senior Professional Staff Member for Near East and South Asia with the U.S. Senate Committee on Foreign Relations, 1992–2002.

Martin Raffel, Senior Vice President, Jewish Council for Public Affairs.

Steve Rosen, Director of Foreign Policy Issues, AIPAC, 1982–2005.

Dennis Ross, Director of Policy Planning in the State Department under President George H. W. Bush; Special Middle East Coordinator under President Bill Clinton; Special Advisor for the Persian Gulf and Southwest Asia to Secretary of State Hillary Clinton.

David Saperstein, Director of the Union for Reform Judaism's Religious Action Center.

Roberta Schoffman, Representative of the Israel Policy Forum in Israel.

Zvika Krieger, former editor at the *New Republic*; Foreign Policy Correspondent at the *Atlantic*; former Senior Vice President of the S. Daniel Abraham Center for Middle East Peace.

Tevi Troy, White House Liaison to the Jewish Community during the George W. Bush Administration.

Matthew Yglesias, liberal blogger at *Talking Points Memo*, the *Atlantic*, Center for American Progress.

Tamara Wittes, Director of the Saban Center for Middle East Policy at Brookings; Deputy Assistant Secretary of State for Near Eastern Affairs, 2009–2012.

Index